I0878599

The Arithmetic of Listening

The Arithmetic of Listening

Tuning Theory and History for the Impractical Musician

KYLE GANN

UNIVERSITY OF ILLINOIS PRESS
Urbana, Chicago, and Springfield

© 2019 by the Board of Trustees
of the University of Illinois
All rights reserved
1 2 3 4 5 C P 5 4 3 2 1

∞ This book is printed on acid-free paper.

Audio examples to accompany the chapters in this book can be found at http://www.kylegann.com/Arithmetic.html.

Publication of this book was supported by a grant from the Dragan Plamenac Endowment of the American Musicological Society, funded in part by the National Endowment for the Humanities and the Andrew W. Mellon Foundation.

Library of Congress Cataloging-in-Publication Data
Names: Gann, Kyle, author.
Title: The arithmetic of listening : tuning theory and history for the impractical musician / Kyle Gann.
Description: Urbana : University of Illinois Press, [2019] | Includes bibliographical references and index.
Identifiers: LCCN 2018061109| ISBN 9780252042584 (hardcover : alk. paper) | ISBN 9780252084416 (pbk. : alk. paper)
Subjects: LCSH: Musical intervals and scales. | Microtonal music—History and criticism. | Microtones.
Classification: LCC ML3809 .G3 2018 | DDC 781.2/6—dc23
LC record available at https://lccn.loc.gov/2018061109
E-book ISBN 9780252051425

To Ben Johnston,
who changed my direction — in memoriam

Contents

Acknowledgments

I must first of all thank Ben Johnston for, with an offhand comment (followed by four years of revelatory teaching), determining the subsequent direction of my life. Ben is a genius, a visionary, and his ten string quartets and many other just-intonation pieces have revealed more about what tuning can achieve than could have been reasonably expected from any one person in a lifetime. Second, for years, editors would ask me what book I was working on, and I would cheerily respond, "Well, I've got a microtonality textbook half finished," just to enjoy the squeamish look on their faces as they changed the subject. Laurie Matheson was the first editor to reply, "Good, let's do it." She's why you're holding this book. Her faith in me has been gratifying. I roamed the world of academic publishing and finally found a home at the University of Illinois Press. Fittingly, Ben taught at the University of Illinois for thirty-two years (though I studied with him privately and was not enrolled there).

I thank my former student Lydia Spielberg, whose classics professors claimed that she knew ancient Greek better than they did and that her senior thesis could have been a doctoral dissertation. Her undergraduate paper on Ptolemy for my tuning class remains the clearest exposition I've been able to find on the subject. A few years later she is already doing postdocs and has gone on to what will doubtless be a stellar academic career. It was my great honor to have the manuscript read by microtonal experts John Schneider (a Partch performer and world's leading expert on the microtonal guitar) and Andrew Granade (an important biographer of Partch), and I benefited from their every suggestion. I thank Kraig Grady, Juhani Nuorvala, Casey Hale, and Paul Erlich for providing materials on Regular Temperament Theory, particularly Paul, who patiently endured and answered many detailed technical questions. He taught me Regular Temperament Theory as he has taught so many others. Stephen Parris, director of Gamelan Encinal, provided me with important documents on gamelan tuning. My Bard College colleague Maria Sonevytsky pulled me back from the brink of ethnomusicological faux pas, and our Baroque specialist, Alexander Bonus, found sources for me and knew exactly when to scoff. I hope I have not embarrassed either of them, nor any of my other benefactors, with further misconceptions. Most of all I thank my lovely wife, Nancy, for so uncomplainingly nurturing a decades-long obsession that began, after all, a few months after we married. She did not see this coming.

THE ARITHMETIC OF LISTENING

INTRODUCTION

> The doors that are closed *because* of education are the saddest doors that humanity never walked through.
>
> —Harry Partch, "A Quarter-Saw Section of Motivations and Intonations"

Dear reader, if you have come to this book, it is perhaps because you have come to question something that it rarely occurs to musicians to question: why there are twelve tones in an octave. I have walked into graduate music classes and asked the question "Why do we have twelve pitches in an octave?," sometimes without finding a single person who could answer, including the professor. It is something musicians seem not to want to know, despite the fact—or because of it—that it governs nearly every aspect of our music making.

It was not always thus. In the fifteenth though eighteenth centuries (in Europe, but much earlier in other cultures), aspects of tuning were widely debated by scholars who had a keen understanding of the issues. Keyboards were constructed that had more than twelve keys to an octave. As recently as Mozart's time, the art of violin playing was taught in a way that distinguished D♯ from E♭ and relied on an understanding of the octave as being divided in from thirty-one to fifty-five parts. The utter amnesia that now generally accompanies the arithmetical relations among musical tones was a result of nineteenth-century practices. It seemed to accompany the creation of a musical canon—for example, now that we know we all have to practice Beethoven's sonatas and Chopin's nocturnes, there's no point in questioning the basis of their performance. (Although even in Beethoven's day, the twelve pitches were tuned differently than they are today.)

So to envision possible futures for music, and also to understand the past as the past saw (and heard) itself, we venture into tuning theory. Tuning theory is widely considered a weird, obscure, esoteric subject. It did not use to be, and it does not have to be. The book you are reading contains material I have taught from many times, and I have been told it is an extremely clear presentation of the topic. I am writing to seduce musicians who don't know anything about microtonality into the field and to empower those who are afraid the subject is difficult.

In tuning theory we use numbers to characterize pitches and their relationships. Doing so simplifies pitch relationships and reveals what they truly mean. If tuning theory seems esoteric today, it is partly because most musicians learn a different set of numbers for pitch relationships: the "perfect fifth," the "minor sixth," the I chord, the IV chord, the V7 chord, the flat 9, and the sharp 11. No musician considers I, IV, V, I an obscure way to describe a musical phenomenon (though nonmusicians find it frightfully confusing). And yet those numbers, whose use dates back to only the seventeenth century, after all, are more arbitrary, complicated, and context-dependent than the ancient, natural system of numbers used in tuning theory.

There is another reason that tuning theory may seem esoteric: it is because *many people in the music world want you to believe that it is esoteric and even obsolete.* Thousands of classical musicians anchor their careers in the music of what is called the "common practice era"—that is, the music of Bach, Haydn, Mozart, Beethoven, Brahms, and so on. All of that music uses twelve pitches per octave. Many more musicians, most of them in universities, have based their careers on the integrity of a style of music invented in 1921 by Arnold Schoenberg called "twelve-tone music," founded on the premise that all intervals of a given rough size (minor thirds, for example) must be equal. The idea that Western European tuning of the last few centuries is only one among an infinite number threatens many of these people. They are afraid that if instruments change, or if people become aware of what alternative tunings can achieve, musical practice will change, and their livelihoods—worse, their prestige!—will be threatened. Whether the fears and insecurities of these people are justified or not, they have no right to prevent you, reader, from learning how many wondrous possibilities exist in the realm of tuning. They possess no license to straitjacket your musical imagination.

In fact, as I shall argue repeatedly in the following pages, such fears are not justified. First of all, Bach and Haydn did not play music in their lifetimes in the same tuning we've been using in the twentieth and early twenty-first centuries. They possessed a richer, more idiosyncratic, more *expressive* tuning than we now impose on their music. If we were truly concerned about preserving the historic European tradition, we would learn how to play music in the tunings the composers intentionally chose for themselves.

Second, it is hardly the heretofore esoteric subject of tuning theory that threatens the hegemony of the European tradition. Ultimately, any tuning can only be justified by the music written for it. Any tuning in which beautiful music has been written has earned its right to exist forever. The twelve-pitch scale of European tradition has spread across the world and is in no danger. If the European repertoire is perceived as endangered, that is because of larger global economic and corporate forces, problems of a post-democratic oligarchy, not because of the modestly sized and sparsely funded community of us alternate-tuning enthusiasts. I won't claim we don't constitute a conspiracy, but our resources are hardly formidable.

Third, the specific tuning of the twentieth-century Western world—twelve-pitch equal temperament—is theoretically necessary only for rigorously atonal music, particularly twelve-tone music. In the first century of its existence, has twelve-tone music gained a sufficiently wide and enthusiastic following to justify granting its preferred tuning permanent priority above all other historical, world, and potential tunings? Common sense, combined with a cursory knowledge of the music world, suggests that the answer to this question is *no*.

And so we embark on an exploration of tuning in defiance of people who are (1) heavily invested in the status quo, (2) afraid of change, and (3) afraid of the truth. Because the truth is that tuning is the secret lens through which the history of music falls into focus. Changes in tuning theory explain why certain chords have been considered dissonant in some eras, consonant in others. Tuning explains why some keys have been commonly used, others avoided. It explains why so many nineteenth-century musicians were convinced that different keys suggested or corresponded to different colors. Tuning lies at the core of divergences in worldview between musics of the West and musics of Asia and Africa. Changes in tuning precede and account for changes in the history of music. Tuning theory explains why (classical) music was tonal in the eighteenth and nineteenth centuries and largely atonal in the twentieth. Tuning helps explain the psychological effects of music and why some musics are so much more viscerally powerful than others. Tuning partly explains why some cultures undergo rapid changes in musical style while others employ relatively static forms for centuries. And, finally, tuning is the great background force determining what kind of music gets made, since composers gravitate toward combinations that sound good in the tuning they have to work with.

Despite all of this, no other musical issue is so ignored, so taken for granted, so shoved into the corners of musical discourse as tuning is in Western musical circles. Everyone takes as God-given the fact that we have twelve pitches to the octave; it's as though the origin of the sacred nature of the number twelve were protected by a conspiracy of silence. And indeed the number itself is arbitrary, a result of historical accident and congealed dogmatism. Seventeenth-century Europe argued long and hard about whether to settle for it, and convenience trumped honesty. The refusal to deal directly with the wider issues of tuning, moreover, prevents musicians from gaining a deeper understanding of music history and from considering how music could conceivably change for the better in the future.

Of the many books written on tuning theory, only a handful are currently in print. Some of the best were written from the viewpoint of English church music, since the English continued tuning their pipe organs to meantone tuning long after the Continent had abandoned it, and they needed tuning manuals to justify and provide instructions for their practices. Piano tuners have written tuning books aimed primarily at other piano tuners, such as Owen Jorgensen's brilliant *Tuning* (1991). Since then, Patrizio Barbieri's *Enharmonic* (2008) has encyclopedically organized the history of tuning disputes concept by concept, though it proves a thorny approach for beginners. Ross W. Duffin's *How Equal Temperament Ruined Harmony (and Why You Should Care)* (2007) has made an elegant argument for returning to historical practices in the performance of older music. A few books have been written about alternate tuning systems in contemporary music; these usually run through a grocery list of different options, treating them all as basically equal in significance and showing little continuity with the great tuning systems of the past.

As someone who has taught tuning theory regularly to young musicians representing a wide variety of interests, I have felt a desperate need for a book written from a standpoint that is historical yet not conservative, theoretical yet acoustically sound, cognizant of the Western and non-Western past yet geared toward possibilities for new composition. The only book in English that has come close in recent decades is Harry Partch's ebullient *Genesis of a Music* (1974), yet for all of its delightfully quirky brilliance and impressive (if slightly outdated) erudition, it primarily seeks to explain only one composer's solution.

Despite promising signs of future developments, music has been enduring a frustrating period of stagnation. As we accustom ourselves to the often baffling twenty-first century, many people sense that some major historical change is on the verge of taking place. But the boundaries of old musical practice are difficult to break through, because so few people understand how much they are caused by mistaken and unquestioned assumptions about what pitches we have available. Today, however, now that we have easily tunable synthesizers, guitars with from sixteen to forty-four frets per octave, and music-making computers that can tune pitches to any arithmetical specifications, there is no longer any reason to be limited to tunings that are convenient on European-originated instruments. The technology has advanced far faster than most musicians' understanding of musical materials. The time has come, and is past due, for a book on tuning theory from a practical composer's standpoint, as well as from the standpoint of a performer who wishes to perform pre-twentieth-century music as it was originally heard.

My personal introduction to microtonality came from the microtonally innovative composer Ben Johnston. I had become a Partch enthusiast without understanding much of Partch's book, and when, after completing my doctorate, I went to study with Ben, I thought to myself, "I love Ben's music, but I'm not going to get into this microtonality stuff; it's too much work." Well, it *has* been a lot of work. Ben never proselytized for microtonality, but he looked at one chord I wrote, commented on how beautiful it would sound if *tuned* properly, and reeled off the related fractions. With a shock I realized that I understood exactly what he was saying, in spite of myself. I had been the trigonometry and algebra star of my high school (president of the math club *and* winner of the regional slide rule competition), and I suddenly became aware that I possessed exactly the talents microtonality needed. It felt like an iron door had clanged shut behind me, and there was no direction to go except forward into microtonality. This was in 1983. Over the next eight years I filled entire notebooks with sets of fractions, and not until 1992 did I write a piece that only made sense in a microtonal tuning. I needed to be able to *feel* all the intervals I was using, and it was admittedly not an easy transition. My hope is that this book will ease that process for others.

When I first decided to write this book, as a text for my microtonality class (titled "The Arithmetic of Listening" since 1998), I initially wanted it to encompass the entire history and theory of tuning. It would have been two thousand pages at minimum. Luckily, I realized at some point that such a book would not only take me at least thirty years to write, but it would be unhelpful; it would present so many approaches to tuning, so much terminological detail, that any reader not already an expert in the field would simply become confused and give up. What was needed was a book for beginners that would proceed far enough to send them off in a particular direction, even allowing that they might not choose the destination implied. I needed to provide general maps to all the available destinations. I envy the scope of Partch's *Genesis*, but he needed to wipe out decades of congealed prejudice with one devastating knock-out punch. Partly thanks to him, I have the luxury of writing for musicians who are not so difficult to convince.

My experience with this book has been that its content, along with supplementary recordings and student tuning projects, fills up a semester of an undergraduate class well. It could also be used to structure a graduate course, in which case additional readings from the historical literature would undoubtedly be required.

The overall theoretical standpoint of the book is that tuning is primarily derived from a multidimensional system in which each dimension correlates to a prime number; thus, the first dimension stems from extension of the third harmonic (producing the Pythagorean system as a line), the second dimension from the fifth harmonic (producing European five-limit tuning, a plane), the third dimension from the seventh harmonic, the fourth dimension from the eleventh harmonic, and so on. Each of these dimensions offers new possibilities for scale and chord construction, and the remaining non-just systems (meantone, equal temperament, and so on) are attempts to incorporate, systematize, and simplify the just systems by approximation. I believe, then, that the entire history of tuning—or at least its most musically fertile aspects—can be encompassed within this one framework in a way that will clarify and simplify it. I treat just intonation—the truth of the natural number system converted to pitch—as central, but swinging into various equal and unequal temperaments has occupied most of musical history and must account for much of the book as well.

The structure of the book, then, starts with basic issues of numerical pitch relationships: concepts of pitch theory (chapter 1), the harmonic series (chapter 2), and the historical development of scales (chapter 3). Chapters 4 through 11 go one by one through the prime numbers 3, 5, 7, 11, and 13 and upward, though chapters 5 through 8 linger in the area of the normative five-limit intervals of European music and their historical temperament forms: meantone, well temperament, and equal temperament. Chapters 12 and 13 explore the more exotic equal temperaments, starting with non-twelve-based ones that have been explored for centuries (such as nineteen tones to the octave, thirty-one, and fifty-three), along with more recent explorations in unconventional equal temperaments, and then moving to twelve-based temperaments that split the half step (quarter tones, sixth tones), which were primarily used in the twentieth century. Chapter 14 is a rather cursory coverage of some tunings outside the Euro-American tradition, whose relevance to Western tuning concepts is ambiguous and questionable but still necessary for an overall view. And chapter 15 details a few recent composers dealing with tuning phenomena (such as glissandos) that are not easily covered in the preceding numerical framework. For reference I have included a glossary of tuning terms used in the book, and an appendix containing a list of interval sizes in a variety of equal temperaments, a list of more than seven hundred important tuning ratios converted to cents (and vice versa), and a table of the conventional frequencies of equal temperament tuned to A 440.

In addition, and very importantly, audio examples for many of the musical examples here can be found at http://www.kylegann.com/Arithmetic.html.

The intended audience for this book is very broad. The book will aid in teaching the underlying principles of music theory. It will offer composers a framework for exploring new (and old) tunings. It will serve to guide performers interested in pre-twentieth-century repertoire in how to choose tunings other than equal temperament and how to match each piece with the tuning that will set it off to best advantage. It will detail the interface between music and mathematics. It will hopefully explain more about *why* music has developed in the directions it has than any standard theory text currently in use. Of all musicians in the Western world, only those who lack curiosity about the practice and theory of their art, and who find the status quo its own justification, will fail to benefit from *The Arithmetic of Listening*.

However impractical it may seem to chase after tunings not found on our panoply of commercially available musical instruments, the impetus behind this book is entirely practical. The intention is not to recount and preserve the dry facts of the history of theory for the sake of scholars already cognizant of them, but to seduce musicians into thinking about and practicing microtonality who have hitherto found the subject forbidding. I am a composer and a professor of music theory and history.

I have no woodworking skills, I cannot build instruments, and I have no training in biology or physics. The reason tuning is perceived the way it is has its counterparts in the construction of the inner ear and in the acoustics of tone interactions, but the reader will not find diagrams of the inner ear, algebraic charts, or calculus equations here. Readers who might appreciate such grounding in the science of hearing I will refer to other books. I have not found it necessary to understand the operation of the inner ear to understand how various tunings work in a musical context. My aim has been to speed and ease the reader into an understanding of how to employ alternate tunings in composition and performance, without extraneous issues, and with the awareness that practical problems of realization will vary with the musicians and their abilities and needs. I hope this book makes clear to a wide range of musicians that tuning arithmetic is not a dark art, but rather the light that makes the whole field fall into place.

CHAPTER 1

THE COSMIC JOKE

Sound is the ear's perception of a vibration. Generally speaking, the human ear perceives a vibration as sound when it vibrates between about 15 times per second and 23,000 times per second. (The upper theshhold decreases as people age, often descending as low as 8,000 vibrations per second.)

A regularly repeating vibration is perceived as a pitch. For example, the A above middle C is often defined as vibrating 440 times per second, or at 440 cycles per second (*cps*, or *Hertz*—Hz). That pitch is referred to as A 440. It is a common tuning standard for instruments in the Western world. In Western twentieth-century tuning, if that A is 440 cps, then our lodestar middle C vibrates at 261.626 . . . cps.

We perceive two pitches as being strongly congruent, almost as identical in a certain way, when one vibrates twice as fast as the other. For example, the pitch at 220 cps is strongly congruent to, and identified with, the one at 440 cps. We call both of those pitches "A." We also call the pitches at 110 cps and 880 cps "A." In a tuning sense,

110 cps = 220 cps = 440 cps = 880 cps = 1760 cps

because we call them all "A." We find it strange to think that 110 = 220 = 440 and so on, and yet musicians are quite used to looking at eight different, evenly spaced notes on the piano keyboard and calling them all "A." It's the same phenomenon.

Because it is so easily intelligible, the *octave* is the interval that most offends the ear when it is out of tune. There is also the interesting fact that it is much easier for most people to sing an octave accurately than to sing slightly smaller intervals such as minor sevenths, major sixths, and so on. Our very larynxes can calculate the ratio 2:1—and unconsciously (as they do when you sing the first two notes of "Somewhere Over the Rainbow" or the sixth and seventh notes of "Way Down Upon the Swanee River").

The perceived pitch distance between any two pitches is called an interval. And for somewhat accidental historical reasons, we call the interval between a pitch and the twice-as-fast pitch above it an octave. Since one of these vibrates twice in the time the other beats once, we could just as easily call it (as Harry Partch insists on) a 2/1. "Octave" is a convenient term largely because it is the term in current use among musicians. (The term evolved from a Latin root connoting the number eight, because in our common major scale the octave, or 2/1, is the tone we reach after ascending through eight steps.)

Every octave, or 2/1, is perceived as the same size interval. That is, the octave from 110 to 220 cps is perceived as being the same size as the octave from 440 to 880. It can be seen from this that *the perceived size of an interval depends on the ratio between the two vibrations*, not the difference between the numbers in cycles per second: 220 minus 110 leaves only 110, while 880 minus 440 leaves 440. But they are still the same interval.

Because of this strong identity of two notes an octave or 2/1 apart, the octave, or 2/1, has been the most basic interval among most musical systems of the world. We say that 2/1 is the most consonant interval possible, except for the unison, or 1/1, which refers to two identical pitches.

One definition of *consonance*—the one used in this book—is that *two pitches are consonant when their vibrations can be related by small numbers*. The smaller the numbers, the more consonant the interval, and there are no natural number ratios smaller than 1/1 and 2/1. Consonance is commonly thought of as a sweet-sounding quality, but it is more accurate to think of it as intelligibility to the ear. *The more consonant an interval is, the easier it is to tune by ear.*

We will find, however, that the human ear can accept a certain fuzziness of approximation, recognizing the meaning of the interval even if the ratio is not exact. Thank goodness—otherwise musical performance would be extremely straitjacketed.

Consonances Other Than 2/1

From 2/1 we can proceed to other intervals. Adding 3 to our repertoire of numbers, we now have the intervals 3/1 and 3/2.

If an A vibrates at 220, then the pitch needed to form a 3/1 interval will vibrate at 660 cps. The pitch needed to form a 3/2 interval will vibrate at 330 cps. Both of those pitches happen to be ones that we call "E." We now have the following group of pitches:

Pitch	Frequency	Ratio
A	880 cps	4/1 (4/1 × 220 = 880)
E	660 cps	3/1 (3/1 × 220 = 660)
A	440 cps	2/1 (2/1 × 220 = 440)
E	330 cps	3/2 (3/2 × 220 = 330)
A	220 cps	1/1

Notice that a second octave exists between E 330 and E 660, because 330 × 2 = 660.

The ratio 3/2 defines an interval that musicians commonly (again through accidental historical reasons, because it is the distance from the first to fifth notes of the scale) call a *perfect fifth*. (If you are unfamiliar or rusty with the names of musical intervals, a chart in chapter 2 will refresh your memory.) The ratio 3/1 defines an octave plus a perfect fifth, called a *perfect twelfth*.

Notice that a third interval exists between E 330 and A 440, which can be defined as the ratio 4/3. Musicians call this ratio a *perfect fourth*. The same interval can also be found between E 660 and A 880. We can also construct a 4/3 interval above A 220—220 × 4/3 = 293.333 . . . —which happens to be the pitch D.

We've now used all permutations of the numbers 1, 2, 3, and 4. It is not necessary to include the ratio 4/2, because, just as in common fractions, 4/2 reduces to 2/1.

Let's go up to the number 5. This adds the ratios 5/1, 5/2, 5/3, and 5/4.

If A vibrates at 220, then those "5" ratios give us the following notes:

Ratio	Frequency		Name
5/1	1100	(5/1 × 220)	C♯
5/2	550	(5/2 × 220)	C♯
5/3	366.666 . . .	(5/3 × 220)	F♯
5/4	275	(5/4 × 220)	C♯

Integrating these notes into our collection, we get:

C♯	1100	5/1
A	880	4/1
E	660	3/1
C♯	550	5/2
A	440	2/1 = 4/2
F♯	366.666 . . .	5/3
E	330	3/2
D	293.333 . . .	4/3
C♯	275	5/4
A	220	1/1

This encompasses all possible ratios among the numbers 1, 2, 3, 4, and 5 with respect to the fundamental A 220. The same ratios, of course, could be rebuilt on any other pitch.

The ratio 5/4 corresponds to the interval that musicians call the major third; 5/3 corresponds to the major sixth; 5/2 is an octave plus a major third (major tenth); and 5/1 is two octaves plus a major third.

Note that in tuning theory *we use a ratio to refer to both an interval and a pitch within a specified tonality*. The *interval* 5/4 refers to two pitches whose frequencies are related by a ratio of 5 to 4. The *pitch* 5/4 is the one whose frequency is 5/4 times that of whatever pitch has been designated, for this context, as 1/1. Until some pitch (and it can be any pitch: E♭, C♯, F𝄪) has been defined as 1/1 for contextual purposes, no other pitch can be named by an interval. We have also surreptitiously introduced the minor third, whose ratio is 6/5: $C_\sharp$ to E (275 Hz to 330 Hz), for instance, and also $F_\sharp$ to A (366.666 . . . to 440).

For now, these are all the intervals we need in order to plunge into our discussion of tuning. In fact, over the course of the sixteenth and seventeenth centuries, the music theorists of Europe decided these were all the consonant intervals we would ever need, and in general Europe has spent four hundred years working with them and not caring much about all the others. (I like to tell students that once they know what sounds the intervals of 1, 2, 3, 4, and 5 make, they can figure out the rest of the history of music by following the implications. I am perhaps given to hyperbole.)

Cents: A Unit of Perceived Pitch Space

Since we aren't yet used to talking about intervals as ratios, we need a unit of measurement that will allow us to specify how large each interval we discuss is.

In the late nineteenth century, Alexander Ellis (1814–1890)—a Cambridge-educated mathematician and philologist who, late in life, made the measurement of absolute pitch across Europe and throughout documentable history his particular study—devised a unit of measurement for perceived pitch space. He set this unit at 1/1200 of an octave, or 2/1. He called that 1/1200 of an octave a *cent*.[1] There are, by definition, 1200 cents in an octave or 2/1.

There's an obvious reason to call 1/1200 of an octave a cent. Musicians of the Western world in the last few centuries have divided the scale into twelve pitches per octave. The distance between any consecutive two pitches in that scale is called a *half step*. Therefore, if there are 1200 cents in an octave, there are (on the average, at least) 100 cents in each of the twelve half steps in that octave. A cent in music is 1/100 of an average half step, the way a cent in American money is 1/100 of a dollar.

It's a conveniently sized unit. One cent is a smaller unit of pitch space than most people can perceive. In certain austere contexts, a difference of 2 cents is perceptible (my piano tuner can distinguish as much), though this is easier in a harmonic context than a melodic one. For instance, given a purely tuned chord, a shift of 2 cents may produce enough beating between pitches (depending on the register and instrument) for a listener to notice that the pitch has changed. Personally, after more than three decades of experimenting with microtones, I can reliably tell that a pitch is mistuned if it is as much as 5 cents off, and I find that two consecutive pitches in a melody need to be at least 10 cents apart for me to register them as discrete steps. It is sometimes averred that, for general musical and melodic purposes, we can perceive as many as about 250 pitches per octave, 1/250 of an octave being 4.8 cents. Why we continue to settle for only 12, then, is a mystery of our culture.

It just so happens that:

> if an octave interval of 2/1 = 1200 cents, then
> a perfect fifth interval of 3/2 = 701.955 . . . cents, and
> a major third interval of 5/4 = 386.31371 . . . cents.

For the moment, let us simply treat this as a scientific fact rather than get bogged down with the mathematics involved at this interesting point. The formula for deriving cents from ratios is explained at the end of this chapter.

The Importance of Perfect Fifths and Major Thirds

Though we will briefly discuss tunings of non-Western musics later in the book (chapter 14), these three intervals—2/1, 3/2, and 5/4—are the intervals that have driven European music theory since the fifteenth century. The reason is that 3/2 and 5/4 make up the major and minor triads that have been the basic building blocks of Western tonal harmony.

Take an A-major triad: A–C♯–E. If A is defined as 1/1, 5/4 will give C♯, and 3/2 will give E. The frequencies in cps of such a triad in the treble clef will be 440, 550, and 660, the logic of which is clear and easy to remember (one of the contingent pedagogical virtues of tuning A to 440).

The minor triad is the major triad turned upside down. In a minor triad A–C–E, there is a 3/2 interval between A and E, but the 5/4 interval is between C and E. What is the interval between A and C? Let's find out.

To add two intervals together, we multiply their ratios. For example, to add a 3/2 and a 4/3, we multiply

$$\frac{3}{2} \times \frac{4}{3} = \frac{12}{6} = \frac{2}{1}$$

We can musically confirm that this is correct, because a perfect fifth (3/2) plus a perfect fourth (4/3) equals an octave (2/1).

So to find what interval added to a major third makes a perfect fifth, we make a formula:

$$\frac{5}{4} \times \frac{A}{B} = \frac{3}{2}$$

Multiplying both sides of the equation by 4/5, we obtain:

$$\frac{A}{B} = \frac{3}{2} \times \frac{4}{5} = \frac{12}{10} = \frac{6}{5}$$

The interval C# to E, then, which musicians call a minor third, is a 6/5. The minor third A to C, then, has the same value.

Clearly it is important in European music to have the 3/2, 5/4, and 6/5 intervals in tune, since those are the basic building blocks of tonal harmony.

HERE'S THE JOKE

If you look at a piano (or harpsichord, or organ, or synthesizer) keyboard, you will see that the major third is four half steps wide (from C to C♯, D, D♯, E). The octave is twelve half steps wide. Therefore an octave should consist of three major thirds: A to C♯, C♯ (D♭) to F, F to A gives you an octave A to A.

But we've already seen that a 5/4 (major third) is 386.31371 . . . cents wide. An octave is 1200 cents.

386.31371 . . . cents × 3 = 1158.9411418 . . . cents

The quantity 1158.9411418 . . . cents falls short of an octave by some 41 cents, almost a quarter tone (half of a half step).

We get a similar result if we multiply the ratios rather than add cents. Three major thirds is three 5/4 intervals multiplied together:

$$\frac{5}{4} \times \frac{5}{4} \times \frac{5}{4} = \frac{125}{64}$$

The fraction 125/64 is a little less than 2/1, which would be 128/64. Three major thirds almost fill out an octave but not quite.

Now let's look at perfect fifths. If you start at the bottom of the piano on A and ascend by perfect fifths, you'll eventually reach A again at the top: A–E–B–F♯–C♯–G♯(A♭)–E♭–B♭–F–C–G–D–A. Go through twelve perfect fifths, and you'll reach a pitch that is seven octaves above where you started. (See ex. 1.1.)

So twelve perfect fifths ought to equal seven octaves. But we've already seen that the perfect fifth is 701.955 . . . cents, and the octave is 1200:

701.955 . . . cents × 12 = 8423.460007 . . .

1200 cents × 7 = 8400.

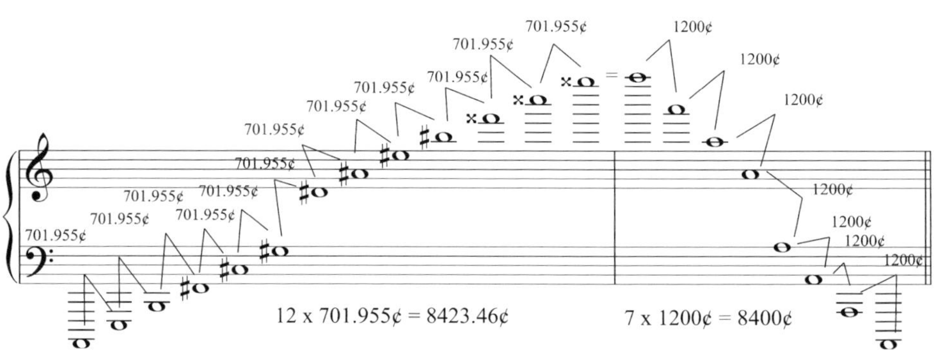

EX. 1.1: Incommensurability between twelve fifths and seven octaves

There is a 23.46-cent discrepancy between twelve 3/2 intervals and seven 2/1 intervals. Looking at ratios instead of cents:

$$\frac{3}{2} \times \frac{3}{2} \times \frac{3}{2} \times \frac{3}{2} \times \frac{3}{2} \times \frac{3}{2} \times \frac{3}{2} \times \frac{3}{2} \times \frac{3}{2} \times \frac{3}{2} \times \frac{3}{2} \times \frac{3}{2} = \frac{531441}{4096}$$

$$\frac{2}{1} \times \frac{2}{1} \times \frac{2}{1} \times \frac{2}{1} \times \frac{2}{1} \times \frac{2}{1} \times \frac{2}{1} = \frac{128}{1} \times \frac{4096}{4096} = \frac{524288}{4096}$$

we find a ratio discrepancy of 531441/524288. (This complicated, difficult-to-remember ratio, we will learn later, is called the *Pythagorean comma* and is a very important ratio in the history of tuning theory. Don't worry, I can't myself reproduce it off the top of my head, and you won't need to either. It is closely approximated by 74/73.)

These discrepancies are the great trick that nature has played on musicians. There are three intervals we particularly want in tune (to begin with—there will be plenty more later): 2/1, 3/2, and 5/4. Our 5/4 is almost a third of the size of our 2/1, *but not quite*. Twelve 3/2 intervals almost fit into seven 2/1 intervals, *but not quite*. They are so close that the temptation to fudge them, to alter them just a minute touch that maybe no one will notice, is well-nigh irresistible.

The problem, sadly, is not at all merely theoretical. Every guitarist deals with it every day. Try tuning the four perfect fourths and one major third that make up the common tuning of a six-string guitar:

E A D G B E

$$\frac{4}{3} \times \frac{4}{3} \times \frac{4}{3} \times \frac{5}{4} \times \frac{4}{3} = \frac{1280}{324} = \frac{320}{81}$$

The ratio between the outer strings should be a double octave, 4/1, which equals 320/80, *not* 320/81. When all the intervals between consecutive strings are perfectly in tune, the outer octaves will not be in tune. This is partly why it is so difficult to get a guitar perfectly in tune by ear and why it usually requires adjustment after an initial pass through the six strings. At least one interval has to be approximated, or rather *tempered*, as we say—that is, taken slightly out of perfect tuning. (I always say this in my microtonality class the first day, and I can tell who the guitarists are from the looks of relief and gratitude on their faces.)

Such difficulties form the great mainspring that has powered tuning theory for the past six centuries in the West, and in the East for much longer than that. For hundreds of years musicians have been trying to make those thirds and fifths and octaves fit together, sometimes cheating the fifths, sometimes cheating the thirds, depending on the musical effect desired (and rarely, of course, cheating the octaves, which most people would find intolerable). And the resulting music has always, always been conditioned by what tuning is offered in any particular era.

The fact that 5/4, 3/2, and 2/1 intervals do not fit with each other has often been lamented, especially by keyboard players and tuners, who are limited to only twelve pitches on their instruments. However, looked at in other ways, the trick that mathematical nature has played on us can be seen as a liberating one. Because actually an infinity of pitches are available to us, and by not fitting together those intervals offer us strategies for organizing that infinity. When we can perceive at least 250 different pitches per octave, why use only 12?

The incommensurability of 5/4, 3/2, and 2/1 points us to a mystery of nature that relates to the natural number series. Basically, those ratios are incommensurate, because no power of 5 (25, 625, 3125 . . .) will ever be divisible by 3 or 2, and no power of 3 will ever be divisible by 5 or 2, and so on. In more mathematical terms, there are no integers a, b, and c larger than zero for which

2^a will ever $= 3^b$, or
2^a will ever $= 5^c$, or
3^b will ever $= 5^c$.

Note that these three numbers are prime. As we will eventually see, every prime number creates and makes available a new series of interval types, and because powers of prime numbers never coincide (as powers of nonprime numbers can), none of those new interval types will be commensurate with the old ones either. The discrepancies between octaves, thirds, and fifths point us toward unexplored infinities of pitch relationships.

But to thus speculate is to jump far ahead of our story. After a detour of a technical but helpful nature, we will return to the origins of our Western musical scale and take a more chronological approach.

Converting Ratios to Cents

Math-phobes may need to brace themselves for the remaining section in this chapter. Be reassured, though, that 90 percent of the complex mathematics in this book appears in the next few paragraphs. If you can absorb the following few principles, the rest of the book will be comparatively easy going.

The problem of measuring perceived interval size is that *perceived pitch doesn't follow a linear scale but rather a logarithmic one*. If perceived pitch followed a linear scale, then the interval 3/2 would be halfway between 1/1 and 2/1. In arithmetic, after all, 3/2 is the halfway point between 1/1 and 2/1. But if 1/1 and 2/1 represent As an octave apart, then 3/2 represents E. Every musician knows, and a glance at a piano keyboard will confirm, that an E between two As is closer to the top one (five half steps away) than to the bottom (seven half steps). In terms of pitch *perception*, 3/2 is closer to 2/1 than it is to 1/1.

Perceived interval size is proportional to the *logarithm* of the ratio between the frequencies. While you multiply the ratios to find an interval sum:

$$\frac{3}{2} \times \frac{4}{3} = \frac{12}{6} = \frac{2}{1}$$

you *add* the logarithms:

$\log(3/2) + \log(4/3) = \log(2/1)$

using base-10 logarithms,

$\log^{10}(3/2) = 0.176\ldots$

$\log^{10}(4/3) = 0.125\ldots$

$\log^{10}(2/1) = 0.301\ldots$

$0.176 + 0.125 = 0.301$

In the centuries before calculators, such calculations were achieved via tables of logarithms; these days, an eight-dollar handheld calculator makes the derivation of logarithms as simple as addition. Note that the logarithm of 3/2, 0.176, is about 7/5 as much as the logarithm of 4/3, 0.125. This makes intuitive sense, since there are five half steps in a perfect fourth and seven in a perfect fifth, the intervals these ratios connote.

These logarithm numbers are not convenient to deal with. The trick Ellis needed was to find a constant to multiply them by that would make an octave, a 2/1 ratio, equal to 1200 cents:

$\log(2/1) \times X = 1200$ cents

So to find X we divide 1200 cents by the logarithm of 2/1 (or simply 2). If we use base-10 logarithms (and any base will work as long as we use it consistently):

$1200/\log^{10}(2) = 1200/.30103\ldots = 3986.3137136\ldots$

Therefore, to make all other intervals correctly proportionate to an octave, we multiply 3986.3137136 . . . by the base-10 logarithms of their ratios:

$\log^{10}(5/4) = .09691\ldots$

$.09691\ldots \times 3986.3137136\ldots = 386.31371\ldots$ cents

$\log^{10}(3/2) = .1760913\ldots$

$.1760913\ldots \times 3986.3137136\ldots = 701.955\ldots$ cents

$\log^{10}(6/5) = .0791812\ldots$

$.0791812\ldots \times 3986.3137136\ldots = 315.64129\ldots$ cents

To perform this operation quickly on your calculator (which must include a constant button and a logarithm button), execute the following operations:

1. Divide 1200 by the logarithm of 2.
2. Save the resulting number as a constant.
3. Enter the ratio whose value in cents you want to find. That is, if 17/13 is your ratio, divide 17 by 13 and obtain the result (continuing with our example, 17/13 = 1.30769 . . .).

4. Take the logarithm of the result (log base 10 of 1.30769 = .1165056 . . .).
5. Multiply that logarithm by the constant you've saved, and the answer will be the size of the interval in cents (.1165056 . . . × 3986.3137136 . . . = 464.42775 . . . cents, the size of a 17/13 interval).

For additional ratios, you need only repeat steps 3 through 5. If your calculator doesn't have a constant button, simply multiply the logarithm of the ratio you're investigating by 3986.3137. Or else multiply it by 1200 and then divide the answer by the logarithm of 2.

If you prefer to use natural (*e*-base) logarithms, the constant will be 1731.2340489 . . . rather than 3986.3137136. . . . The resulting values in cents will be the same.

Mastering this simple formula (which does not necessitate remembering the principles involved every time—muscle memory takes over after a while, trust me) will enable you to easily compare sizes of the hundreds of intervals used in later chapters. And once you have mastered it, the most complex mathematical calculation required in tuning theory will be already behind you. It's downhill from here, math-difficulty-wise.

Converting Cents to Ratios, on the Other Hand

At some point in your life, sadly, you will have an interval size in cents for which you want to find the proper ratio. This is not always so easy. The method is the reverse of the above. Divide the number of cents by 1200/(log 2), or 3986.3137, and then take 10 to whatever power the answer is (which is the opposite of taking the logarithm), which is often possible on a caculator with the 10× key, frequently a secondary-function key. For instance, let's say you want 142.37 cents:

$$142.37 \div 3986.3137 = 0.0357147$$

$$10^{0.0357147} = 1.085712$$

Your calculator, however, will not give you the answer as a fraction, and that's the problem. What ratio equals 1.085712? Not so easy. There are decimal-to-fraction converters on the internet that will give you fractions at whatever level of exactitude you want, and thank god for them. I picked the rather complex interval 38/35 for this one, and 35 × 1.085712 does indeed about equal 38. Unless you are a genius with numbers, it would take you awhile to come up with this on your own.

That's why in this book's appendix I have provided a list of more than seven hundred ratios within an octave called "Anatomy of an Octave." On this chart you can merely look down until you find 142.37¢, and there you will find your ratio, 38/35—also simpler ratios that might be close enough, such as in this case 13/12 (138.57¢). I have kept this chart on my website for many years,[2] and even microtonalists who resent everything else about my approach to tuning love this chart.

Savarts

Just so you know, there is another pitch measurement, not nearly as widely used as the cent, called the *savart*. A savart is 3.986 cents, and there are approximately 301 savarts in an octave. The advantage of the savart is that you can find the logarithm of the ratio and multiply by 1000 instead of 3986.3137, which is easier to do in your head. For example:

log (9/8) = .0511525, ergo 9/8 = 51.1525 savarts

log (3/2) = .1760913, so 3/2 = 176.0913 savarts

log (7/4) = .243038, so 7/4 = 243.038 savarts

Of course, unless you can calculate logarithms in your head, you're still stuck with carrying your calculator (or consulting logarithmic tables, as our forefathers used to). Savarts will not be used in this book, but you will find them in the work of Alain Daniélou (1907–1994, a musicologist who specialized in Asian musical scales) and other earlier, especially French, writers. They were more convenient back in the days before calculators were invented, when everyone relied on logarithmic tables.

CHAPTER 2

The Harmonic Series

The *harmonic series* is something I'd like to expect every musician to know about, but that isn't always the case. If I find a theory text in which the harmonic series is not listed in the index, I disdain it as unreliable. Take any pitch, and let's call that pitch the *fundamental.* A *harmonic* is a higher pitch that vibrates at some whole-number multiple of that fundamental. Thus, 330 cps, 440 cps, and 550 cps are all harmonics of our A vibrating at 110 cps, part of its harmonic series. In most normal cases,[1] when we hear a pitch, we faintly hear some of its harmonics as well, so a harmonic is a physical phenomenon as well as a theoretical construct, and so is a harmonic series.

Historically, it is something of an anachronism to begin our exploration of tuning with the harmonic series, since it wasn't discovered as a physical phenomenon until the seventeenth century. Most of our knowledge of intervals predates its discovery. Yet the harmonic series, or *overtone* series, is an efficient virtual compendium for intervals of all possible sizes. It is possible, I suppose, to make too much of the harmonic series per se, because it has never (until relatively recently) had a major effect on how our music is tuned or how scales developed. The harmonic series is, in effect, an abstract resource that basically contains, in efficient arrangement, all the musical intervals we will ever need. It is simply the natural whole-number series converted into sounding tones.

Credit for the discovery of the harmonic series goes to the mathematician Marin Mersenne (1588–1648), who was perplexed that he could hear faint tones above that made by a plucked string, including the third, fifth, and seventh harmonics. When his colleagues were of little help, he formulated the idea that "it seems it is entirely necessary that [the string] beat the air five, four, three, and two times in the same time."[2] He rejected the idea as implausible, but it turned out to be exactly the case.[3] In fact, an entire harmonic series is faintly or subliminally audible in most musical tones, and the relative strengths of the various tones are one of the determinants of timbre. For instance, a flute tone emphasizes the even harmonics, a clarinet tone the odd harmonics. In a piano tone the loudness of each harmonic is roughly proportional to its place in the series: the octave half as loud as the fundamental, the third harmonic a third as loud, and so forth. This phenomenon was first alluded to by Mersenne in his *Quaestiones celeberrimae in Genesim* of 1623 and attracted more attention in subsequent decades; John Wallis (1616–1703) demonstrated the overtones by studying nodes in vibrating strings, documenting his findings in 1677.[4] One can easily isolate tones from the harmonic series by drawing one's finger lightly along a low string of a grand piano, or guitar, while playing (or plucking) the string; a finger stopping the string at the halfway point will elicit an octave; at the one-third point, the octave plus a fifth; at the one-fourth point, a double octave; and so on, easily audible at least as high as the ninth harmonic.

However, the physical production of the harmonic series is not our theoretical concern. We will discuss it here, instead, as an efficient template for learning how to differentiate interval sizes, as an easily evoked storehouse for all the intervals we might want to refer to. As a theoretical construct, it is the basis for all music in *just intonation*: a term denoting the tuning of musical intervals according to whole-number ratios.

In chapter 1 we considered the ratios between numbers one through six. Example 2.1 extends this process up through the sixteenth harmonic, which, generally speaking, is all we need in dealing with the normative intervals of European music and, in fact, more than we need. This is a harmonic series on the pitch A 110. The large number at the top gives the pitch's position in this harmonic series. The smaller number below that multiplies that number by 110, so the second harmonic is 220 cps, the third 330 cps, and so on. The number below the note shows the number of cents between the note and the A just below (or on) it:

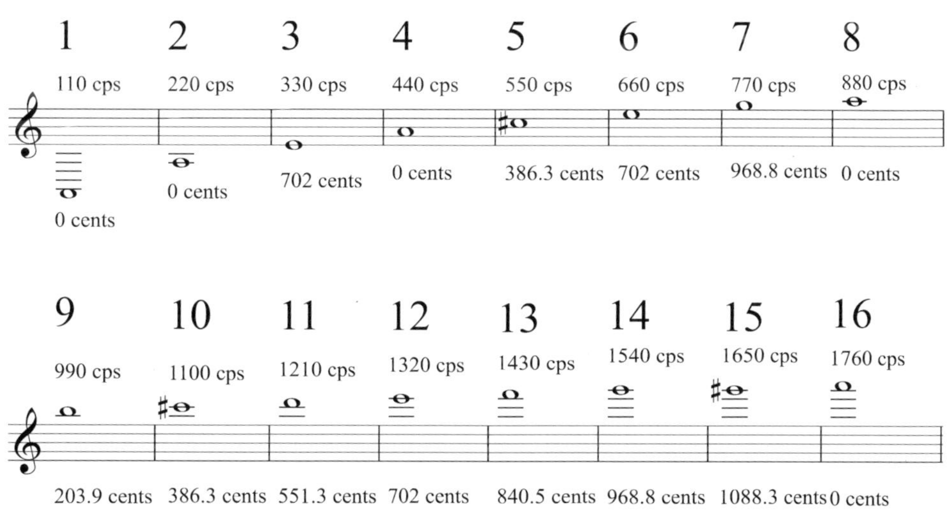

EX. 2.1: The first sixteen harmonics

One will note that the pitches in the harmonic series are perceived as closer and closer as one ascends through the series. For instance we have 203.9 cents between the eighth and ninth harmonics (a 9/8 ratio of a major second), and then:

9 to 10	182.4¢
10 to 11	165¢
11 to 12	150.64¢
12 to 13	138.57¢
13 to 14	128.3¢
14 to 15	119.44¢
15 to 16	111.7¢
16 to 17	105¢
17 to 18	98.95¢
18 to 19	93.6¢

Note that 18/17 is the closest simple, *superparticular* ratio (ratio of the form (N + 1)/N) representing the size of an equal-tempered half step. In previous centuries it was used as a convenient rule of thumb for placing of frets on stringed instruments, each fret being 17/18 of the distance from its predecessor to the bridge.

Also, each octave of the harmonic series doubles the number of pitches:

1st octave	A
2nd octave	A, E
3rd octave	A, C♯, E, G↓
4th octave	A, B, C♯, D↑, E, F↑, G↓, G♯

The fifth octave will contain sixteen pitches; the sixth, thirty-two, the seventh, sixty-four; and so on to infinity. I have added small arrows after the D, F, and G to show that those pitches are either higher or lower than we are used to in our conventional twelve-pitch scale. Such notations will be more accurately specified when we turn to tuning systems using the seventh and higher harmonics.

An unfortunate terminological note: *harmonics*, *overtones*, and *partials* all refer to the same phenomena. However, due to an inelegant tradition, harmonics include the fundamental while overtones and partials do not. Thus the second harmonic is the first overtone, the fifth harmonic is the fourth overtone, and so on. (And the same for "partials.") This book will obviate this difficulty by simply using the term "harmonics" throughout and avoiding the otherwise evocative word "overtone" except in contexts where no specific overtone is referred to.

Example 2.2 uses only the pitches from example 2.1 to show the numerical relationships of the intervals we are all familiar with from any music theory class, here all taken from a harmonic series on A. We can see that (almost) every interval we are used to had its origin in a numerical relationship drawn from the first sixteen harmonics. The quick student will notice a couple of anomalies, however. First, there are two sizes of major second: 9/8 and 10/9, or 204 cents and 182 cents, respectively.

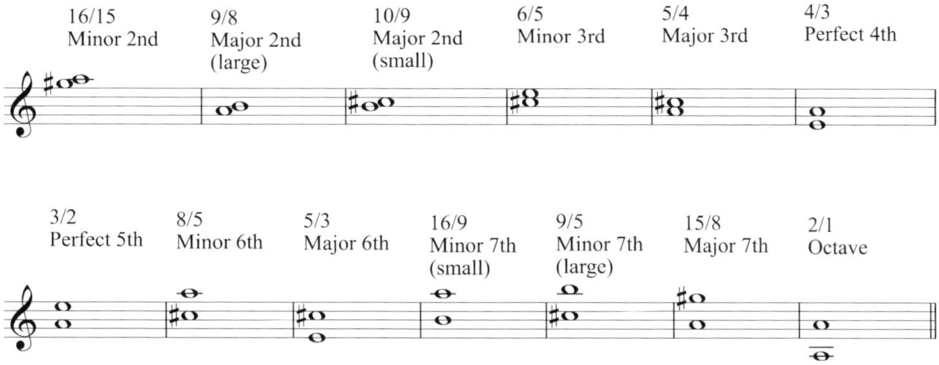

EX. 2.2: Common intervals found within a single harmonic series

Inverting these intervals, we likewise find two sizes of minor seventh: 16/9 and 9/5. Discrepancies between these intervals fuel many of the tuning arguments and accommodations in the history of tuning. Also, one will notice that there is no value given for the *tritone*, the augmented fourth or diminished fifth. The small intervals of the harmonic series actually contain two intervals close to 600 cents: 7/5 (590 cents) and 10/7 (610 cents). But as we will discuss at length in chapter 9, European musicians of the fourteenth through twentieth centuries were highly resistant to employing prime-numbered harmonics higher than five. This is why the tritone has always presented a tuning problem in European music and was referred to during the Renaissance as *diabolus in musica*, the devil in music.

No known scale in common use, however, corresponds to the harmonic series itself. A harmonic-series scale would have eight or sixteen steps to the octave, not seven or twelve. And there are intervals in the harmonic series that have never been used in Western scales (though they have been used in Middle Eastern, African, and Indian scales). The eleventh harmonic of a series on A, for example, is 551 cents above A, a quarter tone between D and D♯. The thirteenth harmonic is 841 cents above A, between F and F♯. Even the seventh harmonic, 969 cents above A, is flatter than the G we're used to. (There are, however, recent works based entirely on overtones of a single fundamental, including La Monte Young's *The Well-Tuned Piano*, James Tenney's *Spectral Canon for Conlon Nancarrow*, and my *Hyperchromatica*. Larry Polansky has also written pieces, such as *B'rey'sheet*, and Robert Carl, such as *Infinity Avenue*, that proceed from one harmonic series to another.)

However, in another way one can say that all the intervals we use in music can be derived from the harmonic series, and for our normative Euro-American tradition, the first sixteen will do. In the early decades of the seventeenth century, Italian, French, and English theorists argued about it but decided, despite some dissension, to forbid use of the seventh, eleventh, and thirteenth harmonics and limit European theory to numbers obtainable by multiples of 2, 3, and 5. Therefore, if you take all the ratios among the numbers 1, 2, 3, 4, 5, 6, 8, 9, 10, 12, 15, and 16, you'll find all the ratios for intervals used (or at least approximated) in European and American music—except for the tritone. All of these intervals are shown in example 2.2. Note, however, that this gives us not a specific scale, but a collection of intervals.

Ultimately, however, since upper octaves of a harmonic series eventually contain 1024 pitches to the octave, then 2048, then 4096 (all powers of two), and so on to infinity, the harmonic series can be said to provide a close approximation of every possible interval. Even the equal-tempered minor seventh on the piano is approximated within about half a cent by the ratio 57/32 (999.468 cents), and 181/128 represents a tritone (599.815 cents) within one-fifth of a cent, enough exactitude for any conceivable human purposes. Thus, within the infinite expanse of the harmonic series we virtually have all possible musical intervals. As I have worked with tuning over several decades, I have become more and more fascinated by the harmonic series as a kind of Theater of Memory containing all possible musical phenomena (even rhythm, since rhythmic ratios are also expressible as whole numbers; for instance, triplet quarter notes make a 3/2 ratio to regular quarter notes).

The Harmonic Series and the Whole-Tone Scale

As a historical note, in the early twentieth century it became common to use the harmonic series as justification for the whole-tone scale, the scale made up of every other step on the chromatic keyboard. However, this reasoning relied on rounding off each harmonic to its closest equal-tempered approximation.

If we take harmonics 8, 9, 10, 11, 13, 14, and 16, we seem to get something approaching a whole-tone scale:

Harmonic	8	9	10	11	13	14	16
Approximate pitch	C	D	E	F♯	A♭	B♭	C

However, if we look at these harmonics in terms of actual pitch differences between adjacent steps, we get a scale of very unequal steps, including a leap of a small minor third between F♯ and A♭ and barely more than a half step between A♭ and B♭:

Harmonic	8		9		10		11		13		14		16
Approximate pitch	C		D		E		F↑		A13		B♭-		C
Cents in each step		204		182		165		289		128		231	

It should be clear from the high quality of various works of Franz Liszt, Nicolai Rimsky-Korsakov, Claude Debussy, Charles Ives, and other composers that the whole-tone scale is justified by its musical use and no longer needs to be justified as a theoretically natural phenomenon—which it is not. It is a peculiarity of the twelve-pitch equal-tempered scale, albeit perfectly usable.

CHAPTER 3

Generating Scales

The origin myth of European music is Pythagoras's allegedly accidental discovery of tuning ratios. (Pythagoras lived in Greece and Italy sometime around 550–500 BCE.) According to Pythagoras's third-century biographer, Iamblichus (c. 250–c. 325 CE), it seems that one day the ancient Greek magus was "intently considering music, and reasoning with himself whether it would be possible to devise some instrumental assistance to the sense of hearing, so as to systematize it." As he mused, Pythagoras "happened to pass by a brazier's (blacksmith's) shop where he heard the hammers beating out a piece of iron on [an] anvil, producing sounds that harmonized. . . . He recognized in these sounds the concord of the octave, fifth, and fourth."[1] With apparent disregard for the smith's work schedule, he took the hammers home, weighed them, and suspended them from four identical pieces of gut string. The heavier the hammer, the more tension it exerted on the string, and the faster the string would vibrate. The strings, when plucked, sounded four pitches:

> that of the lowest string,
> a perfect fourth above the lowest string,
> a perfect fifth above the lowest string,
> and an octave above the lowest string.

In other words, they spelled out the following pitches (or a transposed equivalent), from highest to lowest:

> D′ A G D

Pythagoras weighed the hammers and found that the weights had the following proportions:

6:8:9:12

The heaviest hammer caused its gut string to sound one octave above that of the lightest hammer, and the middle two hammers, having weights 4/3 and 3/2 that of the lightest hammer, created pitches at reciprocal intervals of 3/2 (a perfect fifth) and 4/3 (a perfect fourth) above.

This pretty story has been repeated for at least seventeen hundred years, but there is, of course, no truth to it. In the first place, when one hits an anvil with hammers (as I have found by demonstration), it is the anvil that rings, not the hammers, and the anvil can ring only at one pitch. This part of the story, in fact, is now assumed to come from a Middle Eastern folktale.[2]

The second part stands up to scrutiny just as little. The pitch of a string rises proportionately to the square root of the weight of a pendulum, not to the weight itself. Yet such was the authority of the ancients that no one contested this fact until the 1580s, when Vincenzo Galilei (father of the famous astronomer) tried the experiment and published the correct explanation in his *Discorso particolare intorno alla diversita delle forme del diapason*.[3] In short, for two hammers suspended from strings to create pitches an octave apart, one would have to be four times as heavy as the other, not two.

The origins of European music theory, then rest on fanciful myths. But the numerical nexus that Pythagoras passed down—6:8:9:12—was sound in its significance and became a structural basis for the vast majority of scales across many cultures. The ancient Greeks derived their scales by assuming the 6:8:9:12 structure as a given, and by using mathematics (or the ear) to insert extra scale tones between the 6 and the 8 and, analogously, between the 9 and the 12.

The nexus 6:8:9:12 is geometrically symmetrical. If we apply the ratio to lengths of four strings all having the same tension, then it spells out a descending series: D′ A G D. If we use it to refer to the ratios between the frequencies of four strings, it spells out an ascending sequence: D G A D′. Other factors (tension, thickness) being equal, string length is inversely proportional to frequency of the pitch produced.

The instrument that the Greeks used to observe these ratios was a *monochord*, which Pythagoras is said to have invented.[4] It is a rectangular board or box with a single string attached at each end (although it is convenient to have at least two strings so that the string being stopped can be compared with the unstopped string). The length of the string is divided on the box or board with marks that divide it into a certain number of *parts*, the number sufficient to derive the intervals one is looking for. One might compare it to a guitar whose frets are evenly spaced throughout the length of the strings rather than placed progressively closer as on a normal guitar. Dividing the string into twelve parts is enough to give us the Pythagorean D–G–A–D′ nexus:

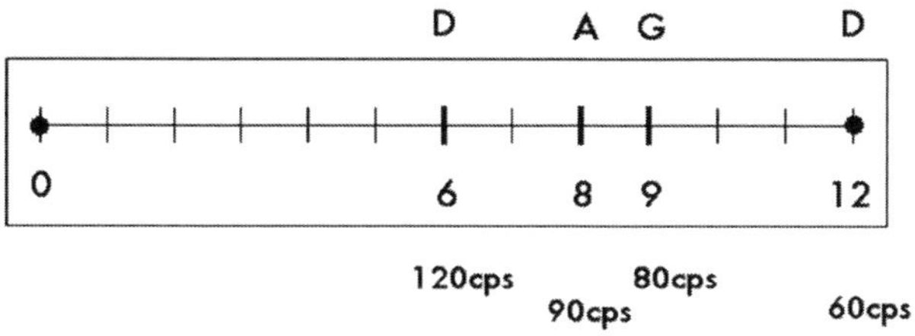

EX. 3.1: Pythagorean D–G–A–D′ nexus on a monochord

The frequencies here are not true to modern-day absolute pitch (60 cps is between B♭ and B; it's not a D) but are chosen to illustrate the reciprocity of frequency and string length. If the string is tuned to D, plucking half the string (six of the twelve parts) gives you a D an octave higher, at twice the frequency. Pressing the string at the nine mark and plucking the longer portion gives you a G, because you are plucking 3/4 of the string and G is 4/3 relative to D. Pressing the string at the eight mark gives you an A, because you are plucking 2/3 of the string and A is 3/2 relative to D. So the ancient Greeks would say (in ancient Greek), twelve parts gives you D, nine produces G, eight A, and six the higher D′. And the frequency in cycles per second is inversely proportional to the string length. (Notice that 6:8 and 9:12 are the same ratios, and thus the same intervals, even though one uses only two of the twelve parts and the other three, because unlike the frets on a guitar, these part lines don't get progressively closer together.)

This also works, more or less, for a flute or other woodwind: closing all holes gives you the fundamental, a hole left open halfway gives you the octave above the fundamental tone, a hole left open at 2/3 gives you A 3/2, and so on. However, in the physics of a woodwind, the exact ratios are somewhat irrationally altered by the material and thickness of material of which the instrument is made. Strings are easier when it comes to making fairly exact determinations. In fact, a monochord will give more exact measurements if, instead of pressing the string (which lengthens it slightly), you construct little movable frets (say, triangular-shaped, sitting on the narrow side) that will allow you to stop the string at a given point without exerting pressure on it.

All of the scales used by the ancient Greeks, all of the medieval European modes, our modern major and minor scales, the ragas for classical Indian music, and most other scales found around the world contain a perfect fourth and perfect fifth within the octave: D G A D′. But D G A D′ itself isn't yet what we call a scale; the gaps between D and G and between A and D′ need to be filled in. How did all of these scales arise?

We will look at three paradigms for the generation of scales that have been invoked, sometimes anachronistically or at least ex post facto, to account for the manner in which the major and minor scales, medieval modes, and twelve-pitch chromatic scale arose. Though perhaps dubious as historically descriptive, these paradigms have value as potential generators of new experimental scales.

SCALE GENERATION PARADIGM NO. 1: THE ANCIENT GREEK GENERA

We can hardly avoid starting with the ancient Greeks, though they did not so much generate scales from a consistent principle as hypthosize various arithmetical ways to achieve the scales they sought. Full octave scales in the Greek theoretical writings all took the Pythagorean 6:8:9:12 as a basis, so in our transposition on D, all of their scales contained the pitches D, G, A, and D′ (or, rather, in reverse order, since they defined scales from the highest note down). The differences lay in the notes that filled in the perfect fourths D–G and A–D′. Since most scales added two steps in the middle, making four pitches in each half, these divisions of a perfect fourth were called *tetrachords*.

The Greeks arrived at three types, or *genera*, of tetrachord: the *diatonic*, the *chromatic*, and the *enharmonic*. Aristoxenus (fourth century BCE, a disciple of Aristotle; more of him in interlude A following this chapter) in his *On Harmonics* (often called *Harmonic Elements*, and first translated into Latin in 1562[5]), was the first to classify them, and he broke with the Pythagoreans by refusing to define them by ratios, believing that measuring intervals by ear was preferable to defining them by lengths of a string.[6] He provided six tunings, two for each type, as defined by fractions of a tone, which in his definition was one-sixth of an octave—*not* given in parts of a string as in the Pythagoras example above, but in a distance we would call 200 cents. (I hope that my more scholarly readers will indulge that I refuse to provide ancient Greek terminology that would add more confusion than clarity to the tuning concepts I hope to get across.[7] Nor will we explore the multi-octave Greater Perfect System as having more to do with Greek notation and performance than tuning concepts.) Thus Aristoxenus's scale assumed, in effect, a seventy-two-tone equal temperament—that is, seventy-two *equal divisions of the octave* (72*edo*, as we will learn to call it in chapter 6).[8] Aristoxenus's definitions of pitches, then, were not based on parts of the string, but in the perceived relative sizes of the intervals, so that a 24 in the following chart is eight times as large as the interval denoted by 3:

Enharmonic	24	3	3
Soft enharmonic	22	4	4
Hemiolic chromatic	21	4½	4½
Tonic chromatic	18	6	6
Soft diatonic	15	9	6
Intense diatonic	12	12	6

Pitchwise, these are to be read downward, with the largest interval always on top, so that each tetrachord (perfect fourth) is divided into thirty parts. All of these groupings add up to thirty units within a perfect fourth (500¢), so by multiplying by 500¢/30, we could translate these tetrachord divisions into modern cents as follows:[9]

Enharmonic	400¢	50¢	50¢
Soft enharmonic	366.7¢	66.7¢	66.7¢
Hemiolic chromatic	350¢	75¢	75¢
Tonic chromatic	300¢	100¢	100¢
Soft diatonic	250¢	150¢	100¢
Intense diatonic	200¢	200¢	100¢

One will note that the enharmonic genus divides the fourth into what we would today call two quarter tones and a major third. It is credited to a seventh-century BCE musician named Olympus and seems to have been extinct by the first century AD[10]; doubt has been cast on whether it was ever used in musical practice at all. However, we will find in the interlude following chapter 12 that it inspired Nicola Vicentino to build an instrument to play it and to compose pieces for it around 1555. Modern composers like Harry Partch (*Two Studies on Ancient Greek Scales*, 1946) and Ivor Darreg (*On the Enharmonic Tetrachord,* 1965) have also written pieces using it.[11]

However, the astronomer, mathematician, and music theorist Ptolemy (c. 83–161) left us the most compendious tome on Greek tuning, the one that proved most influential in subsequent centuries. He criticized Aristoxenus at length for making distinctions that couldn't be backed up by mathematical ratios. Between the Aristoxenians, who started from perception, and the Pythagoreans, who proceeded from mathematical ratios, Ptolemy was in the Pythagorean camp. But unlike some of its more extreme members, he did not consider sonic results irrelevant; he believed in using sounding music to test scales derived from numbers, and if the scales were not aesthetically pleasing, the wrong principles must have been chosen.[12] His *Harmonics* (*Harmonika*) summed up the scales defined by Archytas (early fourth century BCE), Aristoxenus, Eratosthenes (c. 276–196 BCE), and Didymus (early first century BCE), and added several of his own, giving us some twenty scales archived from antiquity. All are defined in terms of string parts, an octave requiring 60 parts of a string divided into 120. (They are given in a table at the end of interlude A.)

So far we have addressed only the division of the tetrachord within a perfect fourth. Greek theory assumed that the octave scale employed two tetrachords separated by a 9/8 tone: one tetrachord in the D′-to-A slot and the other (almost always the same one, at least in theory) in the G-to-D slot. In all such cases, each note in the lower tetrachord has a perfect fifth (3/2) above it in the higher one. Ptolemy, for example, gives Aristoxenus's enharmonic as string lengths of 120, 117, 114, 90, 80, 78, 76, and 60 parts, producing the following ratios and intervals (notice that at 43.8¢ and 45¢, the two smaller intervals are not identical, so Ptolemy has altered Aristoxenus slightly to fit his Pythagorean methodology):

String parts	Interval ratio	Cents between	Ratio from tonic	Cents from tonic
120			1/1	0¢
	40/39	43.8¢		
117			40/39	43.8¢
	39/38	45¢		
114			20/19	88.8¢
	19/15	409.2¢		
90			4/3	498¢
	9/8	203.9¢		
80			3/2	702¢
	40/39	43.8¢		
78			20/13	745.8¢
	39/38	45¢		
76			30/19	790.8¢
	19/15	409.2¢		
60			2/1	1200¢

To play this scale on a monochord, then (as I have demonstrated for students on a dulcimer with the frets removed[13]), one would mark off one-half of the string (an octave) into 60 equal parts numbered from 60 to 120. The open string, equal to 120 parts, gives the tonic. Stopping the string at 117 parts gives the second note, which sounds 40/39 higher, since 120/117 equals 40/39. Fingering at 114 parts produces the next step at 20/19 (120/114 = 20/19), a finger at 90 parts (3/4 of the string, thus 4/3 in pitch) completes the tetrachord, and so on.

The bulk of Ptolemy's scales are not simple ones by any modern definition. His version of what he terms Aristoxenus's hemiolic chromatic uses intervals with a prime number as high as 37, the intervals within the tetrachord being 80/77, 77/74, and 37/30. He has to use fractional parts at times, such as 76⁴⁄₁₁ parts out of 120 in his own tense chromatic scale—clearly not a number a performer is likely to land on accurately. Nevertheless, he has a distinct preference for what are called *superparticular* ratios, ratios of the form (N + 1)/N, in which the numerator is one more than the denominator; only a few of the scales contain ratios not in this category.

It is a poignant fact that only one of Ptolemy's scales was destined for immortality: his own tense diatonic, which became the basis for all European music.

String parts	Interval ratio	Cents between	Ratio from tonic	Cents from tonic
120			1/1	0¢
	16/15	111.7¢		
112½			16/15	111.7¢
	9/8	203.9¢		
100			6/5	315.6¢
	10/9	182.4¢		
90			4/3	498¢
	9/8	203.9¢		
80			3/2	702¢
	16/15	111.7¢		
75			8/5	813.7¢
	9/8	203.9¢		
66⅔			9/5	1017.6¢
	10/9	182.4¢		
60			2/1	1200¢

Let's extract that sequence of consecutive ratios, whose whole-step/half-step pattern gives us, as all the ancient Greek diatonic scales do, what we would think of today as a Phrygian mode:

	16/15		9/8		10/9		9/8		16/15		9/8		10/9	
E		F		G		A		B		C		D		E

If you start with the last 9/8, on the note C, and circle around to the beginning again, you get

9/8 10/9 16/15 9/8 10/9 9/8 16/15

which are the intervals of what is defined as the most basic and consonant just-tuned major scale (called by Harry Partch "the *Ptolemaic sequence*"):

Pitch name	C		D		E		F		G		A		B		C
Step ratios		9/8		10/9		16/15		9/8		10/9		9/8		16/15	
Ratio from 1/1	1/1		9/8		5/4		4/3		3/2		5/3		15/8		2/1

The long process by which ancient Greek modes were transmitted to the West via medieval theorists from Boethius (c. 480–524) on is so tangled by misconception and reinterpretation that we will make no attempt to describe such a comedy of scholarly errors here. Suffice it to say that the medieval modes such as Lydian and Phrygian have no relation to their Greek counterparts. Part of the problem was that the Greeks defined their modes from the top note downward, while the medievals started from the bottom note and ascended (the ancient Greek name for what we would call their highest note, *nete*, meant "lowest."[14]) Somehow only the diatonic genus was transmitted to the medieval world as the basis for our scale systems, and Ptolemy's tense diatonic—having the simplest, most consonant array of intervals in his list, along with Didymus's chromatic—won out as the one the Western world would ultimately base its music on. Even Ptolemy notes that the diatonic was more widely used than the other two: "Now of the genera that have been set out, we would find all the diatonic ones familiar to our ears, but not to the same extent the enharmonic, nor the soft one of the chromatics, because people do not altogether enjoy those of the characters that are exceedingly slackened."[15] He further mentions that within a scale the same tetrachord is not always used throughout.[16] Apparently there was a large gap between theory and musical practice in ancient Greece, so it could well be that the surviving patterns we have laid out here were more the result of arithmetical experimentation than observation.

Scale Generation Paradigm No. 2: Replication of Intervals

Our second paradigm of scale generation comes closer to the musical realities we're used to. This is the practice of generating scales by replication of one or more intervals.

Let's say we start with a pitch, C, and define it as our "tonic" or fundamental pitch, 1/1. Since the simplest intervals, 1/1 and 2/1, will give us only further duplications of the note C at unison or octave, never arriving at a practical scale, we turn to the next simplest interval, 3/1 or 3/2.

We then apply 3/2 to C to obtain our next note, G:

C	G
1/1	3/2

We can then find further pitches by adding another 3/2 above G and one below C—that is, we multiply 3/2 by 3/2 and divide 1/1 by 3/2:

F	C	G	D
2/3	1/1	3/2	9/4

We can then go further, adding more perfect fifths above and below:

B♭	F	C	G	D	A	E	B
4/9	2/3	1/1	3/2	9/4	27/8	81/16	243/32

This gives us a chain of perfect fifths rather than a scale. However, by bringing the notes below C up an octave or two (multiplying them by 2 or 4) and those above

G down by octaves (dividing them by 2, 4, 8, 16), we get a rather nice scale of eight pitches, plus the octave:

Pitch	C	D	E	F	G	A	B♭	B	C
Ratio	1/1	9/8	81/64	4/3	3/2	27/16	16/9	243/128	2/1
Cents	0¢	203.9¢	407.8¢	498¢	702¢	905.9¢	996.1¢	1109.8¢	1200¢

This scale, closely associated with late medieval continental music, is entirely generated by one interval, 3/2. It is called the Pythagorean scale, since it can be generated using only the intervals Pythagoras discovered: 4/3, 3/2, and 2/1. Note also that the numbers of cents are all within ten cents of multiples of one hundred, so it's not far different from the equal-tempered scale on the common piano. (This scale is the subject of chapter 4.) Note that the Pythagorean scale does *not* include the Ptolemaic sequence—E is 81/64 instead of 5/4, A is 27/16 instead of 5/3, and B is 243/128 instead of 15/8. Since those ratio numbers are larger, the intervals are, by definition, not as consonant.

The antiquity of this scale paradigm surely predates recorded history. A Chinese manuscript of the third century BCE records a tuning formula combining both parts of a string or reed flute and duplication of intervals. It directs one to divide the string or reed into eighty-one parts, place a fret or hole at 2/3 that length, another at 4/3 that length, another at 2/3 that length, and another at 4/3 that length (the lengthening representing yin and the shortening yang):[17]

$$81 \times 2/3 = 54$$

$$54 \times 4/3 = 72$$

$$72 \times 2/3 = 48$$

$$48 \times 4/3 = 64$$

This 81:72:64:54:48 nexus gives us a pentatonic scale in Pythagorean tuning:

Parts	81	72	64	54	48
Pitch	C	D	E	G	A
Proportion of length	1/1	72/81	64/81	54/81	48/81
Ratio of pitch	1/1	9/8	81/64	3/2	27/16

Carried out indefinitely, this pattern eventually creates a full chromatic Pythagorean scale, which the Chinese were familiar with thousands of years before Europeans reinvented it. And given that ancient bone flutes with similar tunings found in China have been dated as tens of thousands of years old, one can hardly speculate how long ago the associated concepts of arithmetical parts and duplication of intervals were first determined.

Historically, the perfect fifth is the only interval that has been widely used for one-dimensional scale generation. However, practically any interval capable of producing a variety of intervals (which excludes only the octave, really) could be used.

Experimentally, let's take 13/8 at 840.5 cents, the thirteenth harmonic. From 1/1, one could take powers of 13/8, raising the denominator by powers of two to fit in the octave between 1/1 and 2/1:

1/1 13/8 169/128 2197/2048

And we can do the same for the reciprocal of 13/8—namely, 16/13:

16/13 256/169 4096/2197

Stopping at this point (and we could go further, though the fraction numbers rise quickly) and make a seven-note scale as follows:

Ratio	$\frac{1}{1}$		$\frac{2197}{2048}$		$\frac{16}{13}$		$\frac{169}{128}$		$\frac{256}{169}$		$\frac{13}{8}$		$\frac{4096}{2197}$		$\frac{2}{1}$
Cents	0¢		122¢		359¢		481¢		719¢		841¢		1078¢		1200¢
Steps		122¢		238¢		122¢		238¢		122¢		237¢		122¢	

This is a peculiar scale indeed, but I feel certain some recent composer has experimented with it, and it will create a scale with the same kind of redundancies we find in the Pythagorean scale. For instance, note the 359.5-cent distance (a 16/13 interval, which I have found useful and lovely in my own music) between 0 and 359 cents, 359 and 719 cents, 719 and 1078 cents, 122 and 481 cents, among others. These are intervals unfamiliar to our ears, but the scale, extended far enough, would produce consistent intervallic regularity. Within it one could create a strange, ear-bending musical language that might begin to make its own kind of sense.

Now, there is no reason to limit ourselves to one interval as a basis for scale generation. Let's return to our small chain of perfect fifths, F C G D. No other intervals using the numbers 1, 2, 3, and 4 will increase our repertoire of intervals, but the next number, 5, will. We can construct a tuning as a multidimensional grid, like a mathematical chart with an x axis and a y axis and, if necessary, other axes running at other angles. So we add a 5/4 interval (equivalent to 5/1 and 5/2) above and below the F, C, G, and D, with the horizontal axis representing 3/2 perfect fifths and the vertical axis 5/4 major thirds:

A 5/6	E 5/4	B 15/8	F♯ 45/16
F 2/3	C 1/1	G 3/2	D 9/4
D♭ 8/15	A♭ 4/5	E♭ 6/5	B♭ 9/5

Instead of a one-dimensional chain of perfect fifths, these two intervals create a two-dimensional grid in which the 5/4 major thirds run upward and the 3/2 perfect fifths run from left to right. We can rearrange these twelve pitches (transposing up and down octaves as necessary) into the following scale:

C	D♭	D	E♭	E	F	F♯	G	A♭	A	B♭	B
1/1	16/15	9/8	6/5	5/4	4/3	45/32	3/2	8/5	5/3	9/5	15/8
0	111.7	203.9	315.6	386.3	498	590.2	702	813.7	884.4	1017.6	1088.3

This highly elegant two-dimensional scale (which chapter 5 examines in detail) contains twelve pitches that are fairly evenly spaced throughout the octave. It will become—with great liberty taken in the practice of tempering, or approximation—the basis of European music from the fifteenth century more or less up to the present day. (It even adds in our elusive tritone of F♯.) One will observe that omitting the flat and sharp notes leaves us Ptolemy's tense diatonic—that is, the "Ptolemaic sequence."

Notice that if we extend this grid one more step in any direction, we seem to duplicate pitches in the twelve-step scale:

A	E	B	F♯	C♯
5/3	5/4	15/8	45/16	135/128
F	C	G	D	A
4/3	1/1	3/2	9/4	27/16
D♭	A♭	E♭	B♭	F
16/15	8/5	6/5	9/5	27/20

Here we have an A defined as 5/3 and another as 27/16; 5/3 = 1.6666 . . . and 27/16 = 1.6875, so these are not the same A. Similarly with F 4/3 and F 27/20, and with D♭ 16/15 and C♯ 135/128. All such pairs are separated by a *comma* (from Greek *komma*) with a value of 81/80, 21.506 cents, which is called the *syntonic comma*. The ratio 81/80 equals (3 × 3 × 3 × 3) / (5 × 16). Since the four 3s represent perfect fifths, the 5 a major third, and the 16 an octave displacement, 81/80 is arrived at by rising by four perfect fifths and dropping down a major third (since the 3s are in the numerator and the 5 in the denominator). Thus, if we rise by fifths from F to C, G, D, and A, and drop down by a major third, we find an F that is 21.5 cents away from the F on which we started.

One of the challenges of working with tuning grids of two dimensions or more is the potential duplication of pitch steps and how to define criteria for choosing one pitch over another depending on context. Such problems will come up again and again later in the book, as they have in the history of music theory.

A terminological note: along with the comma, there are other words historically used for very small intervals, and unfortunately their definitions have not been kept clearly distinguished. We have already run into the Pythagorean comma and the syntonic comma, and other tuning discrepancies are sometimes called commas as well, such as the 64/63 "*septimal* comma" of 27.3 cents between a 16/9 minor seventh and a seventh harmonic of 7/4.[18] A *diesis* has had various historical definitions, most recently the 128/125 interval of 41.1 cents between an octave and three stacked major thirds, 5/4 × 5/4 × 5/4 equaling 125/64.[19] *Schisma* is the traditional term for the 32805/32768 interval of only 1.95 cents that separates eight 3/2 perfect fifths plus a 5/4 major third from five octaves. This quantity is also the difference between the Pythagorean and syntonic commas, and we will have occasion to refer to it later. The *kleisma* is a general term for a tiny interval and has been defined in various ways. Then there is the *limma*, which is a part left over, as, say, the 256/243 interval left when two 9/8s are subtracted from a 4/3. The intervals denoted by all of these Greek terms have been the basis for various temperaments, because they are points at which two intervals veer so close in size that the difference between them can be fudged by slight alterations of those intervals' sizes. The distinctions have been so variable and inexact, though, that they are used in this book only when the context is perfectly clear—as, indeed, is generally true of their use in the historical literature as well.

Prime Numbers and Limits

Another name for the tuning of the Pythagorean scale is "three-limit tuning," because it is limited to the ratios you can make by multiplying only 2 and 3. For instance,

81/64 = 3 × 3 × 3 × 3 / 2 × 2 × 2 × 2 × 2 × 2

243/128 = 3 × 3 × 3 × 3 × 3 / 2 × 2 × 2 × 2 × 2 × 2 × 2

The two-dimensional scale just discussed is said to be in "five-limit" tuning, because all of the ratios can be made by multiplying and dividing only the numbers 2, 3, and 5:

16/15 = 2 × 2 × 2 × 2 / 3 × 5

45/32 = 3 × 3 × 5 / 2 × 2 × 2 × 2 × 2

In the course of this book, we will find that as we rise through the number series, each prime number will introduce a new *limit* accompanied by a new quality of tunings. Non-prime numbers do not introduce new intervals but rather octaves, fifths, and other derived intervals from those already encountered.

To obtain intervals outside five-limit tuning, we go to seven-limit. For instance, we can take the two-dimensional grid above and create (though not very extensively on paper) a three-dimensional grid by multiplying and dividing each pitch by 7/4 as in example 9.1. (Following Ben Johnston's notation, which is defined more fully in chapter 9, I have used 7 as an accidental multiplying the starting-note frequency by 7/4, and an upside-down seven, *L*, to indicate a seventh subharmonic, multiplying by 4/7.) We will return to three-dimensional seven-limit tuning in chapter 9.

For a further level, we can take an eleven-based interval, such as 11/8, and multiply and divide every number in our seven-limit three-dimensional grid to create an eleven-limit four-dimensional grid, and so on. As there is an infinity of prime numbers, so there is an infinity of possible dimensions in a grid based on replication of intervals. This rather complex concept is more clearly elaborated in the chapters on seven-, eleven-, and thirteen-limit tuning and is only mentioned now to prepare the ground.

There is, incidentally, no reason to take the prime numbers in consecutive order. La Monte Young derived the tuning of his *The Well-Tuned Piano* (see interlude F following chapter 9) by having 3/2 intervals in one dimension and 7/4 intervals in the other, omitting the 5 axis altogether.

Scale Generation Paradigm No. 3: Arithmetic and Harmonic Means

Our third paradigm for generating scales goes back to Plato's music theorist friend Archytas (first half of fourth century BCE) and also corresponds well to the structure of some of our musical thinking over the last several centuries.[20] It is, in fact, the method used by Pythagoras (or whatever predecessor) in coming up with the pitch nexus 6:8:9:12.

As seen earlier, 8 and 9 divide the octave 6:12 symmetrically—that is, 8 is to 6 as 12 is to 9, and 9 is to 6 as 12 is to 8.

$$8/6 = 12/9 \qquad 9/6 = 12/8$$

This is because 9 is the *arithmetic mean* between 6 and 12, and 8 is the *harmonic mean*.

The arithmetic mean is easy to determine; it is simply what we call the average, given by the formula

$$\frac{A + B}{2}$$

$$6 + 12 = 18, \text{ and } 18 \div 2 = 9.$$

The harmonic mean is, in a way, the inverse of the arithmetic mean and has a more complex formula:

$$\frac{2AB}{A + B}$$

In this example, $2 \times 6 \times 12 = 144$. And $144/(6 + 12) = 144/18 = 8$. The harmonic mean gives an interval that is the inversion of the one given by the arithmetic mean—same size, different direction.

There is also a *geometric mean*, the square root of the product of two numbers—that is, $\sqrt{ab}$. This gives the point halfway between two other pitches, thus giving the midpoint between 1/1 and 2/1 as $\sqrt{2}$, the exact tritone. For instance, 3/2, the perfect fifth, is the geometric mean between 1/1 and 9/4, because 3/2 is the square root of

9/4. Otherwise, since the geometric mean is so often an irrational value, this mean has played a negligible role in just intonation.

Example 3.2 shows the derivation of an almost complete chromatic scale by arithmetic and harmonic means. At each level the pitches are given as pitch names, as ratios to the fundamental C, and as the smallest possible multiples needed to express the ratios in that level as whole numbers.

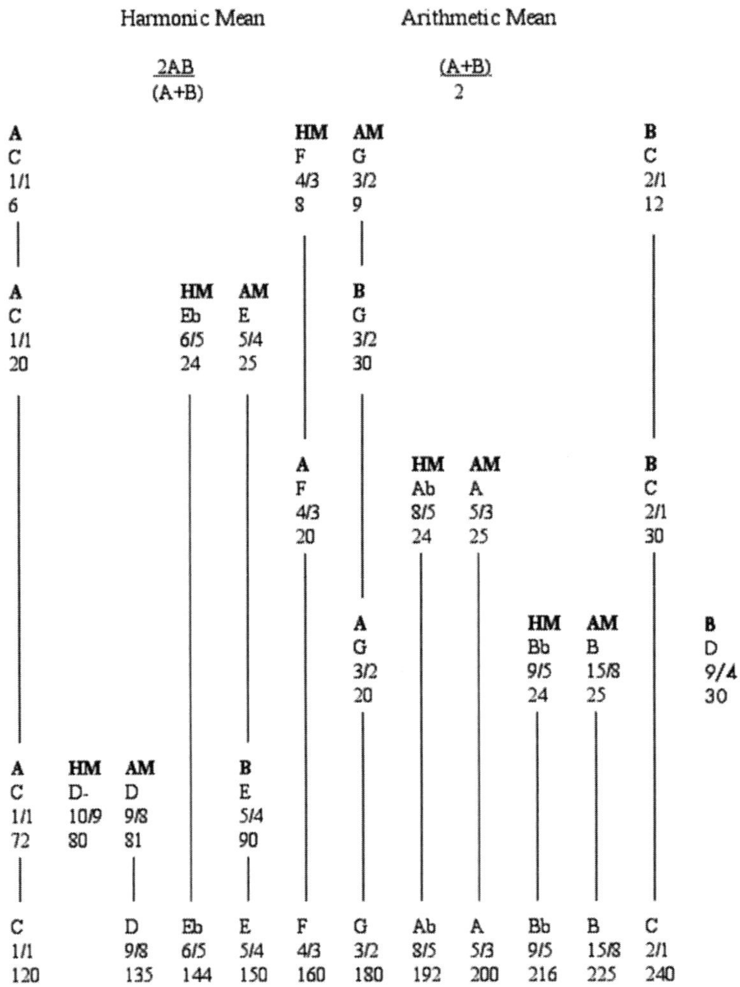

EX. 3.2: Construction of a scale through arithmetic and harmonic means

Here we will construct a scale through arithmetic and harmonic means:

Level 1: In an octave C to C, the arithmetic and harmonic means produce F and G.

Level 2: Within the 3/2 perfect fifth C to G, the arithmetic mean produces E, or 5/4. The harmonic mean produces E♭, or 6/5. The smallest integer by which one can multiply these fractions to express the pitches in terms of whole numbers is 20, giving the pitch nexus:

C		E♭		E		G
20	:	24	:	25	:	30

Level 3: We can duplicate this process with the 3/2 perfect fifth F to C to obtain A♭ and A.

Level 4: To find B♭ and B, we need to extend the process beyond our octave, basing it on G and the D above the higher C.

Level 5: Taking our next most important interval, the 5/4 major third, we find arithmetic and harmonic means between C and E. These means give us two values for the pitch D, 9/8 and 10/9. For reasons explained in chapter 5, 9/8 is considered the more consonant tuning for D in the key of C (and the one contained in the Ptolemaic sequence), but we will run into both of these pitches—only 21.5 cents apart—over and over in our discussions.

Theoretically, one can extend this process into infinity, finding two pitches with which to divide every interval encountered. For instance, within the major second C to D, we find two definitions for the half step:

	HM	AM	
C	C♯	D♭	D
1/1	18/17	17/16	9/8
272	288	289	306

where HM is the harmonic mean, and AM is the arithmetic mean. However, these two inner notes are only six cents apart (ratio 289/288 = 6 cents), too close for any but the most esoteric musical purposes.

Even without subdividing any interval smaller than the major third, however, we have built up enough notes to play fluidly in either C major or C minor. And once again, taking only the natural notes, we've built up a Ptolemaic sequence through different means.

The Tritone: An Archetypal Tuning Problem

Note, too, that example 3.1 provides no F♯ or G♭. The logical thing to do would be to find an arithmetic mean between D and A. However, we see from the bottom row that the ratio D to A is 135:200, which equals 27:40. *D to A in this tuning is not a perfect fifth.*

$$5/3 \div 9/8 \neq 3/2$$

We could solve this problem by substituting our other value for D, 10/9, instead of 9/8. The arithmetic mean between 10/9 and 5/3 is then 25/18, one of the many possible values for F♯ in the key of C. But then our 10/9 D at the bottom of the octave is no longer the same D we have at the top of it, 9/8. In the key of C, D can be consonant with 3/2 G, or it can be consonant with 5/3 A, but it cannot be consonant with both. This is a fundamental problem of the history of keyboard tuning and just intonation.

More generally, though, $F_\sharp$ is the midpoint in the octave C to C′, obtained as an irrational value (the square root of two) via the geometric mean. We will find as we proceed that determining the tuning of a tritone (or augmented fourth, or diminished fifth) is a continual problem in Western theory—one reason it was referred to as *diabolicus in musica*. The arithmetic and harmonic means are two relatively "natural" methods of dividing an interval unequally. Approximating that square root will remain an unyielding bugaboo as we continue to explore five-limit tuning.

The Derivation of Minor Keys

In the following nexus:

		HM		AM		
C		$E_\flat$		E		G
20	:	24	:	25	:	30

it is easy to see that the arithmetic mean within a perfect fifth gives the third of a major triad, and the harmonic mean gives the third of a minor triad. Because of this, the mean paradigm does not privilege the major triad over the minor (nor the dominant V chord over the subdominant IV). Proponents of the harmonic series as a historical origin for harmony (mostly in the twentieth century) have tied themselves in knots trying to explain the existence of minor keys, because the harmonic series spells out the pitches of a major triad. Harmonics 4, 5, and 6 spell out a major triad—C, E, and G in a harmonic series on C—but to find a minor triad we have to go up to harmonics 10, 12, and 15 to find E, G and B. Also within the harmonic series one searches for a subdominant chord in vain. The dominant triad is given by the third, fifteenth, and ninth harmonics, but the subdominant intervals 4/3 and 5/3 are absent from the harmonic series.

Of course, what happened in Europe historically is that one could start on any note of the Ptolemaic sequence to create different modes so that beginning on 5/3 instead of 1/1 yields a natural minor scale, A B C D E F G A. Some twentieth-century composers, starting with Partch, have posited the theoretical existence of an *undertone* or *subharmonic* series as justification for minor keys; the first pitches of a subharmonic series on C are (downward) C F C $A_\flat$ F. Composers Partch, Johnston, and Toby Twining have systematically used the subharmonic series as a substitute for minor keys. (The subharmonic series is discussed at greater length in interlude H following chapter 10.) Since the next pitch is D*L*, however, an 8/7 of 231 cents, this derivation has little historical pedigree. Plus, it is not clear that the subharmonic series occurs commonly as a natural phenomenon. At the very least, emphasis on the harmonic series gives strong primacy to major keys and relegates minor keys and the subdominant to a questionable and subsidiary position. If, however, the thirds of triads are considered as arithmetic and harmonic means, the inequality between major and minor disappears.

Non-Exhaustiveness of the Paradigms

The paradigms given above are far from mutually exclusive; in fact, they are complementary, each offering criteria to limit the proliferation of the others. For instance, as we have shown, the Ptolemaic sequence can be derived using any of them.

The harmonic series, open-ended and infinite in one direction, offers a "natural" basis for considerations of maximum consonance.

The system of Greek parts, based on a 6:8:9:12 structure and opened up to modal variation by starting on different scale steps, gives us a family of related scales.

The replication of intervals paradigm, an ever expanding multidimensional web without theoretical limits, offers a consistent method for expanding a given set of related tones in any direction, with maximum possibilities for transposition of chords.

The mean paradigm, which leads quickly to maximum density and is not open-ended in any practical way, suggests a convenient way to divide intervals within a scale.

Each of these can be used to guide and make choices within the other two.

These paradigms are not the only ways in which scales can be derived, nor do they account for all existing scales. Rather, they are the three primary ways that scales have been generated (or have at times thought to have been generated and discussed as such) in Western culture. Certainly scales can be and have been put together using less rigorous, less mathematically consistent, more intuitive means than those suggested here (as we will see in our consideration of non-Western scales in chapter 14). Taken together, however, these three paradigms provide a flexible and multidimensional framework for the scales and harmonies we will consider throughout most of the rest of the book.

INTERLUDE A

Ptolemy and Ancient Greek "Parts"

This is an interlude. Those who are most interested in tuning theory and not specifically interested in the ancient Greeks may pass to the next chapter with no loss of continuity; the same is true of all the interludes in this book.

The musicologist Wilfrid Perrett mentions a Greek scholar who refused to give him help in translating ancient Greek treatises on music, saying, "Put that stuff away. Nobody has ever made head or tail of ancient Greek music, and nobody ever will. That way madness lies."[1] Today's scholars of the subject are not quite so pessimistic, though it is good to keep in mind that our surviving treatises on ancient Greek music theory, often fragmentary and known only through quotation in later manuscripts, range from a large geographical area and are scattered over a period of some six hundred years. The attempt to pin down a system of music theory correlating to ancient Greek practice is hedged about with ambiguities. We will not attempt to spell out the scale systems of ancient Greece here, which has been done at length in other scholarly works, nor will we attempt to draw examples from the two dozen or so surviving fragments of ancient Greek music. Our only concern, in keeping with our ongoing subject matter, is the tuning of their scales.

Music in the ancient world was part of the *quadrivium*, the quartet of scientific subjects that also included arithmetic, geometry, and astronomy. Writers on music theory also tended to write about the other topics and sometimes made even more lasting contributions in those fields than they did to music. Still, a number of ancient music theorists have had their names kept alive to this day in the history of tuning concepts, and we present them here.

Archytas (first half of fourth century BCE) was a friend of Plato and a student of Philolaus, who publicized Pythagorean music theory. None of his writings survive except fragments contained in the works of others. He is credited with discussing the three mathematical means of music: arithmetic [$(a + b) \div 2$], geometric [$\sqrt{ab}$] and harmonic [$2ab \div (a + b)$].[2]

Aristoxenus (late fourth century BCE) grew up with Pythagorean musical traditions but renounced them at some point, though he retained sufficient affection for Archytas to write the latter's biography. He was a prominent enough disciple of Aristotle (384–322 BCE) for that master to consider appointing him his successor as head of Aristotle's Lyceum, though in the end it didn't happen. His *Harmonic Elements* (*Harmonika stoicheia*) is the oldest Greek musical treatise to have survived largely intact; fragments of a similar work on rhythm have survived in quotation. Aristoxenus achieved a unique fame (or infamy, depending on one's point of view) through his insistence that judging intervals by ear was more important than defining them by ratios. This was his rebellion against the Pythagoreans, which led to a procedural conflict between the Pythagoreans, who depend on numbers, and the Aristoxenians, who judge intervals by ear, that has thundered down through the centuries to the present day. (One can still hear a broad echo of it in the conflict between just intonationists and equal-temperament adherents.) In Stefan Hagel's words, "Of all theorists, he (and his followers) are least restricted by a priori assumptions, and hence most likely to convey unbiased information about ancient music as it was."[3] Aristoxenus was the first to define the enharmonic, chromatic, and diatonic genera.[4]

Eratosthenes (c. 276–c. 196 BCE) was, incidentally, the first person to calculate the circumference of the earth and the angle of its rotation with respect to the sun.[5] His major surviving musical treatise is the dialogue *Platōnikos*, based on the mathematics of Plato's *Timaeus* (or perhaps on an earlier work to which Plato was referring), which draws a distinction between scales derived arithmetically in the Aristoxenian manner and those defined by ratios.[6]

Didymus (latter first century BCE) apparently wrote a treatise, *Concerning the Difference between the Pythagorean and Aristoxenian Theories of Music*, which is quoted by Porphyry (c. 234–c. 305 CE). Didymus was the first to suggest whole tones of different sizes, 9/8 and 10/9, in the diatonic genus, resulting in a ratio of 5/4 instead of equal steps of 9/8 leading to a Pythagorean major third (81/64); thus he contributed to the modern understanding of the just scale. Since the difference between 9/8 and 10/9 is 81/80, the syntonic comma has sometimes been called "the comma of Didymus." It is also in his work that the interval 25/24, now so important as a a chromatic half step, first appears.[7] It was by flipping the order of 10/9 and 9/8 that Ptolemy arrived at his famous tense diatonic.

Ptolemy (c. 83–161 CE) was a Greek mathematician, astronomer, and music theorist who worked at Alexandria. His three-volume work *Harmonika* (*Harmonics*) is the most complete and well-preserved theory treatise we have from the ancient Greek era. He took a middle position between the Pythagoreans and Axistoxenus, arguing that while sense perception could occasionally be fallible, there should be no serious contradictions between mathematics and musical perception. Thus he criticized the Pythagoreans for sometimes entertaining ratio structures that had no relation to musical practice, and the Aristoxenians for defining pitch in terms of perceived distances rather than exact ratios.[8]

The *Harmonika* preserves more than twenty scales based on the enharmonic, chromatic, and diatonic genera as they had been defined by Archytas, Aristoxenus, Eratosthenes, Didymus, and Ptolemy himself. Ptolemy had a conviction that superparticular ratios—ratios of the form (n + 1)/n—were preferable to any others, and most of the scales he lists use only such ratios. He himself defined the enharmonic tetrachord as

5:4 × 24:23 × 46:45 (386.3¢ + 73.7¢ + 38¢),

the "soft" chromatic as

6:5 × 15:14 × 28:27 (315.6¢ + 119.4¢ + 63¢),

the "high" or "tense" chromatic as

7:6 × 12:11 × 22:21 (266.9¢ + 150.6¢ + 80.5¢),

and three diatonic tetrachords: the "tense"

10:9 × 9:8 × 16:15 (182.4¢ + 203.9¢ + 111.7¢),

the "soft"

8:7 × 10:9 × 21:20 (231.2¢ + 182.4¢ + 84.5¢),

and the "even":

10:9 × 11:10 × 12:11 (182.4¢ + 165¢ + 150.6¢).

Ptolemy's *Harmonika* was translated into Arabic in the ninth century, its influence already immortalized through the *De institutione musica* of Boethius (c. 480–c. 524 CE). After Boethius was executed at age forty-four for defending an alleged traitor, his treatise fell into oblivion for a few centuries, and some later chapters were lost forever. It resurfaced, however, in the library of Charlemagne in the ninth century and was subsequently preserved partly or in full in 150 codices. Thus the 6:8:9:12 scale framework of Pythagoras—with Didymus's addition of the syntonic comma between 10/9 and 9/8, then flipped to provide the maximally consonant seven-note diatonic scale as the "Ptolemaic sequence"—bequeathed the just-tuned major scale to the Western world.

For our tuning purposes, Ptolemy's *Harmonika* preserves the three genera in the definitions of his predecessors and himself. His scales, with their definitions in parts and our modern definitions in ratios and cents, are given below. Notice that of the four enharmonic scales given, three use 5/4 for the largest interval, the only place that interval appeared before Didymus suggested dividing the diatonic 5/4 as 9/8 plus 10/9. Didymus's chromatic, with its 1/1, 16/15, 10/9, 4/3 and 3/2, 8/5, 5/3, 2/1 is the only five-limit chromatic scale and the first to distinguish between 16/15 and 25/24 (the half-step interval between 16/15 and 10/9), what we will be calling the *diatonic* and *chromatic half step* (the diatonic being C to D♭ and the chromatic C to C♯). Ptolemy's ditonic diatonic, also used by Eratosthenes, uses only 9/8 for its whole steps, the remaining interval in the perfect fourth being the *limma*, 256/243—the remaining difference between two Pythagorean whole steps and a fourth. This is basically a Pythagorean, three-limit scale. Ptolemy's even diatonic, with its tetrachord of 1/1, 12/11, 6/5, 4/3, is a remarkably evenly spaced scale with all of its intervals between 150 cents and 204 cents, a quarter-tone-inflected scale of eight almost equal steps. With their prime factors of 13, 19, 23, 29, and 31, some of these scales are quite exotic, with intervals that have not been explored much even today. It makes the present-day microtonalist wish that Ptolemy's tense diatonic had not been such a runaway success as to wipe all these others from historical memory.

TABLE 3.1: Scales listed in Ptolemy's *Harmonika*

Enharmonic Genus															
Archytas's enharmonic															
String parts	120		115 5/7		112½		90		80		77 1/7		75		60
Interval ratio		28/27		36/35		5/4		9/8		28/27		36/35		5/4	
Pitch ratio	1/1		28/27		16/15		4/3		3/2		14/9		8/5		2/1
Cents from tonic	0		63.0		111.7		498		702		764.9		813.7		1200
Aristoxenus's and Eratosthenes's enharmonic															
String parts	120		117		114		90		80		78		76		60
Interval ratio		40/39		39/38		19/15		9/8		40/39		39/38		19/15	
Pitch ratio	1/1		40/39		20/19		4/3		3/2		20/13		30/19		2/1
Cents from tonic	0		43.8		88.8		498		702		745.8		790.8		1200
Didymus's enharmonic															
String parts	120		116¼		112½		90		80		77½		75		60
Interval ratio		32/31		31/30		5/4		9/8		32/31		31/30		5/4	
Pitch ratio	1/1		32/31		16/15		4/3		3/2		48/31		8/5		2/1
Cents from tonic	0		55		111.7		498		702		756.9		813.7		1200
Ptolemy's enharmonic															
String parts	120		117 9/23		112½		90		80		78 6/23		75		60
Interval ratio		46/45		24/23		5/4		9/8		46/45		24/23		5/4	
Pitch ratio	1/1		46/45		16/15		4/3		3/2		23/15		8/5		2/1
Cents from tonic	0		38.1		111.7		498		702		740		813.7		1200

Chromatic Genus

Archytas's chromatic

String parts	120		$115\frac{5}{7}$		$106\frac{2}{3}$		90		80		$77\frac{1}{7}$		$71\frac{1}{9}$		60
Interval ratio		28/27		243/224		32/27		9/8		28/27		243/224		32/27	
Pitch ratio	1/1		28/27		9/8		4/3		3/2		14/9		27/16		2/1
Cents from tonic	0		63.0		203.9		498		702		764.9		905.9		1200

Aristoxenus's soft chromatic

String parts	120		116		112		90		80		$77\frac{1}{3}$		$74\frac{2}{3}$		60
Interval ratio		30/29		29/28		56/45		9/8		30/29		29/28		56/45	
Pitch ratio	1/1		30/29		15/14		4/3		3/2		45/29		45/28		2/1
Cents from tonic	0		58.7		119.4		498		702		760.6		821.4		1200

Aristoxenus's hemiolic chromatic

String parts	120		$115\frac{1}{2}$		111		90		80		77		74		60
Interval ratio		80/77		77/74		37/30		9/8		80/77		77/74		37/30	
Pitch ratio	1/1		80/77		40/37		4/3		3/2		120/77		60/37		2/1
Cents from tonic	0		66.2		135		498		702		768.1		836.9		1200

Aristoxenus's tonic chromatic and Eratosthenes's chromatic

String parts	120		114		108		90		80		76		72		60
Interval ratio		20/19		19/18		6/5		9/8		20/19		19/18		6/5	
Pitch ratio	1/1		20/19		10/9		4/3		3/2		30/19		5/3		2/1
Cents from tonic	0		88.8		182.4		498		702		790.8		884.4		1200

Didymus's chromatic

String parts	120		$112\frac{1}{2}$		108		90		80		75		72		60
Interval ratio		16/15		25/24		6/5		9/8		16/15		25/24		6/5	
Pitch ratio	1/1		16/15		10/9		4/3		3/2		8/5		5/3		2/1
Cents from tonic	0		111.7		182.4		498		702		813.7		884.4		1200

Ptolemy's soft chromatic

String parts	120		$115\frac{5}{7}$		108		90		80		$77\frac{1}{7}$		72		60
Interval ratio		28/27		15/14		6/5		9/8		28/27		15/14		6/5	
Pitch ratio	1/1		28/27		10/9		4/3		3/2		14/9		5/3		2/1
Cents from tonic	0		63		182.4		498		702		764.9		884.4		1200

Ptolemy's tense chromatic

String parts	120		$114\frac{6}{11}$		105		90		80		$76\frac{4}{11}$		70		60
Interval ratio		22/21		12/11		7/6		9/8		22/21		12/11		7/6	
Pitch ratio	1/1		22/21		8/7		4/3		3/2		11/7		12/7		2/1
Cents from tonic	0		80.5		231		498		702		782.5		933.1		1200

Diatonic Genus

Archytas's diatonic

String parts	120		$115\frac{5}{7}$		$101\frac{1}{4}$		90		80		$77\frac{1}{7}$		$67\frac{1}{2}$		60
Interval ratio		28/27		8/7		9/8		9/8		28/27		8/7		9/8	
Pitch ratio	1/1		28/27		32/27		4/3		3/2		14/9		16/9		2/1
Cents from tonic	0		63		294.1		498		702		764.9		996.1		1200

Aristoxenus's soft diatonic

String parts	120		114		105		90		80		76		70		60
Interval ratio		20/19		38/35		7/6		9/8		20/19		38/35		7/6	
Pitch ratio	1/1		20/19		8/7		4/3		3/2		30/19		12/7		2/1
Cents from tonic	0		88.8		231.2		498		702		790.8		933.1		1200

Aristoxenus's tense diatonic

String parts	120		114		102		90		80		76		68		60
Interval ratio		20/19		19/17		17/15		9/8		20/19		19/17		17/15	
Pitch ratio	1/1		20/19		20/17		4/3		3/2		30/19		30/17		2/1
Cents from tonic	0		88.8		281.4		498		702		790.8		983.3		1200

Didymus's diatonic

String parts	120		112½		101¼		90		80		75		67½		60
Interval ratio		16/15		10/9		9/8		9/8		16/15		10/9		9/8	
Pitch ratio	1/1		16/15		32/27		4/3		3/2		8/5		16/9		2/1
Cents from tonic	0		111.7		294.1		498		702		813.7		996.1		1200

Ptolemy's soft diatonic

String parts	120		$114\frac{2}{7}$		$102\frac{6}{7}$		90		80		$76\frac{4}{21}$		$68\frac{4}{7}$		60
Interval ratio		21/20		10/9		8/7		9/8		21/20		10/9		8/7	
Pitch ratio	1/1		21/20		7/6		4/3		3/2		63/40		7/4		2/1
Cents from tonic	0		84.5		266.9		498		702		786.4		968.8		1200

Ptolemy's tonic diatonic

String parts	120		$115\frac{5}{7}$		101¼		90		80		$77\frac{1}{7}$		67½		60
Interval ratio		28/27		8/7		9/8		9/8		28/27		8/7		9/8	
Pitch ratio	1/1		28/27		32/27		4/3		3/2		14/9		16/9		2/1
Cents from tonic	0		63		294.1		498		702		764.9		996.1		1200

Ptolemy's ditonic diatonic and Eratosthenes's diatonic

String parts	120		$113\frac{29}{32}$		101¼		90		80		$75\frac{15}{16}$		67½		60
Interval ratio		256/243		9/8		9/8		9/8		256/243		9/8		9/8	
Pitch ratio	1/1		256/243		32/27		4/3		3/2		128/81		16/9		2/1
Cents from tonic	0		90.2		294.1		498		702		792.2		996.1		1200

Ptolemy's tense diatonic

String parts	120		112½		100		90		80		75		66⅔		60
Interval ratio		16/15		9/8		10/9		9/8		16/15		9/8		10/9	
Pitch ratio	1/1		16/15		6/5		4/3		3/2		8/5		9/5		2/1
Cents from tonic	0		111.7		315.6		498		702		813.7		1017.6		1200

Ptolemy's even diatonic

String parts	120		110		100		90		80		73⅓		66⅔		60
Interval ratio		12/11		11/10		10/9		9/8		12/11		11/10		10/9	
Pitch ratio	1/1		12/11		6/5		4/3		3/2		18/11		9/5		2/1
Cents from tonic	0		150.6		315.6		498		702		852.6		1017.6		1200

CHAPTER 4

The Pythagorean Scale

As presented in chapter 3, the Pythagorean, or three-limit, scale is one of the conceptually simplest of all scales, generated from a single and maximally consonant interval. A complete Pythagorean scale can be generated from a series of twelve perfect fifths. The ratios below in the middle column are all powers (including negative ones[1]) of 3/2, those in the right-most scale reducing those fractions to fit into an octave between 1/1 and 2/1:

F♯	729/64	729/512
B	243/32	243/128
E	81/16	81/64
A	27/8	27/16
D	9/4	9/8
G	3/2	3/2
C	1/1	1/1
F	2/3	4/3
B♭	4/9	16/9
E♭	8/27	32/27
A♭	16/81	128/81
D♭	32/243	256/243
G♭	64/729	1024/729

Notice that unlike a series of perfect fifths on the piano, this one does not return to an octave of its starting point: F♯ 729/512 does *not* equal G♭ 1024/729. The difference between them:

$$\frac{729}{512} \div \frac{1024}{729} = \frac{729}{512} \times \frac{729}{1024} = \frac{531441}{524288}$$

is that famous number we've already become acquainted with as the Pythagorean comma: 531441/524288. It is equal to 23.46 . . . cents. It is the amount by which twelve perfect fifths exceed seven octaves, or by which 3/2 to the twelfth power exceeds 2 to the seventh power.

We can rearrange all of these notes resulting from perfect fifths to form a twelve-pitch chromatic scale as follows:

C	D♭	D	E♭	E	F	F♯	G	A♭	A	B♭	B
$\frac{1}{1}$	$\frac{256}{243}$	$\frac{9}{8}$	$\frac{32}{27}$	$\frac{81}{64}$	$\frac{4}{3}$	$\frac{729}{512}$	$\frac{3}{2}$	$\frac{128}{81}$	$\frac{27}{16}$	$\frac{16}{9}$	$\frac{243}{128}$
0	90.22	203.9	294.1	407.8	498	611.7	702	792.2	905.9	996.1	1109.8

If we compare this with the scale commonly used in the twentieth century, the twelve-pitch equal-tempered scale:

C	D♭	D	E♭	E	F	F♯	G	A♭	A	B♭	B
0	100	200	300	400	500	600	700	800	900	1000	1100

we find that it is not far off. The pitch furthest off is the F♯, about twelve cents off, and most of the pitches are within eight cents, which is close indeed. However, as Harry Partch and others have pointed out, the Pythagorean scale may be theoretically simple, but it is not an easy scale for vocal purposes. No one can hear, or measure by ear, the ratio of eighty-one beats against sixty-four clearly enough to sing the 81/64 E in tune against a sounding C 1/1. Its 294-cent minor thirds are bitter and unsatisfying, its major thirds harsh, its sixths equally unsingable. It is a scale not only pure but also a little puritanical.

Unless one is thinking only of the keyboard, of course, there is no reason to limit the Pythagorean scale to twelve pitches. If we continue moving by fifths in both directions, we arrive at not a circle of fifths but a *spiral* of fifths, each divergent from the rung below it by a Pythagorean comma. The following table goes through five "circles" of fifths, from bottom to top, and continuing from left to right, with numbers of cents kept within an octave; pitch names are given until we run out of them (no sign being available for triple sharps or triple flats):

G♭	588	F♯	612	E𝄪	635		659	682
C♭	1086	B	1110	A𝄪	1133		1157	1180
F♭	384	E	408	D𝄪	431		455	478
B𝄫	882	A	906	G𝄪	929		953	976
E𝄫	180	D	204	C𝄪	227		251	274
A𝄫	678	G	702	F𝄪	725		749	772
D𝄫	1177	C	0	B♯	23		47	70
G𝄫	475	F	498	E♯	522		545	568
C𝄫	973	B♭	996	A♯	1020		1043	1066
F𝄫	271	E♭	294	D♯	318		341	365
	769	A♭	792	G♯	816		839	863
	67	D♭	90	C♯	114	B𝄪	137	161

If we examine the points on each rung that return close to any given starting point, we learn which equal divisions of an octave provide close approximations of the perfect 3/2 fifth. For example, let's start at D𝄫 in column 1, at 1177 cents. The points, going up the spiral, at which we come close once again to 1177 are as follows:

Pitches	Cents difference	Number of fifths	Cent deviation from 3/2
D𝄫 1177 to C 0	23.46	12	1.95
D𝄫 1177 to B 1110	–66.8	17	3.93
D𝄫 1177 to C♯ 114	137.1	19	7.21
D𝄫 1177 to B♯ 23	46.9	24	1.95
D𝄫 1177 to A𝄪 1123	–43.3	29	1.49
D𝄫 1177 to B𝄪 137	160.6	31	5.18
D𝄫 1177 to 47	70.4	36	1.95
D𝄫 1177 to 1157	–19.8	41	–0.48
D𝄫 1177 to 161	184.1	43	4.281
D𝄫 1177 to 70	93.8	48	1.95
D𝄫 1177 to 1180	3.615	53	0.068

The "Cents difference" column indicates the difference in cents between the original pitch and a pitch close to it, higher up on the spiral. The "Number of fifths" column shows how many perfect 3/2 fifths we have to go from D𝄫 to reach that new point on the spiral. When we divide the cents difference by the number of fifths, we obtain, in the far right column, the number of cents that needs to be added to or shaved off of our perfect fifths in order to make that pitch in tune with our original D𝄫.

For example, when we climb twelve perfect fifths, we reach a pitch 23.46 cents away from (an octave of) our original pitch. By shaving 1/12 of 23.46 cents off of each fifth, we can make that pitch in tune with the original pitch. Similarly, by climbing twenty-nine perfect fifths, we reach a pitch 43.3 cents lower than our original; but since we can divide twenty-nine fifths into this, we only have to reduce each one by 1.49 cents. The closer the number in the right-hand column is to zero, the better that division of the octave (represented by the "Number of fifths" column) is at accomodating both octaves and close approximations of perfect fifths. So we can see why certain octave divisions have traditionally been championed: not only 12, but 17, 19, 24, 36, and especially 53, which some theorists advocated in the nineteenth century. Fifty-three perfect fifths brings us to a pitch only 3.615 cents away from our starting point, and dividing that tiny difference by 53, we only have to adjust each fifth by .068 cents, just 1/15 of a cent. Fifty-three perfect fifths are almost exactly equal to thirty-one octaves; 3/2 to the 53rd power almost equals 2 to the 31st.

We will return to this notion in chapters 12 and 13 on equal temperaments. For now, it is only important to note that the Pythagorean scale need not be limited to twelve pitches, that it ultimately forms a kind of spiral, and that in each rung of the spiral one finds pitches very close to those of higher and lower rungs. Music teachers will teach you about the "circle of fifths"; try to keep in mind, and be polite when correcting them, that it is actually a spiral.

One can (as Euclid proved and Ptolemy reiterated[2]) obtain the Pythagorean comma by a simpler, different route. It is the amount by which six 9/8 whole steps exceed an octave.

$$9/8 \times 9/8 \times 9/8 \times 9/8 \times 9/8 \times 9/8 \times 1/2 = 531441/524288$$

$$6 \times 203.91\ldots \text{ cents} = 1223.46\ldots \text{ cents}$$

$$1223.46\ldots \text{ cents} - 1200 \text{ cents (an octave)} = 23.46\ldots$$

This means we can visualize Pythagorean tuning more conveniently as a pair of whole-tone scales a perfect fifth apart, as in example 4.1. Each step going horizontally is 203.9 cents; each vertical fifth is 702 cents. It is easier to see here that because 6 × 203.9 cents is more than 1200 cents, the pitch E♭ ends up lower than D♯ by a Pythagorean comma. There is a tradition in string playing (particularly promoted by the great cellist Pablo Casals, 1876–1973[3]) by which sharp notes are played a little higher, as leading tones moving closely into the note they're resolving to, and flat notes are played a little lower, as resolving downward. Though there is no historical continuity between this and the medieval Pythagorean tradition, this is sometimes called *Pythagorean intonation*.

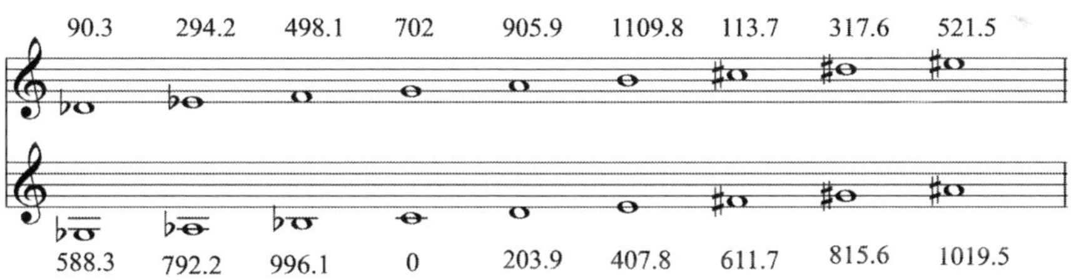

EX. 4.1: The Pythagorean scale as a pair of whole-tone scales

The three-limit Pythagorean scale was the only one tolerated by theorists in medieval France—on the breathtakingly specious reasoning that three was the number of the Holy Trinity. (Arabic scholars had kept alive the mathematical interests of ancient Greece, and the French inherited their tuning knowledge from Arabic treatises, since the Arabic presence in southern France was widespread, leading to a renaissance of interest in the topic at the time.) Pythagorean tuning's problem for composers of the era was that the only common intervals that approach maximum consonance are the fourths, fifths, major seconds, and minor sevenths. The *Pythagorean major third* of 81/64 (408¢) and *Pythagorean minor third* of 32/27 (294¢), and their attendant inversions as sixths, sound harsh to our ears, and apparently did to medieval ones as well, because the thirds were not considered consonances. In fourteenth-century French music, thirds could not be used in final cadences, were avoided on downbeats, and had to be used carefully. In music such as Guillaume de Machaut's (the subject of this chapter's interlude), one can feel the composer's yearning to fill out the chord with thirds, which had to be kept partly repressed. It has been pointed out, though, that the wide major thirds were characterized by an intensity that made the inevitable resolution to fifths all the more satisfying. As discussed in chapter 5, English musicians of the time were not so musically ascetic, so a wave of happier-sounding 5/4s and 6/5s washed down from the north in the early fifteenth century.

INTERLUDE B

Guillaume de Machaut's Notre Dame Mass

Guillaume de Machaut's Notre Dame Mass (or Messe de Nostre Dame, *nostre* being old French for *notre*), probably written in the early 1360s for the Saturday Lady Mass at the Cathedral of Reims, where Machaut served as canon,[1] is one of the great watershed works of music history. It is the earliest known complete (five-movement: Kyrie, Gloria, Credo, Sanctus, Agnus Dei,[2] plus in this case a final *Ite missa est*) mass in which all the movements are by the same composer, and it is remarkable for having elements repeated from one movement to another to create some cyclical unity. It is, then, an early paradigm for a multi-movement work unified by style, motives, and structure. Although we have no firm evidence that fourteenth-century or earlier masses were performed with instruments, the Gloria and the Credo both contain single measures with motives in only the lower two voices with no text, suggesting that instruments might have been used at least to accompany the lower two voices.

Example B.1 gives a reduction of the opening Kyrie. It will be noted that, of the fourteen measures, twelve have only fifths and octaves on the opening downbeat; measures 11 and 13 are the exceptions. In nine of these measures, a third is added to the harmony quickly afterward. Thirds, in the Pythagorean tuning that would have been mandated for a French piece of this era, were considered *dissonances*, being tuned as 81/64 for the major third and 32/27 for the minor third. Thus, they were generally avoided on strong beats, but one can see Machaut's urge to add them on weak beats wherever possible. It has been suggested that the wide Pythagorean major third of 408 cents gave a particular urgency at cadences, resolving outward to a perfect fifth. We also note the double-leading-tone cadences (both notes of a perfect fifth approached in the same direction by half step) at measure 3 going into 4, 5 going into 6, 8 going into 9, and 13 going into 14, in which parallel fifths, chromatically altered as necessary, resolve to the tonic and dominant of the succeeding chord. This type

EX. B.1: Kyrie 1 from Machaut's Notre Dame Mass

of cadence is a stylistic feature of the fourteenth century. (The double leading tone almost always has its third in the bass—that is, in first inversion, as at the end of measure 8, but measures 3 and 4 offer an exception.) The piece vividly suggests how differently thirds and sixths were treated than the more consonant fourths, fifths, and octaves and yet how impatiently the composer's ear wanted to add in thirds and sixths where possible.

CHAPTER 5

The Five Limit, the Second Dimension

History intervenes and alters musical practice. During the Hundred Years' War (1337–1453), northern France was intermittently occupied by the English; the Maid of Orleans, Joan of Arc, turned the tide in France's favor by helping get Charles VII crowned king in 1429, though she was burned at the stake in 1431. Before this high-water mark of the war, however, a great influx of English culture had already invaded France, establishing an English presence at such events as the Council of Constance, which lasted from 1414 to 1418 and reportedly attracted more than seventeen hundred musicians.[1] Unlike the medieval French theorists, who were committed to Pythagoreanism, we have evidence that fifteenth-century English musicians used thirds as consonances in a five-limit tuning. Among other things, an influential English theorist, Walter Odington (fl. 1298–1316), had mentioned in his *Summa de speculatione musice* that major and minor thirds could be sung as consonances of 5/4 and 6/5, respectively, and that they were frequently so altered in actual practice.[2] Also, the music of early fifteenth-century English composers such as John Dunstaple (c. 1390–1453) was noticeably more triadic than the contemporaneous French style; in the precise words of music historian Margaret Bent, in English music of the time, "3rds often seem to be ends in themselves while in contemporary continental music they are still straining for resolution."[3] This fuller, more consonant sound was termed "the *contenance angloise*" by a French contemporary who praised his countrymen Guillaume Dufay and Gilles Binchois for adopting it.[4] The English—historically less theoretically inclined than the French—were happily and intuitively filling their music with major thirds all over the place and tuning them nicely. Pythagorean tuning, so theoretically sound, began to seem practically deficient and, perhaps worse than that, old-fashioned.

Under English influence, then, consonant, five-based thirds began to abound in fifteenth-century music throughout Europe. To deal with them required moving from a one-dimensional tuning concept to a two-dimensional one. Pythagorean tuning is one-dimensional: it can be diagrammed as a line of perfect fifths. In five-limit tuning we must weigh and jostle two desirable intervals: the 3/2 fifth and the 5/4 third. Returning to one of the scale-generating paradigms discussed in chapter 3, we now begin to construct a tuning grid with 3/2 fifths running along our horizontal x axis and 5/4 thirds up our vertical y axis.

We can now also begin using a term that hasn't really been necessary before: *just intonation.* Just intonation is the practice of tuning pitches to pure whole-number ratios. Pythagorean tuning is a kind of just intonation, but since there are no choices to be made among interval sizes in Pythagorean tuning (except for, arguably, the tritone), the term doesn't mean much there. (There is a rather dull argument in the tuning world as to whether Pythagorean tuning—or *temperament*—should be included in the term "just intonation." I decline to take a stance.) From this chapter and in chapters 9, 10, and 11, we will be discussing various levels of just intonation.

Example 5.1 maps out a two-dimensional tuning. Start at any pitch, multiply by 3/2 (move up a perfect fifth), and you'll get the pitch to the right. Move upward, and you'll get the major third above, multiplying by 5/4; 5/4 major thirds run up the columns from bottom to top, and perfect fifths run left to right.

D#- 125/108 253.1¢	A# 125/72 955¢	E# 125/96 457¢	B# 125/64 1158.9¢	Fx+ 375/256 660.9¢	Cx+ 1125/1024 162.9¢	Gx+ 3375/2048 864.8¢	Dx+ 10125/8192 366.8¢
B- 50/27 1066.8¢	F# 25/18 568.7¢	C# 25/24 70.7¢	G# 25/16 772.6¢	D# 75/64 274.6¢	A#+ 225/128 976.5¢	E#+ 675/512 478.5¢	B#+ 2025/1024 1180.4¢
G- 40/27 680.4¢	D- 10/9 182.4¢	A 5/3 884.4¢	E 5/4 386.3¢	B 15/8 1088.3¢	F#+ 45/32 590.2¢	C#+ 135/128 92.2¢	G#+ 405/256 794.1¢
Eb- 32/27 294.1¢	Bb- 16/9 996.1¢	F 4/3 498¢	C 1/1 0¢	G 3/2 702¢	D 9/8 203.9¢	A+ 27/16 905.9¢	E+ 81/64 407.8¢
Cb- 256/135 1107.8¢	Gb- 64/45 609.8¢	Db- 16/15 111.7¢	Ab 8/5 813.7¢	Eb 6/5 315.6¢	Bb 9/5 1017.6¢	F+ 27/20 519.6¢	C+ 81/80 21.5¢
Abb- 1024/675 721.5¢	Ebb- 256/225 223.5¢	Bbb- 128/75 925.4¢	Fb 32/25 427.4¢	Cb 48/25 1129.3¢	Gb 36/25 631.3¢	Db 27/25 133.2¢	Ab+ 81/50 835.2¢
Fbb- 4096/3375 335.2¢	Cbb- 2048/1125 1037.1¢	Gbb- 512/375 539.1¢	Dbb- 128/125 41.1¢	Abb 192/125 743¢	Ebb 144/125 245¢	Bbb 216/125 946.9¢	Fb+ 162/125 448.9¢

EX. 5.1: A two-dimensional grid of five-limit pitches

In the center of the example, enclosing C 1/1, G 3/2, and E 5/4, is a triangle. Move this triangle to any notch on the grid, and it will always encompass the pitches of a major triad. Likewise, one could rotate this triangle 180 degrees to form a triangle pointing downward to enclose C 1/1, G 3/2, and E♭ 6/5. This triangle could then be moved around the page, and it would always enclose the pitches of a minor triad.

Now look at the rectangle in the middle of example 5.1. It encloses twelve different pitches, approximating the twelve-pitch scale we're familiar with, and which could be arranged in scalar order like this:

C	D♭-	D	E♭	E	F	F♯+	G	A♭	A	B♭	B
1/1	16/15	9/8	6/5	5/4	4/3	45/32	3/2	8/5	5/3	9/5	15/8
0	112	204	316	386	498	590	702	814	884	1018	1088

Shift this rectangle around to any position on the grid, and it will always give some transposition of this twelve-pitch scale. You'll notice in the bottom line, which gives the cents above C for each pitch, every pitch in this scale is within 18 cents of a multiple of 100 cents. This is a remarkably evenly distributed scale—so evenly distributed, in fact, that nature almost seems to be begging us to use it.

While this is not per se the historical origin of the twelve-pitch scale, the logic of this three-by-four-place rectangle represents one of the reasons that there are twelve pitches in the European/American musical system. To see why, let's see what happens when we move outside the rectangle.

If we move from D 9/8 another 3/2 (one space to the right), we find an A. But this A, 27/16, is not the same A as we already have inside the rectangle, A 5/3. A 27/16 is 21.5 cents higher than A 5/3. To distinguish them, I have added a plus sign (+) to the 27/16 A. The significance of the plus sign will be made more explicit in chapter 9; it indicates, by definition, that a pitch is raised by 81/80, or 21.5 cents, our syntonic comma. The important thing now, though, is that it and the minus sign (–) distinguish two pitches that have the same letter name but not the same name. A plus indicates a pitch that is 21.5 cents higher; a minus, one that is 21.5 cents lower.

Similarly, if we move from B♭ 9/5 another 3/2 to the right, we find F 27/20—an F that is 21.5 cents higher than the 4/3 F we already have in the rectangle. If we move from A 5/3 *down* a 3/2 (to the left), we find a D different from the D 9/8 we already had: a D at 10/9 and 21.5 cents lower. In fact, if you start from any pitch, move four notches to the right and one down, you'll find another pitch with the same letter name but 21.5 cents higher—and with either a plus sign added or a minus sign taken away. This 21.5 cents, the ratio 81/80, represents the syntonic comma we encountered in chapter 3. Briefly, the syntonic comma could be defined as the difference between the Pythagorean tuning of an interval (say, a 27/16 major sixth) and its five-limit tuning (a 5/3 major sixth). The numerator, 81, is three to the fourth power and thus indicates moving upward by four 3/2s; the 80 in the denominator is an octave of five and indicates going downward by a 5/4.

Move to the left or right of the rectangle, and you find a pitch only 21.5 cents away from one you already have. And with twelve nice pitches *almost* evenly spaced at 100-cent intervals, why would you want to bother with a thirteenth pitch that is only 21.5 cents different from one you've got? This is part of the logic of having only twelve pitches—a fine logic, as far as it goes. We'll find its limitations later.

Moving up or down from the rectangle presents slightly different possibilities. Going upward from A 5/3, we find C♯ 25/24. It's not the same pitch as D♭– 16/15, two notches below the A, but it's close: 41 cents away. You remember how in chapter 1 we said that three 5/4 major thirds were 41 cents short of an octave? Here's the same 41 cents. You'll find the same 41-cent different on the grid between A♭ 8/5 and G♯ 25/16, or E 5/4 and F♭ 32/25.

Now, you might think, *41 cents? That's almost a quarter tone, half of a half step.* It might be worth adding another few keys to our keyboard in order to distinguish between A♭ and G♯, and E♭ and D♯, and so on. After all, string players often do distinguish between those notes (although they're just as likely to play G♯ *higher* and A♭ *lower*, in the kind of intonation mentioned in chapter 4 as Pythagorean). And, as we'll see in interlude C following this chapter, there were attempts in the sixteenth century to reinvent the keyboard with more keys, and with split black keys, to make exactly such distinctions. Harmonically speaking, E♭ and D♯ *aren't* the same pitch, as any music theory teacher will be quick to tell you if you hand him a minor triad spelled C–D♯–G. In tuning, they were *never* the same pitch. They only *became* the same pitch when some genius decided that twelve pitches per octave were enough for a keyboard. (The first such keyboard, with the now-familiar seven lower keys and five raised ones, appeared as the third manual of an organ built in 1361 in Halberstadt, Saxony.[5])

On twelve-pitch keyboard instruments of the Renaissance era there was normally no A♭; there was only G♯. The intervals C–E and E–G♯ are acceptable major thirds, but there was no major third A♭–C. In each of these 41-cent decisions, one pitch is chosen and the other banished to a harmonic underworld where it may be dreamed about but never heard.

Another Derivation of the Twelve-Pitch Scale: The Devilish Tritone

Along with the inherent logic of the two-dimensional pitch grid, the twelve-pitch scale was also determined by the limitations placed by theorists on allowable intervals. The twelve-pitch scale results from two cutoff points. One was to limit allowable intervals to the five limit, which means that every interval ratio has to be expressible by factors of the prime numbers 2, 3, and 5. This is what "five limit" means: no prime numbers allowed larger than five. The other limitation was to allow no numbers of any kind larger than 16. This means we can form ratios from the integers 1, 2, 3, 4, 5, 6, 8, 9, 10, 12, 15, and 16 but not 7, 11, or 13, because those are primes larger than 5. And not 14, because 14 = 2 × 7 and thus involves a prime larger than 5 in its factoring.

	16	15	12	10	9	8	6	5	4	3	2	1
1	1/1	15/8	3/2	5/4	9/8	1/1	3/2	5/4	1/1	3/2	1/1	1/1
2	1/1	15/8	3/2	5/4	9/8	1/1	3/2	5/4	1/1	3/2	1/1	
3	4/3	5/4	1/1	5/3	3/2	4/3	1/1	5/3	4/3	1/1		
4	1/1	15/8	3/2	5/4	9/8	1/1	3/2	5/4	1/1			
5	8/5	3/2	6/5	1/1	9/5	8/5	6/5	1/1				
6	4/3	5/4	1/1	5/3	3/2	4/3	1/1					
8	1/1	15/8	3/2	5/4	9/8	1/1						
9	16/9	5/3	4/3	10/9	1/1							
10	8/5	3/2	6/5	1/1								
12	4/3	5/4	1/1									
15	16/15	1/1										
16	1/1											

Ratio:	Cents:
1/1	0
16/15	111.7
10/9	182.4
9/8	203.9
6/5	315.6
5/4	386.3
4/3	498
3/2	702
8/5	813.7
5/3	884.4
16/9	996.1
9/5	1017.6
15/8	1088.3

Equal temperament:

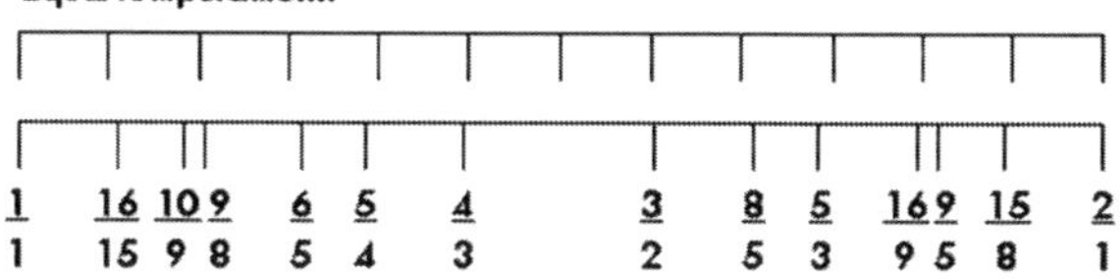

EX. 5.2: All possible ratios among five-limit integers 16 or lower

Example 5.2 gives all possible ratios among the integers 1, 2, 3, 4, 5, 6, 8, 9, 10, 12, 15, and 16. Let's look at what ratios these twelve numbers offer us (assuming octave equivalency):

1/1 and other self-identities	= unison, 0 ¢
2/1, 4/2, 6/3, 8/4, 12/6, 16/8, 4/1, 8/2, 16/4, 8/1, 10/5, 12/3	= octave, 1200 ¢
3/1, 3/2, 6/4, 12/8, 15/10, 6/1, 6/2, 9/3, 9/6, 15/5, 12/1, 12/2, 12/4, 15/10	= perfect fifth, 702 ¢
4/3, 8/6, 12/9, 16/12, 8/3, 16/3, 16/6	= perfect fourth, 498 ¢
5/1, 5/2, 5/4, 10/1, 10/2, 10/4, 10/8, 15/3, 15/6, 15/12	= major third, 386.3 ¢
5/3, 10/6, 15/9, 10/3	= major sixth, 884.4 ¢
6/5, 12/10, 12/5	= minor third, 315.6 ¢
8/5, 16/10, 16/5	= minor sixth, 813.7 ¢
9/1, 9/2, 9/4, 9/8	= major second, 203.9 ¢
9/5	= minor seventh, 1017.6 ¢
10/9	= major second, 182.4 ¢
15/1, 15/2, 15/4, 15/8	= major seventh, 1088.3 ¢
16/9	= minor seventh, 996.1 ¢
16/15	= minor second, 111.7 ¢

This actually gives us thirteen intervals, which, starting them all from the same pitch, could be arranged in a scale as given on the right and bottom in example 5.2. Once again, all of these pitches are within 18 cents of a multiple of 100 cents above the tonic C. Curiously, though, we have two versions of D, 10/9 and 9/8, and two of B♭, 16/9 and 9/5. In a normal musical context, these overly adjacent Ds and B-flats can't be allowed to coexist; one must be chosen and the other banished.

Just as curious, you will note a 204-cent gap between F and G with no pitch to fill it. In the key of C, the pitch halfway between F and G represents the tritone (augmented fourth or diminished fifth). We've already seen the difficulty in obtaining it via the usual scale-building paradigms. Europe was equally unable to find a reasonably simple tuning for it within the five limit, which is why the tritone became *diabolicus in musica*, something to be avoided.

Had European theorists relented and allowed seven as a usable ratio interval, they would have had two fairly consonant tritones at their disposal: 7/5 (582.5 cents) and 10/7 (617.5 cents). But to allow seven would have opened a kettle of tarantulas that the Italian theorists of the late sixteenth and seventeenth centuries shuddered at and collectively slammed shut, not to be opened until Harry Partch decided to take a peek some three-hundred-odd years later. If you look in the rectangle in the center of example 5.1, you'll find an F♯ tritone above C at 45/32, 590 cents, which is a fairly complex ratio in this context. You'll also find others at G♭ 64/45, F♯ 25/18, and G♭ 36/25. None of these were considered singable (and in my experience many singers dislike having to sing tritones up to the present day).

The Justly Tuned Five-Limit Scale

A little arithmetical exploration quickly shows why a twelve-pitch five-limit scale is problematic. Within our central rectangle in example 5.1, there are eight in-tune 5/4 intervals; we have D♭–F and A♭–C, but neither E–G♯ nor A–C♯. Looking for perfect 3/2 fifths, however, we may well recoil to see that we have only nine. The interval F♯–D♭ is easy enough to do without, but we've lost B♭–F, which is now a 40/27 *wolf* fifth, so called for its howling beats. Even more crucially, we've lost D–A, which is a difficult interval to get along without in the key of C. The note D is 9/8, A is 5/3, and the ratio between them is also 40/27. In the key of C we have no ii chord, no V/V. (And D was such a standard key for stringed instruments, involving open strings on violin, viola, and cello.) When we look at usable minor thirds, the pickings are even worse: only six available. This twelve-pitch just scale offers the following six pure major triads at a 4:5:6 ratio: C, D♭–, E♭, F, G, and A♭. Pure minor triads available at a 10:12:15 ratio include c, e, f, g, a, and b. There are some important chords missing there. This was the quandary driving the tuning compromise known as *meantone* temperament, which is the subject of chapter 6.

Of course, there are myriad ways to tune a just scale, even within the five limit and even with only twelve pitches. Using D– 10/9 instead of D 9/8 would have solved the ii chord problem and allowed a pure minor triad D–F–A, but then there would no longer have been a 3/2 ratio between G and D, and the V chord would become useless. Alternatively, you could substitute A + 27/16 for A 5/3 and have your D-major triad back again, but then A+ is no longer in tune with F—81/64 instead of 5/4, and at 407.8 cents even worse than today's major thirds—and you've lost your subdominant chord. Why not raise F to F+ 27/20, to be in tune with D and A+? Then F+ and C are no longer in tune.

You see the vicious circle that begins once you limit your number of pitch steps and try to get them all in tune. In fact, as soon as you have only four pitches related by in-tune 3/2 fifths, you've already lost the purity of a five-limit third, and if you shift a note to get the third right, you lose a fifth. Example 5.3 shows that within the simple pitch nexus C–D–F–G, something is necessarily going to be out of tune in five-limit terms.

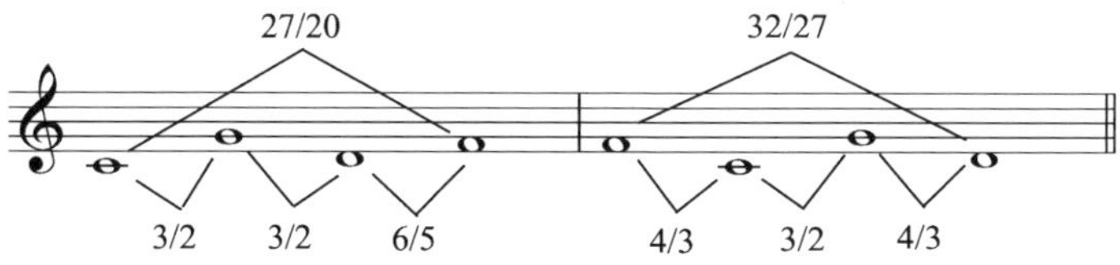

EX. 5.3: Mistuning among four pitches

Of course, string players didn't need to struggle with such incommensurability. All a violinist had to do was play D– 10/9 in a D-minor chord, then switch to D 9/8 if the next chord was G major. String quartet players make this simple kind of adjustment all the time with no theoretical knowledge to spur them to it, just a subtle ear for getting their note to blend with the prevailing chord. Singers in a fine a capella choir have no such problem either, nor do barbershop quartet singers, who aim at maximum resonance.

However, the mathematician, philosopher, and musician Giovanni Battista Benedetti (1530–1590) published, in his *Diversarum speculationum mathematicarum & physicorum liber* of 1585, a stunningly simple demonstration of the impossibility of even strings or voices staying in tune in the simplest five-limit musical context. In the musical passage in example 5.4, the most purely in-tune intonation will result in the progression in example 5.3.[6]

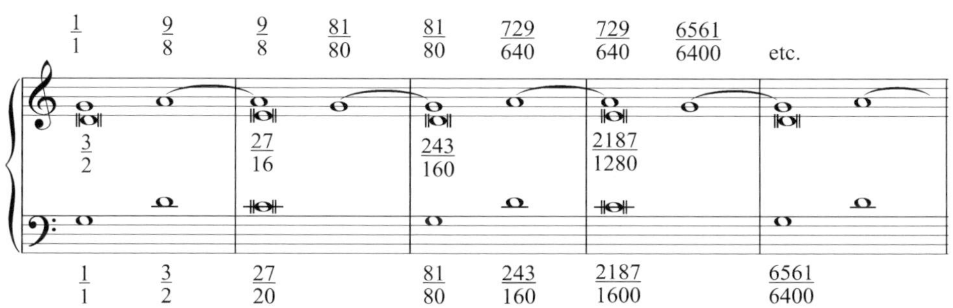

EX. 5.4: Benedetti's demonstration of the impossibility of five-limit tuning

Measure 1, first beat: The D must be 3/2 to be in tune with G 1/1.

M. 1, second beat: The bass's D must be 3/2 to sound with the D still held in the tenor, and the A must be 9/8 to be consonant with it.

M. 2, first beat: Since the A 9/8 is held over, the E a 4/3 fourth below must be tuned to 27/16; the C, to be consonant with both, must be a 5/4 lower than E, therefore 27/20 (27/16 × 4/5).

M. 2, second beat: A 9/8 now resolves down to a G that must be a 3/2 above the still-sustained C 27/20; G, then, will be 27/20 × 3/2 = 81/80.

M. 3: Since G is sustained into measure 3, the bass G must also be 81/80, the D 243/160 (81/80 × 3/2), and the same notes repeat 21.5 cents higher.

In this remarkable little passage using only five pitches, purely in-tune singers will be forced to rise in pitch 21.5 cents every two measures. Within nine repetitions the piece will be in A rather than G, and fifty-six repetitions will cause them to slowly traverse an entire octave without seeming to have changed key! Never have the inherent problems of five-limit tuning been more sharply (you'll excuse the pun) brought into focus. The musician who wants his music meticulously in tune must indeed feel like the gods are laughing at him.

Das I. vnd II. Diſcant-clavier.

EX. 5.5: The seven-plus-five keyboard on the 1361 Halberstadt organ, from Praetorius's *Syntagma Musicum*

INTERLUDE C

Some Modern Five-Limit Notions

Performance in five-limit just intonation was presumably common during the Renaissance and is apparently still practiced by certain early music groups today. Musical examples we could adduce as ostensible illustrations would look too diatonically simple to be revealing. On the other hand, while not much recent microtonal music remains within the five limit, a couple of unusual examples leap to mind.

Terry Riley: *The Harp of New Albion*

One of these examples is *The Harp of New Albion* (1986), a two-hour improvisatory piano piece by the minimalist-pioneer composer Terry Riley (b. 1935). As detailed in the liner notes, *The Harp of New Albion* employs a simple five-limit scale on C♯, differing from the more common form given at the beginning of chapter 5 only by its substitution of 64/45 instead of 45/32:

C♯	D	D♯	E	E♯	F♯	G	G♯	A	A♯	B	B♯
$\frac{1}{1}$	$\frac{16}{15}$	$\frac{9}{8}$	$\frac{6}{5}$	$\frac{5}{4}$	$\frac{4}{3}$	$\frac{64}{45}$	$\frac{3}{2}$	$\frac{8}{5}$	$\frac{5}{3}$	$\frac{16}{9}$	$\frac{15}{8}$

Unusually, however, Riley does not use C♯ 1/1 as a tonic in any of the eleven movements, but rather tonics on A♯, F♯, D, A, B♯, and B, resulting in a series of five-limit modes, here shown with the names of the movements they apply to:[1]

A♯ ("The New Albion Chorale," "The Orchestra of Tao"):

$\frac{1}{1}$ $\frac{16}{15}$ $\frac{9}{8}$ $\frac{6}{5}$ $\frac{32}{25}$ $\frac{27}{20}$ $\frac{36}{25}$ $\frac{3}{2}$ $\frac{8}{5}$ $\frac{128}{75}$ $\frac{9}{5}$ $\frac{48}{25}$

F$_\sharp$ ("The Discovery"):

$$\frac{1}{1}\quad\frac{16}{15}\quad\frac{9}{8}\quad\frac{6}{5}\quad\frac{5}{4}\quad\frac{4}{3}\quad\frac{45}{32}\quad\frac{3}{2}\quad\frac{8}{5}\quad\frac{27}{16}\quad\frac{9}{5}\quad\frac{15}{8}$$

D ("Riding the Westerleys," "Premonition Rag," "Return of the Ancestors"):

$$\frac{1}{1}\quad\frac{135}{128}\quad\frac{9}{8}\quad\frac{75}{64}\quad\frac{5}{4}\quad\frac{4}{3}\quad\frac{45}{32}\quad\frac{3}{2}\quad\frac{25}{16}\quad\frac{5}{3}\quad\frac{225}{128}\quad\frac{15}{8}$$

A ("Cadence on the Wind"):

$$\frac{1}{1}\quad\frac{25}{24}\quad\frac{10}{9}\quad\frac{75}{64}\quad\frac{5}{4}\quad\frac{4}{3}\quad\frac{45}{32}\quad\frac{3}{2}\quad\frac{25}{16}\quad\frac{5}{3}\quad\frac{16}{9}\quad\frac{15}{8}$$

B$_\sharp$ ("Ascending Whale Dreams," "Circle of Wolves") :

$$\frac{1}{1}\quad\frac{16}{15}\quad\frac{256}{225}\quad\frac{6}{5}\quad\frac{32}{25}\quad\frac{4}{3}\quad\frac{64}{45}\quad\frac{1024}{675}\quad\frac{8}{5}\quad\frac{128}{75}\quad\frac{16}{9}\quad\frac{256}{135}$$

B ("Land's End"):

$$\frac{1}{1}\quad\frac{135}{128}\quad\frac{9}{8}\quad\frac{6}{5}\quad\frac{81}{64}\quad\frac{27}{20}\quad\frac{45}{32}\quad\frac{3}{2}\quad\frac{8}{5}\quad\frac{27}{16}\quad\frac{9}{5}\quad\frac{45}{24}$$

The following passage from the beginning of "Premonition Rag" (ex. C.1, transcription by the author), then, follows a dorian mode—1/1, 9/8, 75/64, 4/3, 3/2, 5/3—conventionally tuned except for the 75/64 F, which is highly emphasized and, at a low 274.5 cents, has rather a delicious bite.

EX. C.1: Riley, "Premonition Rag" from *The Harp of New Albion*

The movements in B$_\sharp$ have a more complex set of ratios. "Circle of Wolves" opens by ruminating on C, E, G, B$_\flat$, and B, which I have respelled in example C.2 according to Riley's definition of the tuning, with C as B$_\sharp$. The major third, at 32/25 = 427 cents, is quite sharp, as is the "perfect" fifth at 1024/675 = 721.5 cents. The leading tone, 256/135, is also rather sharp at 1108 cents, and the passage has a nice buzz to it from all the mistuned intervals. With all of these diatonic but unfamiliarly tuned intervals, this movement is a circle of wolves indeed. (In chapter 11 Ben Johnston's modal use of a just-intonation scale applies a similar technique to the nineteen limit.)

EX. C.2: Riley, "Circle of Wolves" from *The Harp of New Albion*

Ben Johnston: Sonata for Microtonal Piano

Ben Johnston's early works managed to wring quite a repertoire of pitches and plenty of buzz from merely five-limit intervals. His Sonata for Microtonal Piano (1964) in particular is a massive, clangorous twelve-tone work with one of the most complex keyboard tunings ever devised, though still within the five limit. The overall principle of the tuning is that fifths are pure and octaves are not. In his notation, minuses lower a pitch 21.5 cents for the syntonic comma and pluses raise it by the same amount. The second colum of pitches in example C.3 contains a string of thirds:

D– F– A– C– E– G– B– D– F A C E G B D F+ A+ C+ E+ G+ B+ D+ F++ A++

in which closely spaced fifths are all pure 3/2s, but notes that would seem to be two octaves apart are always 2421.5 cents apart, or 81/20. Overall there are eighty-one different pitches used on the keyboard.[2] The composition of the piece employs two twelve-tone rows, but which version of a pitch one gets depends on which register of the piano it falls in. Plus, the rows are based on two popular songs, "What Is This Thing Called Love?" and "I'm in the Mood for Love,"[3] both of them characteristic of the insouciant way the European avant-garde and pop-music influences crashed together in experimental music in the 1970s Midwest.

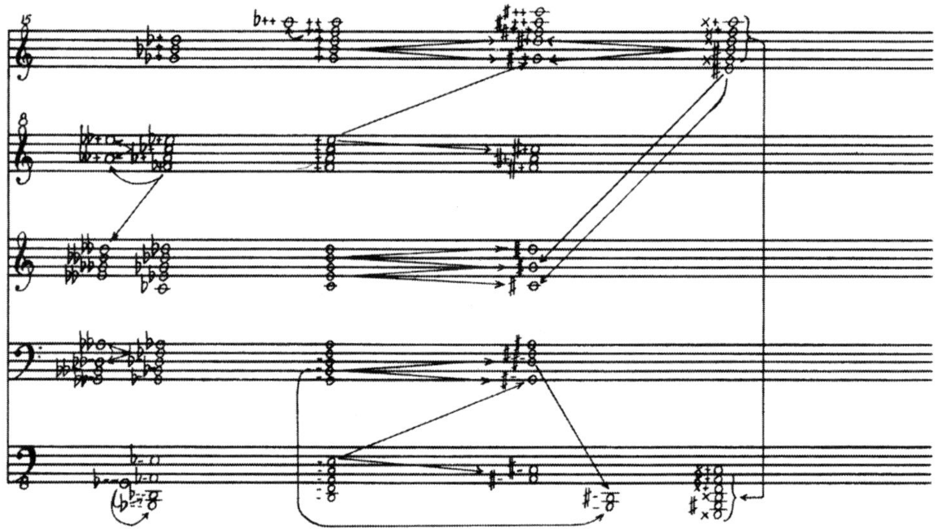

EX. C.3: Johnston, tuning chart for the Sonata for Microtonal Piano

Perhaps never before or since have the simple consonances of five-limit tuning been used at the service of such bristling harmonic complexity.

CHAPTER 6

Meantone Temperament and the Primacy of Thirds

As we saw in chapter 5, the attempt to tune both thirds and fifths simply and perfectly avalanches into a superfluity of pitches, many of them only 21.5 cents apart, inconveniently close for singers and especially for keyboards, which would require many more than twelve keys to play them all. A compromise tuning was needed, and the one that resulted was called *meantone*, for reasons that will be explained shortly. (The word "meantone" is of relatively modern coinage. In earlier centuries it was simply referred to as "keyboard tuning."[1]) It may have been widespread in keyboard tuning by the late fifteenth century, but no description of it survives earlier than a 1523 treatise by Pietro Aron (*Toscanello de la Musica*); even Aron only describes the principle by which fifths are flatted to preserve the justness of the major third and does not detail a full scale.[2] Not until the 1570s did Gioseffo Zarlino (c. 1517–1590) and Francisco de Salinas (1513–1590) provide precise mathematical descriptions. And meantone is more accurately called a temperament than a tuning, because, rather than based on precise intervallic ratios, it is achieved by *tempering* notes, slightly lowering or raising them by ear until they reach an acceptable level of compromise.

The distinction between tuning and tempering used to be crucial in discussions of intonation; it seems less widely insisted on in tuning circles today. Exactly speaking, one *tunes* pitches to whole-number ratios but *tempers* them to approximate, in-between ratios that are theoretically irrational. With modern tuning instruments, however, we can tune an interval to an irrational value with a close approach to exactitude, and the distinction of tempering by ear has lost some of its practical punch. Purist disapproval notwithstanding, the two terms will not be meticulously kept separate in this book.

Meantone temperament prevailed in European music throughout the sixteenth and seventeenth centuries and continued being used in pockets of resistance up through the entire nineteenth century, especially in organ tuning and especially in England.

(According to a common prejudice, the English hadn't produced a great composer since Henry Purcell (c. 1659–1695) in the seventeenth century, and their best musical works dated back to the Renaissance and Baroque, a repertoire they strove to keep alive.) In terms of longevity, then, meantone is the most successful tuning in European history, having lasted more than four hundred years.

The principle of meantone temperament—at least the seminal form we will define first—is that all major thirds in common use must be pure 5/4 intervals of 386.3 cents and that the fifths must be "squeezed" to accommodate the thirds. The central anchor of meantone is the major third C–E. How do we bend fifths to get that third in tune? Well, a series of four perfect fifths will lead from C to E:

Pitches	C		G		D		A		E	
Cents		701.955¢		701.955¢		701.955¢		701.955¢		= 2807.82¢

These four stacked fifths add up to an interval of two octaves and a major third at 2807.82 cents. What we want to end up with instead is an interval of two 1200-cent octaves plus a 5/4 third of 386.3 cents, or 2786.3 cents. Because 2807.8 – 2786.3 = 21.5 cents, each fifth must be "squeezed" by one-fourth of that 21.5 cents in order to get the third in tune. Thus, each fifth is approximately

$$702 - (1/4 \times 21.5) = 702 - 5.375 = 696.625 \text{ cents}$$

Let's look at this construction stated in ratios:

C		G		D		A		E	
	3/2	×	3/2	×	3/2	×	3/2		= 81/16
C		C		C		E			
	2/1	×	2/1	×	5/4				= 20/4 = 80/16

The difference between the Pythagorean third and the meantone 5/4 third is 81/16 to 80/16, or 81/80, 21.506289 . . . cents: the good old syntonic comma. The syntonic comma is the difference between a Pythagorean third or sixth and its simplest five-limit (based on a ratio involving the number five) equivalent. In meantone temperament, we distribute the syntonic comma among the "perfect" fifths by flattening them to accommodate it. There are different ways of distributing parts of that comma; the temperament we are discussing now is called "1/4-comma meantone" because the fifths are each flattened by one-fourth of the comma.

Since that high E vibrates five times as fast as the C two octaves and a third below it (5/4 × 2/1 × 2/1 = 5), the ratio we end up with for each slightly flattened fifth will be defined by this formula:

C		G		D		A		E	
	X	×	X	×	X	×	X		= 5 (20/4)

The fourth root of five, then, is the number that, multiplied by itself four times, will equal the interval two octaves and a third from C to E. The fourth root of five was a standard value of a consonant "perfect" fifth for more than three hundred years of European history.

Let's see what values this gives us for our five pitches so far:

Pitch	C	G	D	A	E
Ratio	1/1	$\sqrt[4]{5}$	$\sqrt[2]{5}$	$(\sqrt[4]{5})^3$	5
Cents	0	696.58 . . .	1393.16 . . .	2089.74 . . .	2786.3 . . .

Now let's transpose by octaves to get all these pitches in the same octave:

Pitch	C	D	E	G	A
Ratio	1/1	$\sqrt[2]{5}/2$	5/4	$\sqrt[4]{5}$	$(\sqrt[4]{5})^3/2$
Cents	0	193.157 . . .	386.313 . . .	696.58 . . .	889.735 . . .

In this sequence the fifths and fourths are all equally (and slightly) out of tune, and the major third C–E is perfectly in tune.

Now that we've arranged the first five tones as a pentatonic scale, there is an easier, more practical way to look at meantone temperament. Notice that the major second C–D is 193.157 . . . cents, which is exactly half of C–E at 386.313 . . . cents: 193.157 . . . × 2 = 386.313. . . . The note D is tuned by ear to the (geometric) *mean*, the midpoint, between C and E. And that's where meantone temperament gets its name. (The meantone major second is also halfway between the 10/9 major second of 182.4 cents and the 9/8 major second of 203.9 cents.) Likewise, we will find that A is tuned to the midpoint between G and B; G, to the midpoint between F and A; F, to the midpoint between E♭ and G; and so on.

C, D, E, G, and A are now tuned. We've got seven pitches left if we're thinking of keyboards (though we will go beyond that limitation later), and we want as many perfect 5/4 thirds as possible. Tuning each of the other seven notes a 5/4 third away from one of our already tuned pitches, we get

D–F♯	=	386.3¢	(tune upward from D)
E♭–G	=	386.3¢	(tune downward from G)
E–G♯	=	386.3¢	(tune upward from E)
F–A	=	386.3¢	(tune downward from A)
G–B	=	386.3¢	(tune upward from G)
A–C♯	=	386.3¢	(tune upward from A)
B♭–D	=	386.3¢	(tune downward from D)

And that completes our twelve pitches. Our scale, then, is as follows:

C	C♯	D	E♭	E	F	F♯	G	G♯	A	B♭	B
0	76.0	193.2	310.3	386.3	503.4	579.5	696.6	772.6	889.7	1006.8	1082.9

Though it is of only academic interest, we can derive the remainder of the ratios by multiplying or dividing by 5/4 from our original five pitches:

C	1/1	=	1	=	0¢
C♯	$5(\sqrt[4]{5})^3/16$	=	1.0449 . . .	=	76.05¢
D	$\sqrt{5}/2$	=	1.118 . . .	=	193.2¢
E♭	$4(\sqrt[4]{5})/5$	=	1.19628 . . .	=	310.265¢
E	5/4	=	1.25	=	386.3¢
F	$2(\sqrt[4]{5})^3/5$	=	1.337 . . .	=	503.42¢
F♯	$5(\sqrt{5})/8$	=	1.398 . . .	=	579.47¢
G	$\sqrt[4]{5}$	=	1.495 . . .	=	696.6¢
G♯	25/16	=	1.5625	=	772.63¢
A	$(\sqrt[4]{5})^3/2$	=	1.672 . . .	=	889.735¢
B♭	$4\sqrt{5}/5$	=	1.789 . . .	=	1006.84¢
B	$5(\sqrt[4]{5})/4$	=	1.869 . . .	=	1082.89¢

Again, the type of meantone temperament we've just described is called 1/4-comma meantone, because each fifth is squeezed by 1/4 of a syntonic comma. When a writer simply refers to "meantone," this is most likely the specific temperament intended.[3] However, there were many other sizes of meantone used and especially theorized about in the seventeenth and eighteenth centuries, and we will consider some of the more common ones below.

I have stopped at a limit of twelve pitches, because I took as a first assumption that we were defining the limits of a twelve-pitch keyboard. But in reality the meantone system (like the Pythagorean) is open-ended, because violins, cellos, trombones, singers, and certain other instruments are not limited to playing or singing only twelve pitches in a scale. If we continue our system outward by major seconds—which are all the same size at 193.15 cents—we can visualize a meantone system (as we did the Pythagorean) as two whole-tone scales, separated here by a perfect fifth of 696.6 cents, in example 6.1.

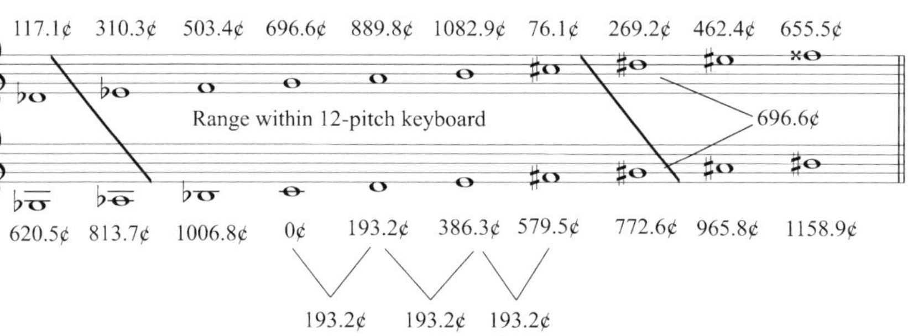

EX. 6.1: 1/4-comma meantone conceptualized as two whole-tone scales

The twelve pitches between the two diagonal lines are all we would have on a twelve-pitch keyboard (and if one starts on the E♭, going diagonally down to the B♭ and then up to the F, and so on, one can understand the scale as a chain of eleven *meantone fifths* of 696.6 cents each). A string quartet, however, has no such limitation, and we see in this example that—since the meantone major second of 193.15 cents is smaller than our equal-tempered second of 200 cents, thus six such major seconds will fall short of an octave—E♭ is 310.3 cents above C, while D♯ is only 269.2 cents above C. The same difference exists between A♭ and G♯, B♭ and A♯, C and B♯, and so on. All the major seconds (notated as such) are 193.15 cents, all the major thirds are 386.3 cents, and all the perfect fifths are 696.6 cents. But every note with a flat (such as E♭) is 41.1 cents above what we think of as its enharmonic equivalent (D♯). Thus a meantone system contains a theoretical infinity of pitches, and all are notated differently, as the correctly spelled whole-tone scale will ascend A♯, B♯, C×, D×, E×, F-triple-sharp, and so on, without ever coming to the same note-spelling twice. It turns out your music theory teacher was wrong: D♯ and E♭ are *not* the same pitch. Didn't sound right, did it?

This is why the eighteenth-century convention of violin playing, as documented for Leopold and Wolfgang Amadeus Mozart among others, mandated that D♯ be played lower than E♭ and similarly for all other enharmonic "equivalents." (In a Pythagorean intonation, as we've seen, the opposite is true: D♯ is higher than E♭, and so on.) In addition, there were, in the seventeenth and eighteenth centuries, occasionally keyboards made with split keys so that fourteen or more pitches were possible, with one key for D♯ and another for E♭ (or G♯ and A♭), in order to facilitate playing in more keys.

Qualities of 1/4-Comma Meantone

Let us limit ourselves, for a moment more, to the twelve pitches of conventional keyboard music, only because early Baroque keyboard music is an exquisite demonstration of how tuning shapes musical expression. Example 6.2 shows the size of major thirds, perfect fifths, and minor thirds built on each of the twelve pitches of the scale. Remember that in considering the major and minor triads of European harmony, we are looking for three optimum interval sizes:

> 386.3 cents for the 5/4 major third;
> 315.6 cents for the 6/5 minor third; and
> 702 cents for the 3/2 perfect fifth.

You'll notice that there are two sizes of major third, two sizes of perfect fifth, and two sizes of minor third. Eight pitches have 386.3-cent major thirds built on them, all but C♯, F♯, G♯, and B. Eleven pitches have pretty good perfect fifths of 696.6 cents, all but G♯. And nine pitches have minor thirds of 310.3 cents, which is not perfect but only 5 cents flat from perfect (which is still three times as good as equal temperament offered us in the twentieth century).

M. 3rd	Cents	P. 5th	Cents	m. 3rd	Cents
C-E	386.3	C-G	696.6	C-Eb	310.3
C#-F	**427.4**	C#-G#	696.6	C#-E	310.3
D-F#	386.3	D-A	696.6	D-F	310.3
Eb-G	386.3	Eb-Bb	696.6	Eb-F#	**269.2**
E-G#	386.3	E-B	696.6	E-G	310.3
F-A	386.3	F-C	696.6	F-G#	**269.2**
F#-Bb	**427.4**	F#-C#	696.6	F#-A	310.3
G-B	386.3	G-D	696.6	G-Bb	310.3
G#-C	**427.4**	G#-Eb	**737.7**	G#-B	310.3
A-C#	386.3	A-E	696.6	A-C	310.3
Bb-D	386.3	Bb-F	696.6	Bb-C#	**269.2**
B-Eb	**427.4**	B-F#	696.6	B-D	310.3

EX. 6.2: Interval sizes on a 1/4-comma meantone 12-pitch keyboard

Any pitch that has a usable fifth and major third built on it can boast a major triad. On a twelve-pitch keyboard, there are eight of these: C, D, E♭, E, F, G, A, and B♭. Any pitch that has a usable minor third and perfect fifth built on it can be the basis for a minor triad: C, C♯, D, E, F♯, G, A, B. So meantone temperament provides us with eight usable major triads and eight usable minor triads. As you might expect, the minor triads all represent the relative minors of the major triads: C major goes with A minor, D major goes with B minor, E♭ major goes with C minor, and so on. That is a larger number of triads, especially more musically crucial triads, than we had with our just five-limit keyboard in chapter 5. We could change which triads are usable by tweaking a pitch here and there, such as tuning all the E-flats down to D-sharp, which would give us B major at the expense of C minor; in any case we will still have only eight of each.

You might also notice that none of the intervals that are unusable are spelled correctly. That is, C♯–F isn't really a major third anyway, but a diminished fourth, and so on for F♯–B♭, G♯–C, and B–E♭. The interval G♯–E♭ isn't a perfect fifth, but a diminished sixth. In fact, in a meantone tuning centered on C–E, there is no A♭, because G♯ is tuned with reference to E, not C. Likewise, there is no A♯, because B♭ is tuned a major third away from D, not F♯. There are no enharmonic equivalents in meantone temperament. The pitches D♭, D♯, G♭, A♭, and A♯ don't really exist here.

And sure enough, if you look through keyboard repertoire from the sixteenth and seventeenth centuries, you won't find pieces in E♭ minor or F♯ major. You'll find pieces in C major or minor, D major and minor, B♭ major, and A minor. For the two hundred or so years that meantone was dominant, composers stayed pretty close to the central keys (in the circle of fifths) of F and C and G and D major, or A minor and E minor so they would have the chords available that they needed to define the tonality. Anything in A♭ major or G♯ minor was just impossible because of that howling 737.6-cent fifth; those keys were avoided entirely. Meantone temperament provided pure major thirds at a sacrifice of transposition possibilities.

If we look, for example, at the *Fitzwilliam Virginal Book*—a massive compendium that is the most important source for seventeenth-century English keyboard music—we will find, among its hundreds of compositions by various composers, no piece whose key signature ranges further from C major/A minor than two sharps or two flats. We will find no Ds, Gs, or As flatted, nor any A-sharps, and only a handful of D-sharps. Most of the D-sharps are left very quickly and not dwelled upon, except for one *Pavana Chromatica* by William Tisdall, which rather daringly begins and ends on B-major triads. Even here, however, the piece seems named for its chromatic melodic progressions (such as C♯–C–B) rather than for any tolerance of extreme dissonance, and, as there are no E-flats in the piece, it would have been a rather simple matter to tune the instrument's E-flats down 41 cents to D-sharps if one wanted to avoid the B-major chords' howling 32/25 major thirds (much easier to do on a virginal or harpsichord than on a modern piano). D-sharps in a Baroque composition may indicate a keyboard tuned in meantone around G as central tonic rather than C. What one will *not* find, however (though we'll see a wild exception in interlude D following this chapter), are enharmonic spellings of the same pitch within one piece.

Interestingly, if one looks at seventh chords in 1/4-comma meantone, most of them have a minor seventh of 1006.9 cents. But two usable seventh chords, those built on B♭ (B♭ D F G♯) and E♭ (E♭ G B♭ C♯) have minor sevenths (more accurately, augmented sixths) of 965.8 cents, which is remarkably close to the pure 7/4 minor seventh of 968.8 cents. This fact had been noted in the eighteenth century. Theorist Giordano Riccati (1709–1790) called the meantone dominant B♭–D–F–G♯ "more tranquil and consonant" than the other dominant sevenths (and one would have to include E♭–G–B♭–C♯ as well), for which reason E♭ was prized as being a particularly expressive key.[4] (The dominant on E♭ would yearn to resolve to A♭, and there was no such key—a poignant thought.) The idea of the different keys having different qualities or colors is one that lasted well through the nineteenth century and seems quizzical in the context of equal temperament, but it has its origins in the resources that different keys had available in meantone.

The nature of this tuning causes Renaissance and early to mid-Baroque music to be suffused throughout with the sweet sound of thirds. The perfect fifth is not quite in tune, which is why a prohibition arises in European music against using a bare perfect fifth without the third filled in: a little experimentation at a meantone keyboard quickly teaches you that you will notice the fifth's out-of-tuneness if the third isn't there but that the third covers it like a charm.

There are acoustic reasons as well why it is better, if one must make a choice, to have the third in tune rather than the fifth. As example 6.3 suggests, beats in an out-of-tune chord typically occur not between the fundamentals, which may be far apart in pitch, but between the overtones that are very close in pitch. The beats in a slightly out-of-tune fifth occur between the third harmonic of the lower note and the second harmonic of the higher note. The beats in an out-of-tune major third, however, occur in a higher octave, between the fifth harmonic of the lower note and the fourth of the higher note. Since, for a given dissonance, beats in a higher octave are faster than those in a lower octave, the quick beats of an out-of-tune third are more disturbing than the slower beats of a slightly out-of-tune fifth.

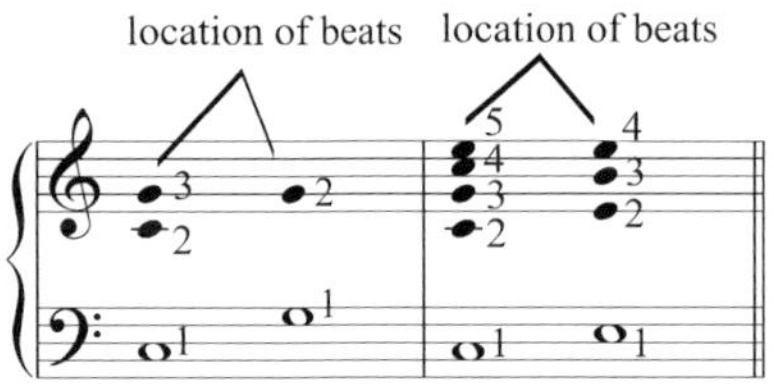

EX. 6.3: Location of beating pitches between a perfect fifth and major third

Tuning a Keyboard in 1/4-Comma Meantone

Just for a moment, let's get practical in this impractical book and look at keyboard tuning. The sixteenth century possessed no method for tuning exact irrational intervals; they proceeded by ear, trying to get D audibly halfway between C and E. Let's examine how this can be done. Owen Jorgensen, in his book *Tuning: Containing the Perfection of Eighteenth-Century Temperament, the Lost Art of Ninteenth-Century Temperament, and the Science of Equal Temperament*, offers piano-tuners' and harpsichord-tuners' rules for tuning to various temperaments, including meantone. His *bearing plan* for tuning 1/4-comma meantone (drawn from and improved from historical tuning manuals) is briefly summarized here, though the reader is referred to Jorgensen's superb tome for the wealth of helpful details and philosophical commentary it contains.

As shown in example 6.4, the steps are as follows:

1. Tune middle C and the E above it to a pure, beatless, 5/4 major third. Then tune the E below these to a pure octave with the high E.
2. Tune G below middle C to a 4/3 perfect fourth, but flatten it slightly until it makes 2.4 beats per second when played with middle C, and 3 beats per second with either the upper or lower E. Piano tuners develop an amazing fluency at judging the precise tempo of beats, somewhat the way good conductors can pinpoint metronome markings. (Beating speeds are further addressed in chapter 8.)
3. Likewise, tune A a perfect 3/2 below the upper E, then sharpen it slightly until it makes 4.1 beats per second when played with middle C, or 2 beats per second when played with either E.
4. Here's the meantone: Tune D above middle C a slightly sharp fourth above A and a slightly narrow fifth above G. The proportion is correct when the D and A beat together at 2.7 beats per second and the G and D at 1.8 beats per second.
5. From this point on, all remaining pitches can be tuned to pure, beatless 5/4 thirds. Tune G♯ upward from the low E, E♭ downward from G, F downward from A, F♯ upward from D, B♭ downward from D, B upward from G, and C♯ upward from A. And tune the rest of the keyboard, of course, in pure octaves.

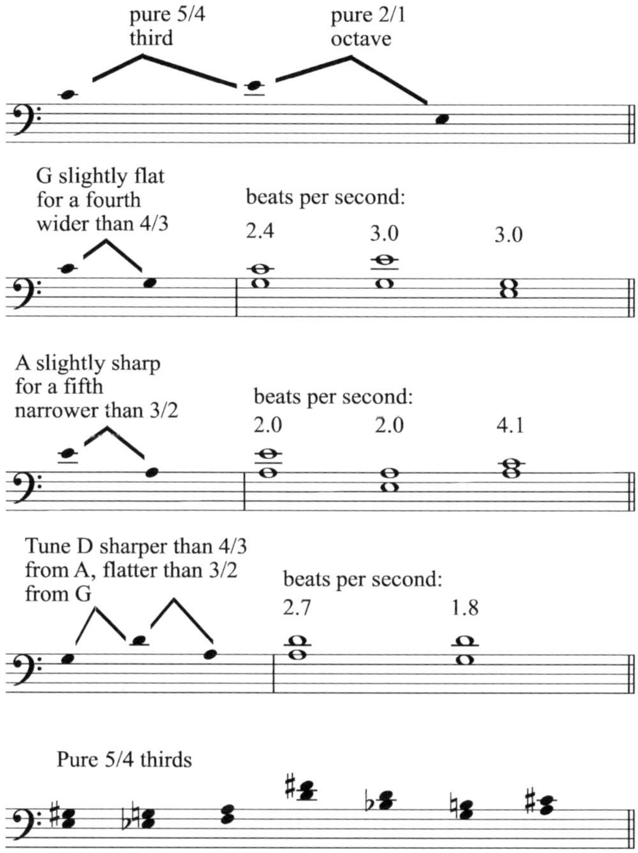

Tune all other pitches by 2/1 octaves

Adapted from Owen Jorgensen's Tuning
(East Lansing: Michigan State University Press, 1991)

EX. 6.4: Bearing plan for tuning a meantone keyboard

OTHER MEANTONE TEMPERAMENTS

Various other meantone temperaments, more or less extreme in their reduction of the size of fifths, were recorded as being used during the sixteenth through eighteenth centuries. Example 6.5 will help visualize their differences and how they are arrived at. All of these follow the same principle as the classic meantone tuning we've outlined and are defined by what portion of a syntonic comma is subtracted from each fifth. Example 6.6 shows the scale in cents for each of the meantones discussed below, in a fifteen-tone system including D♭ as well as C♯, D♯ as well as E♭, and A♭ as well as G♯. Going from left to right across the temperament sizes (which is the mathematical ordering, not the historical one), one can see each pitch gradually converging on a multiple of one hundred.

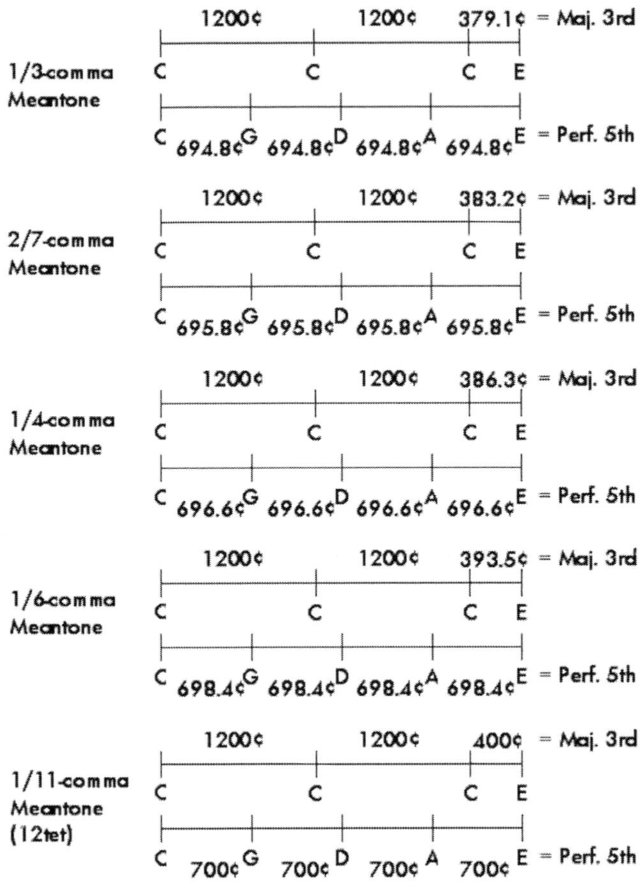

EX. 6.5: Sizes of thirds and fifths in various meantone temperaments

	1/3-Comma	2/7-Comma	1/4-Comma	1/6-Comma
C	0	0	0	0
C♯/D♭	63.5 / 126.1	70.7 / 120.9	76 / 117.1	88.6 / 108.1
D	189.6	191.6	193.2	196.7
D♯/E♭	253.1 / 315.6	262.3 / 312.6	269.2 / 310.3	285.3 / 304.9
E	379.1	383.2	386.3	393.5
F	505.2	504.2	503.4	501.6
F♯	568.7	574.9	579.5	590.2
G	694.8	695.8	696.6	698.4
G♯/A♭	758.3 / 820.9	766.5 / 816.8	772.6 / 813.7	787 / 806.5
A	884.4	887.4	889.7	895.1
B♭	1010.4	1008.4	1006.8	1003.3
B	1073.9	1079.1	1082.9	1091.9

EX. 6.6: Scales in cents of various meantone temperaments

1/3-COMMA MEANTONE This meantone brings not the major third perfectly in tune but the minor third (and thus major sixth). The perfect fifth is squeezed 7.17 to 694.79 cents, which is more than in 1/4-comma, so that the major thirds are slightly narrow (379.15 cents). The temperament is called 1/3-comma because the comma is distributed across only three fifths, C–G, G–D, and D–A. The minor third, then, is 6/5, and the major sixth is 5/3.

2/7-COMMA MEANTONE The ratio 2/7 is the harmonic mean between 1/3 and 1/4, since 1/3 = 2/6, 1/4 = 2/8, and 2/6 > 2/7 > 2/8. This meantone has the distinction of being the earliest to be accurately described, by Zarlino in his *Le institutioni harmoniche* of 1558.[5] Two-sevenths of the syntonic comma is 6.14465 cents, thus the perfect fifth is 695.81 cents. Then 7 × 695.81 cents = 4870.672 cents. If we subtract four octaves (= 4800 cents), we arrive at 70.672 cents, which is the size of the 25/24 chromatic semitone, so that the fifths are squeezed enough to make seven of them arrive at 25/24 instead of 2187/2048 (113.685 cents), which would be the ratio of seven 3/2 fifths. Temperament scholar R. Murray Barbour calls this meantone "a very poor system," but some have valued it because the major and minor thirds and sixths are all equally out of tune by three cents;[6] thus, within a given register the slight beating of thirds and sixths will be approximately the same.

1/6-COMMA MEANTONE This meantone enjoyed a long vogue in the eighteenth century and has the distinction of being the one advocated for violin playing by Leopold Mozart (1719–1787) and his son Wolfgang Amadeus Mozart (1756–1791). It squeezes the fifths by 1/6 of a comma, only 3.584 to 698.37 cents, and since six perfect fifths above C arrive at F♯, the augmented fourths are the five-limit ratio 45/32. The available intervals are much like those of 1/4-comma meantone, but the fifths are not quite so flat and the major thirds, at 393.48 cents, are a little sharper.

All other meantone tunings fall into a similar pattern. In 2/9-comma, 2/9 of the syntonic comma is subtracted from each fifth and so on. To construct a form of meantone temperament, one need only take the size of the perfect fifth and duplicate it for every fifth from E♭ up to G♯. In fact, any amount can be subtracted from the size of the fifths, and within a range from 696.578 cents to 701.955 cents, the flatter the fifths, the more in tune the major thirds will be. The ratio of change is one to four, which means that for every cent the fifths are flattened, the third will be flattened four cents. This is part of meantone's attractiveness, that it takes so little compromise on the fifths to gain so much clarity for the thirds.

Incidentally, 1/11-comma meantone is virtually equal temperament, since 1/11 of the comma is subtracted from each of the eleven fifths. The syntonic comma equals 21.5062896 cents, and 21.5062896 cents/11 = 1.955117 cents, which is almost exactly (1.955000865 cents) the excess of a perfect 3/2 fifth over an equal-tempered fifth of 700 cents.

R.H.M. Bosanquet, in his 1876 work *An Elementary Treatise on Musical Intervals and Temperament*, defined a regular temperament as one whose usable perfect fifths are all the same size.[7] By this definition, all of these meantone temperaments are regular, as are equal temperament and Pythagorean tuning. Furthermore, regular temperaments can be placed within a continuum on the basis of the size of their perfect fifths.

The plethora of theoretically defined tunings in the sixteenth and seventeenth centuries (in 1749 Robert Smith even wrote about 5/18-comma meantone[8]) should not be allowed to obscure the fact that before the twentieth century, tuning was not a science but an art. Each piano tuner was free to make whatever compromise he fancied between perfect fifths and major thirds, one of which always benefited at the expense of the other. It is debatable whether even sixteenth- and seventeenth-century theorists, let alone the average keyboard tuner, could make a practical distinction between 2/7-comma and 1/4-comma meantone, whose difference in the sizes of fifths is 3/4 of a cent. It is possible that they could have mathematically tuned a monochord or organ pipe to an exactly defined comma fraction and then transferred that tuning to a clavichord or harpsichord, but even this process is rife with opportunities for slight deviation from exactitude. We can suppose that mathematical arguments about the best possible meantone lay somewhat on the periphery of everyday keyboard tuning. Even in recent years, I have encountered harpsichord tuners who tune meantone by ear to their taste, without speculation as to what size comma they were using. More important is that meantone temperament represents a simple and elegant logical principle, as a tuning must do in order to give birth to a wide and varied repertoire of music. This is why meantone is one of the world's great tunings, why it was so musically fertile, and why it lasted so long.

Stepping slightly outside our arithmetic, we can give a pictorial demonstration of meantone's superiority to equal temperament. Example 6.7 shows the graph of the vibration of a justly tuned major triad, given by the formula y = sine x + sin 3/2 x + sin 5/4 x. Comparison of the peaks shows a perfectly regular pattern that will repeat indefinitely.

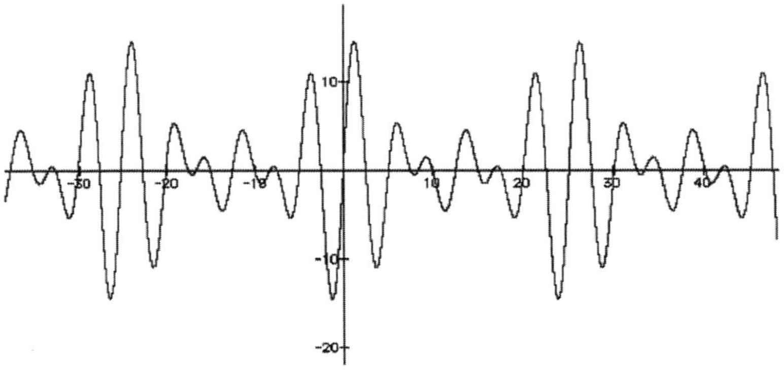

EX. 6.7: Graph of a justly tuned major triad

Example 6.8 is the graph of an equal-tempered triad, with the formula $y = \sin x + \sin 2^{1/3}x + \sin 2^{7/12}x$. Notice how quickly (and in a middle register this graph shows only a few milliseconds' worth) the pattern becomes irregular and non-repeating.

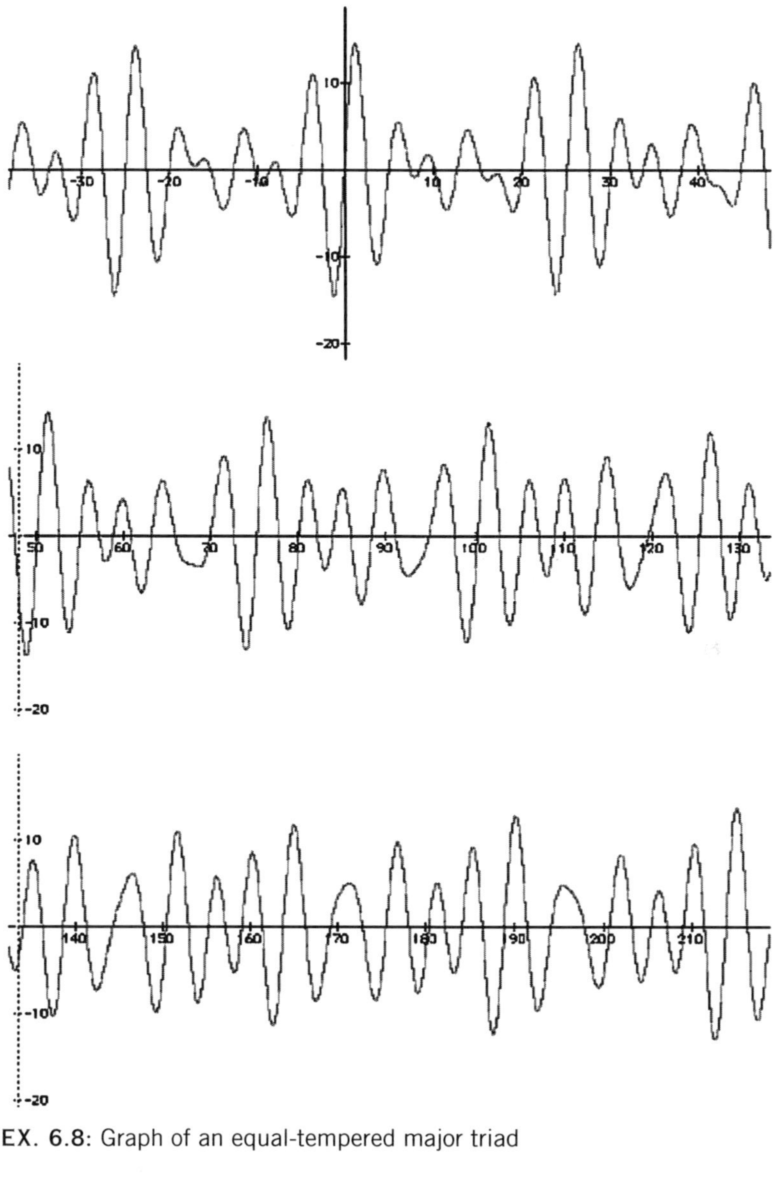

EX. 6.8: Graph of an equal-tempered major triad

Example 6.9 is the graph of a major triad in 1/4-comma meantone, given by the formula $y = \sin x + \sin (5/4\ x) + \sin (5^{1/4}\ x)$. This is slightly less regular than the graph of the justly tuned triad, but it is very close and sustains its regularity much longer. It is apparent to the eye, then, as well as to the ear, that meantone has an effect much closer to just tuning than to equal temperament.

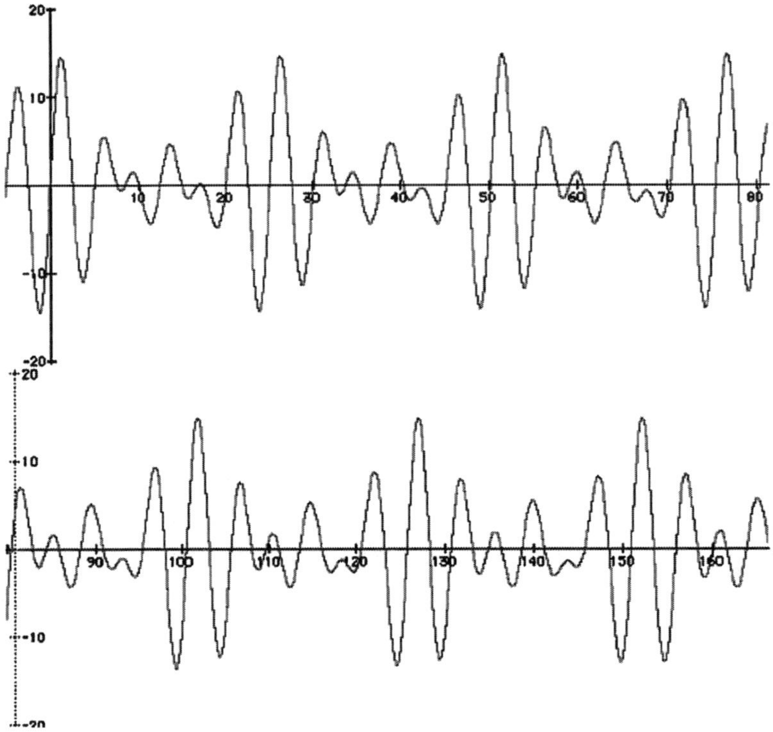

EX. 6.9: Graph of a 1/4-comma meantone major triad

Equal-Tempered Equivalents to Meantone

One of the things that fascinated theorists in the sixteenth through eighteenth centuries, as it continues to fascinate (relatively) many people today, is that certain equal temperaments of greater than twelve pitches provide excellent approximations of various meantones. We will save a fuller discussion of this phenomenon for our chapter 12 on equal temperaments, but let us outline a few basic facts here.

It was realized in the fifteenth century that thirty-one-tone *equal divisions of the octave* (31*edo*) provide an excellent approximation of 1/4-comma meantone. (We use the term "edo" in this instance rather than "31-*tone equal temperament*"—31*tet*—because we're not using all thirty-one steps, merely a division into thirty-one equal parts.) In 31edo, each step is approximately 38.7 cents. Using multiples of 38.7 cents, we arrive at the following sizes for some of our common intervals in 31edo, comparing them to 1/4-comma meantone:

	1/4-comma meantone	**31edo**
Major second	193.2¢	193.5¢ (five steps)
Minor third	310.3¢	309.7¢ (eight steps)
Major third	386.3¢	387¢ (ten steps)
Perfect fifth	696.6¢	696.8¢ (eighteen steps)

Likewise, 1/3-comma meantone is well approximated by 19edo, whose steps are 63.16 cents:

	1/3-comma meantone	**19edo**
Major second	189.57¢	189.47¢ (three steps)
Minor third	315.63¢	315.79¢ (five steps)
Major third	379.15¢	378.95¢ (six steps)
Perfect fifth	694.79¢	694.74¢ (eleven steps)

A 2/7-comma meantone is well served by a 50edo system, with steps of 24 cents:

	2/7-comma meantone	**50edo**
Major second	191.6¢	192¢ (eight steps)
Minor third	312.57¢	312¢ (thirteen steps)
Major third	383.24¢	384¢ (sixteen steps)
Perfect fifth	695.8¢	696¢ (twenty-nine steps)

A 1/6-comma meantone, as Mozart knew and taught, can be conceptualized as a subset of 55edo, whose steps are 21.8 cents (virtually a syntonic comma):

	1/6-comma meantone	**55edo**
Major second	196.74¢	196.36¢ (nine steps)
Minor third	304.89¢	305.45¢ (fourteen steps)
Major third	393.48¢	392.72¢ (eighteen steps)
Perfect fifth	698.37¢	698.18¢ (thirty-two steps)

These near-equivalences have proved useful pedagogically. For instance, we know something about how Mozart taught intonation from the notes taken by an English violinst who studied with him, Thomas Attwood (1765–1838). Mozart referred in letters to Pier Francesco Tosi (1654–1732) as a tuning authority for the idea that flatted notes are tuned lower by a syntonic comma than the enharmonically equivalent sharps, and that the diatonic half step (C–D♭, e.g.) is equal to 5/9 of a whole step, while the chromatic half step (C–C♯) is equal to 4/9 of a whole step. Thus the whole steps in the C-major scale are each divided into nine parts, and the diatonic half steps E–F and B–C have five parts each, adding up to fifty-five parts (these are, of course, not the string parts of ancient Greek monochords, but fractions of a perceived octave).[9]

	C	C♯	D♭	D	D♯	E♭	E	F	F♯	G♭	G	G♯	A♭	A	A♯	B♭	B	C	
Parts:	4	1	4	4	1	4	5	4	1	4	4	1	4	4	1	4	5		= 55

For the young violinist or other string player, this seems to have been a practical method for obtaining accurate intonation in 1/6-comma meantone. We will have more to say about meantone/edo similarities in chapter 12 on non-twelve-based edos.

INTERLUDE D

Meantone Examples

This interlude considers some of the more extreme exploitations of meantone temperament in the classical literature. Most music that was played in meantone looks rather normal on the page today, and musicians can play it in equal temperament without recognizing the qualities that meantone tuning would bring out. For instance, the *Fitzwilliam Virginal Book*, compiled sometime in the early seventeenth century and comprising more than three hundred examples of English keyboard music, contains no pieces written with key signatures of more than two sharps or flats.[1] It is rare to find in it a piece containing more than eleven pitches (although we'll look at one stunning exception below). A-flats are quite scarce. Some pieces feature D-sharps, some E-flats, but virtually never in the same piece. Almost every piece rests easily within a meantone keyboard tuning, though occasionally a virginalist or organist might have wanted to tune the E-flats down to D-sharps for a given piece, which on the virginal would have taken only a minute.

The English composer and keyboardist Orlando Gibbons (1583–1625, curiously absent from the Fitzwilliam collection[2]) wrote some of the most elaborate keyboard music of his time, one of his most impressive examples being *The Lord Salisbury his Pavane and Galliard*. Example D.1 shows the opening, which contains both G and G♯ and F and F♯ in close proximity.

EX. D.1: Gibbons, *The Lord Salisbury his Pavane*, mm. 1–3

Overall the piece contains eleven pitches, with all the accidentals on the sharp side, but including no A-sharps or B-flats. Measures 25 and 26, shown in example D.2, sequence rather tumultously through major triads on A, D, G, C, B, F, and E, requiring F♯, C♯, G♯, and D♯, for an unusual chromatic near-saturation within a brief passage.

EX. D.2: Gibbons, *The Lord Salisbury his Pavane*, mm. 25–26

Since the D♯ lasts only a quarter note, it is imaginable that the piece could be played on an instrument tuned with E-flats, and the dissonant triad would fly by almost too quickly to register as mistuned. But since there are no E-flats, that pitch could be tuned down to D-sharp as well.

We find a more quizzical passage, possibly written as a joke, in a Sonata in E Minor, numbered Kirkpatrick 394/Longo 275, by Domenico Scarlatti (1685–1757). Its middle section, shown in example D.3, following a flourish and a dramatic pause, begins dropping through an alternation of major and minor thirds in the bass, ranging far away from E minor through the black-key side of the circle of fifths. Scarlatti's spellings are quite peculiar. The note B♭ appears as the major third of F♯ (m. 79), E♭ as the third of B major (m. 81), and E♭ as the fifth of G♯-minor (m. 82) on its way to a misspelled German sixth chord of E-flat. One will also notice a D♭ in measure 78 followed by a C♯ in measure 79, so the unusual spelling was clearly not employed for the sake of keeping all the notes within twelve pitches.

EX. D.3: Scarlatti, Sonata in E Minor, mm. 76–83

Assuming this was played on a keyboard without split keys (and the joke becomes only more nefarious if split keys were available, since the chord would be explicitly out of tune), Scarlatti must have known that some of these triads would have been terribly sour, an effect that the trills (indicated by a zigzag line above the note) must have been intended to alleviate. The passage shows an acute awareness of the limitations of meantone keyboard temperament and exploits them with a humor that seems relatively savage for its era.

An even more extreme joke, though, is found from an earlier period in the *Fitzwilliam Virginal Book*, a fantasia on Ut Re Mi Fa Sol La by John Bull (1562/3–1628).[3] The piece starts in C major and moves toward the sharp side through A major and E major, and then, in measure 12 (ex. D.4), makes a bold enharmonic modulation in which D♭ becomes the third of an A-major triad and pivots into G♭ and then E♭ minor and eventually A♭ minor (the same kind of move around the circle of fifths as our Scarlatti example but in a more inescapably sustained manner).

EX. D.4: Bull, fantasia on Ut Re Mi Fa Sol La, mm. 11–16

Overall the piece uses eighteen different pitches: B, F♯, C♯, G♯, and D♯ along with C♭, G♭, D♭, A♭, E♭, and (in a later passage) A♯ as well as B♭. On a twelve-pitch (or even fourteen-pitch) keyboard this passage sounds terrible in meantone. The editor of the modern *Fitzwilliam Virginal Book* writes, "The passage proves that some kind of 'equal temperament' [actually well temperament] must have been employed at this date." But this is very early for such temperament indeed,[4] and it is also possible that Bull was having some arcane fun or that the piece was written as a kind of intellectual exercise, not intended for performance. No other piece in the *Fitzwilliam Virginal Book* remotely approaches any such extreme.

For our last example, let us consider a string quartet to be played in 1/6-comma meantone, for which medium more than twelve pitches are possible. Example D.5 shows the opening of Mozart's "Dissonance" Quartet (composed in 1785 and more formally known as String Quartet No. 19 in C Major, K. 465), chosen for the remarkable range of chromatically related pitches in its slow introduction. Above each note is written the number of cents above C for that pitch in 1/6-comma meantone, the temperament we know Mozart considered suitable for string playing.

EX. D.5: Mozart, "Dissonance" Quartet, K. 465, mm. 1–16

The passage contains fourteen pitches altogether, including C♯ and F♯ along with B♭, E♭, A♭, D♭, and G♭. The "Dissonance" Quartet takes its name from the false relations (notes in different registers with the same pitch name but different accidentals, forbidden in traditional counterpoint), like the A♭ and A in the viola and first violin measures 1 and 2 and the similar G♭ and G in measures 5 and 6. Notice that at 806 and 895 cents, respectively, the A♭ and A are eleven cents closer than they would be in equal temperament and create a more pungent contrast; the same is true for the G♭ and G. The high D♭ in measure 5 is audibly sharper than the C♯ in measure 3. Also note the unequal steps in the chromatic scales at measures 9, 11, 13, and 15, alternating between 89 and 108 cents. Played in 1/6-comma meantone, this slow introduction is marked by a vividness and strangeness that become watered down in an equal-tempered performance. In addition, there is a greater contrast between consonance and dissonance, since the thirds in the triads eventually resolved to are sweeter. For fullest effect, the piece deserves to be heard as Mozart imagined it.

Example D.6, from John Hind Chesnut's article "Mozart's Teaching of Intonation,"[5] partly drawn from Thomas Attwood's notes, gives a circle (spiral, rather) of fifths showing how many cents sharp or flat Mozart recommended playing these pitches. In keeping with meantone practice, the pitches on the flat side are a little sharper than in equal temperament, those on the sharp side a little flatter. The scale of cents running down the left-hand side shows that we are primarily dealing with pitches with ten cents of equal temperament—not an extreme deviation, but enough to provide a marked change of color.

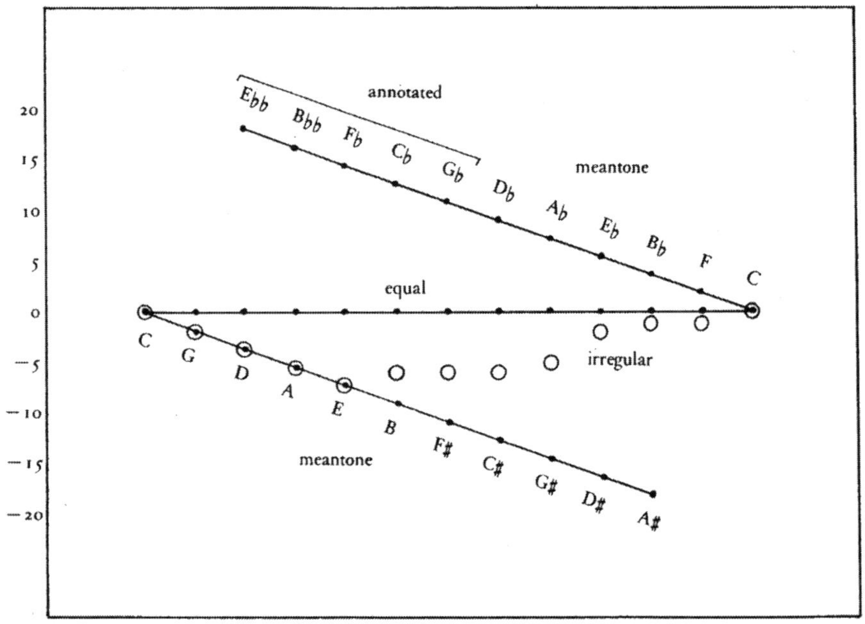

EX. D.6: Mozart's deviations in tuning in 1/6-comma meantone, from Chesnut

CHAPTER 7

WELL TEMPERAMENT AND KEY COLOR

One of the most emblematic images in the history of tuning is that of Johann Sebastian Bach, in September 1746, genially taunting the great organ builder Gottfried Silbermann (1683–1753) about his temperament. Silbermann tuned his organs to meantone, rendering the key of A♭ unusable, since the interval A♭–E♭ (actually G♯–E♭) was an out-of-tune wolf fifth. There are no Bach organ compositions in the key of A♭, nor in any more remote key, though of course his *Well-Tempered Clavier*, written for the more easily tunable harpsichord or clavichord, contains preludes and fugues in that key. According to an old story, when Bach (who played many Silbermann instruments in his day) finally met the master organ builder and played one of his organs, he struck up in the sour key of A♭, gleefully telling him, "You *tune* the organ in the manner *you* please, and I *play* the organ in the key *I* please."[1] We find almost as colorful confirmation from closer to the actual meeting in a 1748 letter from theorist Georg Andreas Sorge (1703–1778), who wrote, "Silbermann's system of temperament cannot be maintained under the conditions of present-day practice. . . . It is therefore to be wished that that superior man [Silbermann], who has acquired so much honor and fame, as well as a good bit of money, with his excellent art, should change his mind about temperament. . . . The four bad triads are of a rough, wild, or, as Capellmeister Bach in Leipzig says, barbaric nature intolerable to a good ear."[2]

This story of two giants in conflict about the future of music, along with the existence of the two books of the *Well-Tempered Clavier* that comprise preludes and fugues in all twenty-four major and minor keys, has tempted some to imagine that it was Bach who single-handedly forced the historical change from meantone to a new tuning capable of accommodating all keys. While this would be an exaggeration, it is certainly in Bach's music that we most clearly find the contrapuntal freedom that seems to yearn to make unlimited modulation possible. In fact, in 1681, even before Bach's birth, the organist Andreas Werckmeister (1645–1706) had begun publishing plans for temperaments in which all triads were bearable.[3] The secret, he wrote, was to widen some of the perfect fifths to pure 3/2 and to temper the rest. This widening of the fifths around F♯–C♯ and squeezing of the fifths around C–G also widens some of the major thirds in the black-note keys, while leaving them more acceptably narrow in the white-note keys. In short, unlike in meantone, where all major thirds are the same size, in well temperament they differ in size depending on the key, creating a variety of triad patterns around the circle of fifths. Well temperaments, then, are *irregular* temperaments, because their fifths vary in size.

Historically speaking, there is no dominant or most typical form of well temperament. Werckmeister came up with several solutions; the most historically influential, called Werckmeister III, employed eight pure fifths nonsymmetrically, on G♭–D♭–A♭–E♭–B♭–F–C and also on A–E–B, with the comma distributed among the other four fifths, C–G–D–A and B–F♯, which are basically the same size as in 1/4-comma meantone. Other theorists such as Johann Georg Neidhardt (1685–1739), Francesco Antonio Vallotti (1697–1780), Johann Philipp Kirnberger (1721–1783), Thomas Young (1773–1829), and many others each came up with their own tempering rules with slight variations (contemporary evidence suggests that Bach preferred Neidhardt's solutions[4]). The basic principle remains the same. Other reference works list dozens of seventeenth- and eighteenth-century temperaments for those whose historical curiosity is inexhaustible,[5] but here we will consider only a handful of temperament plans as representative of the whole. After all and, again, practically speaking, keyboard tuning in this period was an art rather than a science, and it is questionable how far musicians were willing to go in fidelity to one temperament versus another one that differs by only a few cents on certain pitches.

The idea of well temperament is to have a string of from four to eight pure perfect 3/2 (Pythagorean) fifths, often symmetrical around F♯ in the circle of fifths, with the fifths on the "C" side of the circle flattened somewhat to narrow and sweeten the major thirds in keys that contain few sharps or flats. It's as though you took a circle of fifths in equal temperament and squeezed it slightly from C to E, or from F to B, so that the fifths on the opposite side were pulled taut to 701.955 cents and the major thirds under your fingers squeezed down to 391 cents or less. In principle, example 7.1 makes the concept graphically clear. If the reader will imagine a rotatable arc encompassing 120 degrees from C to E, from G to B, from D to F♯, and so on, one can tell from the numbers in such diagrams how much has been subtracted from the fifths to make the major thirds sound better (and also the minor thirds, since the major sixths C–A, G–E, D–B, and so on, are squeezed as well, making the complementary minor thirds larger than 300 cents.

The strategy as given in discussions of temperament is to distribute the comma among some number of the smaller fifths. Technically speaking, it is not always clear whether we are speaking of the *Pythagorean comma* of 23.46 cents (which is the difference between twelve pure fifths and the octave they fail to return to) or the

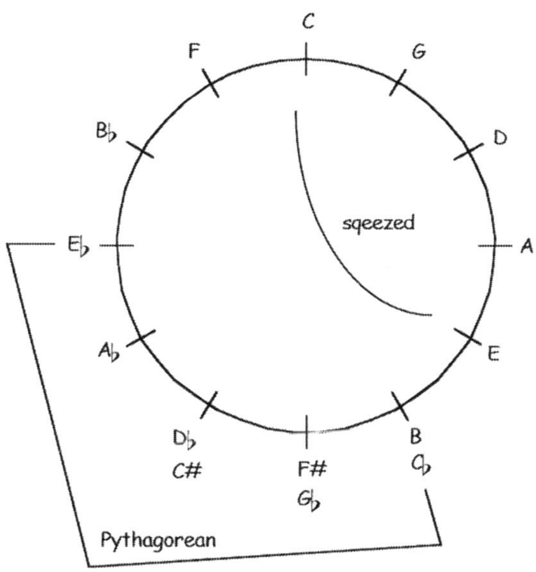

EX. 7.1: The principle of well temperament

syntonic comma of 21.506 cents (the difference between a pure 5/4 major third and a Pythagorean third of 81/64). The discrepancy is admittedly, and thankfully, a tiny one. Whereas in meantone we are explicitly talking about fractions of the syntonic comma, in the circle of fifths we are also concerned with the Pythagorean difference between seven octaves at 8400 cents and twelve perfect fifths at 8423.46 cents. When a writer states that equal temperament is achieved by subtracting 1/12 of a comma from each fifth, it can only be the Pythagorean comma that is meant, since twelve perfect fifths from which 1/12 of the syntonic comma is subtracted would still exceed the octave by 1.95 cents. Within the literature, 1/12 of the comma is taken roughly as two cents, 1/6 as four cents, and 1/4 as six cents, which makes calculations simple and is perhaps, as the saying goes, close enough for jazz. Fine-tuned cent sizes may differ by a few decimal points.

For instance, in the late eighteenth-century temperament known as Kirnberger III (published in 1779 and similar to Werckmeister III, below, with only one interval changed), the fifths C–G–D–A–E are to be tuned to the fourth root of five, as in 1/4-comma meantone. The other eight fifths, E–B–F♯–C♯–G♯–E♭–B♭–F–C are to be tuned as 3/2 Pythagorean fifths. However, strictly speaking, this progression returns to the unison at $5 \times (3/2)^8$, or 32805/32768, an interval of 1.95 cents known as the *schisma*, the minute difference that separates a 5/4 major third from the same interval approached as a series of eight 3/2 fifths. A discrepancy of 1.95 cents was beyond the ears and probably measuring tools of eighteenth-century tuners, but mathematically it has to be factored in somewhere.[6] Either the schisma is divided among the Pythagorean fifths by tuning each one 0.244-cents flat, or each of the meantone fifths must be flattened by one fourth of the Pythagorean comma, to 696.09 cents instead of 696.578 cents (701.955 – (23.46/4) = 701.955 – 5.865 = 696.09). The discrepancies are indeed minute enough that many writers have felt comfortable ignoring the difference between the Pythagorean and syntonic commas.

Today all of these similar temperaments are known as *well temperament* (also *circulating temperament*, since it circulates through all theoretically possible keys), immortalized as such in the title of Bach's *The Well-Tempered Clavier*. Since it made all keys equally possible, and produced a perceptibly equal chromatic scale, it was sometimes referred to in earlier centuries as "equal temperament," starting with William Jones's *Physiological Disquisitions* of 1781[7]—thus the modern confusion. For decades it has been common among musicians to say that Bach's *Well-Tempered Clavier* was composed for equal temperament, but this, as we can demonstrate, is a terminological error and an anachromism. In well temperament all twelve familiar keys, or twenty-four to include major and minor, are usable, *but they do not all sound the same*. Except for certain organs whose tuners held out for meantone, especially in England, well temperament gradually displaced meantone during the eighteenth century. It was actually considered easier to tune, since tuners started from perfect fifths rather than thirds and did not have to bend as many fifths out of tune by just the right amount.

What is most important for us is that in well temperament different keys will have different "colors"—or, more specifically, interval patterns—and therefore beat speeds for each triad. A triad with a major third of 386 to 392 cents will have a restful, sweet sound even if its fifth is slightly flat. A triad with a Pythagorean major third, or one more than 400 cents, will have a zing to it that can be harsh on the ear, although since such triads tend to have perfect 3/2 fifths, they can also achieve a certain stateliness, especially in minor keys. "Sweet" keys tend to be F, C, and G major; harsh or "brighter" keys are F♯, C♯, and B major. In C or F major, emphasizing the full tonic triad and ending a melody on the third scale step can have a lovely, restful effect. Try the same thing in F♯, and that tonic triad with the A♯ emphasized may offend the ear, precluding any feeling of complete resolution. As interlude E following this chapter will demonstrate, eighteenth-century music in F♯ or D♭ tends to skip lightly over the third scale degree, whose complex beat pattern, if not dwelled upon, can create a frisson of liveliness.

For the sake of visual simplicity we will first graph a series of temperaments on tuning wheels of the circle of fifths, first giving 1/4-comma meantone as a basis of comparison. In the circles in example 7.2 we can see that in 1/4-comma meantone limited to twelve pitches, all fifths are the same except for a terribly wide one (usually G♯–E♭) that is 737 cents wide and unusable. Thus in meantone there are no enharmonic equivalents (such as C♯ equaling D♭). The Werckmeister III temperament (published in 1691) distributes the comma among only four fifths, leaving the other eight pure; it is the only one shown whose smaller fifths are basically the size of 1/4-comma meantone. The Vallotti temperament given here subtracts 1/6-comma from six of the fifths

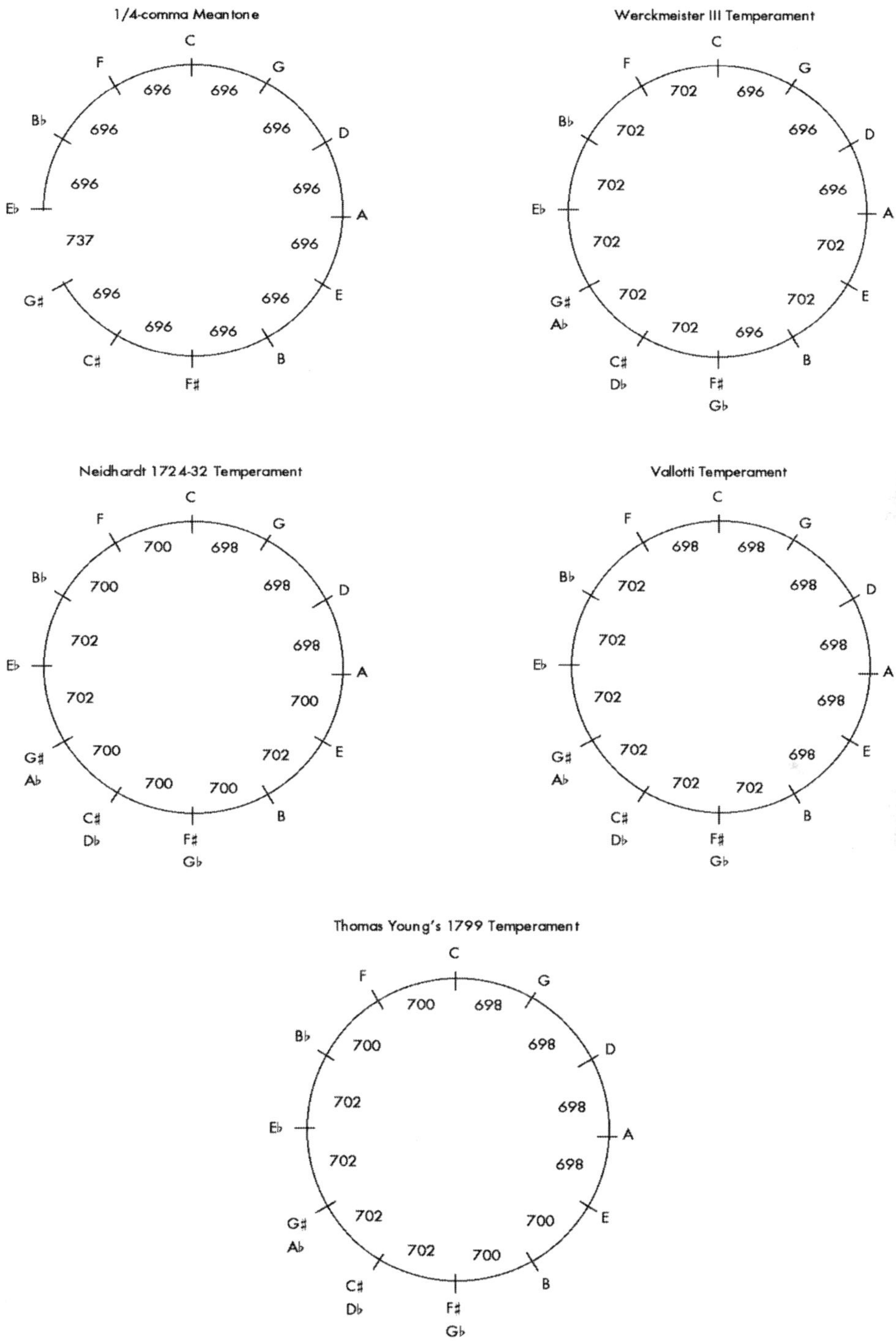

EX. 7.2: Circle-of-fifths wheels for five temperaments

and leaves the other six pure. Neidhardt and Young graduate the fifth sizes from 698 cents (1/6-comma small), to 700 cents (1/12-comma small), to pure 702 cents, though differently distributed. The following table compares cent numbers calculated from C for these four of the most widely used well temperaments, as defined in theoretical writings.

	Werckmeister III	Neidhardt 1724	Vallotti	Young 1799
C	0	0	0	0
C♯	90.2	94.2	94.1	93.9
D	192.2	198	196.1	195.8
E♭	294.1	296.2	298	297.8
E	390.2	390.2	392.2	391.7
F	498.0	498.2	501.96	499.9
F♯	588.3	592.2	592.2	591.9
G	696.1	700	698	697.9
G♯	792.2	794.2	796.1	795.8
A	888.3	894.1	894.1	893.8
B♭	996.1	998.2	1000	999.8
B	1092.2	1092.2	1090.2	1091.9

(In practice, of course, well temperament was subject to considerable variation from one keyboard tuner to another; Neidhardt even recommended a series of different temperaments for different-sized towns.[8]) The first temperament above is the one Werckmeister published in 1691 in his *Musicalische Temperatur*, known to history as Werckmeister III. The next is Neidhardt's temperament published in 1724,[9] followed by that of Antonio Vallotti as computed by Jorgensen based on William Jones's rules for tuning it.[10] And the last is Thomas Young's temperament No. 1 in his paper "Outlines of Experiments and Inquiries Respecting Sound and Light," given in 1799.[11] (A second temperament suggested in that paper resembles Vallotti's, except that the intervals are shifted one notch in the cirle of fifths, and is sometimes referred to, especially on recent electronic keyboards, as Vallotti-Young. Young seems not to have known of Vallotti's work, which was published only in 1779.[12]) None of these scales diverge more than 12 cents from equal temperament on any scale degree; in fact, were one to recalculate the scales from D or G as a reference point, all scale degrees would fall within 7 cents of a 100-cent grid. As one can see from the scales as listed, there's not a nickel's worth of difference between the scale degrees in any of them, and by a nickel I mean 5 cents. Nevertheless, there are some subtle differences in harmonic tendencies, and we shall cursorily explore them.

Our earliest example, Werckmeister III, contains eight perfect 3/2 fifths but not in consecutive order. The fifths G♭–D♭–A♭–E♭–B♭–F–C are tuned just, as well as A–E–B. The Pythagorean comma is distributed among the remaining fourths, C–G–D–A and B–F♯, each of which is reduced to 696.09 cents. (The only difference between this and Kirnberger III is that in the latter the eight 3/2 fifths are consecutive.) The resulting intervals are listed in the following table, listed not according to the chromatic scale but around the circle of fifths, which makes the intended patterns more apparent.

Sizes of Consonant Intervals in Werckmeister III

Major third		Perfect fifth		Minor third	
C–E	390.225	C–G	696.09	C–E♭	294.135
G–B	396.09	G–D	696.09	G–B♭	300.0
D–F♯	396.09	D–A	696.09	D–F	305.865
A–C♯	401.955	A–E	701.955	A–C	311.73
E–G♯	401.955	E–B	701.955	E–G	305.865
B–D♯	401.955	B–F♯	696.09	B–D	300.0
F♯–A♯	407.82	F♯–C♯	701.955	F#–A	300.0
D♭–F	407.82	D♭–A♭	701.955	C#–E	300.0
A♭–C	407.82	A♭–E♭	701.955	G#–B	300.0
E♭–G	401.955	E♭–B♭	701.955	E♭–G♭	294.135
B♭–D	396.09	B♭–F	701.955	B♭–D♭	294.135
F–A	390.225	F–C	701.955	F–A♭	294.135

In general, the numbers in the left-hand column indicate the quality of the major triads (smallest numbers are most consonant), while those in the right-hand column suggest the quality of the minor triads (largest numbers most consonant). The major thirds C–E and F–A are the smallest and most nearly in tune at 390.225 cents, only 3.9 cents sharper than just. In addition, F–C is a perfect fifth, making the F-major triad the one most in tune. Working our way around the circle of fifths in both directions, the next most consonant major thirds are those on G and D on one side, B♭ on the other. At the opposite extreme are three 407.8-cent Pythagorean major thirds on G♭, D♭, and A♭. The most in-tune-sounding major triads, then, will be B♭, F, C, G, and D, and accordingly the best minor triads are the relative minors of the middle three of those keys: D, A, and E. At 311.7 cents, A–C is the minor third that comes closest to being in tune, once again 3.9 cents flatter than a just 6/5.

Werckmeister III attempts to preserve one quality of meantone: similarity of third sizes among keys adjacent in the circle of fifths. One notices that the thirds A–C♯, E–G♯, and B–D♯ are all 402 cents. As the eighteenth century progressed, the tendency grew toward a more gradual modulation from one key to the next. This was achieved by having fewer perfect 3/2 fifths and by making them consecutive. Four consecutive perfect fifths will result in one Pythagorean third, and more 3/2 fifths will increase that number accordingly. Each major third encompasses four fifths in the circle; the more of those fifths are 3/2, the wider the major third will be. A major third whose fifths are a mixture of pure and squeezed will be medium-size, and a third whose fifths are all squeezed will be the smallest of all. Moving an imaginary 120-degree arc around the circle, one can deduce that keeping the perfect fifths contiguous will result in a smoother change in major-third size from key to key. This is the direction in which well temperament evolved.

The next table lists the sizes of consonant intervals in Vallotti temperament. Now there are only six perfect 3/2 fifths, and they fall into a chain: B–F♯–C♯–A♭–E♭–B♭–F. Remnants of the Pythagorean comma are subtracted from the remaining fifths.

Sizes of consonant intervals in Valotti temperament

Major third		Perfect fifth		Minor third	
C–E	392.2	C–G	698.045	C–E♭	298
G–B	392.2	G–D	698.045	G–B♭	302
D–F♯	396.1	D–A	698.045	D–F	305.9
A–C♯	400	A–E	698.045	A–C	305.9
E–G♯	403.9	E–B	698.045	E–G	305.9
B–D♯	407.8	B–F♯	701.955	B–D	305.9
F♯–A♯	407.8	F♯–C♯	701.955	F♯–A	302
D♭–F	407.8	C♯–G♯	701.955	C♯–E	298
A♭–C	403.9	A♭–E♭	701.955	G♯–B	294.1
E♭–G	400	E♭–B♭	701.955	E♭–G♭	294.1
B♭–D	396.1	B♭–F	701.955	B♭–D♭	294.1
F–A	392.2	F–C	698.045	F–A♭	294.1

Of greater aural significance, the major thirds change size in a smooth pattern: the smallest major third is F–A, and from here they grow larger in both directions, from C–E to G–B to D–F♯ and from B♭–D to E♭–G to A♭–C. Since there are still six perfect 3/2 fifths, there are still three major thirds the same size: D♭–F, F♯–A♯, and B–D♯, at 407.2 cents basically the size of Pythagorean 81/64 thirds. At 306.6 cents, A–C is the largest and most consonant minor third. Moving around the circle, they get smaller until the bitter, 294-cent minor thirds on G♯, E♭, B♭, and F, also almost Pythagorean (32/27).

The strategy of Thomas Young's 1799 temperament no. 1 was to smoothe out the circle of fifths even more:[13]

Sizes of consonant intervals in Young's 1799 temperament no. 1

Major third		Perfect fifth		Minor third	
C–E	391.7	C–G	697.9	C–E♭	297.8
G–B	393.9	G–D	697.9	G–B♭	301.9
D–F♯	396.1	D–A	697.9	D–F	304.1
A–C♯	400.1	A–E	697.9	A–C	306.2
E–G♯	404.1	E–B	700.1	E–G	310.3
B–D♯	406	B–F♯	700.1	B–D	304
F♯–A♯	407.9	F♯–C♯	702	F♯–A	301.9
D♭–F	406	D♭–A♭	702	C♯–E	297.8
A♭–C	404.2	A♭–E♭	702	G♯–B	296
E♭–G	400.1	E♭–B♭	702	E♭–G♭	294.1
B♭–D	396	B♭–F	700.1	B♭–D♭	294.1
F–A	393.9	F–C	700.1	F–A♭	295.9

Now there are only four perfect 3/2 fifths: F♯–C♯–G♯–D♯–A♯, and thus only one Pythagorean major third, F♯–A♯. Looking down the column of major thirds, one notices a more gradual progression of major third sizes, from C–E at 391.7 cents, up to F♯–A♯ at 407.9 cents, and back down. Likewise, there is only one optimum minor third, E–G at 310.3 cents, though there are two Pythagorean minor thirds on E♭ and B♭ (this is because a minor third on the circle of fifths encompasses only three perfect 3/2 fifths, and there are four in the circle). Even within the perfect fifths there is a graduated progression from 697.9 to 702 and back. Young described his temperament as what "the best instrument makers" were practicing: "making C:E too sharp by a quarter of a [syntonic] comma, which will not offend the nicest ear; E:G-sharp, and A-flat:C, equal; F-sharp:A-sharp too sharp by a comma; and the major thirds of all the intermediate keys more or less perfect, as they approach more or less to C in the order of modulation."[14]

Piano technician and temperament maven Owen Jorgensen praises Young's 1799 temperament as being "the most perfect idealized form of well temperament ever published." For one thing, its modulation of interval sizes is quite smooth, lending a nuanced flavor to each key. The note C is at one extreme of sweetest; F♯ is unique at the harsh end; middle keys E♭ and A parallel each other in having major thirds the same size as equal temperament, and other keys are arranged in smooth progression in between. No two keys (since a key requires dominant and subdominant chords, among others, as well as the tonic) are quite alike. In addition, as he points out, the intervals are symmetrical around the keys D and A♭ on the keyboard: D–C♯ is the same size as D–E♭, D–C the same as D–E, and so on, and the same around A♭, just as the pattern of black and white keys is also symmetrical around either D or A♭. "The keyboard design," as Jorgensen puts it, "matches the Young temperament interval design."[15]

As noted, to some extent the differences between these temperaments are merely theoretical. Piano tuners were guided by their experience and their own and their patrons' taste throughout the eighteenth and nineteenth centuries, an era in which tuning was an art, not a science. Nevertheless, the advent of well temperament opened the circle of fifths to composition, allowing composers free rein to write in and modulate through twenty-four major and minor keys. Composers could use more distant keys for almost the first time, leading to Arnold Schoenberg's interesting comment about how lucky Chopin was: "When he wanted to do something new, all he had to do was to write in F♯ major."[16]

Those keys were not indistinguishable; each had its own attributes and color, which is important to remember in considering nineteenth-century arguments about the "colors of the keys," which are otherwise seemingly meaningless. Musicians had associations with certain keys: E♭ seeming like the "golden" key, or F♯ seeming tumultuous. The eighteenth century's sole symphony in the key of F♯ is Haydn's "Farewell,"[17] which opens with one of the era's stormiest and most unstable beginnings. The musical creativity of those centuries flowed into well temperament like water into a riverbed, filling up every cranny and taking advantage of every divergence and asymmetry. To play that music today in a bland, even tuning of scientifically equal scale steps is to wash out some measure of the color that the composers intended and that the original audiences enjoyed. It is to diminish the achievements of the famous European composers.

Key Color

Nineteenth-century musical literature is full of discussion of the colors or moods of the different keys. The German poet and composer Christian Schubart (1739–1791) has been widely quoted on the qualities of the various keys. C major, he wrote, is "completely pure," characterized by "innocence, simplicity, naïvety, children's talk." D♭ major is "a leering key, degenerating into grief and rapture. It cannot laugh, but it can smile; it cannot howl, but it can at least grimace its crying.—Consequently only unusual characters and feelings can be brought out in this key." D major is "the key of triumph, of . . . marches, holiday songs and heaven-rejoicing choruses." F♯ minor is "a gloomy key: it tugs at passion as a dog biting a dress. Resentment and discontent are its language." B♭ minor is "surly and very seldom takes on a pleasant countenance. Mocking God and the world; discontented with itself and with everything; preparation for suicide sounds in this key."[18] (And thus Chopin astutely put his famous funeral march of his Second Sonata in B♭ Minor to take advantage of the bitter Pythagorean minor third B♭–D♭ of around 294 cents.) And so on. In an oft-quoted story, Rachmaninoff tells of the time Nicolai Rimsky-Korsakoff and Alexander Scriabin tried to convince him that each key had a color associated with it, both agreeing that D major is golden brown, though disagreeing as to F major, which one considered blue and the other red-purple.[19] Other such stories are common.

This association of keys with moods and colors doubtless comes from a complex web of associations, including historical precedents such as Beethoven's stormy works in C minor and Mozart's Requiem and *Don Giovanni* overture in D minor. Surely D major owes some of its heroic reputation to the fact that stringed instruments get to use their open strings frequently, adding resonance. Synaesthesia, the spontaneous association of colors and tones of the scale to which certain sensitive people are prone, is not a topic we are prepared to embark upon. Nevertheless, the fact that such correspondences were very common in earlier times and not much noticed today suggests that the differences of tuning of various keys in well temperament probably influenced the kinds of moods listeners heard in those keys. It would certainly be worth reviving well temperament to hear the classical repertoire as its first audiences did, and we might find some of those correspondences becoming evident once again.

INTERLUDE E

Bach, Beethoven, and Temperament

We will now apply some of the insights from chapter 7 to selections from two central repertoires of classical music, Bach's *Well-Tempered Clavier* and Beethoven's piano sonatas. Contrary to a belief common among musicians, Bach's *Well-Tempered Clavier* (*WTC*) is not a showcase for equal temperament but rather an exploration of what different qualities one can find among different keys in well temperament. For the purpose of our analyses, keep in mind that the optimum size for a major third is 386.3 cents and for a minor third it is 315.6 cents. Thus, major thirds are more consonant when they are smaller than 400 cents, more dissonant when larger than that; minor thirds are more consonant when they are above 300 cents, and more dissonant when smaller.

Schubart's classification of C major is "innocence, simplicity, naïvety." That certainly characterizes the first prelude of the *WTC* Book I (ex. E.1). (I will deal with only preludes, not fugues, because preludes are more consistently chordal and thus present simpler tuning issues.) We will apply the numbers of the Werckmeister III temperament since, aptly or not, that is the temperament with which Bach is most often associated. C–E, along with F–A, is the narrowest major third in the scale; thus Bach can not only afford to sustain a C and E in the left hand but can also create a lovely effect by emphasizing the E at the top of the melody. The rippling and repetitive motion of this piece is as calm as a flowing brook, but transpose it up to C$_\sharp$ major

EX. E.1: Bach, Prelude in C Major from *The Well-Tempered Clavier*, Book I, mm. 1–3

(with a zinging Pythagorean major third up on top) in well temperament, and the quality becomes a little aggressive.

As one would expect from its key, the Prelude in E♭ Minor (ex. E.2) is particularly colorful. It opens with the repetition of an E♭–G♭ dyad that, at only 294 cents in Werckmeister III, is one of the two narrowest and bitterest minor thirds on the keyboard. The turn to C♭ major at measure 5 is hardly reassuring, since the G♭-major triad is so brightly dissonant and thus hardly restful.

EX. E.2: Bach, Prelude in E♭ Minor from *The Well-Tempered Clavier*, Book I, mm. 1–8

The Prelude in F♯ Major (ex. E.3) trips lightly around that key's harsher consonances. The major third F♯–A♯ has a brash brightness—playing it in well temperament, it can have the effect of a wrong note, and one's hands almost recoil from the keyboard. Notice, then, how in this light two-voice prelude, Bach uses the A♯ melodically but skips away from it quickly when the dissonant (Pythagorean) major third of 407.8 cents is sounded. Each not-so-consonant third or sixth the right hand introduces is quickly abandoned by a dissonance in the left hand. Nevertheless, the slight moments of Pythagorean sharpness give the prelude a lively frisson that disappears when it is played in the calmer key of F major.

EX. E.3: Bach, Prelude in F♯ Major from *The Well-Tempered Clavier*, Book I, mm. 1–6

Likewise, see the Prelude 3 in C♯ Major, whose Pythagorean major thirds are ameliorated by flying by in quick sixteenth notes.

Let us now move to a few passages from Beethoven, taking as our reference point a less extreme well temperament—Thomas Young's well temperament of 1799, which Beethoven may not have used but was typical enough for his generation. (I always feel a little odd talking about how Beethoven wanted his middle and late music to sound, since he couldn't hear it—although certainly he had enough experience in his youth to form strong associations with the various keys.) The calm, slow movement of the his Piano Sonata in F Minor, op. 57, or "Appassionata" (ex. E.4), is an interesting case. Beethoven cast it in D♭ major, and, played in well temperament, the triads bristle with beats, since the D♭–F third is 406 cents, the G♭–B♭ is a Pythagorean 407.9 cents, and the A♭–C is 404.2 cents.

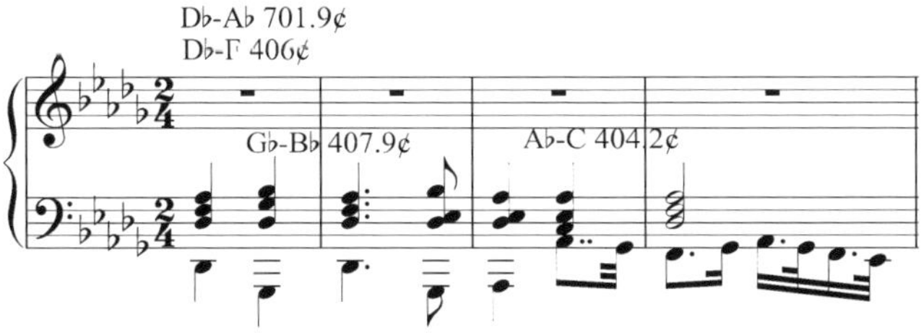

EX. E.4: Beethoven, Sonata in F Minor, op. 57, second movement, mm. 1–4

Play this passage in well temperament transposed a half step down to C major, and it is much calmer—perhaps *too* calm, in fact, for such a tempestuous sonata, and a little lifeless. In C major I find that I involuntarily want to play it faster, as though there's not enough harmonic interest to sustain a slower speed. Thomas Young's 1799 is the temperament I tune my own pianos to, and I can attest that the subdominant G♭ chord has, in itself, a surprising liveliness in this context.

Minor keys on black-note tonics (C♯, F♯, G♯, D♯) can take on an impressive stateliness in well temperament, because while the minor thirds are narrow and a little bitter, the black-key perfect fifths are often perfect 3/2 fifths and quite resonant. Some such consideration must have motivated Beethoven to couch the "Moonlight Sonata," op. 27, No. 2, in C♯ minor (ex. E.5).

EX. E.5: Beethoven, Sonata in C♯ Minor, op. 27, No. 2, mm. 1–5

The note E is a dark 297.8 cents above the C♯, but the C♯–G♯ fifths in the bass are pure and solid-sounding. The more consonant Neapolitan chord on D sounds more like a sudden brightening, quickly subsumed back into the darkness of the G♯ chord. Similar observations could be made about the similarly sad and solemn slow movement in F♯ minor of Beethoven's Piano Sonata No. 29, op. 106, or "Hammerklavier."

The Sonata No. 21, op. 53, "Waldstein" (ex. E.6), is one of the most instructive pieces to examine in terms of its harmonic structure and its relation to the temperament. Both first and second themes in the first movement heavily emphasize the third, which in C is a relatively consonant 391.7 cents.

EX. E.6: Beethoven, Sonata in C Major, op. 53, mm. 1–7

The sudden drop down a whole step to B♭ is a surprise move even in equal temperament, and well tempered it moves to the equally restful key of F major. In this period Beethoven was beginning to contrast his primary and subordinate keys no longer as tonic and dominant, but as tonic and mediant (third scale degree) or submediant (sixth scale degree), which give maximum contrast in terms of the key signature (since going further around the circle of fifths than C to E takes you to B, which, dropping a half step, somewhat decreases the tension rather than ratcheting it up). The contrast between first and second themes in the Waldstein is heightened in well temperament, since the calm 391.7-cent third of the first theme gives way to bright, almost Pythagorean thirds on E–G♯ and B–D♯ in the second (ex. E.7).

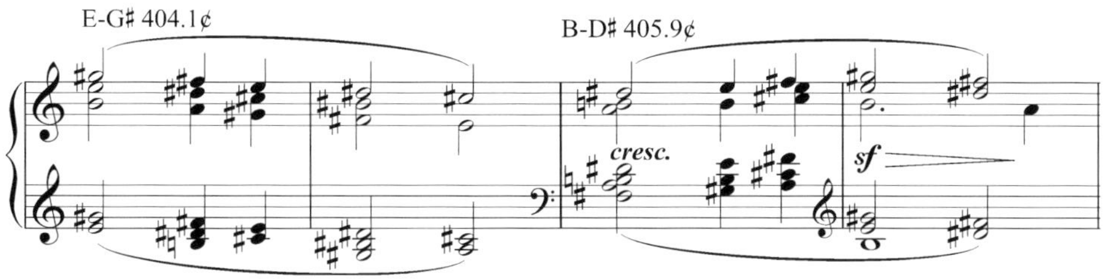

EX. E.7: Beethoven, Sonata in C Major, op. 53, mm. 35–38

This is a sharp key contrast indeed, and the difference in brightness between the C-major opening and E-major climax is entirely lost in equal temperament. Surely the irascible Beethoven would not have been pleased.

CHAPTER 8

Twelve-Step Equal Temperament

If one can't say anything nice about a tuning, it is tempting to say nothing at all. But twelve-step equal temperament has one strength that can't be denied: it has amassed the most effective public relations machine of any tuning in history. Thousands of musicians believe that it is the perfect scientific tuning toward which music has been striving for millennia. Millions more accept it without question. Attacks on it are considered attacks on the Western musical tradition itself—which they are not. It carries an immense weight of historical fallacy. Most musicians probably falsely believe that Mozart and Beethoven wrote and played their works in this tuning. All this despite the fact that it is the blandest twelve-pitch tuning ever conceived, the blandest tuning possible with twelve pitches. And not much more than a century of common use.

The move to 12tet over the course of the nineteenth century was a gradual one and impossible to closely document. Owen Jorgensen, however, has demonstrated that true equal temperament was impossible to achieve on pianos and other stringed keyboards before 1917. Equal temperament was used on seventeenth-century fretted instruments,[1] such as lutes and guitars, because to do otherwise would have required staggering the frets differently for each string (as is now sometimes done for just-intonation and microtonal guitars). It could have been implemented on organs, because the organ pipe lengths were susceptible to exact measurement, but it usually wasn't. The nineteenth century had no way to achieve it on pianos, because there was no way to measure a sounding frequency. In 1869 Alexander Ellis wrote that, on the piano, "'equal temperament' . . . has probably never been attained in this country, with any approach to mathematical precision."[2] Tables of tunings he published sixteen years later, in 1885, confirm that this remained true,[3] and he further wrote in that year, "Tuners of the piano sometimes still intentionally tune unequally, and hence make the effect of A and A-flat really very different."[4]

A degree of confusion was caused by the fact that nineteenth-century writers used the term "equal temperament" to refer to temperaments in which all keys were playable, even those that were not at all equal in the exact scientific sense. This is why the statement that Bach wrote *The Well-Tempered Clavier* to illustrate equal temperament has so often been made. Today the tunings Bach used would fall under what we classify as well temperaments, meaning unequal temperaments in which the keys are all playable but not identical.

Piano tuners in the eighteenth and nineteenth centuries did not listen to beats between simultaneous pitches to judge their tunings and were not yet aware that such beats had any significance. According to Jorgensen, Edward Quincy Norton's *Construction, Tuning, and Care of the Piano-Forte* of 1887 is the first treatise (in English, at least) to allude to the existence of beats between harmonics of played piano tones.[5] Not until William Braid White's *Modern Piano Tuning and Allied Arts* was published in 1917, though, did a method for tuning equal temperament appear that produced scientific accuracy, and it did so by showing a chart (ex. 8.1) for the progressively faster beating of intervals as they were transposed up the scale.[6] Since 1917, piano tuners have used the rate of beating between harmonics of an interval to determine the precise measurements of intervals.

TABLE III. BEATS PER SECOND IN EQUAL TEMPERED INTERVALS (ASCENDING) FROM C_{28} TO C_{52} INCLUSIVE, CORRECT TO 2 PLACES OF DECIMALS.

Name	C. P. S.	Minor Third	Major Third	Fourth	Fifth	Minor Sixth	Major Sixth	Frequency Ratios Ascending
		5:6	4:5	3:4	2:3	5:8	3:5	
		6th & 5th	5th & 4th	4th & 3rd	3rd & 2nd	8th & 5th	5th & 3rd	Coincident Harmonics
		Narrowed by	Widened by	Widened by	Narrowed by	Narrowed by	Widened by	Widened or Narrowed
C_{28}	130.813	7.06	5.19	0.59	0.43	8.26	5.93	
C♯—D♭$_{29}$	138.591	7.47	5.50	0.62	0.46	8.73	6.29	
D_{30}	146.832	7.92	5.82	0.66	0.49	9.25	6.76	
D♯—E♭$_{31}$	155.563	8.39	6.07	0.70	0.52	9.79	7.06	
E_{32}	164.814	8.89	6.53	0.74	0.55	10.38	7.47	
F_{33}	174.614	9.42	6.93	0.79	0.59	10.99	7.92	
F♯—G♭$_{34}$	184.997	9.98	7.34	0.83	0.62	11.64	8.39	
G_{35}	195.998	10.57	7.77	0.88	0.66	12.34	8.89	
G♯—A♭$_{36}$	207.652	11.20	8.26	0.94	0.70	13.08	9.42	
A_{37}	220.000	11.87	8.73	0.99	0.74	13.86	9.98	
A♯—B♭$_{38}$	233.082	12.57	9.25	1.05	0.79	14.68	10.57	
B_{39}	246.942	13.32	9.79	1.11	0.83	15.56	11.20	
C_{40}	261.626	14.12	10.38	1.18	0.88	16.48	11.87	
C♯—D♭$_{41}$	277.183	14.95	10.99	1.25	0.94	17.46	12.57	
D_{42}	293.665	15.85	11.64	1.32	0.99	18.50	13.32	
D♯—E♭$_{43}$	311.127	16.79	12.34	1.40	1.05	19.60	14.12	
E_{44}	329.628	17.79	13.08	1.47	1.11	20.76		
F_{45}	349.228	18.84	13.86	1.58	1.18			
F♯—G♭$_{46}$	369.994	19.96	14.68	1.67				
G_{47}	391.995	21.15	15.56	1.77				
G♯—A♭$_{48}$	415.305	22.41	16.48					
A_{49}	440.000	23.74						
A♯—B♭$_{50}$	466.164							
B_{51}	493.883							
C_{52}	523.251							

EX. 8.1: White's chart of beating speeds in *Modern Piano Tuning and Allied Arts*

Equal temperament is indeed a scientific tuning; to that extent its proponents are on solid ground. But music is an art, not a science, and for the vast majority of music's history, tuning, as well, has been described as an art, not a science.[7] That tuning should now be a science is one of those premises that everyone now assumes without anyone ever having proved it, or having even provided a compelling argument.

Almost needless to point out, equal temperament has the fewest interval sizes of any twelve-pitch tuning. All twelve keys give exactly the same interval pattern, which is supposed to be the tuning's great glory: the fact that no key is distinguishable, in terms of relative pitch, from any other. None of the intervals are consonant except for the 2/1 octave.

> The 3/2 perfect fifth is flat by 1.955 cents.
> The 5/4 major third is sharp by 13.7 cents.
> The 6/5 minor third is flat by 15.6 cents.
>
> All half steps are 100 cents.
> All whole steps are 200 cents.
> All minor thirds are 300 cents.
> All major thirds are 400 cents.
> All perfect fifths are 500 cents.
> All tritones are 600 cents.

And so on. Along with its similarity to a Pythagorean scale, one can add that twelve-pitch equal temperament also provides approximations of the seventeenth and nineteenth harmonics (17/16 = 104.955 cents, and 19/16 = 297.5 cents) but not to the lower, more consonant harmonics. The ratio 18/17, which is 98.954 cents, is commonly taken as the closest reasonably small-number rational approximation of the equal-tempered half step; 89/84 (100.099 cents) is even closer.

There is no need to give examples of music written in 12tet, because they are so common. Yet we can take this opportunity to examine what we're really hearing in our most ubiquitous tuning. As we can see in example 8.2, the perfect fourths and fifths are very close to perfect, less than two cents off. When one plays a C and G in the octave below middle C, the third harmonic of the C and the second of the G ring at 392.4 cents and 392 cents respectively.

EX. 8.2: Beat rates (per minute) of an equal-tempered fifth and fourth

It is the *beats* between the harmonics that make an interval in or out of tune; the ear can't hear beats between the fundamentals, because they are far too slow to register.

But the difference between 392.4 and 392 cents is 4/10 of a cycle per second, which means that over ten seconds the harmonics will go out of phase with each other four times, and there will be four beats. At this pitch register, the interval will beat at a tempo of twenty-four beats per minute, which is pretty unobjectionably slow and measurable with a metronome. Transpose these intervals upward, and the rate of beating will increase; an octave higher, the beats will be forty-eight times per minute; a perfect fifth higher, the rate will be approximately thirty-six. Note in example 8.2 that the perfect fourth G–C beats at the same rate as the fifth C–G. Piano tuners use this equivalence to make sure they've tuned the fourths and fifths accurately in equal temperament.

When we look at the thirds and sixths, however, the situation is much more extreme (ex. 8.3). A major third beats at the fifth harmonic of the lower note and the fourth harmonic of the higher note. When that harmonic is a G above middle C, the difference is 389 cycles per second versus 392, which means the interval will beat three times a second (392 – 389 = 3), a rate of 180 per minute, which is a pretty quick clip.

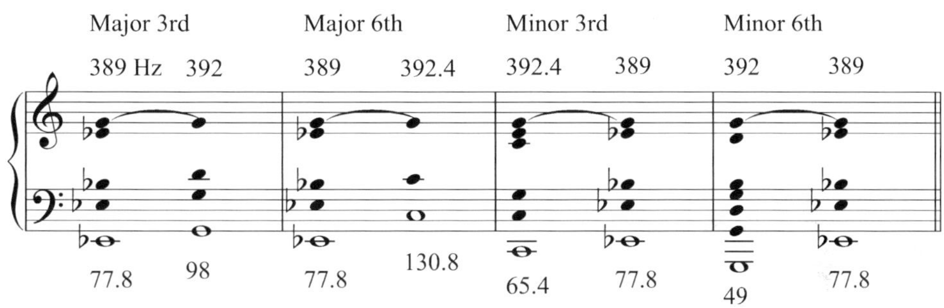

EX. 8.3: Beat rates (per minute) of equal-tempered thirds and sixths

The major sixth E♭–C whose harmonics vibrate at that G will beat 3.4 times a second, or a rate of 204 times a minute. The rate for a minor third matches that for a major sixth, those intervals being complementary, and similarly for a major third and minor sixth.

When playing an interval on a piano, the harmonics that beat usually take a moment to emerge. For instance, if you play, forcefully, a low E♭ and C on the piano, then listen for a moment, the beating G that represents the interplay between their harmonics will slowly emerge, beating, and if you softly play the G to direct your ear to the proper pitch, that G will become easier to perceive, and the speed of the beats will become obvious. Most of us only hear the low E♭ and C, and it requires some training to refocus our ears to hear the actual physical beating. If you loudly play the chord in the bass clef in example 8.4, after a moment you will hear the G in the treble clef emerge quite loudly and beat forcefully as the overtones of the lower notes coincide at that spot.

EX. 8.4: Undertones ringing at G in the treble clef

Piano tuners use these rates of beat speed to tell whether an equal-tempered piano is correctly out of tune. According to Jorgensen, piano tuners in the nineteenth century were unaware that the beats emitted by out-of-tune intervals were beats between the harmonics of those notes. Edward Quincy Norton's *The Construction, Tuning, and Care of the Piano-Forte* (1887) represents a turning point in this respect. "Tune middle C to the desired pitch," begin his tuning instructions, "then tune F—fifth below—sharp of C, until between C and F there result three beats in five seconds."[8] It was William Braid White's *Modern Piano Tuning and Allied Arts* that published, for the first time, the exact beating rates for fourths, fifths, thirds, and sixths for different notes on the piano (see ex. 8.1).[9] The book was destined to become "the leading textbook of its century," still in print today, and the word "modern" was dropped from the title for the 1938 edition.[10] This means, as Jorgensen argues from a wide array of (English-language) sources, that exact equal temperament could not be obtained on pianos before 1917.

White gives a *bearing plan* (what piano tuners call the order in which they tune an octave or more of notes), which I adapt in example 8.5. The numbers on the lower staff give correct frequencies in 12tet. The numbers below the upper staff give the cycles per second for the second and third, or third and fourth (depending on whether a fourth or fifth is being tuned), for the harmonics at which the interval beats. The lower number above the upper staff gives the difference in cycles per second, and the top

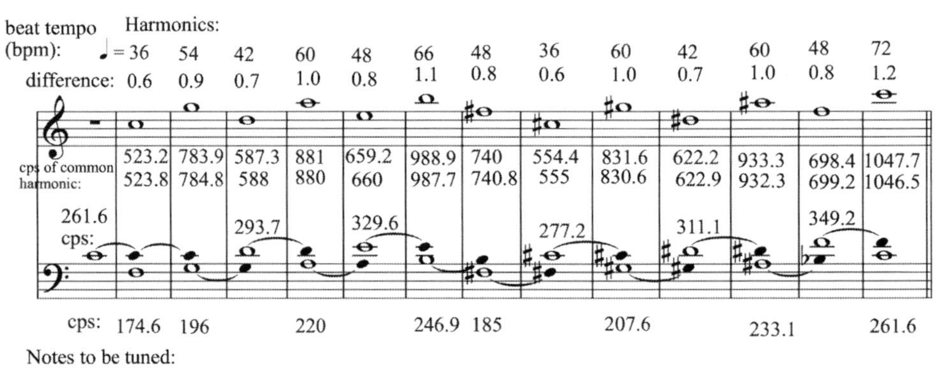

EX. 8.5: White's bearing plan for equal temperament

number (the difference number times sixty) gives the number of beats per minute. All values in cycles per second are rounded to the nearest 0.1, which means that they are approximate but also that the number of beats per minute is easily correlated with a metronome. This does not indicate that piano tuners used only fourths and fifths to tune with. In a longer table White adds the much faster beating numbers for thirds and sixths and lists at what point tuners should check these intervals to make sure the fourths and fifths are tuned accurately.

Parenthetically, I have found piano tuners fascinating to talk with. For one thing, they are musicians, which generally means nonconformists, but they are musicians who avoid the limelight and work in the shadows, rarely seeking attention, so by and large they're a pleasantly odd and non-egocentric bunch. Second, they are not habituated, as most of us us are, to concentrate only on the fundamentals and filter out the overtones, but quite the opposite: they are intensively trained such that the overtones are very real and obvious to them, so they truly hear music differently. I envy their richness of auditory experience. The important point for us is that when they get intervals *out of tune* to the right extent, they know that they've tuned 12tet correctly.

The musicologist A. H. Fox-Strangways admitted to Harry Partch, in a moment of resigned candor, that the spread of equal temperament has ruined singing (because singers have to veer away from, and even learn not to hear, the natural consonances they would otherwise gravitate toward) and also threatened with oblivion the various flavors of Indian ragas.[11] And yet he gives the standard reasoning that is universally given for using equal temperament: that without it, modulation from one key to another becomes impossible. As already seen in the chapters on meantone (ch. 6) and well temperaments (ch. 7), this is a manifest falsehood. Haydn's keyboard sonatas modulate, yet Haydn's clavichord was not tuned in equal steps. And Partch, in rebuttal, describes his experiments showing that modulation can be entirely convincing even on his own instruments in just intonation.[12]

In the logic of twelve-tone music, an idiom developed by Arnold Schoenberg in the 1920s and which became something of an international lingua franca for a few decades, all major sevenths are intended as interchangeable, all tritones are interchangeable, and so on. This premise is believed with an unquestioning religious faith. And yet no one has ever demonstrated that the meaning of a twelve-tone piece by Schoenberg or Anton Webern would be fatally compromised if the major sevenths were slightly different sizes, as they would be in well temperament. (I play Webern and Charles Ives on my well-tempered pianos and find them even more beautiful in Young 1799.) Equal temperament is indeed the tuning that matches, isomorphically, the inner logic of twelve-tone music. It is a striking example of historical synchronicity that equal temperament became available on pianos in 1917, and Schoenberg wrote his first twelve-tone row only four years later, in 1921. Twelve-tone thinking and its derivatives dominated compositional thought in America and Europe throughout the 1950s, '60s, and '70s. In the 1980s composers began to turn away from twelve-tone practice in droves. And yet music continues to flounder for a new direction, partly because 99 percent of Western musical practice—and increasingly musical practice in the rest of the world as well—is glued, seemingly irrevocably, to a tuning that is theoretically appropriate only to atonal music of the period 1921 to circa 1990. This rigid mind-set is one that we need not remain trapped in.

CHAPTER 9

The Seven Limit and Johnston Notation

We leave music's past now and begin to peer into its future. Just over the other side of the great barrier of European tuning theory lies the three-dimensional seven limit, the ratios based on numbers involving seven as a factor. Four hundred years ago, the possibility of using seven as a tuning ratio was still up in the air in Europe. Gioseffo Zarlino, in his *Le institutioni harmoniche* of 1558, had enshrined the *numero senario*, the number six, as the "sonorous number" beyond which no consonances were possible (although he had to create an exception for the minor sixth 8/5 as an acceptable inversion of the 5/4 major third).[1] Over the next couple of centuries, though, various theorists and musicians made an argument for septimal (seven-based) intervals, only to retreat in the face of common practice. The mathematician Marin Mersenne (1588–1648) claimed in 1636, "I have not the slightest doubt that the dissonant intervals of which I have spoken . . . i.e., the ratios 7:6 and 8:7 that subdivide the fourth—may become pleasing if one accustoms oneself to hearing and bearing them . . . for diverse effects that ordinary music lacks." Later, however, he changed his tune and his tuning, writing that because 7/6 "is neither a consonance nor a difference of consonances, nature—which is harmonic—rejects it and prefers to interrupt its series of intervals and melodies than to move through an interval that serves no purpose except to wound the ear and the spirit." [2] The astronomer and scientist Christiaan Huygens (1629–1695) likewise wrote that the number seven "is not unable to produce a consonance" but then dismissed 7/6 and 8/7 as being "incompatible with the consonances already established."[3] The Jesuit Honoré Fabri (1607–1688) wrote in 1670 that "if 8:1 is a consonance, I do not see 7:1 should not also be . . . nor will this be a disagreeable consonance, but, quite the contrary, more pleasing to the ear than 8:1: let anyone try for himself."[4] Then he dismisses septimal intervals on the same incompatability argument. And so it went, writer after writer admitting that septimal intervals could please the ear before deciding that employing them was inconvenient. It was as though if you came out publicly for the number seven, a couple of thugs from the Six-Based Mafia showed up at your office for a little persuasion. Ah, well.

Nevertheless, in 1746, in his oratorio *Judas Maccabeus*, George Frederick Handel wrote some Cs into a part for D trumpet, which in those pre—valve trumpet days could only be played as a seventh harmonic. An English commentator condescended to this attempt at originality and mentioned that for that reason the song in question was often omitted from performances.[5] In 1754 the violinist and composer Giuseppe Tartini (1692–1770) proposed that on the violin a seventh harmonic should be played in a dominant chord rather than the syntonic seventh 9/5 or Pythagorean 16/9, both because it is more consonant and because, since it is closer to the major third or the tonic it is mostly likely to resolve to, it has an effect "so pleasing that nothing can be more so."[6] (In the example I have used Ben Johnston's notation instead of the odd squiggle Tartini uses as a makeshift accidental. I have also indicated the cents in the melody above the tonic F.)

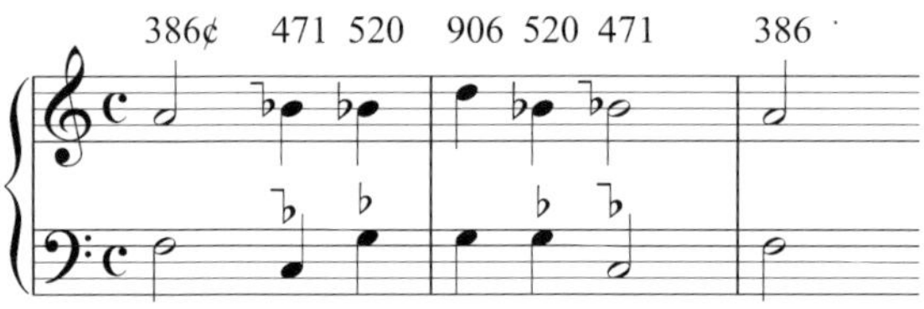

EX. 9.1: Tartini's example for the septimal seventh

Also in the 1750s, Giordano Riccati, in his *Le leggi del contrappunto*, laments: "To tell the truth, it is very strange that . . . though the ear derives pleasure from the most simple proportions in which the number 7 appears—the musical theorists should have such difficulty in realizing that this number does not deserve that banishment from harmony and melody to which they have unjustly condemned it."[7] I heartily concur.

The idea of opening up European music to the seventh harmonic died a thousand little deaths over a period of some four centuries, each death rendering the next more inevitable. For all of its admitted charms, the divine number seven was closed off to Western music for three centuries while Arabic musicians, jazz singers, and others around the world went on to explore its beauties. Finally, sometime around 1930, a young proofreader named Harry Partch (1901–1974), who had dropped out of music school, burned all of his previous music in a big potbellied stove in New Orleans and began work on a twenty-nine-pitch scale (later expanded to forty-three) that took into account both the seventh and eleventh harmonics.[8] The seventh harmonic was finally unleashed into a modern musical tradition. (Partch was not, however, the first

Western composer to use microtones; the Czech composer Alois Hába had begun working with quarter tones a few years earlier.)

We find the simple ratios of seven-limit tuning by combining 7 as a numerator and denominator with the numbers already used in five-limit tuning. Limiting ourselves once again to numbers no greater than 16, the ratios are:

7/1 = 7/2 = 7/4
7/3 = 7/6
7/5
8/7 = 16/7
9/7
10/7
12/7
15/7 = 15/14

Note that we do not yet include 11/7 or 13/7, for both involve prime numbers larger than seven; they are not within the seven limit. Two of the intervals given—9/7 and 15/14—do not yet have complements, so we add 14/9 as a complement of 9/7 and, going above 16, 28/15 as a complement of 15/14. This gives us a scale of ten seven-based intervals as follows:

15/14 = 119.443¢
8/7 = 231.174¢
7/6 = 266.871¢
9/7 = 435.084¢
7/5 = 582.512¢
10/7 = 617.488¢
14/9 = 764.916¢
12/7 = 933.129¢
7/4 = 968.826¢
28/15 = 1080.557¢

These ten intervals are the basic new intervals of seven-limit tuning. Using ever higher numbers, we find an infinity of newly derived intervals (27/14, 63/32) as well.

There are at least three interesting observations we can make about this progression of intervals:

1. Using twelve-step equal temperament as a background grid, we note that six of the ten intervals—8/7, 7/6, 9/7, 14/9, 12/7, 7/4—lie approximately one-third of a half step away from a multiple of one hundred cents. These are the intervals that use only 2 and 7 as factors, and not 5. As we will see upon further consideration of more finely divided equal-tempered scales, a scale that divides each half step into three steps—thirty-six-tone equal temperament, in other words—provides very good

approximations of the seven-limit intervals, which is one reason the thirty-six-tone has gained a few adherents. Each new prime-number limit, we will find, provides a new type, a new *personality*, of intervals, and the seven limit gives us intervals a third of a half step away from the pitches we are used to.

2. Two of the other intervals, 7/5 and 10/7, provide us with perfectly good (i.e., relatively consonant) values for the tritone, or the pitch equivalent of the square root of 2: 582 cents and 618 cents, respectively. When we turn to seven-limit tuning, the tuning of the tritone ceases to be problematic. In fact, by definition, the 7/5 tritone is more consonant than some of the five-limit intervals we are used to, such as 8/5 and 9/5, because it uses smaller numbers.
3. These seven-limit intervals give us new values for most of the usual intervals of the five-limit scale, all but the perfect fourth and perfect fifth. We can label these new intervals by the word "septimal," or seven-based.

   15/14 = septimal half step
   8/7 = septimal whole step
   7/6 = septimal minor third
   9/7 = septimal major third
   7/5 = septimal augmented fourth
   10/7 = septimal diminished fifth
   14/9 = septimal minor sixth
   12/7 = septimal major sixth
   7/4 = septimal minor seventh
   28/15 = septimal major seventh (or also 27/14)

   By replacing five-limit intervals with these new values, we get an exotic language of intervals that can replace or add variety to the sizes we're used to.

In the world of seven-limit tuning, all intervals can be expressed as factors of the numbers 2, 3, 5, and 7. As 2, 3, and 5 gave us a two-dimensional grid (2 being an identity function and not a discrete dimension), seven-limit tuning requires a three-dimensional grid. In example 9.2, the 3/2 perfect fifths run once again from left to right, the 5/4 major thirds run from bottom to top vertically, and the 7/4 septimal minor sevenths (7/4 being equivalent to the simplest seven-based interval, 7/1) run diagonally from the plane on the lower left to the one on the upper right.

In Ben Johnston's tuning notation (which we will finally introduce in full in this chapter), sharps and flats, modified by pluses and minuses, suffice for all five-limit intervals. For seven-limit intervals we need a new accidental. Johnston's solution is to use a 7 before notes that are lowered from a 9/5 minor seventh to a 7/4 minor seventh.

$$7/4 \div 9/5 = 7/4 \times 5/9 = 35/36$$

Thus, a 7 before a pitch multiplies its frequency by 35/36, lowering it by 48.77 cents. An upside down 7 (approximatable typographically by an italic capital *L*), referred to

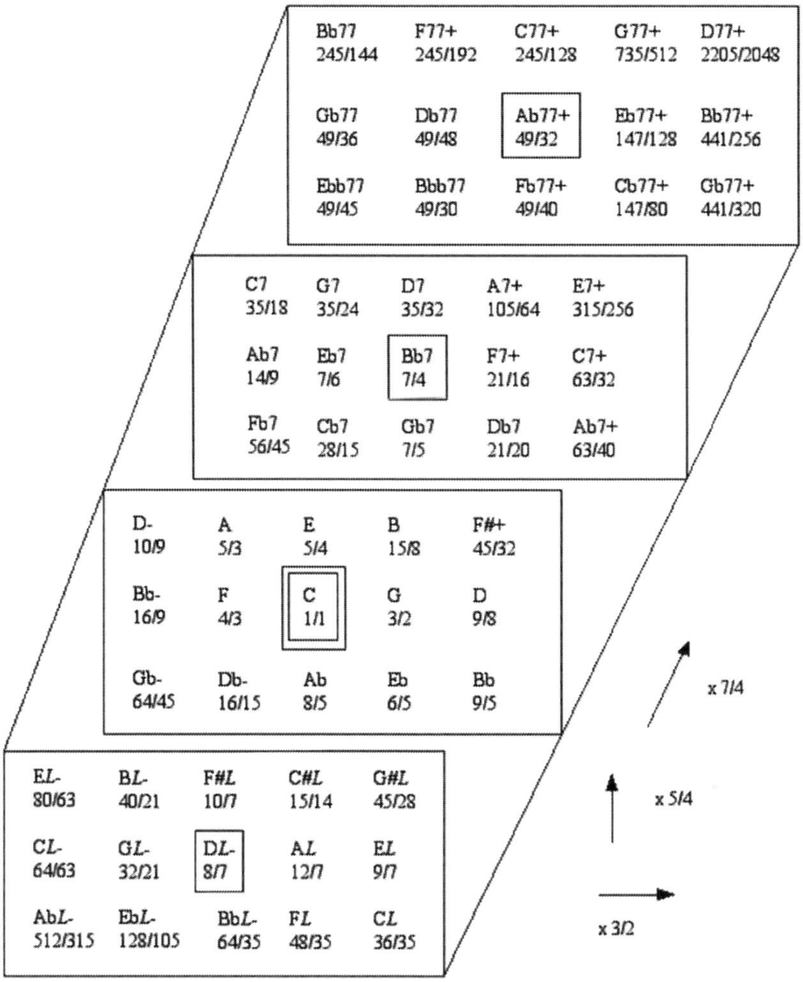

EX. 9.2: A three-dimensional, seven-limit grid

as a *sub-seven*, multiplies the frequency by 36/35, *raising* it by 48.77 cents. In example 9.2 all the pitches in the plane second from the top are marked by a seven, and all of those in the top panel by two sevens. All the pitches in the plane to the lower left are marked by a sub-seven (*L*).

Let us look at the implications of a few of these intervals. Seven-limit tuning is based on the quite consonant interval 7/4; adding this interval to the pure major triad forms a dominant seventh chord with ratios of 4:5:6:7. Combined with these pitches, however, the 7/4 blends in, making a stable, unified sonority, one not necessarily creating the need for resolution that the seventh of a dominant traditionally does in a tonal context. It is questionable (dependent on context and the musician's taste, of course) whether in retuning music couched in classical tonal syntax, the higher, less consonant 9/5 or 16/9 might still be more appropriate as the seventh of a dominant seventh chord intended to seek resolution.

There has been widespread speculation that three degrees, at least, of the septimal scale—7/6, 14/9, and 7/4—might represent the intention of "blue" notes in blues and jazz performances.[9] Each of these is about a third of a half step flatter than the corresponding scale degrees in twelve-pitch equal temperament. It is often noted in textbooks on jazz that the third, sixth, and seventh scale degrees are often flatted in jazz performance as the "blue" notes. The septimal tritones beloved of blues singers could also fall into this category. In theory, some use of these intervals, so well known in some non-Western musics, could have survived in the singing of Africans who were brought to America as slaves, thence infiltrating blues and jazz performance. Since so much jazz performance employs equal-tempered instruments such as the piano, this is not an easy aspect of performance to generalize about. My experience in measuring the pitch of jazz singers like Billie Holliday and Sarah Vaughan on recording suggests that at times they do flatten the third, sixth, and seventh scale degrees to an extent that closely matches septimal interval values and at other times, even within the same song performance, will be in tune with the piano. This is an area in which more study is needed and facile generalizations are probably best avoided. However, it is an evocative field for creative speculation, and Johnston has made string quartet transcriptions of jazz classics relying heavily on septimal intervals.

Isolated from cultural context, one can say something about the character of the intervals themselves. If 7/4 has a warm, well-blended sound, striking in its use as the first sound of La Monte Young's *The Well-Tuned Piano*, 7/6 has a "bitter" quality in contrast to the more *neutral* 6/5 minor third, at least in conventionally melodic and triadic usage. Use of five- versus seven-limit intervals gives us two possibilities for quite consonant minor seventh chords, one using 6/5 and 9/5, the other with 7/6 and 7/4:

Five-limit minor seventh		**Seven-limit minor seventh**	
B♭	9/5	B♭7	7/4
G	3/2	G	3/2
E♭	6/5	E♭7	7/6
C	1/1	C	1/1

The five-limit minor seventh has a more consonant minor third, but the seven-limit has a more consonant minor seventh. The full ratios are as follows:

Five-limit minor seventh	**Seven-limit minor seventh**
C E♭ G B♭	C E♭7 G B♭7
10 : 12 : 15 : 18	12 : 14 : 18 : 21

so that the five-limit minor seventh is a little more consonant overall, but the septimal minor seventh contains beautiful possibilities, and the two can form an interesting contrast within a piece of music. Far more complex is the minor seventh mixing the more consonant third and seventh, with a septimal wolf fifth of 35/24 (653.18 cents):

C		E♭		G		B♭7
1/1		6/5		3/2		7/4
20	:	24	:	30	:	35

A beautifully consonant half-diminished seventh chord is possible using the fifth, sixth, seventh, and ninth harmonics of any pitch (in this case an A♭):

C		E♭7		G♭7		B♭7
1/1		6/5		7/5		9/5
5	:	6	:	7	:	9

However, another fairly simple (in principle if not in beat pattern) half-diminished seventh chord is also possible using the ratios 1/1, 7/6, 7/5, and 7/4:

C		E♭7		G♭7		B♭7
1/1		7/6		7/5		7/4
60	:	70	:	84	:	105

As evident in the progression of denominators (7/7 [1/1], 7/6, 7/5, 7/4), this is an undertone series, the harmonic inversion of the septimal dominant seventh chord.

Just as every interval using a 7 as an accidental, or with a 7 factor in the numerator of a ratio, is by implication a seventh harmonic of some other pitch in a given context, every pitch using a *L* and with a 7 factor in the denominator is by implication a seventh undertone, or subharmonic. Three of these ratios in particular—8/7, 9/7, and 12/7—provide intervals a third of a half step wider than we are used to in twelve-tone equal temperament. The 8/7 is a 231-cent whole step that can easily be learned to sing and perceive, so persuasive is its position as complement of the 7/4, and as the distance between the seventh and eighth harmonics. The ratio 9/7 provides a major third of 435 cents, even wider than Pythagorean, and opens up possibilities for different major triads and seventh chords:

Pitch	C		E*L*		G		
Ratio to C	1/1		9/7		3/2		
Composite ratio	14	:	18	:	21		
Cents from C	0		435		702		
	C		E*L*		G		B*L*
	1/1		9/7		3/2		27/14
	14	:	18	:	21	:	27
	0		435		702		1137

Personally, I have found these chords less usable, more difficult to hear as stable, than the chords based on seven as an overtone of the fundamental or fifth, even though the beat relationships are not much more complex. Still, others may have had other experiences, and such triads are widely used to excellent effect in La Monte Young's *The Well-Tuned Piano*, one of the most important and revealing works ever written in seven-limit tuning, which will be discussed in interlude F following this chapter.

Barbershop Quartet: The Ultimate Seven-Limit Vernacular Performance Tradition

It could be said, I think, that the leading American tradition of just-intonation performance practice is barbershop quartet. This tradition of singing started in the late nineteenth century with a strong African American influence and soared to popularity in the early decades of the twentieth century. Today it remains widely practiced as an amateur but vibrant pastime in rural parts of the country. Barbershop quartets rehearse in small rooms so that they can hear their mutual resonance and become maximally in tune with each other. They don't practice with a keyboard, because the notes they sing aren't on the keyboard, and a piano would throw them off.[10] They fill their arrangements with dominant seventh chords and sing those seventh chords as 4:5:6:7 in the harmonic series. As the web page of the Barbershop Quartet Society puts it, "Barbershop singers adjust pitches to achieve perfectly tuned chords (instead of tempered tuning like the piano) in just intonation while remaining true to the established tonal center."[11]

Example 9.3 shows a passage from the 1918 popular song "I'm Forever Blowing Bubbles" as officially harmonized by the Society for the Preservation and Encouragement of Barber Shop Quartet Singing in America (SPEBSQSA—seriously, they use the acronym). Traditionally, the second tenor sings the main tune. Also, the two higher tenor parts are generally notated an octave higher in the treble clef; I have restored them to actual pitch. In the example, with B♭ as the 1/1 tonic, the ratio of most notes is given above the note, and the cents above the tonic are given below each note. I have based my calculations here on the maintaining of pivot notes from one chord to the next. Also, for convenience I have assumed, at the double-bar line between measures 24 and 25, that the pitch reverts to 1/1 on the tonic chord, causing a syntonic comma shift from the bass F of 40/27 back to 3/2 in the alto. One can see that the pitches that give the seventh of a dominant seventh chord will need to be lowered; the soprano C in measure 16 and tenor C in measure 19 drop down to 155 cents above B♭; the tenor G in measure 18 is 857 cents rather than the 884 cents just sung; the soprano F in measure 20 is 653 cents rather than the expected 702 cents; and so on. Compared to 12tet, some of the sevenths are virtually quarter tones, and the second-scale degree can be 182 cents or 204 cents depending on whether the chord is on F or G.

Barbershop harmony has its own distinctive chord syntax, for which classical analysis is sometimes inadequate. One typical chord is a dominant seventh chord on the leading tone, used as a kind of neighbor-note chord to the tonic, apparent in example 9.4 on the word "blowing."

EX. 9.3: "I'm Forever Blowing Bubbles," mm. 13–32

EX. 9.4: "I'm Forever Blowing Bubbles," mm. 57–60

I have speculatively kept the leading tone A at 1088 cents, but if the tenor voice wants to maintain its G at 884 cents instead of dipping down to 857 cents, the whole chord could come up 27 cents. Frequently (though not in this case), the seventh of this chord avoids parallel octaves that would occur between two As and two B-flats. In any case, barbershop quartets find their pitches intuitively through intensive rehearsal, and it would be of interest to study via recordings what adjustments tend to be actually made. I occasionally receive notes of gratitude from barbershop singers thanking me for explaining on my tuning website why the chords they sing can't be found on a piano. The tradition certainly deserves more serious study as a body of phenomenally well-performed vernacular microtonal music.

Ben Johnston's Notation

The composer Ben Johnston (b. 1926, my teacher for four years and the dedicatee of this book) developed an efficient notation for just-intonation music up to the thirty-one limit and beyond. I have been sneaking bits of it into the text already, and as we will be using it for the next three chapters and the accompanying interludes, it is time to introduce it in full. It is based on the idea, recognized in the sixteenth century, that an accidental multiplies the frequency of a note by some fraction; in a just-intonation context, a sharp multiplies a frequency by 25/24 (C to C♯, say), and a flat multiplies it by the inverse, 24/25, lowering it 70.67 cents as the sharp raises it by that amount. The symbols up through thirty-one-limit tuning (Johnston has ventured higher) are given in example 9.5, along with their ratios, cent difference, and basic purpose. The notation is centered on the key of C in the sense that C–E–G and its dominant and subdominant chords, G–B–D and F–A–C, are all purely tuned to 4:5:6 ratios.

Perhaps the most difficult aspect of the notation (it certainly still seems so after I've used it for three and a half decades) is the use of pluses and minuses to adjust for the syntonic comma. You will note at the bottom of example 9.3 that the ratio given for F to D (plus an octave) is 16:54. Moving those numbers into the same octave gives 32/27, which is a Pythagorean minor third, not a five-based one. The F that makes a 6/5 with D is notated as F+. Likewise, D– is a 6/5 below F. To extend the chain of 5/4 and 6/5 thirds given in the example requires pluses above D and minuses below F:

B♭– D– F A C E G B D F♯+ A+ C♯+

Thus the user of this notation has to keep in mind that triads such as D F A, B♭ D F, and B D♯ F♯ are not pure, nor is D to A a perfect fifth. The purely consonant forms are D F+ A+, B♭– D– F (or B♭ D F+), and B D♯ F♯+.

The remainder of the notation is easier to keep track of intuitively. A seven before a note lowers it by 35/36 (48.77 cents) to turn a 9/5 minor seventh into a septimal seventh. Likewise, an upside-down seven, or sub-seven (rendered typographically by an italicized capital *L*) does the opposite, raising a note by 36/35 to make it the

Sign	Ratio	Cents Difference	Purpose	Sign	Ratio	Cents Difference
+	81/80	21.51¢	10/9 to 9/8	-	80/81	-21.51¢
♯	25/24	70.67¢	6/5 to 5/4	♭	24/25	-70.67¢
7	35/36	-48.77¢	9/5 to 7/4	L	36/35	48.77¢
↑	33/32	53.27¢	4/3 to 11/8	↓	32/33	-53.27¢
13	65/64	26.84¢	8/5 to 13/8	ƐL	64/65	-26.84¢
17	51/50	34.28¢	25/24 to 17/16	LL	50/51	-34.28¢
19	95/96	-18.13¢	6/5 to 19/16	6L	96/95	18.13¢
23	46/45	38.05¢	45/32 to 23/16	ƐZ	45/46	-38.05¢
29	145/144	11.98¢	9/5 to 29/16	6Z	144/145	-11.98¢
31	31/30	56.77¢	15/8 to 31/16	LƐ	30/31	-56.77¢

Ratio Values of Natural Notes

F A C E G B D
4 : 5 : 6
4 : 5 : 6
4 : 5 : 6
16:20:24:30:36:45:54

EX. 9.5: Ben Johnston's just-intonation notation

septimal sub-seventh of something. Thus G7 is the seventh harmonic of A, and A*L* is the seventh subharmonic of G. Notice in example 9.3 that the seven turns a 9/5 minor seventh septimal but not a 16/9 seventh. The seventh harmonic of G, then, is not F7, but F7+.

This is similar with all the other accidentals. A small arrow pointing upward before a note adjusts it by 33/32 for an eleventh harmonic; F↑ is the eleventh harmonic of C. A downward arrow lowers a note by 32/33 for a sub-eleventh harmonic, so D↓ is the eleventh subharmonic of G. (This is convenient because the eleventh harmonic is understood as a quarter tone, and arrows up and down have so often been used in quarter-tone notation.) A 13 before a note raises it from an 8/5 to a 13/8 to obtain a thirteenth harmonic. An upside-down 13 (ƐL) lowers it for a subharmonic. And so on. These accidentals can also be combined, so that a 7-flat is 7♭ (B7♭ is the seventh harmonic of C), a 13-flat is 13♭, the seventh harmonic of a thirteenth subharmonic is 7 over ƐL, the seventh subharmonic of an eleventh harmonic is ↑L, and so on in many configurations. One might even come to remember that the value of 7♭ is 14/15, that of ♯L (sharp plus sub-seven) is 15/14, that of 13♭ is 39/40, that of *L*– is 64/63. (In thirty-one-limit tuning, as in Johnston's Ninth String Quartet, the 13s and upside-down 31s can be a little hard to keep distinguished.) By convention, the pluses and minuses are always separate and closest to the notehead.

Example 9.6 is a chart that has helped me to locate the proper intervals, and keep the syntonic comma in the right place, when I was getting started. It shows the odd-numbered harmonics on each natural note up to thirty-one. So if, for example, you're looking for the harmonics above D♭, you can start with the D line and add a flat to every note. If you're looking for harmonics above A*L*+, you can go to the A line and add *L*+ to every note (the *L* canceling out any 7 that might be found). If you want an eleventh subharmonic below A♭, you can find the eleventh harmonic that is an A (it's on the E line), and add both a down arrow and a flat to both the A♭ and the E to get the E♭↓ that is the subharmonic. It took me a few years to become fluent in this notation, but now I habitually think in it. It does exactly specify every possible note in a thirty-one-limit system. *No two pitches that differ by ever so little can have the same notation, and no two notes notated differently can be the same pitch.*

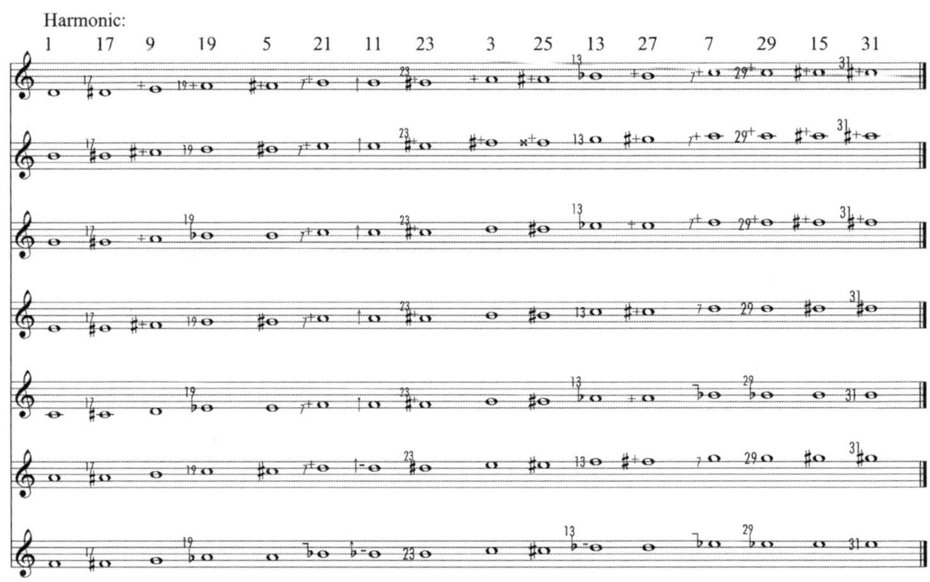

EX. 9.6: The odd harmonics up to thirty-one of all seven natural notes in Ben Johnston's notation

Deriving the Notation from Ratios

The student, in my experience, sometimes finds it difficult at first to start with a desired ratio and imagine what its pitch expression would be. The process is rather simple once the few principles are understood. Keep in mind that when we multiply a pitch by 7 we are moving to its seventh harmonic, which is an octave of a minor seventh; when we divide a frequency by 11, we move to its 11th subharmonic, which is some octave of a fourth below. Also, each accidental is intended to modify a specific interval; for instance, the up-arrow changes a 4/3 interval to an 11/8, and since 4/3 is a perfect fourth, for an 11/8 we always start with a perfect fourth and add an up-arrow. Likewise, the 13 (65/64) changes an 8/5 to a 13/8, and since 8/5 is a minor sixth, we always start with a minor sixth and add the 13. Generally speaking, if there is an 11 in the numerator there *must* be an up-arrow in the accidental; if there is a 13 in the denominator, there *must* be an upside-down 13 in the accidental, and similarly for each prime factor larger than 5.

The rules for starting with an initial pitch, applying a ratio to it, and deriving a resulting pitch name, up through the 19-limit, are as follows:

Sort the ratio into its prime factors. We can disregard 2 and all powers of 2 as octaves, signifiers of register rather than pitch name. For our purposes, 12/11 is effectively 3/11.

For every 3 in the numerator, ascend one perfect fifth. (Add a plus to the perfect fifth note if starting on any kind of B or D, including B♭, D♯, B–, whatever. If the original note had a minus, the plus will merely cancel it out on the new note.)

For every 5 in the numerator, ascend one major third. (Add plus if starting on a D.)

For every 7 in the numerator, ascend one minor seventh and add a 7. (Add plus if starting on a G, B, or D.)

For every 9 in the numerator, ascend one major second. (Add plus if starting on an E, G, B, or D.)

For every 11 in the numerator, ascend one perfect fourth and add ↑. (Add minus if starting on an A or F.)

For every 13 in the numerator, ascend one minor sixth and add a 13. (Add minus if starting on an F.)

For every 17 in the numerator, add a sharp and a 17.

For every 19 in the numerator, ascend a minor third and add a 19. (Add plus if starting on a D.)

For every 3 in the denominator, descend one perfect fifth. (Add minus if starting on an A or F.)

For every 5 in the denominator, descend one major third. (Add minus if starting on an F.)

For every 7 in the denominator, descend one minor seventh and add a ㄥ. (Add minus if starting on an F, A, or C.)

For every 9 in the denominator, descend one major second. (Add minus if starting on an F, A, C, or E.)

For every 11 in the denominator, descend one perfect fourth and add ↓. (Add plus if starting on a B or D.)

For every 13 in the denominator, descend one minor sixth and add a ƐƖ. (Add plus if starting on a D.)

For every 17 in the denominator, add a flat and a ㄥƖ.

For every 19 in the denominator, descend a minor third and add a 6Ɩ (though difficult to distinguish from a 61). (Add minus if starting on an F.)

Here are two examples. In example 9.7, for the ratio 21/13 we need a 3 and a 7 going up, and a 13 coming down.

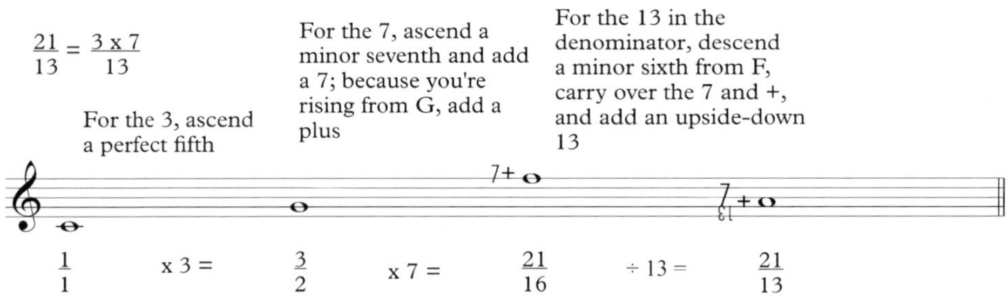

EX. 9.7: Finding 21/13 from C

In example 9.8, for the ratio 44/25 we need an 11 going up (we can ignore the 4 as denoting two octaves), and two 5s coming down.

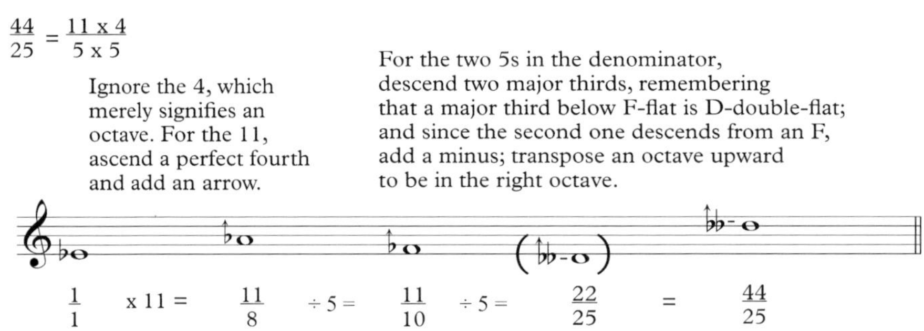

EX. 9.8: Finding 44/25 from E♭

From multiplying all the primes in the numerator, and dividing by all the primes in the denominator, some facility at musically notating ratios should be quickly gained, and with experience, correctly placing the pluses and minuses becomes intuitive as well.

HEWM Notation

A competing version of Johnston's notation has grown up, called HEWM notation—after Helmholtz, his translator Alexander Ellis, and two current composers involved with it, Daniel James Wolf (b. 1961) and Joe Monzo (b. 1962). Some people have not liked the variability among different scales of Johnston's pluses and minuses. Instead of the FACEGBD triads, HEWM notation starts with the Pythagorean scale so that all notes that look like perfect fifths are pure 3/2. The pluses and minuses, then, are invariably correlated with ratios that contain a five. A C-major triad is spelled C E– G, the minus lowering the Pythagorean major third by a syntonic comma. Likewise, a C-minor triad is C E♭+ G, the plus raising the Pythagorean minor third of 32/27 up to 6/5. To make a chart for HEWM notation like that in example 9.3, FACEGBD should be replaced with the string of fifths FCGDAEB in Pythagorean values; the value of the sharp is 2187/2048 instead of 25/24; the 7 connotes 63/64 instead of 35/36; and other accidentals defined with fives must be similarly Pythagorized. This notation does possess an admirable mathematical consistency. So much important music, though—including Johnston's entire output, the extant transcriptions of Partch's music, and Toby Twining's *Chrysalid Requiem*—that HEWM notation will need to develop its own comparably important repertoire if it is to ever displace Johnston's notation.

The HEWM concept is also embodied in the Extended Helmholtz-Ellis JI pitch notation developed by Marc Sabat and Wolfgang von Schweinitz, which has gained some traction, especially in Europe.[12] As with HEWM, the conventional natural, sharp, and flat notes imply Pythagorean tuning. Otherwise, the accidentals differ from HEWM. A syntonic comma alteration is indicated by an arrow up or down:

C to E = 81/64	C to E♭ = 5/4
C to E♭ = 32/27	C to E♮ = 6/5

Multiple arrows for multiple syntonic commas are possible: ♮♭. Seventh, eleventh, and thirteenth harmonics and subharmonics are indicated by the following accidentals, the fractions sometimes differing from Johnston's because they are intended to alter the Pythagorean tuning of the natural notes rather than the five limit:

Septimal	꜒	64/63	꜖	63/64
Undecimal	↑	33/32	↓	32/33
Tridecimal	↑	27/26	↓	26/27

In addition, a T above an accidental indicates a pitch in the 12tet scale, above which a number of cents to be played sharp or flat can be attached. So while the intent of the notation is to enable just intonation, it can actually accommodate any pitch desired and many types of tuning strategies. An example of the notation in a Sabat score can be seen in example 9.9, and more complete information about this notation can be found on Sabat's website at http://www.marcsabat.com/pdfs/notation.pdf.

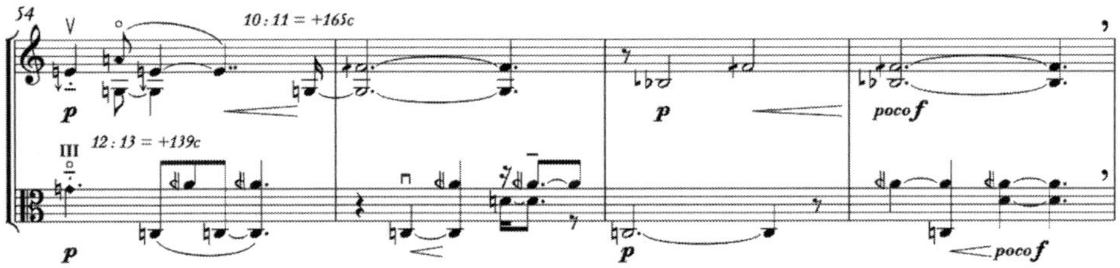

EX. 9.9: Marc Sabat, *Bob Gilmore, Elizabeth Smalt* (2015), mm. 54–57

INTERLUDE F

La Monte Young's *The Well-Tuned Piano*

One of the most famous and instructive seven-limit works is *The Well-Tuned Piano* by La Monte Young (b. 1935), who is widely considered the father of the minimalist movement in music. Lasting five to six hours in performance, *The Well-Tuned Piano* is not a fixed score, but a work improvised from about eighty themes, cadences, scales, and chordal areas. Young first performed it in 1964, in a version that contained only chords, which Young rippled with his fingers like raindrops, and lasted about forty-five minutes. From that point, the piece grew in length and complexity in a process of continual addition and development. For years the only way to hear the work was to go to Young's Manhattan performance space. Then, in 1987, a five-hour recording of a 1981 performance was issued and, more recently, a six-hour DVD of the last 1987 performance. The work requires so much in terms of performer stamina and performance conditions that performances have been rare, and 1987 was the last series. Aside from Young, only one other person—his protégé Michael Harrison—has performed the work. *The Well-Tuned Piano* is one of the great monuments of American piano music and an amazing and revelatory achievement in seven-limit tuning.

Through improvising on overtones with his underground group, the Theater of Eternal Music, in the 1960s, Young became interested in working with intervals based on the number seven. Idiosyncratically, he has always expressed a dislike for intervals based on the number five. (This could be a result of the buzziness that major and minor thirds have in twelve-pitch equal temperament. It could also be a result of the general disfavor that thirds and sixths fell into during the high-modernist atonal era as being too sweet and tonality-defining.) Seven-limit tuning generally requires a three-dimensional grid, but by eliminating the five axis, Young was able to build up his tuning in a two-dimensional grid analogous to that of European just intonation.

The tuning of *The Well-Tuned Piano* is based in perfect 3/2 fifths in one direction and septimal 7/4 sevenths in the other, as in example F.1.

× 3/2

	$\frac{49}{32}$ B	$\frac{147}{128}$ F♯	$\frac{441}{256}$ C♯	$\frac{1323}{1024}$ G♯	
× 7/4	$\frac{7}{4}$ C	$\frac{21}{16}$ G	$\frac{63}{32}$ D	$\frac{189}{128}$ A	$\frac{567}{512}$ E
	$\frac{1}{1}$ E♭	$\frac{3}{2}$ B♭	$\frac{9}{8}$ F		

EX. F.1: Tuning grid for *The Well-Tuned Piano*

The pitch names given represent the keys on the piano that are to be played, but they obscure the true intervallic relationships. In Johnston's notation (see chapter 9), the grid would be rendered thusly:

C77♭+	G77♭+	D77♭+	A77♭++	
D7♭	A7♭+	E7♭+	B7♭+	F7++
E♭	B♭	F+		

This notation makes the septimal sevenths between horizontal rows more consistent and obvious (for instance, each note in a row contains one more 7 in its accidental than the one below it), but it leaves confusion as to which piano keys to play. Laid out as a scale with ratios and cents, the scale appears as in example F.2.[1]

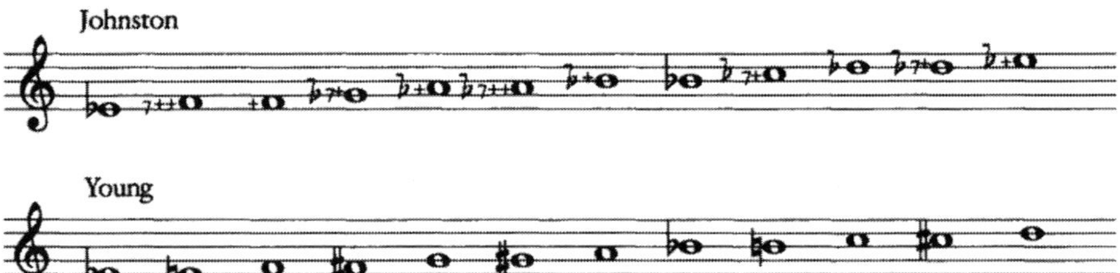

ratio:	$\frac{1}{1}$	$\frac{567}{512}$	$\frac{9}{8}$	$\frac{147}{128}$	$\frac{21}{16}$	$\frac{1323}{1024}$	$\frac{189}{128}$	$\frac{3}{2}$	$\frac{49}{32}$	$\frac{7}{4}$	$\frac{441}{256}$	$\frac{63}{32}$
cents:	0	177	204	240	471	444	675	702	738	969	942	1173

EX. F.2: The tuning of *The Well-Tuned Piano*

Note that the pitches do not uniformly ascend: G♯ is lower than G, and C♯ is lower than C, by the same amount. The reason for this was so that all perfect 3/2 fifths in the scale would be played as perfect fifths on the keyboard, seven "half steps" in size.

Mapping the scale against a 12tet grid reveals how unequal the steps are (ex. F.3).

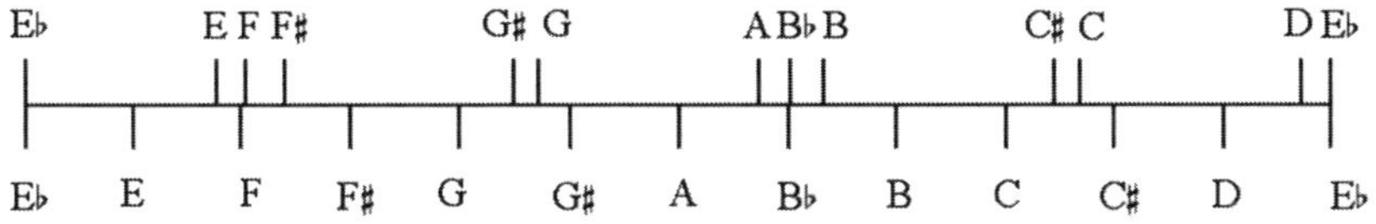

EX. F.3: Tuning graph for *The Well-Tuned Piano*

The scale is virtually pentatonic, with variants for each note. No pitches appear in the areas representing E (100 cents), G♭ (300), G (400), A (600), B (800), C (900), or D (1100). The pitches are grouped around 0, 200, 450, 700, and 950 cents above the tonic, with three tunings each for two of those pitches and two each for the remaining three. (Interestingly, the original 1964 version employed the thirty-first harmonic: C♯ was 31/16, G♯ was 93/64, and E was 279/256. The thirty-first harmonic was a favorite in the Theater of Eternal Music improvisations.)

In twelve-pitch equal temperament there are eleven interval sizes within an octave, or only six if we do not count complements (minor third = major sixth). In *The Well-Tuned Piano*'s scale we have thirty-eight interval sizes (each here paired with its inversion), listed here from the most consonant to the most dissonant:

3/2	702¢	4/3	498¢
7/4	969¢	8/7	231¢
7/6	267¢	12/7	933¢
9/7	435¢	14/9	765¢
9/8	204¢	16/9	996¢
21/16	471¢	32/21	729¢
27/14	1137¢	28/27	63¢
27/16	906¢	32/27	294¢
49/32	738¢	64/49	462¢
49/36	534¢	72/49	666¢
49/48	36¢	96/49	1164¢
63/32	1173¢	64/63	27¢
81/56	639¢	112/81	561¢
81/64	408¢	128/81	792¢
147/128	240¢	256/147	960¢
189/128	675¢	256/189	525¢
441/256	942¢	512/441	258¢
567/512	177¢	1024/567	1023¢
1323/1024	444¢	2048/1323	756¢

In practice, however, Young primarily uses the most consonant intervals in performing the piece. The vast majority of the intervals heard in *The Well-Tuned Piano* can be accounted for by intervals with ratios using numbers less than sixteen: the 3/2 perfect fifth, the 4/3 perfect fourth, the 7/4 septimal minor seventh, the 7/6 septimal minor third, the 9/7 septimal major third, the 12/7 septimal major sixth, and the 14/9 septimal major sixth. (In addition, Young retunes the piano by lowering pitches, never raising them, and the note A, tuned to 440, is the highest pitch relative to its place in the scale. If you try tuning along with the recording, the E♭ is actually about 75 cents flat, closer to D than to E♭; the E♭ below middle C is 148.9947 cps.)

Harmonic Structure

One of the most brilliant aspects of *The Well-Tuned Piano* is its large-scale harmonic structure. Generally speaking, the piece alternates between two harmonic areas, called the Opening Chord and the Magic Chord (ex. F.4).

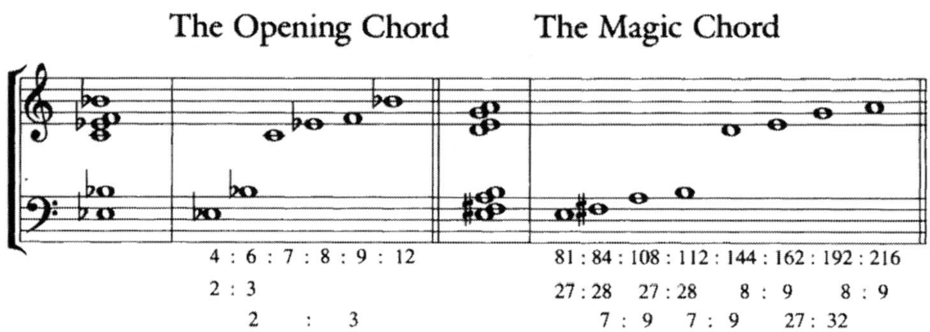

EX. F.4: The Opening Chord and the Magic Chord

The Opening Chord is simply two perfect fifths with a septimal seventh added. The primary theme, the "Theme of the Dawn of Eternal Time" (every entity in *The Well-Tuned Piano* is given a name) takes place entirely in this chord. Since these four notes are adjacent in the tuning grid for the piece, one can move its shape through the grid and see that there are four transposition levels for the Opening Chord within the tuning:

on E♭	1/1	3/2	7/4	9/8
on C	7/4	21/16	49/32	63/32
on G	21/16	63/32	147/128	189/128
on D	63/32	189/128	441/256	567/512

So in the course of the piece, the "Theme of the Dawn of Eternal Time" appears at three of these transposition levels, on E♭, G, and D, in the traditional manner of a symphonist moving his theme into different keys as the piece develops.

The sections in the Magic Chord offer a more complex tonality, often over a drone note on B or F♯. This can be seen as a kind of extended pentatonic scale, alternating seconds and thirds, although two of the seconds are narrowly minor at 28/27 (63 cents), two of the thirds are widely major, 9/7 (435 cents), and the other is a Pythagorean minor third of 32/27. The Magic Chord is a subset of a Romantic Chord, in which are played themes of a Romantic and ornamental nature, usually over a drone on G (ex. F.5).

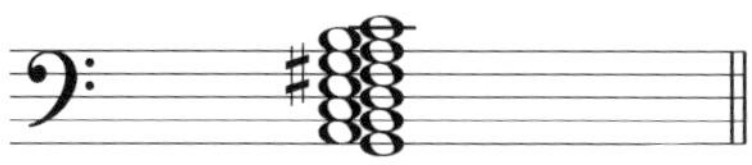

48:54:56:64:72:81:84

EX. F.5: The Romantic Chord

Generally speaking, F♯ and B are especially low in the scale relative to their notation, so what looks like D major and G major sounds minor instead.

Entities in *The Well-Tuned Piano* include clouds, themes, cadences, and sequences, all of which can occur in various harmonic areas. *Clouds* are chords articulated through the rapid reiteration of pitches. They sometimes continue for quite a long time, and, because the intervals are tuned so perfectly and some of the pitches are so close together, when heard live they create amazing aural illusions that can't be picked up by microphones and thus can't be heard on a recording; one seems to hear voices, foghorns, machines. *Themes* are sometimes merely pitch sequences or rows, such as the "Theme of the Magic Chord," shown in example F.6 (all transcriptions here are by the author) in what Young calls a "Subtractive Variation." Fractions above the notes in the example give ratios over the F♯ pedal point, including the seven-limit intervals 12/7, 8/7, 9/7, and 27/14 (an 1137-cent major seventh).

EX. F.6: The Subtractive Variations of the "Theme of the Magic Chord" (4:33:47 on the 1981 recording)

Some of the themes are sequences of dyads (two-note chords), sometimes merely notated in Young's score as as a string of available dyads to improvise on. Such is the case in example F.7, the "Theme of the Lyre of Orpheus in the Elysian Fields."

EX. F.7: The "Theme of the Lyre of Orpheus in the Elysian Fields" (at 4:08:56 on the 1981 recording)

Sometimes one harmonic area will transition into another through thematic fragments. This happens between the Opening Chord and the Magic Chord at eleven minutes into the 1981 recording (ex. F.8). The dyads E♭–B♭ and C–F are from the Opening Chord; B–D and F♯–A are from the Magic Chord. Notice that this passage is a string of parallel 9/7 thirds (and later 12/7 sixths) with an occasional perfect fifth.

EX. F.8: Transition from the Opening Chord to the Magic Chord (at 0:10:58 on the 1981 recording)

The sequences are occasional chord progressions that are dwelt on, usually cadentially, and the cadences are closing formulas, such as the "Cadence of Paradise" shown in example F.9.

EX. F.9: The "Cadence of Paradise" (as heard at 0:28:33 on the 1981 recording)

Despite its improvisatory nature, the overall structure of *The Well-Tuned Piano* is quite simple and elegant. Example F.10 shows the harmonic progression of the 1981 recording, passing among the Opening, Magic, Magic-Opening, Magic Harmonic Rainforest, Romantic, and Elysian Fields (over a D drone) Chords (a "harmonic chord," in Young's terminology, is one extended through additional octaves). Notice that the pitch C♯ appears only in the Elysian Fields and that the pitch G♯ doesn't appear on that recording at all (though it does in the 1987 recording, during the Brontesaurus Boogie section—this is why I never found those pitches when I first ascertained the tuning).

Sec.	*Timing*	*Pitch Classes Present*	*Name*
1	0:00:00–0:09:38	E♭ F B♭ C	Opening Chord
2	0:09:38–0:21:47	E♭ E F F♯ G A B♭ B C D	[Transition]
3	0:21:47–1:02:29	E F♯ G A B D	Magic Chord
4	1:02:29–1:21:54	E♭ E F F♯ G A B♭ B C D	Magic Opening Chord
5	1:21:54–2:06:06	E♭ F G♭ (G) B♭ C	Magic Harmonic Rainforest Chord
6	2:06:06–3:01:15	E♭ E F F♯ G A B♭ B C D	[Transition]
7	3:01:15–4:01:51	E F♯ G A B C D	Romantic Chord
8	4:01:51–4:59:41	E F♯ G A B C C♯ D	Elysian Fields
9	4:59:41–5:01:22	E♭ E F G B♭ B C	Ending

EX. F.10: Harmonic structure of the 1981 recording of *The Well-Tuned Piano*

From a tuning standpoint, *The Well-Tuned Piano* is a remarkable sustained exercise in seven-limit tuning, one with no five-based intervals to dilute the strangeness. My personal experience with the piece was that it can sound unsettlingly peculiar for the first few hours, but by the fifth hour the ear forgets that a piano has ever been tuned any other way. Also, since Young tunes the three strings on each piano key to absolute unison (unlike most modern pianos, on which the pitch is slightly varied to obscure the out-of-tuneness), the piano can sound more like bells than like a normal piano. For much more information, consult my article "La Monte Young's *The Well-Tuned Piano*" in the Winter 1993 issue of *Perspectives of New Music*.[2]

INTERLUDE G

Ben Johnston's String Quartet No. 4

Ben Johnston's Fourth String Quartet (1973) is one of the most beloved of microtonal works, a rare avant-garde piece that has found, and can thrill, a wide audience. Much of the reason for its appeal is that it is based on a tune known to almost everyone, the old hymn "Amazing Grace." It is, however, one of the most difficult works in the repertoire to play, due to the combination of its seven-limit scale with two dozen pitches and its extreme rhythmic difficulties, which mirror the pitch relationships. Henry Cowell, in his seminal book of American music theory, *New Musical Resources* (1930), had suggested that we could structure rhythms analogously to the way we think about pitch—that is, in different tempos at the same time, such as four-against-five-against-six-against seven to mirror the ratios of a just-intoned dominant seventh chord. In response, many American composers (myself included) have written pieces combining similar pitch and rhythmic relationships. Johnston's Fourth Quartet is by far the best-known result.

The "Amazing Grace" Quartet is played in a slight *scordatura*—that is, each string player tunes his or her strings to exact 3/2 fifths, notated C–, G–, D–, A, and E (D– to A being a perfect 3/2 fifth in Johnston's notation). The piece is, then, in the key of G minus and takes the form of a theme with eight variations.

The opening statement of the theme is meant to be as rustic as possible, played in a Pythagorean pentatonic scale tuned to perfect fifths: G– 1/1, D– 3/2, A 9/8, E 27/16, and B 81/64. As one can see in example G.1 at the intervals marked by brackets, Johnston generally avoids thirds (81/64 and 32/27), except as neighbor notes, and harmonizes with fifths and major seconds (at 9/8, more consonant than the thirds) as much as possible.

Variation 1 elaborates the theme in the first violin and adds the cello, still emphasizing Pythagorean fourths and fifths. Variation 2 (ex. G.2) splits the instruments into different tempos analogous to the ratios of a Pythagorean-tuned string instrument.

EX. G.1: Johnston's String Quartet No. 4, mm. 1–7

The cello, in 2/4 meter, plays a 2:3 ratio by plucking fifths in dotted eighth notes in the lower register and bowing an upper line in regular eighth notes. The viola, marked in 6/8 meter, plays triplets against the cello's upper line. The second violin is in 9/8, playing triplet sixteenth notes against the viola's eighth notes. And the first violin (its apparent rhythm marked above the staff) is effectively in 27/32 meter across two measures, keeping as background a tempo 3/2 as fast as the second violin's sixteenth notes.

EX. G.2: Johnston's String Quartet No. 4, var. 2, mm. 5–7

So just as the pitches C– G– D– A E have relative ratios of four 3/2s in a row, the tempos here take as their beats fractions of a measure in the pattern 3/8, 1/4, 1/6, 1/9, 2/27, which, inverted and multiplied by 3, give us 8, 12, 18, 27, and 40.5, each multiplied by 3/2 to arrive at the next. Using a Pythagorean pentatonic scale, Johnston has also given us a pentatonic scale of tempos.

Variation 3 elaborates the theme by adding in five-limit ratios to make a conventional major scale (1/1, 9/8, 5/4, 4/3, and so on) and also adds in rhythmic quintuplets in order to mirror the increase in pitch diversity. Variation 5 begins in 7/8, adding sevens to the rhythmic spectrum, and finally achieving a 35:36 polyrhythm between dyads in the first violin and viola over virtual 9/8 in the cello and 2/4 in the second violin (ex. G.3).

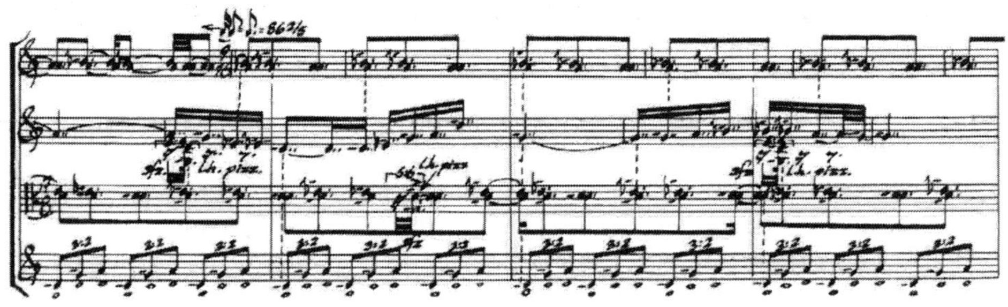

EX. G.3: Johnston's String Quartet No. 4, var. 5, mm. 3–6

The ratio 36:35, it will be remembered, is the ratio of Johnston's 7 accidental.

Variation 6 (ex. G.4) is based on the inversion of "Amazing Grace" (starting on the second note in the first violin) and thus appropriately uses subharmonic seven-based intervals such as 8/7, 12/7, and 27/14.

EX. G.4: Johnston's String Quartet No. 4, var. 6, mm. 1–3

The final two variations of the piece combine the extended "major" scale of variation 4 with the "minor" one of variation 6 into a twenty-two-pitch complement as follows:

22-pitch scale var. 7		Cents	"Major" var. 4	"Minor" var. 6
G–	1/1	0.000	1/1	1/1
A7♭–	28/27	62.96	28/27	
A♭–	16/15	111.73		16/15
A–	10/9	182.4	10/9	
A*L*–	8/7	231.17		8/7
B7♭–	7/6	266.87	7/6	
B♭–	6/5	315.64		6/5
B–	5/4	386.31	5/4	
B*L*–	9/7	435.08		9/7
C7	21/16	470.78	21/16	
C	27/20	519.55		27/20
C♯	45/32	590.22	45/32	
C♯*L*	81/56	638.99		81/56
D–	3/2	701.96	3/2	3/2
E7♭–	14/9	764.92	14/9	
E♭–	8/5	813.69		8/5
E–	5/3	884.36	5/3	
E*L*–	12/7	933.13		12/7
F7	7/4	968.83	7/4	
F	9/5	1017.6		9/5
F♯	15/8	1088.27	15/8	
F♯*L*	27/14	1137.04		27/14
G–	2/1	1200.00	2/1	2/1

One can see this hyperchromatic scale in action in example G.5 as the first violin plays it at the climax. After this ecstatic rendering, the rhythmic complexities and pitches gradually diminish and fall away until the music ends up in a gentle cadence with the pentatonic scale, the final sonority containing not even a third, just G and D, coming to a rather precipitous rest where it began.

EX. G.5: Johnston's String Quartet No. 4, var. 8, first violin, mm. 22–24

Example G.6 shows the cumulative progression of pitches among the eight variations, from pentatonic to diatonic to chromatic to hyperchromatic, with page numbers from the score given.[1] Despite the work's tremendous difficulties, it has been widely performed because it is so well loved; there have been at least three commercial recordings. Johnston's ten string quartets, numbers 2 through 10 of which are in just intonation, form one of the most formidable bodies of string quartet repertoire from the twentieth century. As we will see in interlude I following chapter 11, though, the Fourth String Quartet is hardly the most complex or difficult in the series.

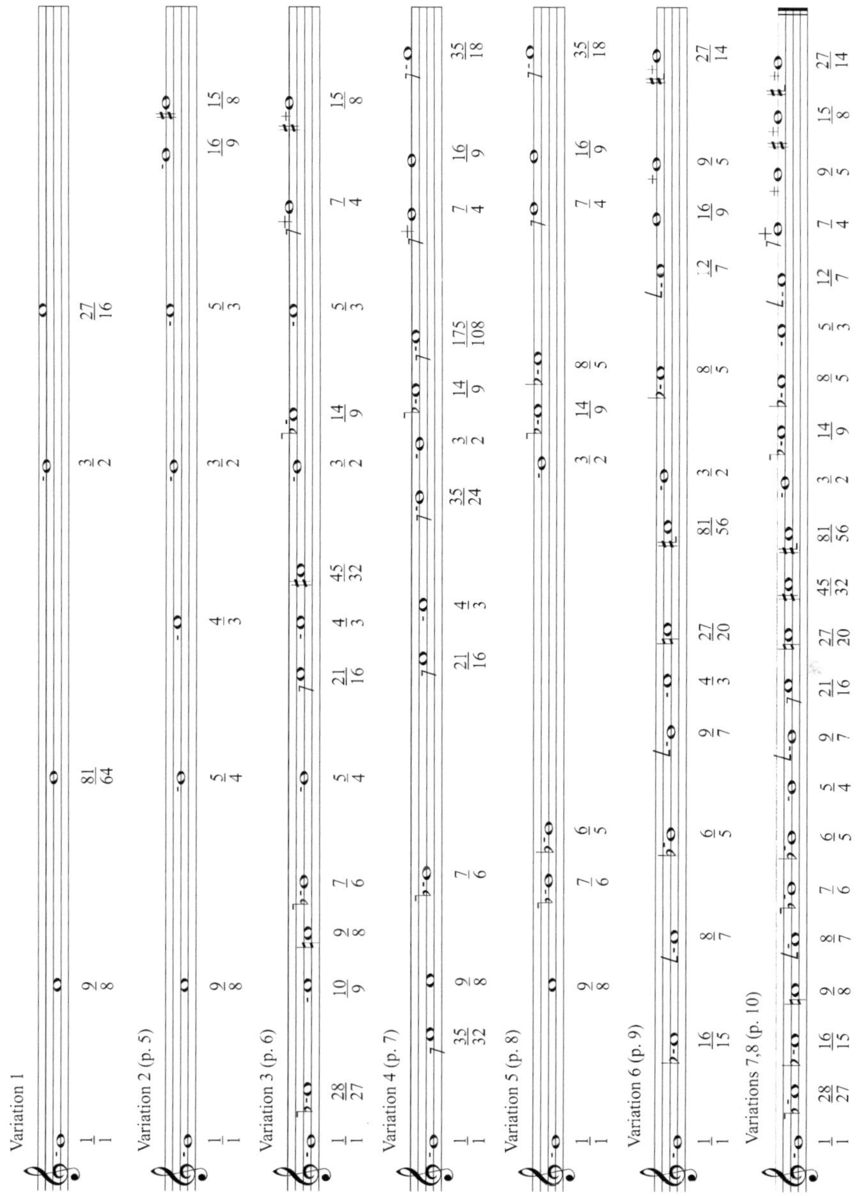

EX. G.6: Pitches used in each variation of Johnston's String Quartet No. 4

CHAPTER 10

THE ELEVEN LIMIT AND THE FOURTH DIMENSION

The number eleven brings an intriguing new flavor to music, as many intervals based on it fall halfway between our twelve equal-tempered pitches and are suggestive of quarter tones. The eleventh harmonic is 551.318 . . . cents above an octave of the fundamental, an 11/8 interval. Over C it falls almost exactly halfway between F and F♯. Limiting ourselves once again to numbers under sixteen, eleven generates the following ratios:

11/1 = 11/2 = 11/4 = 11/8
11/3 = 11/6
11/5 = 11/10
11/7
11/9
12/11
14/11
15/11
16/11

Among these, 11/10, 11/9, and 15/11 are without complements, so we add 20/11, 18/11, and 22/15 to get the following scale of twelve eleven-based intervals:

12/11 = 150.64¢
11/10 = 165¢
11/9 = 347.41¢
14/11 = 417.51¢
15/11 = 536.95¢
11/8 = 551.32¢
16/11 = 648.68¢
22/15 = 663.05¢
11/7 = 782.49¢
18/11 = 852.59¢
20/11 = 1035¢
11/6 = 1049.36¢

Of these twelve intervals, nine are within fifteen cents of a quarter tone (fifty cents between two equal-tempered steps), and six of those—12/11, 11/9, 11/8, 16/11, 18/11, and 11/6—are within three cents. These six are the ones that use only 2, 3, and 11 as factors. Eleven-limit tuning gives us a field rich in what we think of as quarter tones. Consequently, the personality of eleven-limit tuning can be to smooth out the scale by giving us mediating pitches halfway between the equal-tempered, or even five-limit, pitches we're used to. In particular, 11/9 is a useful *neutral* third between major (5/4) and minor (6/5), while 11/6 is a similarly neutral seventh. As we will see in chapter 14, Arabic music uses approximations of some of these eleven-based intervals.

To raise a perfect 4/3 fourth to an undecimal fourth, we can use the upward arrow (↑) as defined by Ben Johnston, indicating a comma of 33/32, or 53.27 cents. Likewise, a downward arrow (↓) indicates a lowering by the same amount, 32/33, to create an eleventh subharmonic of something. The use of arrows to create eleventh harmonics and undertones is consistent with the widespread use of arrows to indicate quarter tones in the notations of many composers. Note that the accidental converts three-limit ratios to eleven-based ones; five-limit ratios (such as the 27/20 wolf fourth) will require a plus or minus.

Historically, the quarter-tone scale (which is the main topic of chapter 13) was the first non-twelve-pitch scale to be explored in European music. Urged as a possibility by Franz Liszt and Ferruccio Busoni, it was copiously experimented with in the 1920s and '30s by Alois Hába, Hans Barth, Ivan Wyschnegradsky, Julián Carrillo, and to a lesser extent by Charles Ives. Quarter-tone notation has even become comparatively standardized (this is also dealt with in chapter 13). From a just-intonation standpoint, the theoretical problem with the twenty-four-pitch quarter-tone scale is that it provides basically a Pythagorean scale approximation plus the eleventh harmonics of those notes, leaving out the more audible fifth and seventh harmonics in between—it "goes around our elbows to reach our thumbs," as Partch eloquently puts it.[1] Nevertheless, as works by Ives, Hába, and Wyschnegradsky prove, there is something spine-tingling about the irreducible in-betweenness of quarter tones, and the simpler intervals based on the number eleven can be used to the same effect.

The most important of these, of course, is what we might call the "undecimal" fourth, 11/8. Within a given tonality, the pitch works smoothly as the fourth degree of a so-called overtone scale (such as was approximated by Béla Bartók as C D E F♯ G A B♭—or in jazz the Lydian dominant scale—in both his Music for Strings, Percussion, and Celesta and Sonata for Two Pianos and Percussion). My students, immersed in jazz terminology (if not always jazz itself), are used to recognizing chords with "sharp elevens"—why must they always be fully sharp rather than more consonantly half sharp? In Partch's words, "The musician will undoubtedly ask: if we concede that the 'seventh of the chord' sometimes implies the Identity 7, and the 'ninth of the chord' sometimes implies the Identity 9, why cannot the 'eleventh of the chord' imply the Identity 11?"[2]

Within triads and seventh chords, the eleven limit offers a "neutral" third, 11/9, between major and minor, and a neutral seventh, 11/6, between major and minor. This possibility of a chord between major and minor was what fascinated Charles Ives in the third of his Three Pieces for Two Quarter-Tone Pianos, and he gives it as an example (though as a quarter-tone chord and without ratios, of course) in his quarter-tone essay, "Some Quarter-Tone Observations." (See example 13.2.)

The neutral triad is made up of the ratios 18:22:27:

Pitch	C		E♭↑−		G
Ratio to C	1/1		11/9		3/2
Composite ratio	18	:	22	:	27
Cents from C	0		347		702

In Johnston's notation, we have to add a minus in E♭↑−. The up arrow is intended to raise 4/3 to 11/8, but by itself it raises 6/5 to 99/80, which, multiplied by the 80/81 comma, gives us 11/9. The up arrow by itself will raise a Pythagorean 32/27 third to 11/9. The neutral seventh chord is as follows:

C		E♭↑−		G		B♭↑−
1/1		11/9		3/2		11/6
18	:	22	:	27	:	33
0		347		702		1049

I have also found these mediating, ambiguous chords quite usable and fertile.

Eleven-limit intervals also offer two undecimal seconds between the whole step and half step: 12/11 (150.6 cents) and 11/10 (165 cents), the former more exactly in between. The complement of the former, 11/6 (1049 cents) is the neutral seventh we've already seen in the neutral seventh chord. We have already run across 12/11 and 11/10 in Ptolemy's "even diatonic." The seventeenth-century theorist Giambattista Doni (1594–1647) tried to resurrect these in music for viol consorts around 1635 and even added in the 15/11 fourth (537 cents), the 20/11 seventh (1035 cents), and a 45/44 comma (39 cents) to support them consonantly.[3] Though less insistently than seven, even eleven has been waiting on the horizon for centuries to make its appearance in musical practice.

For what it's worth, since many 11-based intervals approximate quarter tones, 121-based intervals (11 × 11) approximate twelve-pitch equal-temperament. The eleventh harmonic of the eleventh harmonic, 121/64, is 1102.6 cents, virtually an equal-tempered major seventh. Likewise,

12/11 × 12/11	=	144/121	=	301.3 cents (a minor third)
11/9 × 11/9	=	121/81	=	694.8 cents (a fifth)
18/11 × 18/11	=	324/121	=	1705.2 cents (an eleventh)
11/6 × 11/6	=	121/36	=	2098.7 cents (a major thirteenth)

The great champion of eleven-limit tuning in just intonation was Harry Partch, whose work we will discuss in interlude H following this chapter.

INTERLUDE H

Harry Partch

Harry Partch (1901–1974) is a towering figure in the history of tuning and microtonality. In terms of theory and performance, he not only single-handedly rescued just intonation from the obscurity it had languished in for hundreds of years, but he also went far beyond any previous musician by inventing and manufacturing an entire orchestra of instruments in which he could play all of the pitches he wanted. In 1930, at age twenty-nine, he burned all the music he had written up to that point, including an unfinished piano concerto, in a potbellied stove in New Orleans. Armed with a viola he had modified to play in accurate just intonation by nailing tacks in the fretboard, he turned his back on acoustic falsehood forever. No other composer has proved such an inspiration to so many twentieth- and twenty-first-century microtonalists. He is our Moses who led us from the wilderness farther into the promised land than it seemed like one man should have been able to go, particularly in those days of predigital technology. And the book he wrote to explain his theories and instruments, *Genesis of a Music*, for all of its idiosyncrasies, remains one of the best and most readable introductions to the history and theory of tuning. As his biographer Bob Gilmore aptly writes, "It comes as a sobering corrective to the anarchic, irreverent aspects of Partch's creativity to realize how many hours he must have spent poring over Helmholtz's book and leafing through innumerable lesser works, drier than dust, on music theory and acoustics."[1]

The scale associated with Partch's music famously contains forty-three tones to the octave, yet over and over he lamented that music writers had latched on to that number as though he considered it the natural endpoint of some airtight system; he didn't. It was a convenience and a compromise. What Partch did was to extend the harmonic series up through the eleventh harmonic. Partch thought that if the harmonic series approximated and justified major keys in conventional tonality, the subharmonic series (the harmonic series inverted, ex. H.1) provided a just-intonation analogue to minor keys. As the first six harmonics of C consist of C, E, and G, the first six subharmonics produce C, A♭, and F, a minor triad on the subdominant. The existence of subharmonics in the natural acoustic world has been long debated. Apparently, bowed string instruments can be made to produce undertones if enough pressure is applied, and in *New Musical Resources* Henry Cowell claims to have met a professor in Moscow who had invented an instrument "on which at least the first nine undertones could be heard without the aid of resonators."[2] As the harmonic series is based on the integers 1, 2, 3, 4, 5, and so on, the subharmonic series is based on their reciprocal fractions: 1/1, 1/2, 1/3, 1/4, and 1/5, and so on. (The fractions 4/3 and 8/5 will render 1/3 and 1/5 within the 1/1–2/1 octave.) Extended through the eleventh harmonic of C it will reach D*L* (8/7 in terms of C 1/1) as a seventh subharmonic and G↓ (16/11) as an eleventh subharmonic.

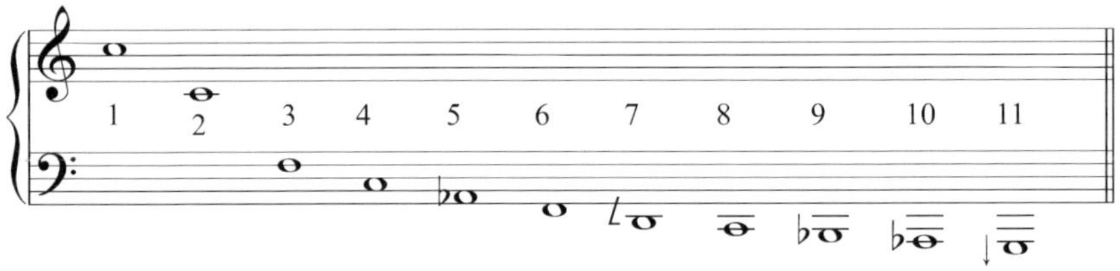

EX. H.1: The subharmonic or undertone series

The ratios so produced will all have powers of two in the numerator rather than the denominator as in the harmonic series.

In any case, Partch considered the subharmonic series as basic as the harmonic series, and his typical pitch structures tend to be symmetrical by inversion (a tendency also inherited by Partch's protégé Ben Johnston). Partch referred to his harmonic series as an "otonality" (since it was based on overtones) and a subharmonic series as a "utonality" (based on undertones). The structural basis of his tuning consists of the odd-numbered harmonics up to eleven, also transposed to the pitches of the subharmonic series down to eleven. Twenty-nine different pitches result, in a grid shown in example H.2. This is not only a diagram but the actual tuning of the central section of two of Partch's primary percussion instruments, the Diamond Marimba and the Quadrangularis Reversum. As you can see, the upper-left diagonal is a series of thirds encompassing the first, fifth, third, seventh, ninth, and eleventh harmonics (specifically of G 392 Hz, the pitch Partch decided to tune to, which is almost exactly 200 cents lower than A 440 and thus matches the G on our pianos). The bottom-left diagonal in the opposite direction gives the inversion of that, with the first, fifth (8/5), third (4/3), seventh (8/7), ninth (16/9), and eleventh (16/11) subharmonics. Then he transposed the upper diagonal, the otonality, on to each of the notes of the lower diagonal, the utonality. Note that some pitches are duplicated at more than one point on the grid, notably the 1/1 that runs across the center horizontal line.

					11/8					
				9/8		11/10				
			7/4		9/5		11/6			
		3/2		7/5		3/2		11/7		
	5/4		6/5		7/6		9/7		11/9	
1/1		1/1		1/1		1/1		1/1		1/1
	8/5		5/3		12/7		14/9		18/11	
		4/3		10/7		4/3		14/11		
			8/7		10/9		12/11			
				16/9		20/11				
					16/11					

EX. H.2: Partch's twenty-nine-pitch tonality diamond

As a scale, this structural framework of twenty-nine pitches is very uneven, making it difficult to move in even roughly parallel intervals. Some steps between consecutive pitches were as small as 14 cents (for instance, the 121/120 between 12/11 and 11/10), while others were as large as 151 cents (between 1/1 and 12/11, and reciprocally between 11/6 and 2/1). So Partch added some fourteen further pitches, consonant with some of those twenty-nine, that filled in the gaps. The total resulting forty-three-tone scale is as follows:

Ratio	Cents	Name, if any	Johnston notation[3]
1/1	0.000	tonic	G
81/80	21.506	syntonic comma	G+
33/32	53.273	undecimal comma	G↑
21/20	84.467		A♭7+
16/15	111.731	five-limit half step	A♭
12/11	150.637	undecimal neutral half step	A↓+
11/10	165.004	undecimal neutral half step	A♭↑
10/9	182.404	minor whole tone	A
9/8	203.910	major whole tone	A+
8/7	231.174	septimal whole tone	A*L*
7/6	266.871	septimal minor third	B♭7
32/27	294.135	Pythagorean minor third	B♭-
6/5	315.641	five-limit minor third	B♭

Ratio	Cents	Name, if any	Johnston notation[3]
11/9	347.408	undecimal neutral third	B♭↑–
5/4	386.314	five-limit major third	B
14/11	417.508		C7↓+
9/7	435.084	septimal major third	B*L*
21/16	470.781	septimal fourth	C7+
4/3	498.045	perfect fourth	C
27/20	519.551	"wolf" fourth	C+
11/8	551.318	undecimal tritone	C↑
7/5	582.512	septimal tritone	D♭7
10/7	617.488	septimal tritone	C♯*L*
16/11	648.682		D↓
40/27	680.449	dissonant five-limit fifth, "wolf" fifth	D–
3/2	701.955	perfect fifth	D
32/21	729.219		D*L*–
14/9	764.916	septimal minor sixth	E♭7
11/7	782.492	undecimal minor sixth	D↑*L*–
8/5	813.686	five-limit minor sixth	E♭
18/11	852.592	undecimal neutral sixth	E↓+
5/3	884.359	five-limit major sixth	E
27/16	905.865	Pythagorean major sixth	E+
12/7	933.129	septimal major sixth	E*L*
7/4	968.826	septimal minor seventh	F7+
16/9	996.090	five-limit small minor seventh	F
9/5	1017.596	five-limit large minor seventh	F+
20/11	1034.996		F♯↓+
11/6	1049.363	undecimal neutral seventh	F↑
15/8	1088.269	five-limit major seventh	F♯+
40/21	1115.533		F♯*L*
64/33	1146.727		G↓
160/81	1178.494		G–

A four-dimensional *lattice* for Partch's tuning is shown in example H.3, with each of four directions showing the intervals 3/2, 5/4, 7/4, and 11/8, respectively. That this scale ended up with forty-three steps, Partch said many times, is "in fact the one-half truth of the one-fourth factor" and "totally misleading."[4]

Partch's scores are difficult to read for the uninitiated (which includes almost everyone aside from his experienced performers), because they are all written in tablature notation—that is, the notation shows the player what notes to play on the instrument but not the actual pitch names. (The most common forms of tablature notation are guitar tab and lute tablature, which show the player where to stop each string but not what pitch will result.) Since so many of the instruments are widely different in technique of performance, each instrument has a different tablature. Transcribing each instrument into pitch notation requires knowing how the instrument is played.

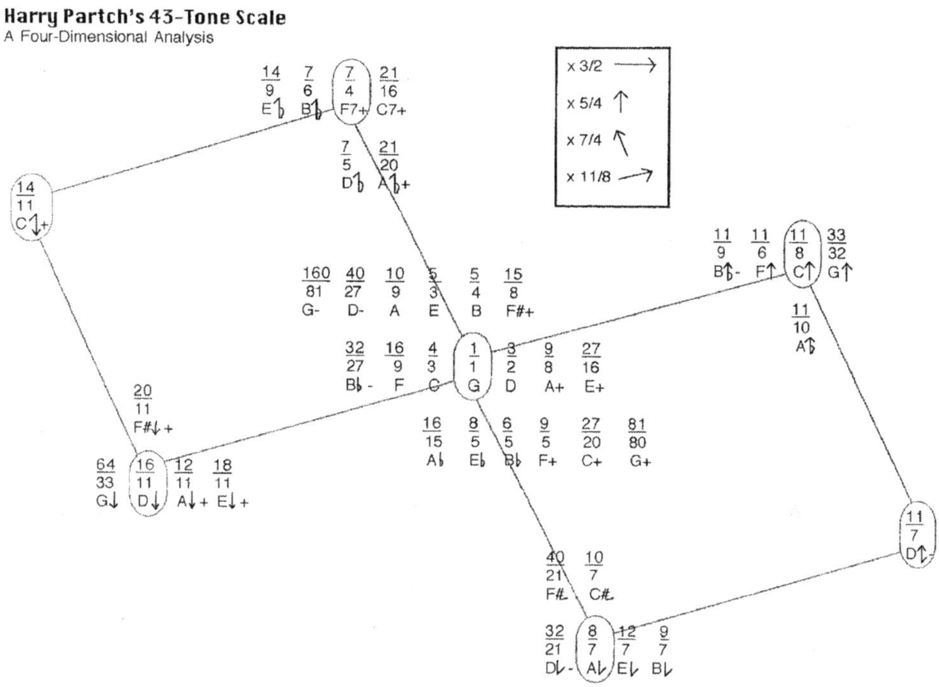

EX. H.3: Partch's forty-three-tone scale in lattice notation

Thus when one looks at a Partch score, one is seeing only instructions for the player, and the musical content can be extracted only with difficulty. For instance, example H.4 shows the opening of Partch's *Barstow*.

EX. H.4: Partch, *Barstow*, mm. 1–4 in manuscript

The voice part, following Partch's usual custom, is notated conventionally, without great exactitude of pitch—sometimes ratios are added. The Surrogate Kithara, which doesn't play in these measures, is given directions as to where to place the sliding glass rods for the strings that will first be played: the green row for the otonality on 8/5 and the orange row for 16/15. The Chromelodeon, a modified reed organ, is notated with the pitches that a keyboard player would play on a normal keyboard. And the Diamond Marimba, using otonalities in measures 1 and 2 and utonalities in measure 3, has notes indicated in each row of that instrument; otonalities are indicated by numbers above the staff, and utonalities are underneath. A transcription of the actual pitches is seen in example H.5.

EX. H.5: Partch, *Barstow*, mm. 1–5, Richard Kassel's transcription

One of the potential effects Partch clearly enjoyed in his tuning was something he called "tonality flux," the interlocking of different triads through slight movements of voice leading. One of his examples comes from the beginning of "The Letter," a movement of *The Wayward*.[5] Throughout the piece the kithara plays a six-note ostinato that alternates between a minor triad on the 7-otonality and a major triad on the 7-utonality. As seen in example H.6, in ratios to G, Ben Johnston's notation, and cents from G, the pitches undulate so narrowly that a casual listener might think the same triad is repeating over and over.

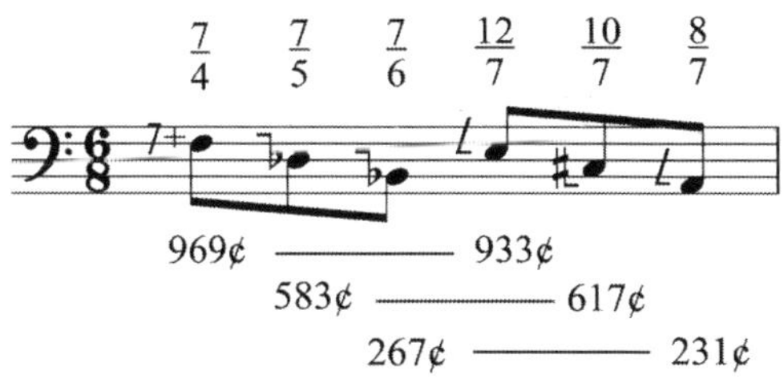

EX. H.6: Ostinato of "The Letter"

The F7+ drops only thirty-six cents to the E*L*, and similarly the B♭7 to the A*L*, but the D♭7 *rises* thirty-four cents to the C♯*L*. The other example (and if this comes from one of his pieces, I haven't found it) is a minor triad on F↑ 11/6 to a major triad on D↓ 16/11, from the 11-utonality to the 11-otonality (ex. H.7).[6] Here the C↑ rises a half step to D↓, while the other two pitches descend by only fourteen cents.

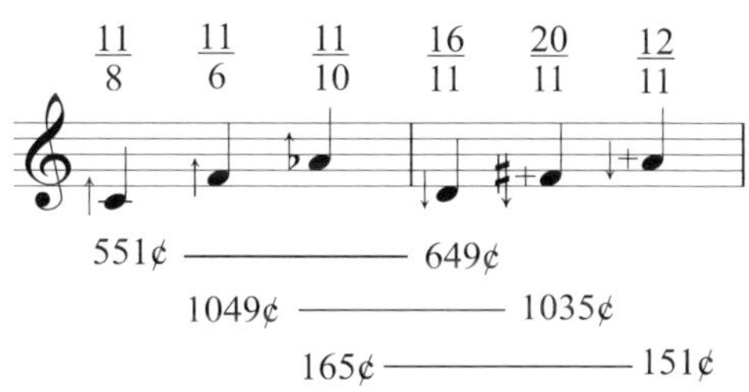

EX. H.7: Another example of tonality flux

To say that much work remains to be done toward the understanding of Partch's scores would be a gross understatement. As I was not a performer in his ensemble, my own ability to transcribe his scores is limited. Richard Kassel helpfully includes transcription guides to several of the instruments in his edition of *Barstow*. When Partch died, many feared that his music would not survive, but the instruments (currently at the University of Washington in Seattle) have been duplicated, and authentic performances have actually increased in recent years. His incredibly original music created its own tradition, and we have much left to learn from it.[7]

CHAPTER 11

THE THIRTEEN LIMIT AND BEYOND

Harry Partch felt deeply that his stopping at the eleventh harmonic was somewhat arbitrary. He explained his rationale in typically colorful terms: "When a hungry man has a large table of aromatic and unusual viands spread before him he is unlikely to go tramping along the seashore and in the woods for still other exotic fare. And however skeptical he is of the many warnings regarding the unwholesomeness of his fare—like the 'poison' of the 'love-apple' tomato of a comparatively few generations ago—he has no desire to provoke further alarums."[1] Partch knew that the thirteenth harmonic was out there beckoning and that someday it would be added to our musical vocabulary.

The series of prime numbers is infinite. There can be no largest prime number, as the following mathematical proof shows:

> Assume n is the largest prime number, and let x = n! + 1. Then x cannot be prime, since x > n. Thus x must have a prime divisor, p. But since n is the largest prime, p <= n, so p occurs in the product n!. So x and n! are both divisible by p, which means x – n! is divisible by p. But x – n! = 1, and 1 is not divisible by p, so we have a contradiction, and thus there cannot be a largest prime number.

Thus tuning, as defined by prime-number limits, is an infinitely expandable world, infinite in its dimensions. Without some way of organizing that infinity, we can't be pragmatically creative within it. I hope it will be seen that some of the methods shown so far are extendable tools that can be applied to much greater length to universes not yet explored.

THE THIRTEEN LIMIT

For the basic intervals formed by prime numbers above eleven, we should probably go beyond our upper limit of sixteen and find ratios of numbers up to thirty-two.

Exploration of small-number ratios involving thirteen (and no higher primes) yields the following results:

13/1 = 13/2 = 13/4 = 13/8
13/3 = 13/6 = 13/12
13/5 = 13/10
13/7
13/9
13/11
14/13 = 28/13
15/13 = 30/13
16/13 = 32/13
18/13
20/13
21/13
22/13
24/13
25/13
27/13 = 27/26

These give us the following sixteen thirteen-based, or tridecimal, ratios:

		Otonality	Utonality
27/26	=	65.34¢	
14/13	=	128.3¢	
13/12	=		138.57¢
15/13	=	247.74¢	
13/11	=		289.21¢
16/13	=	359.47¢	
13/10	=		454.21¢
18/13	=	563.38¢	
13/9	=		636.62¢
20/13	=	745.79¢	
21/13	=	830.25¢	
13/8	=		840.53¢
22/13	=	910.79¢	
24/13	=	1061.43¢	
13/7	=		1071.7¢
25/13	=	1132.1¢	

Since we've gone as high as thirty-two, the remaining four complementary ratios are complex indeed:

26/25	=	67.9¢
26/21	=	369.75¢
26/15	=	952.26¢
52/27	=	1134.66¢

Once again, ratios involving factors of only 2, 3, and 13 have a somewhat consistent relationship to twelve-tone equal temperament, being from 35 to 41 (or subharmonically, 65 to 59) cents off from the pitches we're used to:

27/26	=	65.34¢
13/12	=	138.57¢
16/13	=	359.47¢
18/13	=	563.38¢
13/9	=	636.62¢
13/8	=	840.53¢
24/13	=	1061.43¢

We have a thirteen-limit, or tridecimal, "quarter tone," 27/26; two large tridecimal half steps, 13/12 and 14/13; a narrow tridecimal minor third of 13/11; complementary tritones of 13/9 and 18/13; two minor sixths of 21/13 and 13/8; a major sixth of 22/13; and major sevenths of 13/7 and 25/13. In addition, several thirteen-limit intervals create approximate quarter-tone relationships: 15/13, 16/13, 13/10, 26/15, and 20/13.

One composer I know who has made the thirteenth harmonic her especial study is Mayumi Tsuda. Several of her works are based on a twelve-pitch scale she calls the Harmonic 13th, given here:[2]

Ratio	Cents
1/1	0
14/13	128.3
13/12	138.6
16/13	359.5
13/10	454.2
18/13	563.4
13/9	636.6
20/13	745.8
13/8	840.5
22/13	910.8
13/7	1071.7
208/105	1183.4

Example 11.1 shows all possible intervals in the scale as ratios. Since some scale degrees are based on the 13 otonality and some on the utonality, the scale splits pretty cleanly into simple intervals (between two pitch steps with 13 either in both numerators or both denominators) and highly complex ones, such as 320/169 or 1352/735, with 1/1 as an intermediary. Were a composer to be guided by the pattern of relative consonances in the scale (not the only strategy for composing in it), clear scales on various scale steps would emerge as materials:

on 14/13	8/7, 9/7, 10/7, 11/7, 13/7
on 13/12	6/5, 4/3, 3/2, 12/7
on 16/13	9/8, 5/4, 11/8, 7/4 . . .

and so on. Like most microtonal scales (like all scales, ultimately), this one suggests ways to begin composing in it.

	1/1	14/13	13/12	16/13	13/10	18/13	13/9	20/13	13/8	22/13	13/7	208/105
1/1	1/1	14/13	13/12	16/13	13/10	18/13	13/9	20/13	13/8	22/13	13/7	208/105
14/13	13/7	1/1	169/168	8/7	169/140	9/7	169/126	10/7	169/112	11/7	169/98	1352/735
13/12	24/13	336/169	1/1	192/169	6/5	216/169	4/3	240/169	3/2	264/169	12/7	64/35
16/13	13/8	7/4	169/96	1/1	169/160	9/8	169/144	5/4	169/128	11/8	169/112	169/105
13/10	20/13	280/169	5/3	320/169	1/1	180/169	10/9	200/169	5/4	220/169	10/7	32/21
18/13	13/9	14/9	169/108	16/9	169/90	1/1	169/162	10/9	169/144	11/9	169/126	1352/945
13/9	18/13	252/169	3/2	288/169	9/5	324/169	1/1	180/169	9/8	198/169	9/7	48/35
20/13	13/10	7/5	169/120	8/5	169/100	9/5	169/90	1/1	169/160	11/10	169/140	676/525
13/8	16/13	224/169	4/3	256/169	8/5	288/169	16/9	320/169	1/1	176/169	8/7	256/105
22/13	13/11	14/11	169/132	16/11	169/110	18/11	169/99	20/11	169/88	1/1	169/154	1352/1155
13/7	14/13	196/169	7/6	224/169	7/5	252/169	14/9	280/169	7/4	308/169	1/1	16/15
208/105	105/104	735/676	35/32	210/169	21/16	945/676	35/24	525/338	105/64	1155/676	105/56	1/1

EX. 11.1: All intervals in Mayumi Tsuda's Harmonic 13th scale

The Seventeen Limit

The seventeenth harmonic is 104.955 cents above the octave; 17/16 = 104.955 cents. The nineteenth harmonic is 297.513 cents above the octave, and 19/16 = 297.513 cents. Since 17/16 is within 5 cents of an equal tempered half step, and 19/16 is within 3 cents of an equal-tempered minor third, these prime numbers offer fewer thrills for those in our equal-tempered culture who are looking for exotic-sounding intervals than do 7, 11, and 13. In musical practice these numbers represent something of a barrier beyond which few microtonal composers will pass. Beyond them lies 23, which, since 23/16 is 628.274 cents, offers a 1/8-tone quality. A few composers, however, have found 17 and 19 useful numbers for creating scales and musical structures. And it is no fault of the numbers themselves that twelve-tone equal temperament rendered them, to our ears, quotidian.

Combining the number 17 with seventeen-limit (*septemdecimal*) numbers up to 32 yields the following results:

17/1 = 17/2 = 17/4 = 17/8 = 17/16
17/3 = 17/6 = 17/12
17/5 = 17/10
17/7 = 17/14
17/9
17/11
17/13
17/15
18/17
20/17
21/17
22/17
24/17
25/17
26/17
27/17
28/17
30/17
32/17

These pitches yield the following scale:

		Otonality	Utonality
18/17	=	98.95¢	
17/16	=		104.96¢
17/15	=		216.69¢
20/17	=	281.36¢	
17/14	=		336.13¢
21/17	=	365.83¢	
22/17	=	446.36¢	
17/13	=		464.43¢
24/17	=	597¢	
17/12	=		603¢
25/17	=	667.67¢	
26/17	=	735.57¢	
17/11	=		753.64¢
27/17	=	800.91¢	
28/17	=	863.87¢	
17/10	=		918.64¢
30/17	=	983.31¢	
32/17	=	1095.05¢	
17/9	=		1101.05¢

Two intervals derived from seventeen are of particular historical and mathematical interest. Just one cent away from an equal-tempered half step, 18/17 was the interval used in the sixteenth and seventeenth centuries to calculate placement of frets on lutes, theorbos, and other fretted instruments. It was known that 18/17 to the twelfth power came very close to 2 (1.9855599), and a method evolved by which an instrument maker would divide a string into eighteen parts and place the top fret at the seventeenth division from the bridge; then divide the remainer into eighteen parts again and place the second fret at the seventeenth division from the bridge; then divide the remainder into eighteen parts; and so on, the frets getting closer and closer together and each representing 17/18 of the remainder of the string. This would result in a series of equal half steps, twelve to the octave.

The other interesting seventeen ratio is 17/12 (and its complement 24/17), which is three cents away from the equal-tempered tritone. The fraction 17/12 squared is almost exactly 2 (2.0069444), and it is the closest relatively small-whole-number-ratio approximation of the square root of 2. (The ratio 181/128 is 599.815 cents, even closer.)

In addition, 17/9 is only a cent wider than an equal-tempered major seventh, and 27/17 is within one cent of an equal-tempered minor sixth. As one can see, the flavor of the seventeen limit is bound up with that of twelve-tone equal temperament. There are also intervals like 17/14, a third of a half step above a minor third, and 17/11, a quarter tone sharper than a perfect fifth. These intervals derive their distance from twelve-tone equal temperament from the numbers in the denominator, 7 and 11, respectively.

THE NINETEEN LIMIT

Combining the number 19 with nineteen-limit numbers up to 32 yields the following results:

19/1 = 19/2 = 19/4 = 19/8 = 19/16
19/3 = 19/6 = 19/12
19/5 = 19/10
19/7 = 19/14
19/9 = 19/18
19/11
19/13
19/15
19/17
20/19
21/19
22/19
24/19
25/19
26/19
27/19
28/19
30/19
32/19

The basic intervals added by nineteen-limit tuning, then, are as follows:

		Otonality	Utonality
20/19	=	88.8¢	
19/18	=		93.6¢
21/19	=	173.27¢	
19/17	=		192.56¢
22/19	=	253.8¢	
19/16	=		297.51¢
24/19	=	404.44¢	
19/15	=		409.24¢
25/19	=	475.11¢	
19/14	=		528.69¢
26/19	=	543.01¢	
27/19	=	608.35¢	
19/13	=		656.99¢
28/19	=	671.31¢	
30/19	=	790.76¢	
19/12	=		795.56¢
32/19	=	902.49¢	
19/11	=		946.2¢
19/10	=		1111.2¢

As with seventeen, the ratios involving only 2, 3, and 19 have a 12tet quality to them, while those derived from seven and eleven as well are more exotic.

The most prominent piece I know of in nineteen-limit tuning is Johnston's Suite for Microtonal Piano (1977). The keyboard is tuned to twelve harmonics of the pitch C:

Keyboard:											
C	C♯	D	E♭	E	F	F♯	G	A♭	A	B♭	B
Ratios:											
$\frac{1}{1}$	$\frac{17}{16}$	$\frac{9}{8}$	$\frac{19}{16}$	$\frac{5}{4}$	$\frac{21}{16}$	$\frac{11}{8}$	$\frac{3}{2}$	$\frac{13}{8}$	$\frac{27}{16}$	$\frac{7}{4}$	$\frac{15}{8}$
Johnston notation:											
C	C17♯	D	E19♭	E	F7+	F↑	G	A13♭	A+	B♭7	B

These represent the 16th, 17th, 18th, 19th, 20th, 21st, 22nd, 24th, 26th, 27th, 28th, and 30th harmonics of C, but since 19 is the highest prime number involved, the scale is in nineteen-limit tuning. The piece's first and fifth movements are in the key of C, the first making pervasive reference to the spacing of a harmonic series. The second movement, however, is in the key of D, and the third in E, giving more exotic scales to work with. The scale on D, for instance, is 1/1, 19/18, 10/9, 7/6, 11/9, 4/3, 13/9, 3/2, 14/9, 5/3, 16/9, and 17/9. The fourth movement retains a degree of consonance by employing a Phrygian mode on E, and the third movement is complexly twelve-tone. We abstain from further analysis here in favor of an interlude on Johnston's more monumental Seventh String Quartet, but more information can be found in my article "Key Eccentricity in Ben Johnston's Suite for Microtonal Piano."[3]

The Twenty-Three Limit and Above

Using the same method, we find a series of basic intervals based on 23:

24/23 = 73.68¢
23/22 = 76.96¢
25/23 = 144.35¢
23/21 = 157.49¢
26/23 = 212.25¢
23/20 = 241.96¢
27/23 = 277.59¢
23/19 = 330.76¢
28/23 = 340.55¢
23/18 = 424.36¢
30/23 = 459.99¢
23/17 = 523.32¢
32/23 = 571.73¢
33/23 = 625¢
23/16 = 628.27¢
34/23 = 676.68¢
35/23 = 726.87¢
23/15 = 740¢
36/23 = 775.64¢
23/14 = 859.45¢
38/23 = 869.24¢
39/23 = 914.21¢
40/23 = 958.04¢
23/13 = 987.75¢
42/23 = 1042.51¢
44/23 = 1123.04¢
23/12 = 1126.32¢
45/23 = 1161.95¢

Many of these intervals (particulary ones using only 2, 3, and 23 as factors) create eighth tones, tones near 25 cents and 75 cents sharp or flat in relation to 12tet.

Chapter 11

The Harmonic Series Returns

The device of creating scales from all possible ratios within a certain number limit is a useful procedure for five-, seven-, and eleven-limit scenarios, but clearly by the time one gets to the twenty-third harmonic it has become an unwieldy paradigm. Higher harmonic ratios generate so many pitches per octave, and harmonics above the thirteenth are so difficult to perceive as such, that such scales increasingly tend to generate arbitrary-sounding microtonal pitch arrays for which various equal-tempered divisions of the scale might be a more practical substitute. There are doubtless people who will find these very qualities useful or attractive, generating scales this way and writing melodies along ratios like 31/17 and 50/31, or perhaps using computer software to negotiate among the ten dimensions that full use of thirty-one-limit tuning would require. Ben Johnston's String Quartet No. 9 is a revelatory work in thirty-one-limit just intonation, although it tends to use the thirty-first harmonic primarily as a passing tone between the thirtieth and thirty-second and does not venture into more complex ratios; plus, as noted earlier, some of the improvisations of the Theater of Eternal Music in the 1960s employed the thirty-first harmonic along with even-limit intervals. An improvisation of theirs from the mid-1960s called *Pre-Tortoise Dream Music* (retroactively so named in light of a subsequent group of works titled *The Tortoise, His Dreams and Journeys*, performed over the drone of the terrarrium in which Young's turtle lived) has all performers playing/singing the pitch row in example 11.2 over a D drone.[4]

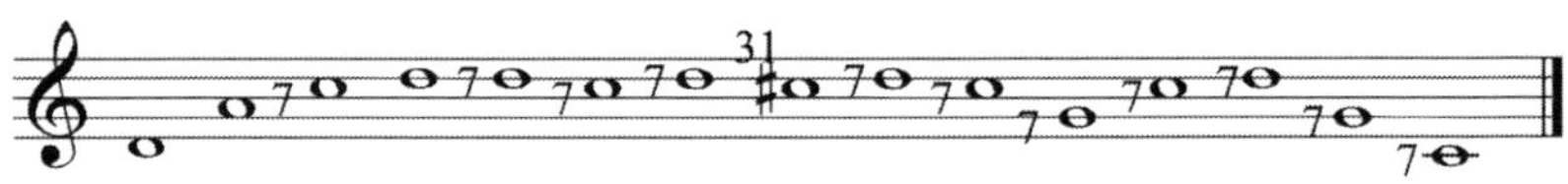

Harmonic number:	32	48	56	64	63	56	63	62	63	56	42	56	63	42	28
Ratio to fundamental:	1/1	3/2	7/4	2/1	63/32	7/4	63/32	31/16	63/32	7/4	21/16	7/4	63/32	21/16	7/4

EX. 11.2: Pitch sequence in the Theater of Eternal Music's *Pre-Tortoise Dream Music*

Johnston has gone at least up to the fifty-third harmonic in his music for acoustic instruments, and La Monte Young in his sine-tone installations has experimented with prime numbers between 1792 and 2304.[5] So far, however, most composers who have ventured above thirteen-limit tuning have abandoned the limit concept as such and dealt directly with the harmonic series or with combinations of different harmonic series.

In the following list of new prime harmonics up through sixty-one, one can quickly get an idea of where, in relation to 12tet, each harmonic will produce new tones in combination with Pythagorean intervals:

29/16 = 1029.58¢
31/16 = 1145.04¢
37/32 = 251.34¢
41/32 = 429.06¢
43/32 = 511.52¢
47/32 = 665.51¢
53/32 = 873.5¢
59/32 = 1059.17¢
61/32 = 1116.88¢

Note that 31 and 37 produce new quarter-tone approximations, and so on, each new prime number producing an ever larger and finer grid of intervals, ever less intelligible to the ear. A list of such intervals up to thirty-one-limit can be found included in the appendix, "Anatomy of an Octave."

Array Notation for Higher-Limit Ratios

Eleven-limit tuning requires a four-dimensional grid or lattice; tridecimal tuning, five dimensions; seventeen-limit, six dimensions; and so on. This is unwieldy on paper, if not impossible. But computers deal nicely with many dimensions and can do so via exponential array notation, using a series of positive and negative whole numbers that are indicative of what factors are present. Each number in the array stands for an exponent that some prime number is taken to in the ratio, according to a prearranged scheme. For example, let's assume we are going to use ratios within the thirteen-limit. We then need a series of numbers, one to indicate what power of 2 is present, another which power of 3, and others for 5, 7, 11, and 13. The ratio 1/1 would be indicated by a series of zeros, since in 1/1 all those primes are taken to the zeroth power (anything to the zeroth power = 1):

Since $1/1 = 2^0 \times 3^0 \times 5^0 \times 7^0 \times 11^0 \times 13^0$,
1/1 = 0, 0, 0, 0, 0, 0

3/2 equals $2^{-1} \times 3^0 \times 5^0 \times 7^0 \times 11^0 \times 13^0$ (since $2^{-1} = 1/2$), so in array notation
3/2 = −1, 1, 0, 0, 0, 0

$22/21 = 2^1 \times 3^{-1} \times 5^0 \times 7^{-1} \times 11^1 \times 13^0$, and so in array notation
22/21 = 1, −1, 0, −1, 1, 0

Conversely, the array −3, 1, −2, 1, 1, 0 would indicate $2^{-3} \times 3^1 \times 5^{-2} \times 7^1 \times 11^1 \times 13^0$, or $1/8 \times 3 \times 1/25 \times 7 \times 11 = 231/200$. Example 11.3 shows the beginning of Harry Partch's scale in array notation. It's certainly not the easiest notation to read, but it does give six- (or more) dimensional values in a linear, easy-to-store form and may be the key to dealing with ratio tuning in the future via computer.

Ratio:	Exponential expression:	Array notation
1/1	$2^0 \times 3^0 \times 5^0 \times 7^0 \times 11^0 \times 13^0$	0, 0, 0, 0, 0, 0
81/80	$2^{-4} \times 3^4 \times 5^{-1} \times 7^0 \times 11^0 \times 13^0$	-4, 4, -1, 0, 0, 0
33/32	$2^{-5} \times 3^1 \times 5^0 \times 7^0 \times 11^1 \times 13^0$	-5, 1, 0, 0, 1, 0
21/20	$2^{-2} \times 3^1 \times 5^{-1} \times 7^1 \times 11^0 \times 13^0$	-2, 1, -1, 1, 0, 0
16/15	$2^4 \times 3^{-1} \times 5^{-1} \times 7^0 \times 11^0 \times 13^0$	4, -1, -1, 0, 0, 0
12/11	$2^2 \times 3^1 \times 5^0 \times 7^0 \times 11^{-1} \times 13^0$	2, 1, 0, 0, -1, 0
11/10	$2^{-1} \times 3^0 \times 5^{-1} \times 7^0 \times 11^1 \times 13^0$	-1, 0, -1, 0, 1, 0
10/9	$2^1 \times 3^{-2} \times 5^1 \times 7^0 \times 11^0 \times 13^0$	1, -2, 1, 0, 0, 0
9/8	$2^{-3} \times 3^2 \times 5^0 \times 7^0 \times 11^0 \times 13^0$	-3, 2, 0, 0, 0, 0
8/7	$2^3 \times 3^0 \times 5^0 \times 7^{-1} \times 11^0 \times 13^0$	3, 0, 0, -1, 0, 0
7/6	$2^{-1} \times 3^{-1} \times 5^0 \times 7^1 \times 11^0 \times 13^0$	-1, -1, 0, 1, 0, 0
32/27	$2^5 \times 3^{-3} \times 5^0 \times 7^0 \times 11^0 \times 13^0$	5, -3, 0, 0, 0, 0
6/5	$2^1 \times 3^1 \times 5^{-1} \times 7^0 \times 11^0 \times 13^0$	1, 1, -1, 0, 0, 0
11/9	$2^0 \times 3^{-2} \times 5^0 \times 7^0 \times 11^1 \times 13^0$	0, -2, 0, 0, 1, 0
5/4	$2^{-2} \times 3^0 \times 5^1 \times 7^0 \times 11^0 \times 13^0$	-2, 0, 1, 0, 0, 0
14/11	$2^1 \times 3^0 \times 5^0 \times 7^1 \times 11^{-1} \times 13^0$	1, 0, 0, 1, -1, 0
9/7	$2^0 \times 3^2 \times 5^0 \times 7^{-1} \times 11^0 \times 13^0$	0, 2, 0, -1, 0, 0

EX. 11.3: Beginning of Partch's scale in array notation

Of course, many microtonal musicians tune out of the harmonic series long before reaching this chapter. For many, dividing the octave into equal parts is the more reasonable approach. Our next two chapters address many possible ways and reasons to achieve this, after a few interludes involving thirteen-limit music.

INTERLUDE I

Ben Johnston's String Quartet No. 7, Movement 3

The following analysis is not for the faint of heart. If your eyes begin to glaze over, feel free to skip it. Only a few people on earth need to know how this piece is composed. Ben Johnston's String Quartet No. 7 has the reputation of being the most difficult string quartet ever written. Its third and final movement contains more than twelve hundred pitches to the octave, more than one per cent. The piece was completed in 1984 and not played, apparently, until the Kepler Quartet finally recorded it in 2016. It is a towering achievement of just-intonation conceptualization, one of the most complexly designed pieces in the world. Theorist Timothy Ernest Johnson heroically managed to analyze it for his doctoral dissertation (to which I refer those interested[1]), and it took him three computer programs simply to keep track of all the pitches.

Nine of Johnston's string quartets (all but the first) are written in just intonation. From the second one on, Johnston's strategy is to introduce new pitches by tuning them consonantly to previous notes, moving successively from one consonance to another to range quite far afield. If you imagine the pitch web as a lattice, with perfect 3/2 fifths running along one dimension, 5/4 major thirds a second dimension, 7/4 septimal sevenths another dimension, and so on, Johnston's quartets generally move their way around a lattice by adjacent steps. The challenge for the players is to learn to hear these basic intervals so securely that they can constantly tune each new note to those they're already hearing. In the Seventh Quartet, this technique is taken to an unprecedented level of complexity.

The final movement is called "Variations." It is 177 measures long. The structure is based on a 176-pitch, "hyperchromatic" tone row with no repeated pitches, each pitch forming the key pitch of one measure. In the first "macro-variation," which is 30 measures long, the key pitch starts in the viola and is always found there, on the downbeat of each measure. There are seven macro-variations (and micro-variations within those). In the first, the key pitch rises gradually from C 1/1 to D 9/8; in the second, it rises from D to E 5/4; in the third, from E to F 4/3; and so on through the just major scale (Ptolemaic sequence), ending on a triumphant C-major chord.

The 176-note row underlying the piece proceeds through only six intervals, from two to ten cents in size, all of them kleismas or schismas (inexact names for tiny intervals):

Ratio	Size	Factors
896/891	10¢	$2^7 \times 7/3^4 \times 11$
176/175	10¢	$11 \times 2^4/5^2 \times 7$
32805/32768	2¢	$5 \times 3^8/2^{15}$
385/384	4¢	$5 \times 7 \times 11/3 \times 2^7$
729/728	2¢	$3^6/13 \times 7 \times 2^3$
325/324	5¢	$13 \times 5^2/3^4 \times 2^2$

The viola begins the first measure on C, and then the players all play intervals that will allow them to arrive at the second pitch of the scale, D♭7↓– 896/891, only ten cents higher. The factors involved in an interval of 896/891 are $2^7 \times 7/3^4 \times 11$—that is, 896 equals $2^7 \times 7$, and 891 equals $3^4 \times 11$. We can ignore the 2^7, since that only denotes octaves of the same pitch. To get from C to D♭7↓–, we need to go upward by one 7/4, since there is a 7 factored in the numerator; and we need to go down by four perfect fifths (3^4 in the denominator), plus down by one 11/8 interval to account for the 11 in the denominator. We can thus proceed downward by perfect fifths (or upward by perfect fourths, which is the same thing) from C down to A♭–, then up by a seventh harmonic from A♭- to G♭7–, and then down by an eleventh harmonic (8/11) to D♭7↓–, as follows:

C		F		B♭–		E♭–		A♭–		G♭7–		D♭7↓–
	–3		–3		–3		–3		7		–11	

Going down four perfect fifths, up one seventh harmonic, and down by an eleventh harmonic equals multiplying the initial frequency by $2^7 \times 7/3^4 \times 11$, with the 2^7 accounted for by raising the pitch upward seven octaves to keep it in the same register.

As you can see in example I.1, all of these pitches are found in the opening measure:

EX. I.1: Johnston, String Quartet No. 7, movement 3, mm. 1–4

Those are not the only pitches found, for to fill out the texture and make it more lush, Johnston adds other, harmonizing pitches as well, as seen in example I.2.

					D7♭-	D7♭-	D7♭-	|	E7♭♭-
			B♭-	B♭-	B♭-	C7♭-		|	F7♭-
		F	F	F	G7♭-	G7♭-	G7♭-	|	G7♭-
C	C	C	C	C	C	C7♭-	E7♭♭-	|	D7♭↓-
	G	G	G	E♭-	E♭-			|	
				A♭-	A♭-			|	

EX. I.2: Pitches in m. 1 of Johnston's String Quartet no. 7, movement 3

The boldface pitches in the example are the ones needed to navigate from C to D♭7↓–, entirely via perfectly tuned perfect fourths plus one seventh harmonic and one eleventh subharmonic. That may sound like a difficult thing for a string quartet to do—it is—and after they've accomplished that, they have 175 more such negotiations to go.

The extreme difficulty is slightly mitigated by the fact that the pitch row rises through only six intervals, and every time the interval is 896/891 the same relationships come into play. The key pitches for the first macro-variation, each found in the viola, are as found in table I.1. As you can see in the sixth column, "Ratio to next note," measures 1, 5, 9, 13, 15, 18, 22, 26, and 30 all proceed through a ratio of 896/891. The last eight of those nine measures, then, aside from some slight variations, are all basically transpositions of measure 1, measure 5 being transposed upward 26 cents; measure 9, 53 cents; and so on. So out of the first thirty measures, the quartet is playing the same relationships in nine of those measures. This is hardly a matter of simple repetition, of course, since different strings are involved in each case. But for the players, once they've learned to hear the first measure securely, they're looking for the same interval patterns in the other eight measures as well. The listener, meanwhile, hears the same first-measure pattern come back again and again, with its characteristic rising perfect fourths in the violins followed by a chord of two perfect fifths, separated by a 7/4, in the cello and second violin. For instance, measure 9 in example I.3, which except for the first notes in violin 1 (resulting from the previous measure) looks like measure 1, transposed upward by only a 33/32.

EX. I.3: Johnston, String Quartet No. 7, movement 3, m. 9

Measure 2 moves the key pitch upward by 176/175, which equals $11 \times 2^4/5^2 \times 7$. The intervals involved (once again ignoring the power of 2) include a rising eleventh harmonic and a descent through one 7/4 and two major thirds of 5/4, as follows:

D♭7↓–		G♭7–		A♭–		F♭–		D𝄫––
	11		–7		–5		–5	

One will find these pitches in measure 2 (ex. I.1), with the D♭7↓– in the viola, the G♭7– sustained in violin 2, the A♭– in the cello (tenor clef), and the F♭– in violin 1, enabling the viola to land on D𝄫–– at the beginning of measure 3. Measures 8, 12, 16, 19, 23, and 29 also rise through a 176/175 interval, and those measures are all similar to measure 2, transposed slightly upward (and with a few rhythmic differences)—and so on, 174 more times. It is indeed an incredible feat of endurance, hearing exact intervals, and keeping one's place in the freest pitch space of any carefully notated piece I know of.

TABLE I.1: Ben Johnston's String Quartet no. 7, Movement 3, analysis

M.	Pitch	Ratio to C	¢ → C	Factors	Ratio to next note	¢ to next note (8ths in m.)	Factors of ratio to next note
m. 1	C	1/1	0	1	896/891	10	$2^{7}\times7/3^{4}\times11$
m. 2	D♭7↓–	896/891	10	$2^{7}\times7/3^{4}\times11$	176/175	10	$11\times2^{4}/5^{2}\times7$
m. 3	D𝄫––	2048/2025	20	$2^{10}/3^{4}\times5^{2}$	32805/32768	2	$5\times3^{8}/2^{15}$
m. 4	C+	81/80	22	$3^{4}/5\times2^{4}$	385/384	4	$5\times7\times11/3\times2^{7}$
m. 5	C7↑+	2079/2048	26	$7\times11\times3^{3}/2^{11}$	896/891	10	$2^{7}\times7/3^{4}\times11$
m. 6	D♭77	49/48	36	$7^{2}/3\times2^{4}$	729/728	2	$3^{6}/13\times7\times2^{3}$
m. 7	C♯713++	1701/1664	38	$7\times3^{5}/13\times2^{7}$	325/324	5	$13\times5^{2}/3^{4}\times4$
m. 8	C♯7+	525/512	43	$3\times5^{2}\times7/2^{9}$	176/175	10	$11\times2^{4}/5^{2}\times7$
m. 9	C↑	33/32	53	$3\times11/2^{5}$	896/891	10	$2^{7}\times7/3^{4}\times11$
m. 10	D♭7–	28/27	63	$7\times4/3^{3}$	729/728	2	$3^{6}/13\times7\times2^{3}$
m. 11	C♯13+	27/26	65	$3^{3}/2\times13$	325/324	5	$13\times5^{2}/3^{4}\times2^{2}$
m. 12	C♯	25/24	70	$5^{2}/3\times8$	176/175	10	$11\times2^{4}/5^{2}\times7$
m. 13	CL↑–	22/21	80	$11\times2/3\times7$	896/891	10	$7\times2^{7}/11\times3^{4}$
m. 14	D♭––	256/243	90	$2^{8}/3^{5}$	32805/32768	2	$5\times3^{8}/2^{15}$
m. 15	C♯+	135/128	92	$5\times3^{3}/2^{7}$	896/891	10	$7\times2^{7}/11\times3^{4}$
m. 16	C7↓	35/33	102	$5\times7/3\times11$	176/175	10	$11\times2^{4}/5^{2}\times7$
m. 17	D♭–	16/15	112	$2^{4}/3\times5$	32805/32768	2	$5\times3^{8}/2^{15}$
m. 18	C♯++	2187/2048	114	$3^{7}/2^{11}$	896/891	10	$7\times2^{7}/11\times3^{4}$
m. 19	D7↓+	189/176	124	$3^{3}\times7/2^{4}\times11$	176/175	10	$11\times2^{4}/5^{2}\times7$

M.	Pitch	Ratio to C	¢ → C	Factors	Ratio to next note	¢ to next note (8ths in m.)	Factors of ratio to next note
m. 20	D♭	27/25	134	$3^3/5^2$	325/324	5	$13{\times}5^2/3^4{\times}2^2$
m. 21	D♭13–	13/12	139	$13/3{\times}2^2$	729/728	2	$3^6/13{\times}7{\times}2^3$
m. 22	C♯*L*+	243/224	141	$3^5/2^5{\times}7$	896/891	10	$7{\times}2^7/11{\times}3^4$
m. 23	D↓	12/11	151	$3{\times}2^2/11$	176/175	10	$11{\times}2^4/5^2{\times}7$
m. 24	D♭*L*–	192/175	161	$3{\times}2^6/5^2{\times}7$	325/324	5	$13{\times}5^2/3^4{\times}2^2$
m. 25	D♭*L*13––	208/189	166	$13{\times}2^4/3^3{\times}7$	729/728	2	$3^6/13{\times}7{\times}2^3$
m. 26	C♯*LL*	54/49	168	$3^3{\times}2/7^2$	896/891	10	$7{\times}2^7/11{\times}3^4$
m. 27	D*L*↓–	256/231	178	$2^8/3{\times}7{\times}11$	385/384	4.5	$5{\times}7{\times}11/3{\times}2^7$
m. 28	D–	10/9	182	$5{\times}2/3^2$	32805/32768	2	$5{\times}3^8/2^{15}$
m. 29	C♯♯++	18225/16384	184	$5^2{\times}3^6/2^{14}$	176/175	10	$11{\times}2^4/5^2{\times}7$
m. 30	C♯L↑+	8019/7168	194	$11{\times}3^6/7{\times}2^{10}$	896/891	10	$7{\times}2^7/11{\times}3^4$
m. 31	D	9/8	204	$3^2/2^3$			

m. 1: $2^7{\times}7/3^4{\times}11$

C F B♭– E♭– A♭– G♭7– D♭7↓–
–3 –3 –3 –3 7 –11

m. 2: $11{\times}2^4/5^2{\times}7$

D♭7↓– G♭7– A♭– F♭– D♭♭––
11 –7 –5 –5

m. 3: $5{\times}3^8/2^{15}$

D♭♭–– F♭– C♭– G♭– D♭– A♭ E♭ B♭ F+ C+
5 3 3 3 3 3 3 3 3

m. 4: $5{\times}7{\times}11/3{\times}2^7$

C+ F+ A+ G7+ C7↑+
–3 5 7 11

m. 5: $2^7{\times}7/3^4{\times}11$

C7↑+ F7↑+ B♭7↑ E♭7↑ A♭7↑ G♭77↑ D♭77
–3 –3 –3 –3 7 –11

m. 6: $3^6/13{\times}7{\times}2^3$

D♭77 E♭7 B♭7 F7+ C7+ G7+ D7+ A7++ C♯713++
–7 3 3 3 3 3 3 –13

Another interesting aspect: you will notice in table the following distances above C in the first seven measures:

m. 1	C	0
m. 2	D♭7↓–	10
m. 3	D♮♭––	20
m. 4	C+	22
m. 5	C7↑+	26
m. 6	D♭77	36
m. 7	C♯713++	38

The pitch differences in cents are as follows:

0		10		20		22		26		36		38
	10		10		2		4		10		2	

Johnston "serializes" the rhythm of the piece, in effect, by making the length of each measure proportional to the number of cents between the key pitches. Thus, as can partly be seen in the table, the sequence 10, 10, 2, 4, 10, 2 is reflected by having the opening meters corresponding to those numbers of eighth notes (5/4 containing ten eighth notes):

5/4	5/4	2/8	4/8	5/4	2/8

Thus the number of eighth notes per measure is determined by the number of cents between the key pitches of those measures. So over a temporal distance of 1200 eighth notes, the pitch gradually rises 1200 cents from the opening C to the closing C.

I'm just giving you the gist of the first macro-variation, for the third, fourth, and fifth macro-variations are texturally contrasting: the third and fourth climactic and the fifth almost entirely in harmonics, after which the last two sections basically repeat the first two in transposition.[2] It's a remarkable-sounding piece, unlike anything else in the repertoire, with plenty of unpredictably varied repetition and a sense of floating through utterly open, grid-less pitch space. For those with a stomach for the math involved, I highly recommend Johnson's brilliant and extremely detailed dissertation for more information.

INTERLUDE J

KYLE GANN'S *HYPERCHROMATICA*

My *Hyperchromatica* (2015–2017) is a work for three retuned, computer-driven pianos (Disklaviers, made by Yamaha, although other player-piano systems and even computer realization are possible). The piece is in seventeen movements and lasts two hours and thirty-five minutes, making it the longest fully notated microtonal work I know of. The scale contains thirty-three pitches, all of them harmonics of E♭.[1] The basic scale is a harmonic series from the eighth to the fifteenth harmonic. This eight-note set is then replicated on each of the original eight notes (I call this my 8 × 8 tuning; I am apparently not the first to employ it but can specify no precedents). In short, one takes the odd numbers 1, 3, 5, 7, 9, 11, 13, and 15, and multiplies them all by those same numbers, and those are the harmonics of E♭ needed. Only thirty-three pitches result from 8 × 8, because some multiplications overlap: $3 \times 5 = 15 \times 1$, for instance. Example J.1 gives the pitch names in a typographically convenient version of Ben Johnston's just-intonation notation, the ratio of each pitch, its distance from E♭ in cents, and the arrangement of pitches within the harmonic series of E♭, F+, G, A♭↑, B♭, C13♭, D7♭, and D, the harmonic scale of E♭.

Pitch name	Ratio	Cents	1/1	3/2	5/4	7/4	9/8	11/8	13/8	15/8
Db^^-	121/64	1103						11		
D	15/8	1088	15	5	3					1
Db13	117/64	1044					13		9	
C#+	225/128	977								15
Db7	7/4	969	7			1				
C^	55/32	938			11			5		
C+	27/16	906		9			3			
C7+	105/64	857				15				7
Cb13	13/8	840	13						1	
B	25/16	773			5					
Bb^	99/64	755					11	9		
Cb77+	49/32	738				7				
Bb13	195/128	729							15	13
Bb	3/2	702	3	1						
Bbb713	91/64	609				13			7	
A+	45/32	590		15	9		5			3
Ab^	11/8	551	11					1		
Abb1313	169/128	481							13	
Ab7+	21/16	471		7		3				
G^	165/128	440						15		11
G+	81/64	408					9			
G	5/4	386	5		1					
Gb13	39/32	342		13					3	
Gb7^	77/64	320				11		7		
F#+	75/64	275			15					5
F+	9/8	204	9	3			1			
Fb13^	143/128	192						13	11	
F7+	35/32	155			7	5				
E+	135/128	92					15			9
Eb^	33/32	53		11				3		
Eb13	65/64	27			13				5	
Eb	1/1	0	1							
Eb7+	63/32	1173				9	7			

EX. J.1: The 8 × 8 tuning of *Hyperchromatica*

One structure that recurs in many of the movements is a twenty-four-chord sequence harmonizing the twenty-four pitches that occur in major or minor triads (ex. J.2; the cents refer to the top note of each chord and its distance above E♭). Often these chords have sevenths, elevenths, or (less often) ninths added, and the close spacing provides a maximum of tonality flux (defined in interlude H). Some notes are harmonizable more than one way, and the chord may vary according to context.

EX. J.2: Twenty-four-chord sequence used in *Hyperchromatica*

This chord progression is the basis of the rather minimalist "Dark Forces Signify," as well as of two middle sections of "Ride the Cosmos" (ex. J.3; the top and bottom lines here slide down through 204¢, 155¢, 92¢, 53¢, and are harmonized by triads or seventh chords).

EX. J.3: Gann, "Ride the Cosmos" from *Hyperchromatica*, mm. 84–85

I have renotated the originals here in Ben Johnston's notation; in the score for three retuned pianos, it was of course only necessary to indicate the keys played.

One fertile source of tonality flux (out of many here) is the contrast between the first and thirteenth harmonics. Example J.4 shows how close the E13♭-minor triad and seventh chord are in pitch to the E♭ triad and seventh chord, with the third and seventh descending where the tonic and fifth rise. This tonality difference marks the climax of the second movement, *Futility Row* (ex. J.5), where at measure 225 a suspension on a 16/13 interval resolves by forty-two cents down to 6/5. Notice also the hyperchromatic scale flourish in measure 226, a frequent feature of the piece. This may be the first piece written in the key of E13♭-minor—that is, E♭ is 1/1, and the tonic of this movement is the sixty-fifth harmonic, twenty-seven cents above 1/1.

15/8 117/64
3/2 195/128
5/4 39/32
1/1 65/64

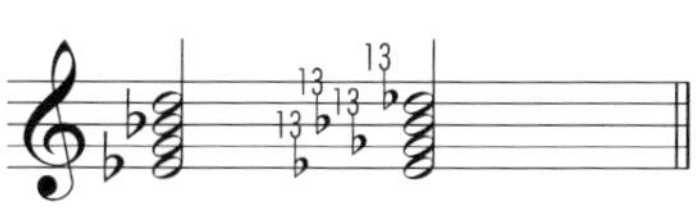

cents: 1088 1044
702 729
386 342
0 27

EX. J.4: Voice leading between seventh chords on E♭ and E13♭

EX. J.5: Gann, "Futility Row" from *Hyperchromatica*, mm. 224–226

The harmonic series tends to support major keys, as we've seen, and does not contain a subdominant. In so long a piece with so many movements, this constant major-ness would have proved tedious, so I hit upon the idea of using the harmonics 8 through 15 as a *mode*, with any point as tonic. In "Pavane for a Dead Planet," and elsewhere, I achieved a kind of minor key by starting on the fifth harmonic:

Original:	$\frac{1}{1}$	$\frac{9}{8}$	$\frac{5}{4}$	$\frac{11}{8}$	$\frac{3}{2}$	$\frac{13}{8}$	$\frac{7}{4}$	$\frac{15}{8}$	
"Minor" mode:			$\frac{1}{1}$	$\frac{11}{10}$	$\frac{6}{5}$	$\frac{13}{10}$	$\frac{7}{5}$	$\frac{3}{2}$	$\frac{8}{5}$	$\frac{9}{5}$

Likewise in "Dark Forces Signify," "Spacecat," and especially "Rings of Saturn," I started on the third harmonic for a scale with a subdominant: 1/1, 13/12, 7/6, 5/4, 4/3, 3/2, 5/3, 11/6. And in "Reverse Gravity" I put the simpler harmonic series on 1 and 3 above bass notes of 11 and 13 to get more exotic modes like 14/13, 15/13, 16/13, 18/13, 20/13, 22/13 and 12/11, 13/11, 14/11, 15/11, 16/11, 18/11, 20/11, and so forth (ex. J.6, with ratios to the bass note given above the melody notes; the bass note moves from the thirteenth to the eleventh harmonic in the middle of measure 5).

EX. J.6: Gann, "Reverse Gravity" from *Hyperchromatica*, mm. 1–6

One thing I love to do in microtonal pieces is move between the major and minor third of a chord via the 11/9 neutral third. This tuning provided me no such opportunity, but I realized that between the twenty-fourth and twenty-fifth (also forty-eighth and fiftieth) harmonics there is a forty-ninth right in between, so that in the key of G I could progress between major and minor from B♭ (6/5 or 48/40 in that key) through C77♭ (49/40) to B (5/4 or 50/40)—in cents, 316–351–386. I based the movement "Busted Grooves" on this smooth major-to-minor undulation.

And so on. Seventeen movements allowed me to explore the scale in a larger variety of contexts, both conventional-looking and texturally unusual. In addition to the microtonal aspect, most of the movements employ polytempo structures that render the piece unplayable by humans.

INTERLUDE K

TOBY TWINING'S *CHRYSALID REQUIEM*

Toby Twining (b. 1958) is a singer/composer who studied with Ben Johnston, and who, in the 1990s, had a small vocal group that specialized in innovative pieces in just intonation. In 2002, after five years of work on it,[1] he released a recording of a more ambitious piece than anyone would have expected: *Chrysalid Requiem*, a twelve-part requiem mass in very extended just intonation. The piece is so complex in its pitch (and rhythm) explorations that the singers are required to perform it by wearing headphones and listening to a synthesized recording giving them the tunings and pulse. The result, sung acoustically and in perfect polyrhythms and tuning, is one of the strangest and most magnificent demonstrations of just-intonation choral work ever achieved. I cannot begin to do the work justice in this short interlude. However, I include a few examples to give a few hints of Twining's achievement, make you aware of it, and urge you to listen to it.

Example K.1 is the beginning of the second movement, the Kyrie. The singers are an alto, a tenor, and two baritones, and between the alto and tenor parts you can see the taped synthesizer part, which is heard by the singers but not by the audience. Twining ranges far afield in his tonalities, and it will be apparent that the key here is (in Johnston's notation) F77+. Although the piece is officially thirteen-limit overall, the third and especially seventh harmonics are emphasized far more than the thirteenth or fifth.[2] Here the synthesizer gives the singers the first, third, ninth, and seventh harmonics of F77+ at the beginning, switching to a dominant ninth chord on C77+ in measure 4. Baritone 1's part is notated with the low pitch he sings, and with the tune he rather whistles above that through overtone singing, with the harmonic numbered on each note. Note that at measure 3 going into measure 4, baritone 1 is expected to sustain the ninth harmonic of F77+ and sustain it while changing the drone note to C77+, of which the harmonic is now the third. The dotted thirty-second notes that ensue suggest a kind of polytempo effect inherited from Johnston.

II. *Kyrie*

EX. K.1: Twining, Kyrie from *Chrysalid Requiem*, mm. 1–5

For example K.2 I draw on Timothy Ernest Johnson's doctoral dissertation, which analyzes the "Gradual/Tract" movement (along with Johnston's Seventh Quartet). According to Johnson, Twining's rhythmic structures as well as his structural harmonies are pervasively based on the numbers three and seven. The piece is based on a harmonic series segment 4:6:7:9:21:63, which Johnson calls the "G/T [Gradual/Tract] hexachord." Note that 4:6:9 gives a pair of perfect fifths, as does 7:21:63, with a 7:4 ratio between the two sets. This hexachord on the pitch C gives, in Johnston's notation, C G B♭7 D F7+ C7+, a chord that is heard in polytempo pulses at the close of the movement. As Johnson points out, the first twenty-two measures follow a sequence of six tonalities:[3]

F77+ utonal
B♭77 utonal
G7 utonal
A otonal
C7 otonal
G7 otonal

The tonalities are symmetrical around a G7/A axis, F77+ utonal paired with G7 otonal, B♭77 utonal with C7 otonal, and G7 utonal with A otonal. Example K.2 shows an exciting moment in the middle of this passage, when, at the center of measure 12, the tonality shifts from G7 utonal to A otonal at the words "Eternal rest grant them,

Lord, / and let light perpetual shine on them"—the darkness of the three utonalities giving way to the brightness of harmonic series on A (then C7 and G7).

EX. K.2: Twining, "Gradual/Tract" from *Chrysalid Requiem*, mm. 11–13 (simplified)

In this perpetual motion passage it is easy to see the threes, fours, and sevens in the rhythm—dotted eighths, quarters, and double-dotted quarter beats—mirroring the threes, fours, and sevens that permeate the tuning. The scale in measure 11 and the first half of measure 12 is the G7 utonality: G7, F7, E7♭, D↓, C7, BƐ⅂, A. After that follows an A otonal scale: A, B, C♯, (D↑), E, (F13), G7, G♯. The tonality pivots around the G7 and A, which are in both scales. This is actually one of the clearer and simpler passages in the *Chrysalid Requiem*, at least conceptually. You can see how the synthesizer part, heard only by the singers, helps them get both their pitches and rhythms. That the audience can hear such a complicated structure executed by singers, and can't perceive the process by which they're doing it, makes for a truly otherworldly sound.

Example K.3 shows a passage from the Libera me in which harmonies are made from stacked 7/6 intervals for a pair of 36:42:49 sonorities; accidentals are placed only in the vocal parts, not in the synthesizer part. Lasting some sixty-three minutes, Twining's *Chrysalid Requiem* is one of the most ambitious, mystifying, and deeply moving works, if not indeed *the* most, that has ever been penned and performed using microtonal methods. It is also an exciting early look into how the world of digital technology might be used to expand the range of acoustic performance.

EX. K.3: Twining, Libera me from *Chrysalid Requiem*, mm. 109–111

CHAPTER 12

NON-TWELVE-DIVISIBLE EQUAL TEMPERAMENTS

To work in just intonation is to move back and forth between notes and fractions. It's not a process with which all musicians can be comfortable. For many composers and theorists, equal temperaments of more than twelve pitches to the octave provide a way to get purer (or more exotic) intervals of many kinds while obviating the need for constant recalculations of fractions and cents (although we will see that exotic equal temperaments can acquire their own math obsession). Chapter 13 discusses quarter tones, sixth tones, and other systems of dividing the half step or whole step, derived from 12tet. But first, in this chapter, we explore divisions of the octave not divisible by twelve, which actually have a longer and more august history. (Readers might find it helpful to consult the appendix, which contains a number of selected equal temperament scales given in cents.)

Over the centuries certain equal divisions of the octave have strongly recommended themselves and garnered adherents: particularly nineteen tones to the octave, thirty-one tones, and sometimes even fifty-three. The reason for this, simply stated, is that these particular equal divisions provide close approximations of the 702-cent perfect fifths and 386-cent major thirds desired in European music.

Equal division	Available perfect fifth	Available major third
12	700 ¢	400 ¢
19	694.74 ¢	378.95 ¢
31	696.77 ¢	387.10 ¢
53	701.89 ¢	384.91 ¢

Notice that the major third in thirty-one-tone equal temperament (ET) is nearly perfect and that the perfect fifth is diminished to the same size as in meantone tuning. This makes thirty-one-tone ET particularly attractive to proponents of meantone.

Historically, it has been acknowledged for centuries that certain equal temperaments provide close approximations of certain meantone temperaments and thus of the consonances used by European music. Thirty-one divisions of the octave, for instance, lines up very well with 1/4-comma meantone—though we're really talking about 31edo (equal divisions of the octave) rather than 31tet (31-tone equal temperament), since not all thirty-one tones are necessary for most meantone pieces. However, in example 12.1 we give conventionally notated equivalents for all thirty-one steps of the scale, with a unique pitch name for every scale step. The columns on the right show the pitches arranged vertically as whole-tone scales, each whole tone equal to five of the thirty-one steps (= 193.55 cents) and each major third equal to ten steps (= 387.1 cents). A chromatic half step (C–C♯) is two steps, and a diatonic half step (C–D♭) is three. All perfect fifths are 696.77 cents (eighteen steps), which is within a fifth of a cent of the meantone perfect fifth.

Mean-tone:	31 edo:	Cents:	Pitch name:	Meantone major seconds (vertically):				
1200	1	1200	C	C				
	31	1161.29	B#		B#			
	30	1122.58	Cb			Cb		
1082.9	29	1083.87	B				B	
	28	1045.16	Ax					Ax
1006.8	27	1006.45	Bb	Bb				
	26	967.74	A#		A#			
	25	929.03	Bbb			Bbb		
889.7	24	890.32	A				A	
	23	851.61	Gx					Gx
813.7	22	812.90	Ab	Ab				
772.6	21	774.19	G#		G#			
	20	735.48	Abb			Abb		
696.6	19	696.77	G				G	
	18	658.06	Fx					Fx
620.6	17	619.35	Gb	Gb				
579.5	16	580.65	F#		F#			
	15	541.94	Ex/Gbb			Ex/Gbb		
503.4	14	503.23	F				F	
	13	464.52	E#					E#
	12	425.81	Fb	Fb				
386.3	11	387.10	E		E			
	10	348.39	Dx/Fbb			Dx/Fbb		
310.3	9	309.68	Eb				Eb	
269.2	8	270.97	D#					D#
	7	232.26	Ebb	Ebb				
193.1	6	193.55	D		D			
	5	154.84	Cx			Cx		
117.1	4	116.13	Db				Db	
76.1	3	77.42	C#					C#
	2	38.71	Dbb	Dbb				
0	1	0.0	C		C			

EX. 12.1: Near-equivalence of 31edo with 1/4-comma meantone

Correlation of 1/6-Comma Meantone with 55edo

1	1200	C	C					
55	1178.18	B#		B#				
54	1156.36							
53	1134.54							
52	1112.72	Cb				Cb		
51	1090.91	B					B	
50	1069.09	Ax						Ax
49	1047.27							
48	1025.45							
47	1003.63	Bb	Bb					
46	981.81	A#		A#				
45	960.0							
44	938.18							
43	916.36	Bbb				Bbb		
42	894.54	A					A	
41	872.72	Gx						Gx
40	850.91							
39	829.09							
38	807.27	Ab	Ab					
37	785.45	G#		G#				
36	763.63							
35	741.81							
34	720.0	Abb				Abb		
33	698.18	G					G	
32	676.36	Fx						Fx
31	654.55							
30	632.73							
29	610.91	Gb	Gb					
28	589.09	F#		F#				
27	567.27	Ex			Ex			
26	545.45							
25	523.64	Gbb				Gbb		
24	501.82	F					F	
23	480.0	E#						E#
22	458.18							
21	436.36							
20	414.55	Fb	Fb					
19	392.73	E		E				
18	370.91	Dx			Dx			
17	349.09							
16	327.27	Fbb				Fbb		
15	305.45	Eb					Eb	
14	283.63	D#						D#
13	261.82							
12	240.0							
11	218.18	Ebb	Ebb					
10	196.36	D		D				
9	174.54	Cx			Cx			
8	152.72							
7	130.91							
6	109.09	Db					Db	
5	87.27	C#						C#
4	65.45							
3	43.63							
2	21.82	Dbb	Dbb					
1	0.0	C		C				

EX. 12.2: Near-equivalence of 55edo with 1/6-comma meantone

As already discussed in chapter 6, 55edo provides a close approximation to the 1/6-comma meantone preferred by Mozart. In example 12.2 the major third is eighteen of the fifty-five steps, not quite as pure at 392.73 cents. A chromatic half step is four steps, and a diatonic half step is five. We cannot give every step in 55edo a pitch name without going into triple sharps and triple flats, for which there is no conventional notation. (With seven natural notes, seven sharps, seven flats, seven double sharps, and seven double flats, there are only thirty-five note names in a conventional meantone system.) However, to more fully explore the resources of various equal temperaments, and become able to predict which divisions will give us which optimal interval sizes, we will expound a general theory of equal temperaments derived in the nineteenth century.

R.H.M. Bosanquet's Theory of Temperaments

In his 1876 book, *Elementary Treatise on Musical Intervals and Temperament*—consulted by Partch in writing his *Genesis of a Music*—English scientist and music theorist Robert Holford MacDowell Bosanquet (1841–1912) outlined a general theory of divisions of the octave. His theory is given in terms of mathematical theorems and corollaries, which I will simplify here, both for readability and because not every point Bosanquet makes retains significance for our purposes.[1]

Given any division of the octave, there will be a number of those divisions that most closely corresponds to the perfect fifth. As a formula, we could express this as

$$n = \text{nint}(m \times 701.955/1200),$$

where n is the number of units in a perfect fifth, m is the the number of units in an octave, and "nint" signifies the *nearest* integer (not necessarily the greatest integer, as in the computer software usage of "int"; we could alternatively use int[m + .5]). For example, if we divide the octave into fifty-three equal parts, then

$$\text{nint}(53 \times 701.955/1200) = \text{nint}(31.003) = 31$$

So in a division of fifty-three-tone ET, thirty-one of the fifty-three units will constitute our most perfect fifth. To find the size of that fifth, we take 31/53 of 1200 cents, which is 701.887 cents—an exemplary fifth indeed, only .068 cents away from beatless 3/2 perfection. The size of the fifth can be generalized by the formula

$$n/m \times 1200 = \text{fifth size in cents},$$

where m is the number of units in an octave, and n is the number of such units in the best available fifth.

Applying these formulas, we get the following fifth sizes in various equal temperaments:

m-division ET		n units in fifth		fifth size in cents
12	nint(m × 701.955/1200) =	7	n/m × 1200 =	700
13	″	8	″	738.46
14	″	8	″	685.71
15	″	9	″	720
16	″	9	″	675
17	″	10	″	705.88
18	″	11	″	733.33
19	″	11	″	694.74

And so on. Notice that 12, 17, and 19 give us acceptable perfect fifths and that the other divisions really don't.

This much, I hope, is clear. The next step Bosanquet takes is a little more abstract: he classifies divisions of the octave in terms of how closely octaves and fifths coincide. The goal that was generally pursued, in 3/2 fifth-oriented temperament, was to make seven octaves line up with twelve fifths. In 12tet the octave is twelve units and the fifth is seven units.

12 fifths = 12 × 7 units = 84 units
7 octaves = 7 × 12 units = 84 units

Because 84 – 84 = 0, Bosanquet calls 12tet a *zeroth-order ET division*, or a division of the order 0.

In seventeen-tone ET, ten units make up the perfect fifth, while seventeen units make up the octave. Here, then,

12 fifths = 12 × 10 units = 120 units
7 octaves = 7 × 17 units = 119 units

The units of 120 – 119 = 1, so 17edo is a first-order division, or a division of the order 1. In eighteen-tone ET, there are eleven units in the fifth:

12 fifths = 12 × 11 units = 132 units
7 octaves = 7 × 18 units = 126 units

A unit quantity of 132 – 126 = 6, so 18edo is a sixth-order division. Divisions can have a negative order number, as does 26edo, in which there are fifteen units in the fifth.

12 fifths = 12 × 15 units = 180 units
7 octaves = 7 × 26 units = 182 units

And 180 minus 182 = –2, so 26 is an ET division of order –2.

To find the order of an ET division, we always subtract the number of units in seven octaves from the number of units in twelve fifths. If twelve fifths in a given division are larger than seven octaves—if the fifth is larger than 700 cents, in other words—that answer will be a positive number, and the order number will be positive. If twelve fifths are smaller than seven octaves—if the fifth is smaller than 700 cents—that answer will be a negative number, and the order number will be negative. In other words, Bosanquet calls ET divisions positive if the fifth is larger than 700 cents, and negative if it is smaller, a distinction that need not overly concern us here.

The table below shows statistics for a number of ET divisions, starting with the number of pitches per octave, the number of steps in a fifth, the size of the fifth in cents, the number of steps or units in twelve fifths, the number of steps or units in seven octaves, and finally the order number of that particular ET division, arrived at by subtracting the previous column from the one before it.[2]

Pitches per octave m	Units per fifth nint(701.955m/ 1200) = n	Cents in fifth 1200n/m	12 fifths 12n	7 octaves 7m	Order (Bosanquet) 12n – 7m
12	7	700.00	84	84	0
13	8	738.46	96	91	5
14	8	685.71	96	98	–2
15	9	720.00	108	105	3
16	9	675.00	108	112	–4
17	10	705.88	120	119	1
18	11	733.33	132	126	6
19	11	694.74	132	133	–1
20	12	720.00	144	140	4
21	12	685.71	144	147	–3
22	13	709.09	156	154	2
23	13	678.26	156	161	–5
24	14	700.00	168	168	0
25	15	720.00	180	175	5
26	15	692.31	180	182	–2
27	16	711.11	192	189	3
28	16	685.71	192	196	–4
29	17	703.45	204	203	1
30	18	720.00	216	210	6
31	18	696.77	216	217	–1
32	19	712.50	228	224	4
33	19	690.91	228	231	–3
34	20	705.88	240	238	2
35	20	685.71	240	245	–5
36	21	700.00	252	252	0
37	22	713.51	264	259	5

Pitches per octave m	Units per fifth nint(701.955m/ 1200) = n	Cents in fifth 1200n/m	12 fifths 12n	7 octaves 7m	Order (Bosanquet) 12n – 7m
38	22	694.74	264	266	–2
39	23	707.69	276	273	3
40	23	690.00	276	280	–4
41	24	702.44	288	287	1
42	25	714.29	300	294	6
43	25	697.67	300	301	–1
. . .					
53	31	701.89	372	371	1
. . .					
55	32	698.18	384	385	–1
. . .					
65	38	701.54	456	455	1
. . .					
118	69	701.69	828	826	2
. . .					
301	176	701.66	2112	2107	5

The point of assigning an order number is this: in general, the smaller the order number, the more closely the fifths and octaves in an ET division will coincide, and the more closely the fifth will approximate 700 cents. As we look down the chart of example 12.3, certain tunings will have an order of 0. These are the divisions divisible by twelve: 12, 24, 36 tones to an octave and so on. The next most preferable divisions are those of orders 1 and –1, which still have fifths of about 700 cents. And since divisions that are multiples of twelve do not approximate 5/4 major thirds very well until we get into very high divisions, these 1 and –1-order divisions have the best chance of approximating both fifths and thirds.

As we look down the right-hand column of example 12.3, we see that in the line of consecutively increasing ET divisions, the order numbers follow a repeating pattern, starting with 12edo, 0, 5, –2, 3, –4, 1, 6, –1, 4, –3, 2, –5.

Starting with twelve-tone ET, we get a division of order 0 every twelve divisions, at 24, 36, 48, and so on.

Starting with seventeen-tone ET, we get a division of order 1 every twelve divisions, at 29, 41, 53, and so on.

Starting with nineteen-tone ET, we get a division of order –1 every twelve divisions, at 31, 43, 55, and so on.

Starting with twenty-two-tone ET, we get a division of order 2 every twelve divisions, at 34, 46, 58, and so on.

Historically, the divisions of order 1, 0, and –1 have excited the most interest. Divisions of order 3, –3, 4, –4, 5, –5, and 6 offer the weakest correspondence of fifths and octaves, and thus the most compromised fifths, so they have not been considered useful in a music based on simple consonances, however interesting they might be for other purposes. The ET divisions considered to offer the best possibilities, then, are:

0-order:
12, 24, 36, 48, 60, 72, 84, 96 . . .

1-order:
17, 29, 41, 53, 65 . . .

–1-order:
19, 31, 43, 55, 67 . . .

Not surprisingly, these are generally the same scales that recommended themselves in our Pythagorean explorations in chapter 4. Now, if we extract from example 12.3 only the 1-order and –1-order divisions, we find the following progression in fifth sizes:

17tet	**has a fifth of**	**705.88¢**
19	"	694.74¢
29	"	703.45¢
31	"	696.77¢
41	"	702.44¢
43	"	697.67¢
53	"	701.89¢
55	"	698.18¢
65	"	701.54¢
67	"	698.51¢
77	"	701.30¢

These numbers will asymptotically approach 700 cents from either side. But the true perfect fifth is 701.955 cents, not 700 cents, so it is clear that among these equal temperaments., fifty-three-tone ET gives us the closest approximation to a perfect fifth of any reasonably small and efficient division of the octave, thus part of that division's appeal to certain tuning theorists.

We ought to note that, ultimately, order number is significant only for relatively small divisions of the octave. Once we get into several hundred equal steps per octave, the grid becomes so fine that we can reach good approximations of intervals regardless of order number. For instance, 1206-tone ET is order 6, but 705 units of it give a fifth of 701.49 cents, which is a better value for a 3/2 fifth than many smaller 1- or 2-order divisions. Order number, then, is a concept of limited usefulness, though it is helpful for explaining why certain relatively small divisions of the octave have inspired enthusiasm over the centuries.

Having chosen these divisions of the octave for their optimum-size perfect fifths, we can then compare them in terms of the purity of other intervals we want to use. Example 12.3 shows most of the 0-, 1-, and –1-order equal temperaments below 100 along with their closest approximations to the intervals 5/4, 6/5, 7/4, 11/8, and 13/8.

m-division E.T.	closest 5/4 major third	closest 6/5 minor third	closest 7/4 seventh	closest 11/8	closest 13/8
optimum size:	386.3	315.6	968.8	551.3	840.5
0-order:					
12	400 cents	300	1000	600	800
24	400	300	950	**550**	850
36	400	300	**966.67**	566.7	833.3
48	375	325	**975**	**550**	850
60	380	**320**	960	560	**840**
72	**383.33**	**316.67**	**966.67**	**550**	833.3
84	**385.71**	**314.29**	**971.43**	557.1	**842.9**
96	**387.5**	**312.5**	**975**	**550**	**837.5**
1-order:					
17	352.94	282.35	988.24	564.7	847.1
29	372.41	331.03	951.72	537.9	827.6
41	380.49	321.95	**965.85**	**556.1**	848.8
53	**384.91**	**316.98**	**973.58**	543.4	**837.7**
65	**387.69**	**313.85**	978.46	**553.8**	849.2
77	**389.61**	**311.69**	**966.23**	545.5	**841.6**
-1-order:					
19	378.95	**315.79**	947.4	568.4	821.1
31	**387.10**	309.68	**967.7**	541.9	851.6
43	**390.70**	306.98	976.7	558.1	**837.2**
55	392.73	305.45	960	545.5	850.9
67	394.03	322.39	**967.2**	**555.22**	**841.8**
79	379.75	**318.99**	**972.2**	**546.8**	**835.4**

EX. 12.3: Interval sizes in 0, 1, and –1-order edos

Approximations within five cents appear in boldface. Note that 72tet offers excellent 5/4, 6/5, 7/4, and 11/8 intervals; 96 excels at all five. ETs of 53 and 79 are also fertile in this respect. Of course, most of these 1- and –1-order edos provide all of these intervals in better resolution than 12tet does the simple 5/4 major third, at its damnable expense of fourteen cents.

Bosanquet designed and had built a "Generalised Harmonium" capable of playing a 53tet scale in such a way that parallel chords required no change in position of the hands as they ascended and descended the scale.[3] As he pointed out, by 1850 British parliamentarian and major general T. Perronet Thompson had already designed and built an "Enharmonic Organ" to play forty tones chosen from 53edo, allowing modulation in all keys with virtually just–tuned intervals. (The amount of keen interest taken in tuning and temperament by nineteenth-century British musical amateurs is rather astonishing.) The Enharmonic Organ's terribly complicated-looking three-manual keyboard of knobs, levers, and buttons is shown in example 12.4,[4] and Bosanquet's explanation of its tuning is in example 12.5. In Bosanquet's notation, a downward diagonal before the note name lowers its pitch by 22.6 cents (1/53 of an octave), and an upward diagonal similarly raises it by that amount. The back cover of Bosanquet's book bears an advertisement by his organ builder offering harmoniums with twenty-four keys per octave at a price of 36 pounds, thirty-six keys per octave at 52 pounds, and so on up to eighty-four keys per octave at 126 pounds. The ad makes it clear that the purpose of this variety in harmoniums is for trying out different brands of meantone temperament, not for quarter tones, sixth tones, and such. I'm afraid such prices could not possibly be matched today.

Front View and Profile of the Finger-boards, on a Scale of One Fourth

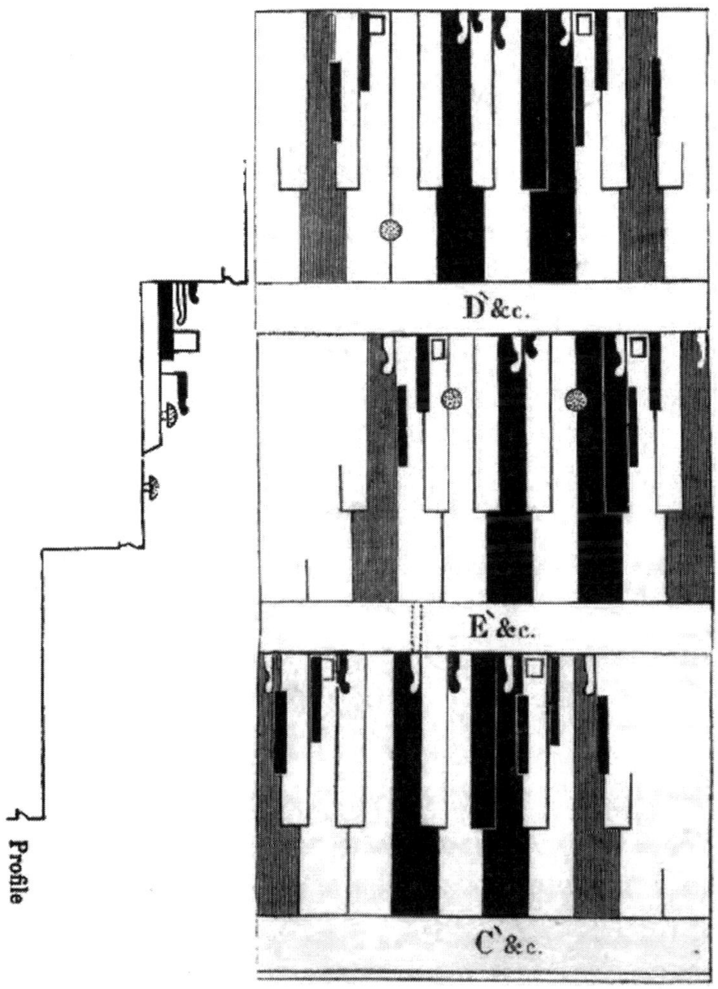

EX. 12.4: Diagrams of T. Perronet Thompson's fifty-three-tone keyboard

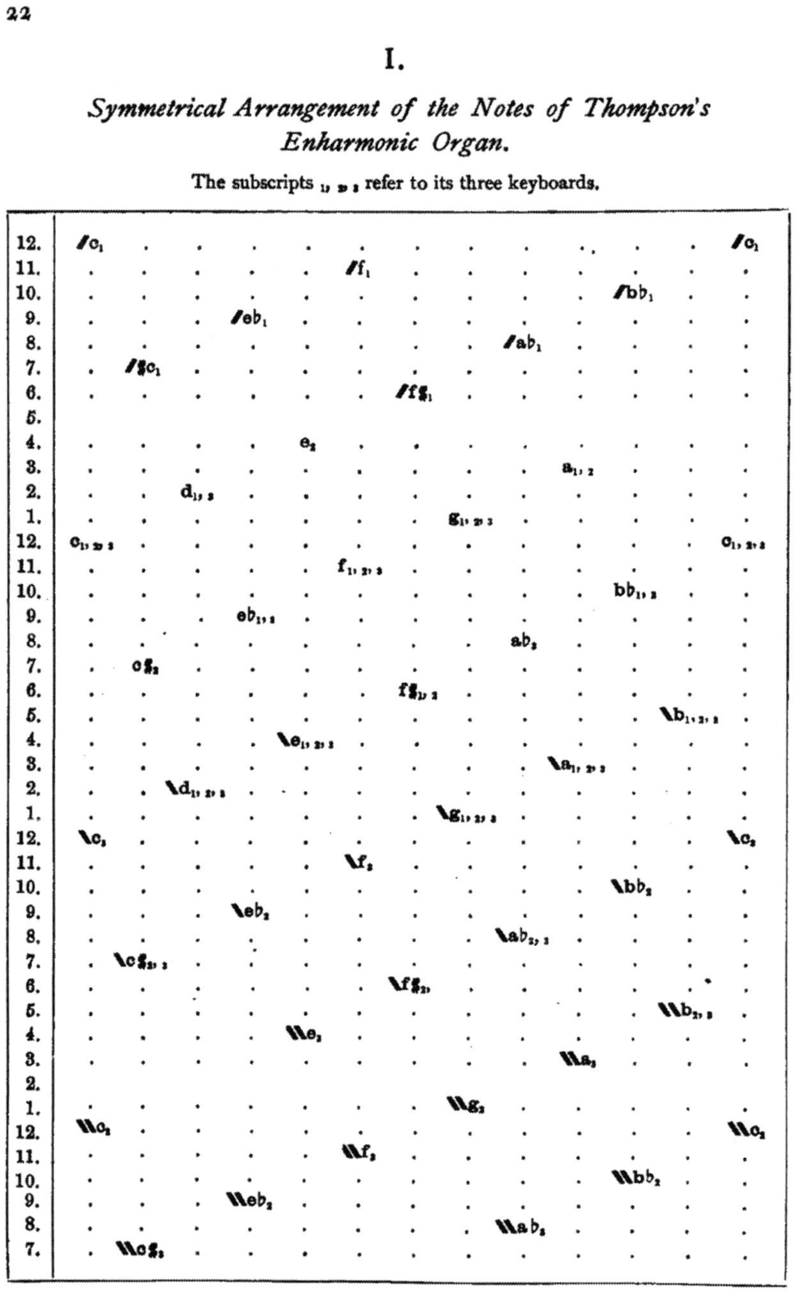

EX. 12.5: Bosanquet's chart of Thompson's Enharmonic Organ tuning

Twentieth-century composers have expermented with many equal temperaments above and even below twelve, sometimes in search of approximations of the seventh, eleventh, and thirteenth harmonics. One of the most amazing performances I've ever heard was by the New York group Music for Homemade Instruments in 1999. They first played a melody in 13tet several times and then *sang* the same melody, without instruments, in perfect 13tet intonation. Thirteen-tone equal temperament contains vitually no intervals we're accustomed to, but the frisson of such weird intervals well performed is undeniable.

Easley Blackwood's Twelve Microtonal Etudes, Ivor Darreg, Neil Haverstick

One of the works most often used to demonstrate diverse equal temperaments is the Twelve Microtonal Etudes for Electronic Music Media, op. 28 (1980) of Easley Blackwood (b. 1933). The etudes are in equal temperaments from thirteen to twenty-four (quarter tone). Each etude has a different set of accidentals, sometimes simply differentiating between conventional enharmonics so that C♯ is different from D♭ and F𝄪 from G, at other times adding an accidental, which is an arrow (up or down) drawn through a circle.

Realized on a synthesizer (back in the days when this was a labor-intensive task), the etudes are in a rather neo-Baroque idiom. The music emphasizes intervals that the edo shares with 12tet (for instance, 15tet and 12tet, both divisible by three, both contain major thirds, while 16tet and 12tet both have minor thirds). Example 12.6 shows the notation key and opening of the Etude in twenty-three-tone equal temperament. With its stodgy rhythms and old-fashioned organ timbres, the piece is not terribly compelling on musical grounds alone but remains in the microtonal canon as a unique and commercially available demonstration.

EX. 12.6: Notation and beginning of Easley Blackwood's Etude in twenty-three-tone equal temperament

More interesting, though less reliably available, is the music of California composer and instrument builder Ivor Darreg (1917–1994), who wrote music in a wide variety of equal and unequal tunings, such as his Suite for Microtonal Keyboard, op. 62 in 22tet (1975) and Preludes for 19tet guitar, as well as a group of works titled *Beyond the Xenharmonic Frontier* in 13tet, 17tet, 19tet, and so on up to 51tet and 53tet.[5] He built instruments (guitars, metallophones, and a string instrument called the Megalyra) in 10-, 14-, 15-, 16-, 17-, 19-, 21-, 22-, 24-, 31-, and 34-tone equal temperaments. He wrote essays prolifically, and coined the term *xenharmonic*, now often used in some microtonal circles, to refer to tunings outside of the familiar twelve-pitch grid.[6] For instance, of some of the more extotic edos, he wrote:

> I could explain here that the seventeen-tone system turns certain common rules of harmony upside-down: major thirds are dissonances which resolve into fourths instead of the other way round: certain other intervals resolve into major seconds; the pentatonic scale takes on a very exciting mood when mapped onto the 17 equally-spaced tones, and so on; but I can't expect you to believe me until you hear all this yourself. If you try to play these pieces in another system, it just doesn't work; they lose their punch; the magic is all gone.
>
> Quite as much, if not more as, when certain pieces composed in and for 19 are tried in 31. They go flabby, no punch. On the other hand, certain pieces composed in 31, when tried in 19, become too crude or coarse-textured. They lose their finesse, their subtlety, and the restful calm of 31 is replaced by the aggressiveness of 19.[7]

In addition, Neil Haverstick (b. 1951) has made a career based on his music for his 19tet and 34tet guitars, along with other tunings (some nonequal).[8] His piece "Birdwalk" is a 19tet guitar blues, the rhythms of which are humorously subverted by the longer time it takes for the blues conventions to traverse the more subdivided scale. He notates his 19tet music in conventional sharps and flats (also guitar tab),[9] but without enharmonics, so that E♯, F, F♯, and G♭ are four different pitches.

Regular Temperament Theory

Many composers have experimented with non-equal scales derived from equal divisions of the octave—or, more specifically, generated by equal intervals. A particular class of such scales is characterized by *moments of symmetry*, a term used by the music theorist Ervin Wilson (1928–2016), who has been a major influence on West Coast microtonalists in particular. In his seminal 1975 paper on the topic (actually a handwritten letter that devolves into a long series of charts),[10] Wilson shows how the penatonic, diatonic, and chromatic scales can be generated by adding perfect fourths to preexisting notes to create new scale steps (ex. 12.7; the numbers in the top row show how many fourths are needed to reach that pitch from C).

0	5	10	3	8	1	6	11	4	9	2	7
C											
C					F						
C					F					Bb	
C			Eb		F			Ab		Bb	
C	Db		Eb		F	Gb		Ab		Bb	
C	Db	D	Eb	E	F	Gb	G	Ab	A	Bb	B

EX. 12.7: Pentatonic, diatonic, and chromatic scales generated by fourths

That the pentatonic (fourth line) and diatonic (fifth line) scales comprise contiguous subsets of the circle of fifths is hardly in itself a new insight, but Wilson (and his followers), armed with a belief that the characteristics of the pentatonic and diatonic might come in handy in future yet unknown scales as well, have used this pattern to generate scales with more than twelve pitches using one interval as a generator and filling out the scale until it contains only two interval sizes, just as the diatonic scale uses only whole and half steps.

One of Wilson's examples is a series of scales generated in seventeen-tone equal temperament by a generator of seven units, a slightly small perfect fourth of 494.12 cents (ex. 12.8).

0	1	2	3	4	5	6	7	8	9	10	11	12	13	14	15	16	17	
0																	0	1 step
0							1										0	2 steps
0							1							2			0	3 steps
0				3			1				4			2			0	5 steps
0	5			3			1	6			4			2			0	7 steps
0	5	10		3	8		1	6	11		4	9		2	7		0	12 steps
0	5	10	15	3	8	13	1	6	11	16	4	9	14	2	7	12	0	17 steps

EX. 12.8: MoS (moment of symmetry) scales generated in 17edo by taking every seventh step

Here the numbers in the *lower* part of the chart give the order in which new scale steps are generated, and the scales included (omitting, for instance, eight steps, fourteen steps) are the ones in the system that offer moments of symmetry—that is, scales in which only two step sizes result. (In the five-step line the intervals are three and four units; in the seven-step, one and three units; in the twelve-step, one and two units.) The seven-step scale, for example, comprising steps 0, 1, 4, 7, 8, 11, and 14, contains only intervals of one and three steps, for the following scale in cents:

0	70.6	282.4	494.1	564.7	776.5	988.2

Consecutive intervals within the scale are either 70.6 or 211.8 cents.

For another instance, a twenty-one-pitch scale known as Blackjack temperament has been widely used. It can be generated by an interval of 116.666 . . . cents, which is 7/6 of an equal-tempered half step, resulting in steps on the following cent amounts:

0		
83.33 . . .	116.66 . . .	200
233.33 . . .	316.66 . . .	350
383.33 . . .	466.66 . . .	500
583.33 . . .	616.66 . . .	700
733.33 . . .	816.66 . . .	850
933.33 . . .	966.66 . . .	1050
1083.33 . . .	1166.66 . . .	1200

All the adjacent steps in this scale are either 83.33 . . . cents or 33.33 . . . cents, and the scale is a subset of seventy-two-tone equal temperament. One can easily see, in this arrangement, that equal-tempered major seconds, perfect fourths, and perfect fifths are retained, as are excellently in-tune major thirds of 383.33 cents and septimal minor sevenths of 966.66 cents. Also we find the neutral (virtually eleven-based) third of 350 cents, the neutral sixth of 850 cents, and the neutral seventh of 1050 cents. Wilson used the letters L and S to denote large and small steps in a scale pattern, and the pattern here is LSLSLSSLSLSLSLSLSLSLS. One will note that there are two consecutive small steps, and the 116.66 . . . –cent generator could be extended to create more steps (or retracted to have fewer). Joseph Pehrson (b. 1950) is probably the best-known composer associated with Blackjack temperament. He notates it using Ezra Sims's 72tet notation, which is outlined in chapter 13.

Overlapping with many of Wilson's ideas, microtonal theorists have created a body of tuning theory often known as Regular Temperament Theory (RTT). (As with the names of so many musical movements, some of its practitioners have cautioned against this one as not quite accurate, but no other term has acquired a consensus, and this one seems to be adequately widely recognized.) Just as Ben Johnston, La Monte Young, and other just intonationists have gone back to a pre-meantone moment in history and continued up the harmonic series for new intervals, the RTT musicians have gone back to meantone and generalized its method to create new scales by tempering out other commas than the syntonic comma (81/80) that meantone was crafted to obviate. Frequently these scales offer better approximations of seventh, eleventh, and thirteenth harmonics than 12tet does and are chosen to take advantage of them. Theorists and composers working in this area have given the resulting scales rather fanciful names.

For instance, a temperament called Porcupine temperament is intended to temper out the comma 250/243. What does this mean exactly? First of all, let's factor out the comma: 250/243 = 2 × 5 × 5 × 5 / 3 × 3 × 3 × 3 × 3. As we know, the 2 signifies an octave, the 5s are major thirds, and the 3s are perfect fifths. Thus 250/243 is the 49-cent comma found by going up an octave and three major thirds (C–C–E–G♯–B♯) and then down by five perfect fifths (B♯–E♯–A♯–D♯–G♯–C♯).

This may sound arcane, but in his seminal RTT paper, "A Middle Path: Between Just Intonation and the Equal Temperaments,"[11] Paul Erlich gives an example of a justly tuned chord progression (attributed to Jason Yerger) used to generate Porcupine temperament. The chord progression begins on F♯ minor and moves conventionally through triads on A, E, G, D, and F to end in F minor. Example 12.9 shows the chord progression given in just intonation, with ratios and cents, and with a Johnstonian plus sign marking the A in measure 6 to differentiate it from the A at the beginning. The ending triad is lower than the opening one by forty-nine cents, the 250/243 comma. (This looks somewhat like Benedetti's example, given in chapter 5, demonstrating the need for temperament, with the ratios quickly requiring larger and larger numbers.)

Ratios:									
	3/2	9/5	9/5	9/5	81/50	81/50	81/50	729/500	729/500
	6/5	3/2	27/20	27/20	27/20	243/200	243/200	243/200	1458/1250
	1/1	6/5	6/5	27/25	27/25	27/25	243/125	243/125	243/125

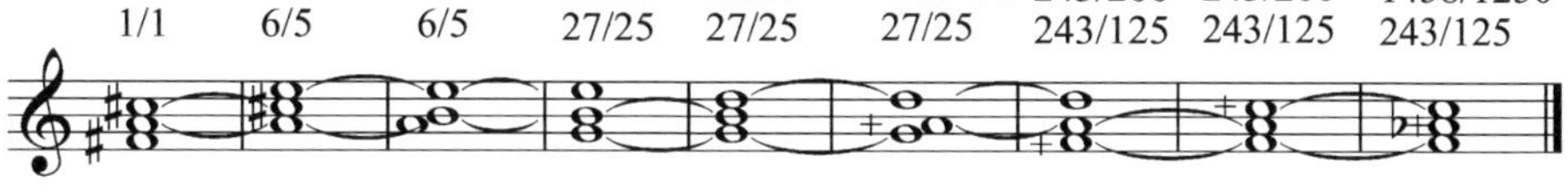

Cents:									
	702	1018	1018	1018	835	835	835	653	653
	316	702	520	520	520	337	337	337	266
	0	316	316	133	133	133	1151	1151	1151

EX. 12.9: Yerger's chord progression for tempering out 250/243

But, Erlich suggests, what if we wanted to temper out that comma, thus ending up on the same chord we started on? So just as to achieve meantone we narrowed the fifths and (except in 1/4-comma) widened the thirds to get the syntonic comma out of the way, now we're going to do the same thing, basically nudging our interval sizes and dividing up the forty-nine cents of the comma among them. We know from our factoring that the comma results from going up by three major thirds and then down by five perfect fifths (discounting the octave). Example 12.10 gives the notes in a two-dimensional array, fifths going left to right and thirds up and down, in the order in which they appear in Yerger's chord progression. So from F♯ we're going up a fifth to C♯, down a third to A, up two fifths to E and B, down a third to G, up two more fifths to D and A, and then down a third to F, which we want to make equal to our F♯. (Having reached our comma note, we don't need to worry about the A♭ and C that harmonize it.)

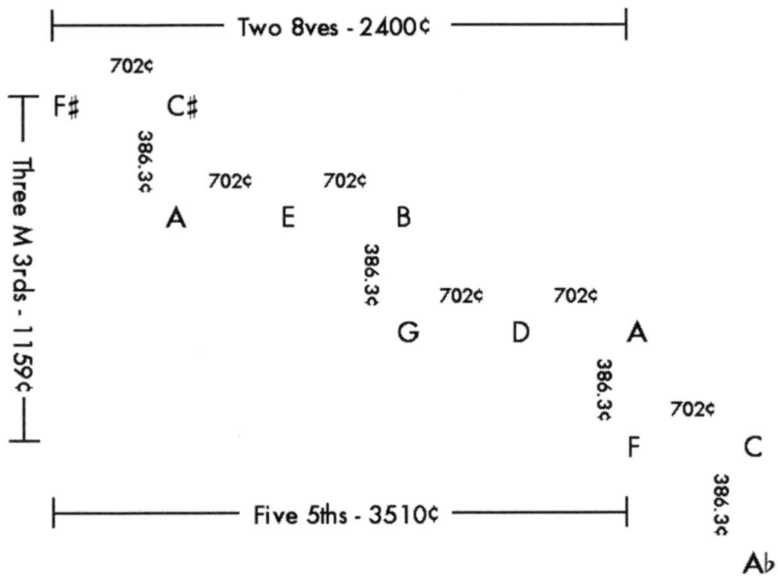

EX. 12.10: Tempering thirds and fifths to remove 250/243

Example 12.10 shows that we want two octaves—2400¢ between our F♯ and F. We're going up five fifths (3510¢) and coming down by a major third three times (1159¢) and want the difference to be 2400¢. But 3510¢ – 1159¢ = 2351¢, which is 49¢ flat, and that's our comma. So we need a fifth size around 702, which we'll call A, and a third size around 386, which we'll call B, such that

$$5A - 3B = 2400$$

If we keep A at 702¢, 3510¢ – 3B = 2400¢, and B = 370¢. Using F♯ as 0¢, 702¢ for all fifths, and 370¢ for major thirds, we will obtain the following tuning in cents for the progression above:

		1034	–	1034	–	1034		868	–	868	–	868		702	–	702
702	–	702		536	–	536	–	536		370	–	370	–	370		332
332	–	332	–	332		166	–	166	–	166		0	–	0	–	0
0																

Our major seconds, so notated, have been reduced to 166 cents (top line: 1034—868—702), so we go up a large minor third of 332 cents from C♯ to E in the top line and descend by two "major seconds" of 166 cents each back to our starting point. (You can hear the somewhat discomfiting result at http://www.kylegann.com/Porcupine-ex.mp3.)

If we collect all the pitches used in this example, we come up with the following scale:

F(♯)	1200
E	1034
D	868
C(♯)	702
B	536
A	370
A(♭)	332
G	166
F(♯)	0

All of the scale steps are 166 cents except for the one between A(♭) and A, which is only 38 cents. Having only two step sizes (in a pattern LLSLLLLL), and being generatable by repeating the interval size of 166 cents, this qualifies as a moment of symmetry. Of course, we would have to come up with some ad hoc notation for such a chord progression, because there is no way in normal notation to make F♯ equal to F, nor to bisect the minor third C♯–E with a note in the middle.

The general practice among RTT composers has been to find equal divisions of the octave that approximate, or at least support, scales derived in this manner. For some this can simplify the math somewhat or at least make returning to it unnecessary; also, if one wishes, the scale can be transposed within the equal temperament without altering it. In the case of eight-step Porcupine, the LLSLLLLL pattern requires that we have seven large steps and one small step both divisible by the same scale step. So if the large step is number of units A, and the small step is a smaller number of units B, we need a temperament (edo) such that 7 × A plus 1 × B equals the number of steps in the equal division.

If A = 2 and B = 1, the edo = 15 (7 × 2 plus 1 × 1)
If A = 3 and B = 1, the edo = 22 (7 × 3 plus 1 × 1)
If A = 3 and B = 2, the edo = 23 (7 × 3 plus 1 × 2)
If A = 4 and B = 1, the edo = 29 (7 × 4 plus 1 × 1)
If A = 5 and B = 1, the edo = 36 (7 × 5 plus 1 × 1)

So all of these equal divisions of the octave—15edo, 22edo, 23edo, 29edo, and 36edo—will "support" an eight-step Porcupine scale.

If we look through the chart of twenty-two-tone equal temperament in the appendix, we will find values very close to the fifth of 709 cents and the major third of 381.667 cents: 22edo has intervals of 709.09 cents and 381.82 cents. Thus 22edo provides a framework for a subset of pitches that will effect this temperament at the following values:

0
163.64
327.27
381.82
545.45
709.09
872.73
1036.36
1200

And as 31edo gives a simulacrum of 1/4-comma meantone, and 55edo well represents 1/6-comma meantone, Erlich urges 22edo as a close simulacrum of Porcupine temperament.

Porcupine temperament is not limited to the eight-pitch scale above, however. If we use the 22edo definition of this temperament, we can generate the eight-pitch scale by repeating steps of 163.64 cents upward from our starting point as in example 12.11.

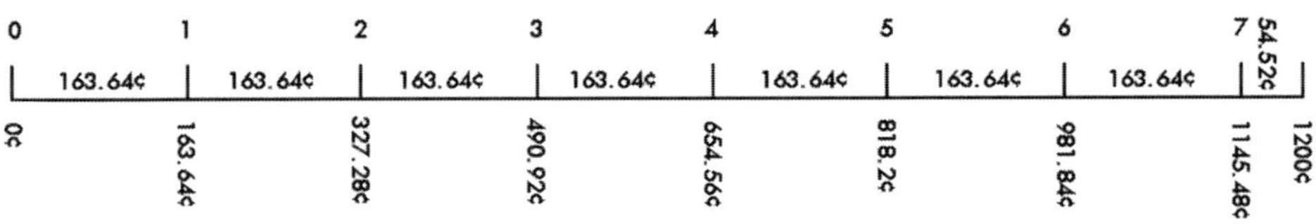

EX. 12.11: Eight-step Porcupine temperament

This is in the form LLLLLLLS, a permutation (or, more simply, mode) of the LLSLLLLL scale above. Then we can keep going, adding 163.64 cents and wrapping around the octave. Thus our last step was 1145.48 cents, to which we add 163.64 cents. This gives us 1309.12 cents, from which we subtract an octave of 1200 cents to get 109.12 cents. That's our eighth step of 163.64 cents, and we keep going up by the same step size as in example 12.12.

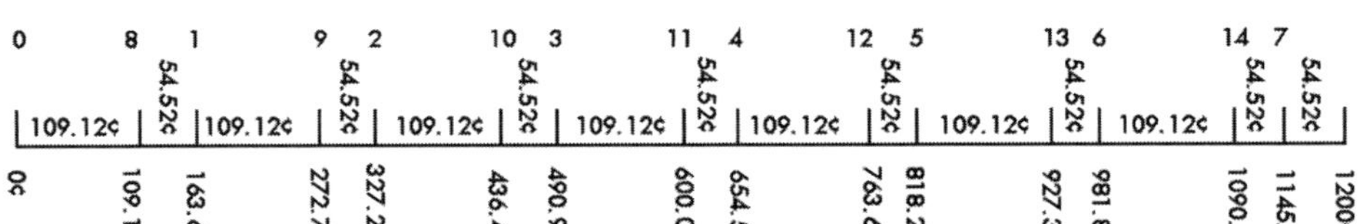

EX. 12.12: Fifteen-step Porcupine temperament

We reach another moment of symmetry at fifteen steps, in a pattern LSLSLSLSLSLSLSS. Both the eight-tone scale in example 12.11 and this fifteen-tone scale in example 12.12 are examples of the class of Porcupine temperaments. We can still express this scale in 22edo, because if the L is two steps and the S is one, 7L + 8S will equal 22. And I chose a fifteen-step scale because for Porcupine temperament it represents the next moment of symmetry after eight steps. (Any number of steps between eight and fifteen will leave you with at least one step not the same size as the other two, steps of 163.64 cents from the original eight-step line.) Continuing to replicate the 163.64 cents generator through another octave will fill out a 22tet scale, so if we want to continue to our next Porcupine moment of symmetry of twenty-two steps, we will have to go up to a higher edo (such as 37edo or 52edo).

One of the perceived virtues of Porcupine in 22edo is that a "harmonic seventh" of 981 cents can be divided into three "minor thirds" of 327 cents; likewise, a "perfect fourth" of 490 cents is divided into three equal steps (the excluded comma 250/243 is the difference between three 10/9 seconds—1000/729—and a 4/3 fourth).[12] Once again, there is no obvious or commonly accepted musical notation for 22edo, so composers are left to their makeshift devices. (George Secor and Dave Keenan developed a notation called Sagittal that has become somewhat popular because it can be adapted for various temperaments.[13])

Other subtleties are possible. RTT composers sometimes even adjust the octave size a little (so that 5A − 3B would equal a number other than 2400), and one can apply the same method to intervals other than the octave, such as the 3/1 perfect twelfth (called a *tritave* in such instances). In essence, two consistently sized intervals are going out of phase with each other in pitch space, one usually being the octave but not necessarily, just as 12tet results from 700 cents going out of phase with 1200 cents, or 1/4-comma meantone results from 696.6 cents going out of phase with 1200 cents. One could conceivably proceed more simply by, say, taking every eleventh note in 29edo and repeatedly adding in the 455.17-cent intervals (11/29 × 1200 cents) until a scale appears that seems aesthetically pleasing.

The preceeding gives the derivation of one temperament from the comma it seeks to temper out, and a similar logic can be applied to any other comma. We'll take a look at one more worked-out example, after which readers can test their own experiments and find plenty of other information (not always clearly presented) on the internet. Mavila temperament is defined as tempering out the comma 135/128. That equals 3 × 3 × 3 × 5 / 2 × 2 × 2 × 2 × 2 × 2 × 2. In short, then, this comma gives the difference from the closest octave (128) found by rising by three perfect fifths and one major third: C–G–D–A–C♯. The ratio 135/128 is 92.18 cents, so it's a pretty large comma. The two-dimensional just-intonation grid that brings us from 128 to 135 is as follows:

E	B	F♯	C♯	
5	15	45	135	
386¢	1088¢	590¢	1292¢	
C	G	D	A	E
1	3	9	27	81
0¢	702¢	204¢	906¢	408¢

We want the two-octave distance from C (up through G, D, and A) to C♯ to equal 2400 cents. While we could take any route through the grid, ultimately the three fifths add up to 2106 cents, the major third is 386.3 cents. And 2106¢ + 386.3¢ = 2492.3¢. Both thirds and fifths need to be narrowed, so if A is the size of a fifth and B that of a third, 3A + B = 2400¢. If A = 680, then B = 360 (very close to the just intervals 40/27 and 16/13). Optimized for thirds and fifths but not for octaves (which we will keep pure), the third is 356.07 cents and the fifth is 681.31.[14] Replacing the 702 in the above grid with 681, and the 386 with 356, we get the following scale in cents:

C	0
D	162.62
E–	325.24
E	356.07
F♯	518.69
G	681.31
A	843.93
B	1037.38
C♯	1200

A chord progression on the above scale, then, could be

G	681	—	G	681		F♯	519		E–	325
E	356		D	163	—	D	163		C♯	1200
C	0		B	1037		A	844	—	A	844

And the C♯ at the end would be equivalent to the C at the beginning. The eight-note scale is a subset of a nine-note moment of symmetry; to complete the subset we would have to add another A at 874.76 cents. This has a step pattern of LLSLLLSLL, and its two intervals between adjacent notes are 162.62 cents and 30.83 cents. For an equal temperament supporting its 7 Ls and 2 Ss, we can use 16edo (7 × 2 plus 2 × 1), 23edo (7 × 3 plus 2 × 1), 30edo (7 × 4 plus 2 × 1), or 37edo (7 × 5 plus 2 × 1). We can compare these nine-note Mavila scales through four edos as follows:

Optimum	16edo	23edo	30edo	37edo
0	0	0	0	0
163	150	156.5	160	162.2
325	300	313	320	324.3
356	375	365.2	360	356.8
519	525	521.7	520	518.9
681	675	678.3	680	681.1
844	825	834.8	840	843.2
875	900	887	880	875.7
1037	1050	1043.5	1040	1037.8

Note that in general, though not always, the more pitches per octave, the closer approximation to the original. The ratio between the optimal steps 162.62 cents and 30.83 cents is about 5.27/1, so at a ratio of five to one in step sizes, 37edo is very close indeed, within a cent on every step.

We can find similar definitions for other temperaments: Dicot (tempering out the chromatic half step 25/24), Augmented (128/125, the difference between three major thirds and an octave), Srutal (2048/2025), Ripple (6561/6250), Helmholtz (32805/32768, the schisma), and many others. Example 12.13, a chart by Paul Erlich, comprises in compact form a wealth of information about the five-limit temperaments that have been used. At the very center of the nested hexagons, if you can find it, is a small six-pointed star; this represents just intonation, the point at which the intervals are exact whole-number ratios. The numbers represent various edos. The lines with names attached represent the various temperaments. The closer a line comes to that central star, the more faithfully that temperament preserves the intervals of just intonation. These are called "low-damage" temperaments, in contrast to the outer "high-damage" temperaments that don't represent the third and fifth harmonics as well but may approximate higher harmonics better. Closest to the star, for instance, is the 53 on the Helmholtz line (just above 19 on the meantone line), since 53edo provides five-limit intervals almost perfectly in tune; other edos on the meantone line, such as 17, 19, and 31, have been closely associated with meantone. Along each line are given the

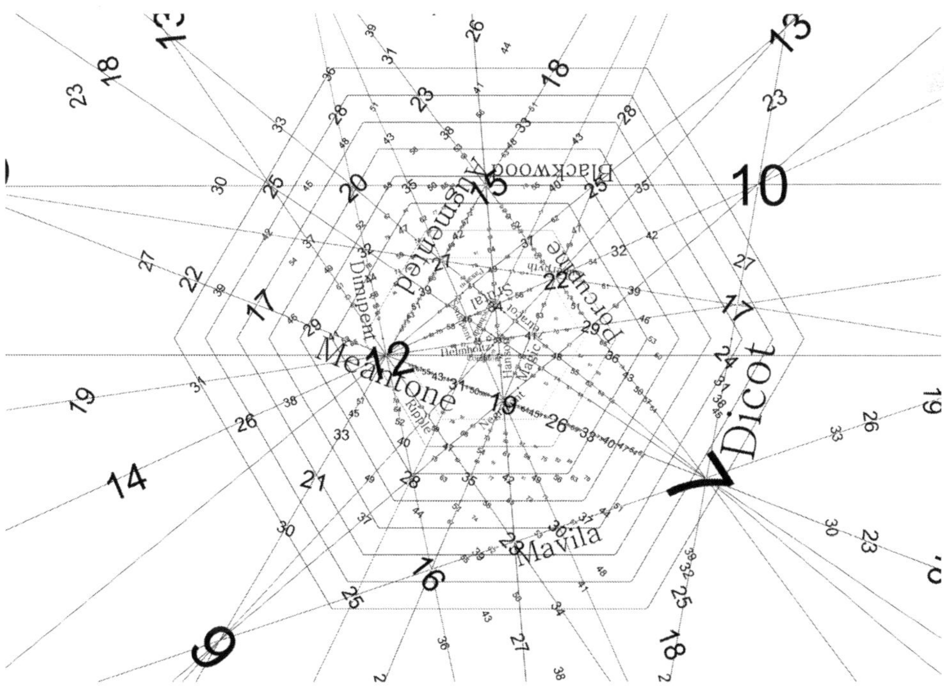

EX. 12.13: Paul Erlich's chart for the relationships of five-limit temperaments

numbers of the edos that support that temperament; the font size of each number is inversely proportional to the quantity, small numbers being printed the largest. So, for instance, one can see that Augmented temperament is supported by 15edo, 21edo, 27edo, 33edo, and so on. On the Porcupine line we find the edos 15, 22, 23, 29, and 36 that were given above; likewise 16, 23, 30, and 37 for Mavila. I thank Erlich for permission to use this extremely helpful chart, which contains far more information than I can afford to explicate here; I refer interested readers to his "Middle Path" article.[15]

I will provide raw data for three more temperaments, in case readers want to experiment.

Magic temperament tempers out the comma 3125/3072 ($5 \times 5 \times 5 \times 5 \times 5 / 3 \times 2^{10}$, the 29.6-cent comma obtained by ascending through five major thirds and descending by a perfect fifth, meaning a difference, in just intonation, between C and B_{x}). It is optimally generated by the interval 380.39 cents going out of phase with an octave. Magic temperament is almost perfectly accommodated by a 41edo, so I give those values for it here. The seven-step, SLSLSLS moment of symmetry (MoS) contains intervals of 58.54 cents and 321.95 cents (two steps and eleven steps); the ten-step MoS, SLSSLSSSLS, has intervals of 58.54 cents and 263.41 cents (two steps and nine steps); and the thirteen-step MoS, SSLSSSLSSSLSS, has intervals of 58.54 cents and 204.88 cents (two steps and seven steps):

Seven-step MoS		Ten-step MoS		Thirteen-step MoS	
58.54	S	58.54	S	58.54	S
				117.07	S
		321.95	L	321.95	L
380.49	L	380.49	S	380.49	S
439.02	S	439.02	S	439.02	S
				497.56	S
		702.44	L	702.44	L
760.96	L	760.96	S	760.96	S
819.51	S	819.51	S	819.51	S
		878	S	878	S
				1082.93	L
1141.5	L	1141.5	L	1141.5	S
1200	S	1200	S	1200	S

Blackwood temperament tempers out the comma 256/243, the 90 cents discrepancy between five perfect fifths (C–G–D–A–E–B) and the nearest C octave. In its fifteen-step form it is virtually identical to 15tet and is named for the composer Easley Blackwood, who wrote pieces in that division of the octave, including one of the Microtonal Etudes. The ten-step moment of symmetry is interesting for being similar to the octatonic (or diminished) scale, but with ten alternating whole and half steps instead of eight, so each step is 4/5 the size of the equivalent octatonic:

160	240	400	480	640	720	880	960	1120	1200

Beatles temperament works well in 27edo. It tempers out several seven-limit intervals, and since seven-limit tuning requires a three-dimensional grid, two intervals must be tempered out to generate the entire scale from one interval. (Being a seven-limit temperament, it is omitted from example 12.13.) It can be optimally generated by an interval of 844.42 cents going out of phase with an octave. Its seven-step MoS, SLSLSLS, uses intervals of 133.33 cents and 222.22 cents (three steps and five steps); the ten-step MoS, LSLLLSLLSL, uses intervals of 88.89 cents and 133.33 cents (two steps and three steps); and the seventeen-step MoS, LSLSLLSLSLSLLSLSL, uses intervals of 44.44 cents (4/9 of an ET half step, one 27tet step) and its double 88.89 cents (two steps):

Seven-step		Ten-step		Seventeen-step	
				88.89	L
133.33	S	133.33	L	133.33	S
		222.22	S	222.22	L
				266.67	S
355.56	L	355.56	L	355.56	L
				444.44	L
488.89	S	488.89	L	488.89	S
				577.78	L
		622.22	L	622.22	S
711.11	L	711.11	S	711.11	L
				755.56	S
844.44	S	844.44	L	844.44	L
				933.33	L
		977.78	L	977.78	S
1066.67	L	1066.67	S	1066.67	L
				1111.11	S
1200	S	1200	L	1200	L

The most obvious differences among these scales are the size ratio between the large and small steps (the L-to-S ratio, which can vary widely within one temperament) and the number of steps present, as well as the LS pattern. Some composers also take into account the kinds of harmonic progressions made possible by the comma that is tempered out, as our initial two examples attempted to make clear, though this is not always obvious in the music.

One can see that using such methods an infinity of scales can be generated. The initial impulse is often to create regular scales, analogous to the diatonic, based on tempered versions of just-intonation intervals (and not always the most consonant or obvious ones), though it's clear that some of the scales will consist of intervals not approximating any of our familiar small-ratio intervals. Whether the limitation to two interval sizes, insisted upon by some RTT composers, satisfies some such inherent perceptual need, as was exhibited by the diatonic scale, is open to question.[16] On this point Wilson wrote: "These [two-interval] structures are so rich in properties that one is hard put to isolate one, and say 'this is the raison d'etre.' I think that as part of the pattern-making process we latch onto cycles. That anywhere a cycle has the potential of forming, it will tend to do so. Having asserted itself, its own inertia re-affirms it, and gives it remarkable durability."[17] And as composer Kraig Grady (b. 1952), one of Wilson's main explicators and a proponent of such scales, adds, "I have received numerous comments from listeners about how the scales I use hold together, not knowing or being concerned that they are Moments of Symmetry."[18] For many composers, the use of such subsets of equal-tempered scales comes as a welcome limitation, freeing them from either dealing with a smooth continuum of too many pitches or juggling the open-ended ratios of just intonation. Theoretical explorations of such scales have a widespread presence on the internet, having generated their own, often quite forbidding jargon (see, for instance, Joe Monzo's Tonalsoft website at http://tonalsoft.com, and the Xenharmonic wiki at http://xenharmonic.wikispaces.com, "xenharmonic" being Ivor Darreg's term for any tuning outside the usual twelve-note scale). Be warned, however, that some people in this field get carried away by the math and bewildering terminology,[19] and that the ultimate musical purpose of their ratiocinations can be difficult to divine within the thickets of equations, lattices, and elaborate diagrams.

In any case, both camps, the just intonationists and the RTT composers, want to continue some aspect of traditional musical practice, but they differ on which aspect. The RTT composers want to achieve scales that are analogous to the diatonic and pentatonic but within different flavors of diatonic tonality devoid of the familiar clichés. The just intonationists, generally speaking, want to retain harmonies that are already familiar (such as the major and minor triads) but be able to expand that harmonic syntax via the seventh, eleventh, thirteenth harmonics, and so on, often retaining commas for microtonal voice leading, to have a continuous range of nuance between familiarity and exoticism. Both have their musical uses.

INTERLUDE L

NICOLA VICENTINO'S ARCHICEMBALO

Nicola Vicentino (1511–1576) is certainly not one of the famous names of music history, but for microtonalists he has become a hero, one perhaps not surpassed until Harry Partch some four centuries later. In his pursuit of a greater range of tones within the octave, he built, in 1555, a harpsichord he called the archicembalo, with 132 keys, comprising thirty-six different pitches per octave (31tet plus five more tuned to just intonation).[1] He later followed it with a similarly tuned portable organ called the arciorgano. In his accompanying treatise, *L'antica musica ridotta alla moderna prattica* ("Ancient music restored to modern practice," 1555), Vicentino boldly made clear that his impulse was largely inspired by what we would today call multicultural concerns:

> Everybody will be able to set in music his manner of singing with the intervals of the division of our instrument. With the music used nowadays one can write no French, German, Spanish, Hungarian, Turkish, Hebrew songs, nor one in another language, because the steps and skips of all the nations of the world do not proceed according to their maternal pronunciations exclusively through the intervals of whole tones and natural and accidental semitones, but through diesis and enharmonic semitones, whole tones, and skips. So that with this division of ours we have accommodated all the nations of the world who will be able to write their accents and set them in as many voices as they will see fit.[2]

Vicentino's music is sometimes loosely referred to as "Renaissance quarter-tone music," and while we will see that this is an inaccurate formulation, his music does have a bracing freshness that sounds like someone has introduced quarter tones into an otherwise conventional choral style.

Vicentino was a student of the great Netherlandish composer Adrian Willaert (c. 1490–1562), from whom he apparently imbibed some ideas about the ancient Greek genera. He was particularly impressed by claims that the enharmonic genus, with its perfect fourth divided by two quarter tones (as we would call them today) and a major third, was superior in expressive capacity to the other genera. As Plutarch wrote in his *De musica*, which had been translated in 1507, "The musicians of our times, though, disdained completely the most beautiful genus of all [the enharmonic] and the most fitting, which the ancients cherished for its majesty and severity."[3] "Compared to the ancient ratios," wrote Vicentino, "ours are not only more numerous but more sonorous. But why, then, in our times do we not observe musicians producing those effects that authors claim were made in antiquity?"[4]

So Vicentino rather brilliantly fused his search for the enharmonic genus with another, equally attractive project, creating a closed system in which thirty-one closely approximated meantone fifths would result in an equal scale allowing any sonority to be transposed to any level.[5] Thus the tuning seems to have been based on 31edo, although, as I have already written, there are thirty-six pitches per octave. This discrepancy will be explained presently.

The theoretical description Vicentino gives of his tuning is inconsistent and at times paradoxical, and many writers have puzzled to arrange its details in order.[6] Vicentino inconsistently named some of his intervals by fractions, as though he were thinking in just intonation rather than meantone temperament. For instance, he gives the ratio of his smallest interval, the minor diesis, as 40/39, which is 43.8 cents,[7] thus larger than the 38.7-cent step of 31edo. I refer the reader interested in more detail to the many scholarly articles I cite in the notes, but I am going to cut through the Gordian knot by giving the cents values of the tuning in pure 31edo. Any deviations resulting from values I've seen in other charts are no more than three cents.

The keyboard comprises two manuals, each with three rows of keys—that is, the usual seven "white" keys per octave plus two rows of split raised keys, as in example L.1.

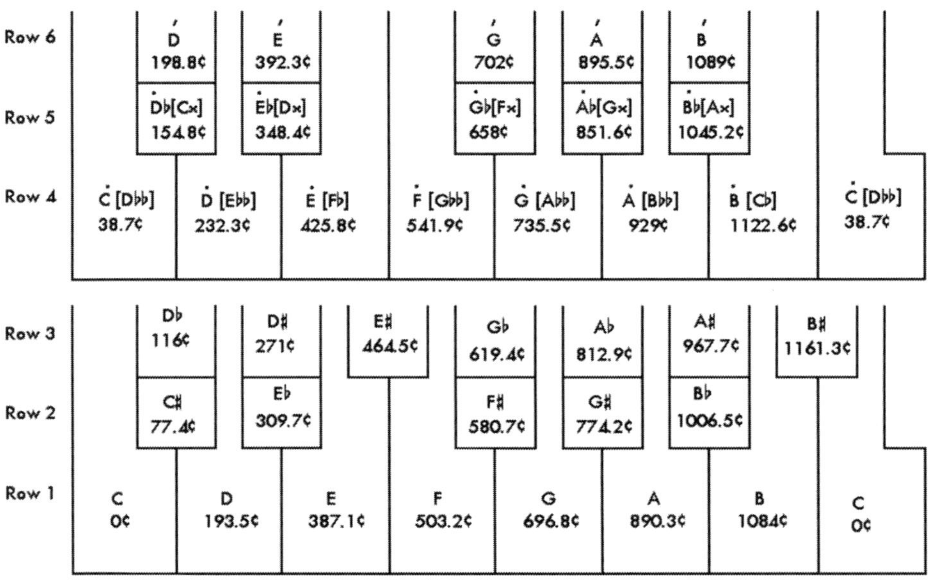

EX. L.1: Diagram of Vicentino's archicembalo keyboard

The seven natural keys in row 1 constitute the usual meantone major scale. The five "black" keys in row 2 are the sharps and flats most commonly used in Renaissance music: C♯, E♭, F♯, G♯, and B♭. Their enharmonic "equivalents" (D♭, D♯, G♭, A♭, and A♯) are in row 3, along with two more keys between E and F and B and C—namely, E♯ and B♯. The concession is a brilliant one; the bulk of early Baroque keyboard music could be performed on the first two rows alone, and almost all of it only on the lower manual, with the upper manual reserved for more exotic effects.

In row 4 of the upper manual we find the major scale with a dot above each pitch name, which was Vicentino's way of indicating a note raised by the smallest interval, which he called a *minor diesis*; a minor diesis, then, is 38.7 cents, and a major one is 77.4 cents, twice as large. The chromatic semitone (C to C♯) is also a major diesis, and a diatonic semitone (C to D♭) is equal to three minor dieses. Row 5 contains the pitches that are a minor diesis above the flat notes in rows 2 and 3. Disregarding row 6 for a moment, we see that each whole tone in the natural scale is divided into five minor dieses:

C Ċ C♯ D♭ Ḋ♭ D

and thus also from D to E, F to G, G to A, and A to B. In example L.1, I have also given each pitch with a dot above it its meantone equivalent in brackets. Using the dots made Vicentino's notation more intuitive for the performer; every note with a dot above it is to be played on the upper manual. It leads to some curious notations, though, since, for instance, a major triad on Ḋ is spelled Ḋ–G♭–Ȧ and one on Ȧ as Ȧ–D♭–Ė. Using the meantone equivalents results in a scary-looking but more logical E𝄫–G♭–B𝄫 and B𝄫–D♭–F♭.

Row 6 exists outside the 31edo structure. The D, E, G, A, and B are tuned to perfect 3/2 fifths above the respective G, A, C, D, and E in row 1 so that perfect just-intonation triads can be played on the most common pitches if desired. (Evidence exists in *L'antica musica* that Vicentino had also planned for extra keys on the C and F a 3/2 fifth above F and B♭, but these were not incorporated in the final instrument design.[8]) Written with a comma above the note name to indicate that they are raised by a comma—though actually raised only one fourth of a syntonic comma—these notes are not alluded to in any of Vicentino's music.

Vicentino appears to have written only a few pieces in this notation, all of them included (some only fragmentarily) in his *L'antica musica*.[9] Of these, his *Musica Prisca Caput* is particularly interesting for being in three sections, the first part demonstrating the diatonic genus; the second, the chromatic genus; and the third, the enharmonic genus. For Vicentino, and based on his researches in Greek music, the enharmonic genus consists of a minor diesis, a major diesis, and a major third[10] (although when one looks into the question of modes and tetrachords, the picture grows enormously more complicated); for instance:

C	Ċ	D♭	F	G	Ġ	A♭	C
0¢	39¢	117¢	503v	697¢	735¢	813¢	1200¢

Musica Prisca Caput shows, however, that he was concerned with using this ancient Greek scale not as a melodic resource but as a background structure that allows for subtle, hyperchromatic voice leading among chords. Example L.2 gives the third, enharmonic section of the piece (without lyrics), with cents above C marked on each note.

EX. L.2: Vicentino's *Musica Prisca Caput*, mm. 29–48

One will note that the triads are all tuned conventionally, however peculiar some of them look. Also, we see Vicentino taking a distinctly modern pleasure in harmonizing hyperchromatic scale passages. From the middle of measure 40 in the soprano we see a gradual pitch rise as follows, taking eight steps to cover less than a perfect fourth:

Pitch	Ȧ	B♭	B	Ḃ	C	Ċ	C♯	D♭	D
Cents	930	1006	1084	1123	0(1200)	39	77	116	193

As mentioned before, this could be renotated with standard sharps and flats (and double flats) in conventional meantone notation, as in example L.3.[11]

EX. L.3: Vicentino, *Musica Prisca Caput*, mm. 41–48, renotation in meantone notation

If one follows the strict rules for meantone pitch relationships, this notation will yield the same results as Vicentino's, and the music goes much further outside our normal musical experience, while maintaining consonance, than the examples by Bull and Scarlatti shown in the interlude to chapter 6 and at a considerably earlier date.

Vicentino's influence continued in Ferrara, where he was based, in the music of Luzzasco Luzzaschi (c. 1545–1607, who was said to perform beautifully on the archicembalo),[12] and ultimately on Don Carlo Gesualdo (1566–1613),[13] long celebrated for the pungent, almost atonal passages of some of his late madrigals. Outside Ferrara, however, he garnered less support, and Vincenzo Galilei (1520–1591), known less for his participation in the birth of opera than for fathering the famous scientist Galileo Galilei) wrote of him:

> Don Nicola had some students, who, while he played, especially in the enharmonic genus, sang this sort of music composed by him. He had this music performed in all the principal cities of Italy and I have heard it often, in various times and places. Let it be the sign of whether this music pleased or not that after his death it was practiced neither by his students nor by anyone else. . . . If by misfortune one of the singers lost his way while singing, it was impossible to put him back on the right track. Thus this kind of music necessarily required an instrument that could guide the voices of the singers through unknown tracts (not to say through precipitate cliffs), not letting them proceed according to the nature of singing and through a straight path. These particular sounds of the enharmonic . . . could only be unpleasant to the senses. . . . After Don Nicola's death the music was not sung any

> more; the instruments were no longer played in that manner and his students completely abandoned the enharmonic, not finding anyone who wished to listen to it.[14]

Nevertheless, Vicentino's fame has blossomed in the last few decades. Marco Tiella and Barthélemy Formentelli achieved a reconstruction of the archicembalo in 1974,[15] and several performances of Vicentino's pieces, some with voices and some with instruments, have been made available on the internet in recent years, proving what a lively and bracing effect Vicentino's microtonal excursions can have. Vicentino, who spent his life combating the small-mindedness of his colleagues, has been posthumously vindicated.

CHAPTER 13

Twelve-Based Equal Temperaments

We have saved for last what used to be, when I was a student, the best-known type of microtonality of all: quarter tones, along with other divisions based on the twelve-pitch equal scale. Earlier much-studied equal temperaments such as 19tet, 31edo, 53edo, and 55edo were pursued because of their capacity to include close approximations of just intervals such as the major and minor thirds and perfect fifth. Over the nineteenth century a kind of tuning amnesia crept in, as an irrevocable European musical canon arose grounded in the no-longer-questioned twelve pitches to the octave. When composers once again began thinking about increasing the number of pitches in the early twentieth century, they dared not fight against the implacable dominance of the piano keyboard. Instead, they opted for compromise: splitting the 100-cent half step instead of the octave. Two pianos could be tuned 50 cents apart to achieve twenty-four tones per octave; three pianos could be tuned in 33.3-cent increments to obtain thirty-six tones. Starting in 1917 a tradition of quarter tones and sixth tones arose that continues to the present day. The historical priority of other equal divisions is worth keeping in mind, but for most of the twentieth century, quarter tones were the more dominant form of microtonality. This is beginning to change again.

Beethoven's childhood friend Anton Reicha (1770–1836), who became a famous pedagogue at the Paris Conservatoire, suggested the possibility of quarter tones as early as 1824.[1] The great pianist-composer Franz Liszt (1811–1886), late in his life, prophesied that the saturation of the chromatic scale would necessitate turning to quarter tones and "half-quarter-tones."[2] Not long after, the terribly underrated Italian composer Ferruccio Busoni (1866–1924), who had met with the aging Liszt early in his own life, called for a scale of thirty-six equal steps to the octave, writing the following in his 1911 "Sketch for a New Esthetic of Music":

> The tripartite tone (third of a tone [i.e., 66⅔ cents]) has for some time been demanding admittance, and we have left the call unheeded. Whoever has experimented, like myself

> (in a modest way), with this interval, and introduced (either with voice or with violin) two equidistant intermediate tones within the extremes of a whole tone, schooling his ear and his precision of attack, will not have failed to discern that tripartite tones are wholly independent intervals with a pronounced character, and not to be confounded with ill-tuned semitones.[3]

So far this description outlines an 18tet scale, but Busoni goes on to expand it to thirty-six so as not to lose such familiar intervals as the minor third and perfect fifth (unavailable in an 18tet scale).[4] The call was heeded; in the second and third decades of the 1900s, several composers began working indepedently with scales of 24, 30, 36, 72, and even 96 equally spaced pitches per octave.

As we observed in chapter 11, the virtue of quarter tones is that they render possible close approximations of several basic eleven-limit intervals: 11/8 (551¢), 11/9 (347¢), 11/6 (1049¢), 16/11 (649¢), 12/11 (151¢), and 18/11 (853¢). The limitation of a quarter-tone system is that it introduces intervals based on eleven without allowing as intermediaries those based on seven or five. Thus the ear must accommodate itself to more complex ratios than musicians are used to without the benefit of the slightly easier to digest intervals that are omitted from 12tet; for instance, a major triad can be fitted with its eleventh harmonic but not its seventh or a better-tuned fifth harmonic. Thus it has always seemed to me that there is something irrevocably dissonant and incommensurable, perhaps even inherently atonal, about the quarter-tone gamut. This does not, of course, mean that quarter-tone music can't exhibit its own thrills and pleasures, its frisson of unfamiliarity, nor that it can't, in the hands of a good composer, build up its own new kind of syntax. In the early days of atonality and Schoenberg's "liberation of the dissonance," when differentiation between consonance and dissonance was waved aside, quarter-tone intervals seemed as good a repertoire of intervals as any.

The history of splitting the half step begins with the Czech composer Alois Hába (1893–1973), who used quarter tones in his Suite for String Orchestra of 1917.[5] Hába's mother was a folksinger, and in the songs she sang from the Moravian Wallachia region of the Czech Republic, the young Hába noticed that not all the pitches fit within the twelve-tone scale. On January 20, 1917, he heard a lecture about quarter tones by Willi von Möllendorf (1872–1934), at which the latter demonstrated a keyboard for bichromatic harmonium, but Hába had already written a quarter-tone work of his own.[6] Returning to Prague in 1923 from his studies in Berlin, Hába established a department of microtonal music at Prague Conservatory, teaching a course in quarter tones in 1924. The center operated fully from 1934 until 1949, save for an interruption during World War II. Hába was important for the construction of quarter-tone and sixth-tone instruments, including pianos, harmoniums, clarinets, trumpets, and guitars.[7] Of his sixteen string quartets, six are in a quarter-tone system, three in sixth tones, and two in fifth tones (30tet).

The Mexican violinist, conductor, and composer Julian Carrillo (1875–1965) claimed to have begun experimenting with sixteenth tones (12.5 cents) on his violin as early as 1895, but as his biographer Alejandro Madrid points out, we have only his word for that,[8] and he was rather addicted to mythologizing his life. He began writing about microtonal theoretical issues in 1923 and dubbed his microtonal system *el sonido trece* (the thirteenth sound),[9] using that phrase throughout his long career as kind of a logo standing for his brand of microtonality in general. Madrid argues persuasively that, unlike Hába, Carrillo did not come to microtones through observation of non-European music but through theoretical readings in Busoni, Schoenberg, and others whom he encountered through his studies in Leipzig.[10] Carrillo's early works are in the Germanic romantic idiom in which he was trained, but in 1924 he managed a performance of what has remained his best-known work, *Preludio a [Cristobal] Colón* (which he claimed to have written in 1922). In order to accommodate a ninety-six-tone line, he used numbers from zero to ninety-five to indicate pitches, with stems to specify rhythms. Scored for flute, violin, soprano, quarter-tone guitar, harp, and octavina (a guitar-shaped Philippino instrument), the piece undulates in tiny intervals around an E (note 32, C being 0) in a kind of proto-minimalist way and has a far more lonely and haunting atmosphere than the inexpressive notation, seen in example 13.1, would lead one to imagine.

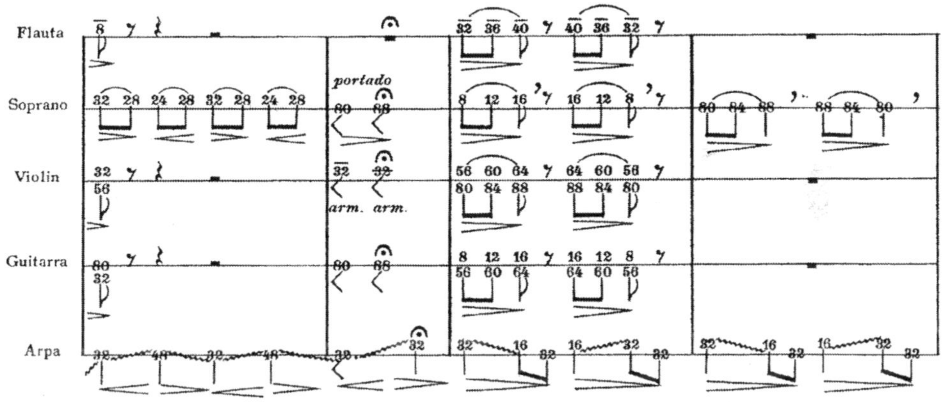

EX. 13.1: Carrillo, *Preludio a Colón*, mm. 23–26

Carrillo's rather arrogant self-promotional style hindered his career, and the bulk of his music awaits resurrection. However, in 1958 he presented a series of fifteen microtonal pianos he had built, illustrating intervals from the third tone to the sixteenth tone, at the 1958 World's Fair in Brussels and appeared with fellow microtonalists Hába, Wyschnegradsky (of whom more below), and Adriaan Fokker (1887–1972). His late string quartets employ quarter tones, and in 1962 he wrote a remarkable quarter-tone, a capella Mass a S.S. Juan XXIII, in honor of Pope John XXIII, which has been released on commercial recording.

German pianist-composer Hans Barth (1897–1956) lived in the United States from the age of ten and, under Busoni's encouragement, helped to invent a quarter-tone piano.[11] He came in contact with Charles Ives (1874–1954), who was newly arrived in the New York composition scene after a reclusive twenty-year absence. Ives, whose day job as an insurance executive had made him a rich man, helped fund Barth's quarter-tone piano project. In return, Barth rekindled Ives's interest in quarter tones, and when Ives wrote his Three Quarter-Tone Pieces (for two pianos), Barth was one of the pianists who premiered it. Nevertheless, Ives later wrote in his *Memos*, "I must say that I think Hans Barth went at the matter in the wrong way. . . . The concerts he has given and the way he has used the piano, to my way of thinking, have done more harm than good in interesting people in quarter-tones, or developing a natural sense and use for them."[12]

Ives thought quarter tones would become better accepted if grafted more gradually onto tonal principles that were already well established. In 1925 he wrote his only theoretical article, "Some 'Quarter-Tone' Impressions." With little historical knowledge at his disposal (by today's standards), he tried to reason out by what natural acoustic laws quarter tones might be worked into our music, though he also stressed that resistance to them was probably based more in habit, education, and prejudice than in acoustics. He recalls his father's experiments with quarter tones and other divisions of the octave and says, "After working for some time he became sure that some quarter-tone chords must be learned before quarter-tone melodies would make much sense."[13] Ives quite rightly, I think, posits that four-note (at least) chords are essential to quarter-tone harmony, because in a three-note chord, if two tones have a conventional interval and the other is a quarter tone, the quarter tone may seem merely out of tune, but if each note is paired with another in the same chromatic scale, more of a balance is maintained.[14] Ives then suggests five chords for use, mostly made up of pairs of fourths or fifths balanced between the normal scale and quarter tones. In order to demonstrate his chords, we will use the quarter-tone notation that has become rather standard on today's music notation software, shown in example 13.2; several earlier composers had developed their own, but this one seems superior in logic and simplicity.

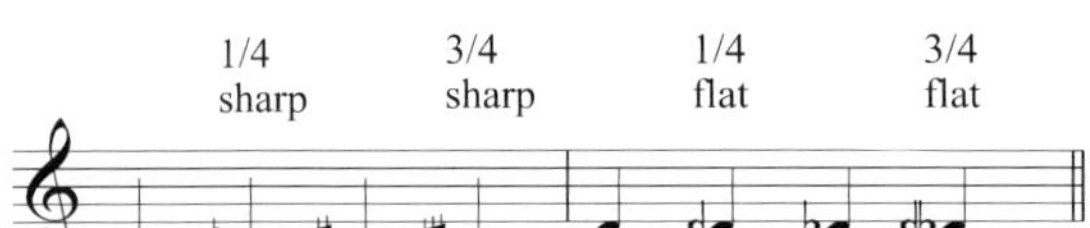

EX. 13.2: Today's quarter-tone notation

Chord A in example 13.3 is made up of two perfect fifths separated by an interval of five quarter tones. Ives writes of it, "If listened to several times in succession, it gathers a kind of character of its own—neither major, minor, nor even diminished.

. . . It gives a feeling of finality and supports reasonably well a simple quarter-tone melody."

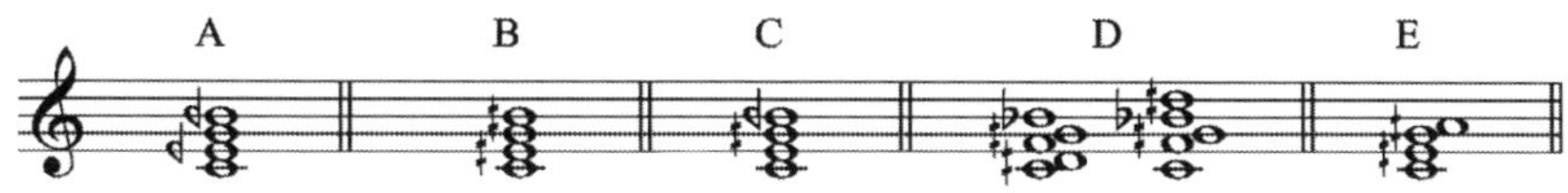

EX. 13.3: Ives's suggestions for useful quarter-tone chords

We note that chord A comes quite close to a "neutral" just-intonation seventh chord of 1/1, 11/9, 3/2, 11/6. Chord B Ives calls "stronger in itself than the one [A] we have outlined above, but the narrow interval B (quarter) with the octave makes it rather impracticable, especially in inversions." (This is close to a thirteen-limit chord 1/1, 13/10, 3/2, 39/20.) Chord C, he says, since it contains no perfect fifth, "throws the mind into a kind of diatonic expectancy which the upper intervals resist." Chord D, based on evenly divided perfect fourths (and we could compare it to 1/1, 15/13, 4/3, 20/13, 16/9), he finds "malleable" and "useful," especially if the D‡ is taken up an octave. He finally throws in a final chord, E, as a "third or subsidiary chord," "comparatively weak-sounding and therefore pliable."[15] (We could parse this as 1/1, 13/10, 4/3, 26/15, or, more simply, 1/1, 9/7, 3/2, 12/7.) We will look at Ives's use of these chords in interlude M following this chapter.

In 1927 Alois Hába published his *Neue Harmonielehre*, his *New Theory of Harmony of the Diatonic, Chromatic, the Quarter-Tone, the Third-Tone, the Sixth-Tone, and the Twelfth-Tone Systems*, which was translated into English in 1980 by Suzette Mary Battan as part of her doctoral dissertation.[16] For all of its detailed exegesis, it is really, as Battan notes, "little more than an inventory of scales and chords that contain quarter tones with little discussion of their possible harmonic or structural function in a composition."[17] A far more methodical and exhaustive, and yet more concise, theoretical work on quarter tones appeared in 1932: Ivan Wyschnegradsky's *Manuel d'harmonie á quarts de ton* (*Manual of Quarter-Tone Harmony*). Luckily, this latter was translated from the French and republished, by Noah and Rosalie Kaplan in 2017,[18] in the nick of time for my researches. Wyschnegradsky (or Vyschnegradsky, 1893–1979) was a disciple of Alexander Scriabin, who in 1916 had a mystical experience showing him his musical path. As his official website puts it, Scriabin realized that "music can tend towards cosmic consciousness only by blending into the *sound continuum*,"[19] and he began searching for ways to hear quarter, sixth, and twelfth tones. In November 1918 he bought two upright pianos, tuned one a quarter tone higher than the other, and began to compose. He eventually wrote several works for string quartet in quarter tones (First Quartet, 1923; Second, 1930–1931), many works for quarter-tone pianos and some quarter-tone works for four pianos (including a "symphony," *Ainsi parlait Zarathoustra*, in 1929–1930 and *Cosmos* ten years later), and some works for three pianos tuned a sixth tone apart (such as *Dialogue à trois*, 1973–1974). Wyschnegradsky designed the first piano tuned in quarter tones that was actually built, by the August Forster firm in Czechoslovakia in 1924.[20]

For someone with a rather mystical reputation, Wyschnegradsky's manual on quarter-tone harmony is admirably systematic and thorough, not prejudicing the student toward any particular approach. He first comes up with names for all the intervals not found in the chromatic scale (ex. 13.4).

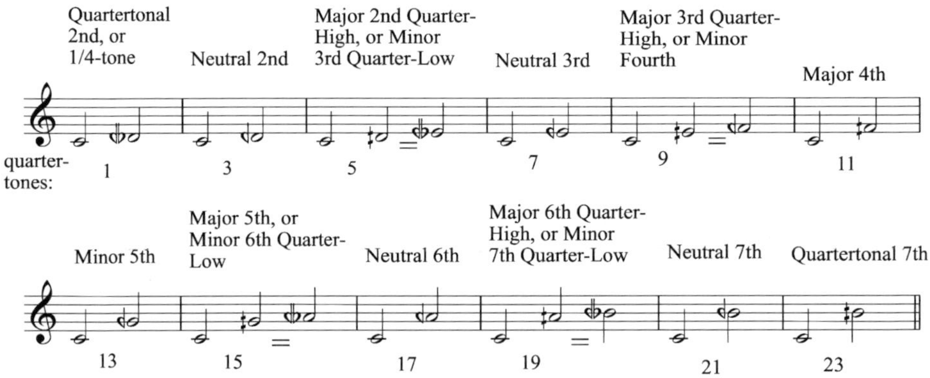

EX. 13.4: Wyschnegradsky's quarter-tone interval nomenclature

He then devises scales and harmonic cycles based on only on one interval, or replicating patterns symmetrically within an octave (ex. 13.5).

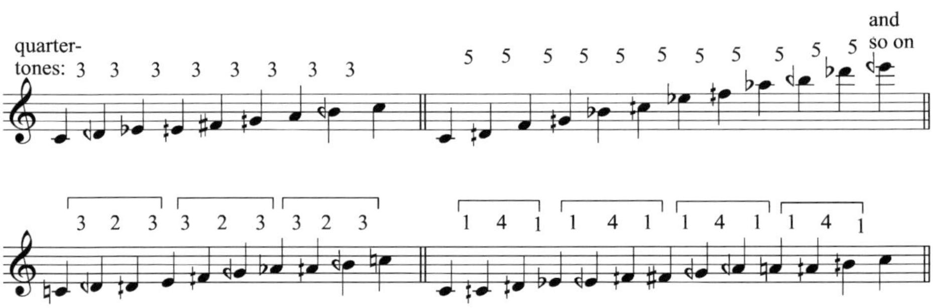

EX. 13.5: Some of Wyschnegradsky's scales

Next he provides examples of the ornamental use of quarter tones as neighbor notes, appoggiaturas, passing tones, and so on, both as single notes and parallel or contrary-motion chords. He suggests all the ways in which triads and seventh chords could be altered (ex. 13.6).

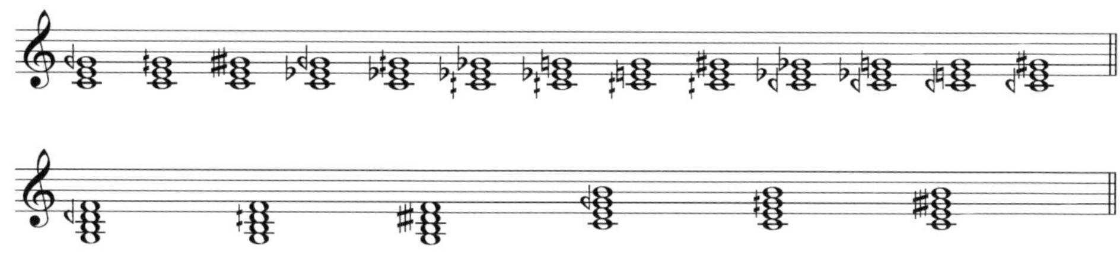

EX. 13.6: Wyschnegradsky's quarter-tone-altered triads and seventh chords

He then provides examples of triadic quarter-tone modulations in traditional voice leading (ex. 13.7).

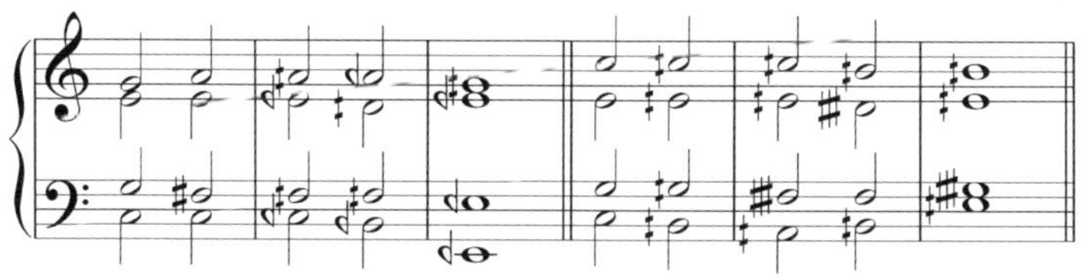

EX. 13.7: Wyschnegradsky's examples of modulating via quarter tones

Wyschnegradsky's final chapter explores free composition with quarter tones, with some composed examples, and closes with an appendix showing the acoustical derivation of quarter tones from the natural eleventh harmonic. In a way, Wyschnegradsky starts more traditionally than Ives, with conventional triads in both scales and ornamental passing tones, and proceeds to go much further afield, anticipating the kinds of limited-transposition modes in Olivier Messiaen's book *Technique de mon langage musical* of 1944. It is difficult to imagine a musical use of quarter tones that Wyschnegradsky failed to anticipate.

Other important composers in a quarter-tone idiom include Mildred Couper (1887–1974), an American although born in Buenos Aires, whose best-known pieces at this point are probably her *Xanadu* (1930) for two pianos tuned a quarter tone apart and *Dirge* for violin and piano, the latter published in Henry Cowell's *New Music Edition* in 1937;[21] and the American Tui St. George Tucker (1924–2004), who played the recorder and wrote many pieces with quarter tones for recorder ensemble.[22] In general, quarter-tone music per se (by which I mean saturated use of the 24tet scale) went out of fashion in the final third of the twentieth century, though higher divisions based on twelve, particularly 72 and 96, continue to thrive.

Hába wrote in both fifth tones (based on dividing the whole step rather than half step) and sixth tones. The fifth-tone notation used in his String Quartet No. 16 (1967) is shown in example 13.8.[23]

EX. 13.8: Hába's fifth-tone notation

Note that he reassigned his quarter-tone accidentals to do service as a fifth tone higher or lower and that F♯ is now forty cents lower than G♭, no longer enharmonic. Thirty-tone equal temperament, with its forty-cent steps, possesses the following approximations of common intervals (tridecimal intervals are particularly precise):

5/4	400¢
4/3	480¢
3/2	720¢
7/4	960¢
11/8	560¢
13/8	840¢ (pure 840.53¢)
13/9	640¢ (pure 636.62¢)
16/13	360¢ (pure 359.47¢)

The lack of a consonant perfect fifth may be found troubling, but the use of redefined quarter-tone accidentals could easily be applied to double the tuning to 60tet.

Sixth-tone tuning, or 36tet—as Busoni pointed out in 1911—provides an excellent approximation of seven-limit tuning. The interval 7/6 is almost perfect at 266.67 cents instead of 266.87, 7/4 is 966.67 cents instead of 968.83, 9/7 is 433.33 cents rather than 435.1, and so on. Hába used different notations for sixth tones in different works; example 13.9 shows his notation in the 1955 Suite for Violoncello, and example 13.10 gives that for his Suite for Bass Clarinet Solo of the same year.[24]

EX. 13.9: Hába, notation for Suite for Violoncello

EX. 13.10: Hába, notation for Suite for Bass Clarinet Solo

The methods Wyschnegradsky devised to develop quarter-tone scales and harmonies would work just as well for fifth and sixth tones. For instance, since thirty is divisible by three, a nine-note scale in fifth-tones of 3–4–3–3–4–3–3–4–3 would divide the octave in three segments transposable at the major third, while 2–1–3–2–1–3–2–1–3–2–1–3–2–1–3 would provide a fifteen-note scale with five segments transposable at an interval of 240 cents. A 36tet octave could be divided in sixth tones as 4–3–5–4–3–5–4–3–5, or 3–4–3–5–3–3–4–3–5–3, and so on. Hába, in his treatise, generated scales and chords in a third-tone scale by taking every seventh pitch, every eighth, every eleventh, every thirteenth.[25] The possibilities are vast and leave much to be explored.

Ezra Sims (1928–2015), the late and colorful grand old man of New England microtonalism, has been the leading composer in the field of 72tet composition. He and improvising saxophonist-clarinetist Joe Maneri (1927–2009), founder of the Boston Microtonal Society, have been responsible for turning Boston into a veritable hotbed of 72edo activity; it is virtually the town's official microtonal tuning. Sims contributed a notational system that has been widely adopted by his students and that (despite not being intuitively obvious) has led to more consistency of performance practice than most microtonal notations have afforded (ex. 13.11).

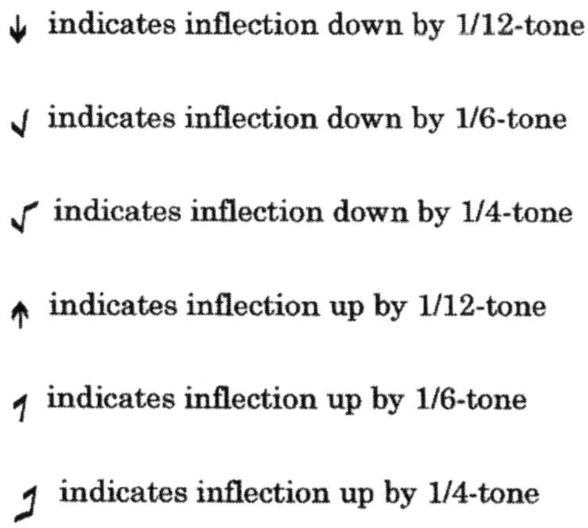

EX. 13.11: Sims's 72tet notation

Seventy-two equal steps per octave has the virtue of accommodating eleven-limit tuning quite well. It allows for quarter tones, which approximate eleven-based intervals; sixth tones, which approximate seven-based intervals; and twelfth-tones, which approximate five-based intervals and even come close to some of the thirteen-based intervals:

Ratio	72tet value	Just intonation value
13/12	133.33¢	138.57¢
12/11	150¢	150.64¢
5/4	383.33¢	386.3¢
9/7	433.33¢	435.1¢
4/3	500¢	498¢
11/8	550¢	551.3¢
13/8	833.33¢	840.5¢
12/7	933.33¢	933.13¢
14/9	766.67¢	764.9¢
7/4	966.67¢	968.9¢
15/8	1083.3¢	1088.27¢

Indeed, in the 1960s Sims gradually came to rely on an assymetrical eighteen-pitch scale (ex. 13.12, in Sims's handwriting—what appears to be 13/9 is actually 13/8) transposable throughout his 72tet gamut, which he realized had a close relationship to the harmonic series, the just values as noted.[26]

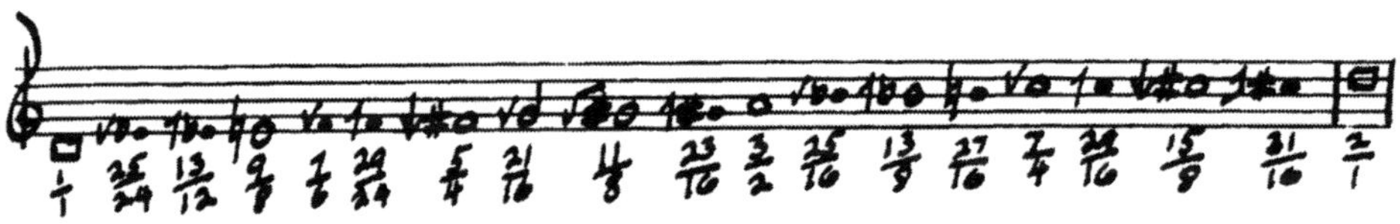

EX. 13.12: Sims's eighteen-pitch scale in 72edo

In the 72tet scale this would correspond to steps 0, 4, 8, 12, 16, 20, 23, 28, 33, 38, 42, 46, 50, 54, 58, 62, 65, 69, and 72, or to 72tet intervals of 4, 4, 4, 4, 4, 3, 5, 5, 5, 4, 4, 4, 4, 4, 3, 4, and 3. Expressed in cents that would be:

0	383.33	833.33
66.67	466.67	900
133.33	550	966.67
200	633.33	1033.33
266.67	700	1083.33
333.33	766.67	1150
		1200

Like the Regular Temperament composers (but earlier), Sims derived an unequal scale from his 72edo (though not a regular one). We will consider his Fifth String Quartet in Interlude N following this chapter.

Spectralism

Spectralism is a musical movement that began to coalesce (initially mostly in Europe) during the 1970s, first named in a 1979 article by Hugues Dufourt.[27] Inspired by electronic music and particularly new computer possibilities, composers such as Tristan Murail (b. 1947), Gerard Grisey (1946–1998), Claude Vivier (1948–1983), and others used spectrographic computer analyses of sonic phenomena as a guide for orchestrating sound complexes based in nature. Spectralism came about partly as a reaction against twelve-tone serialism, which had come to be regarded as abstract and arbitrary in its processes, something not based in nature. As a result, the spectralists found themselves approximating harmonic series, which led to an embrace of microtones. However, rather than turn to just intonation, the general practice has been to base the music on 12tet and to inflect certain pitches with quarter tones, sixth tones, and eighth tones to approximate harmonics.

Grisey's Prologue for viola solo (1976) is one of the seminal works of the movement and also the introduction to his large work *Les espaces acoustiques*. His microtonal notation for this piece involves only sharps, no flats, and uses conventional notation for quarter tones plus arrows upward and downward for eighth tones away from the other pitches; thus, 48tet (ex. 13.13).

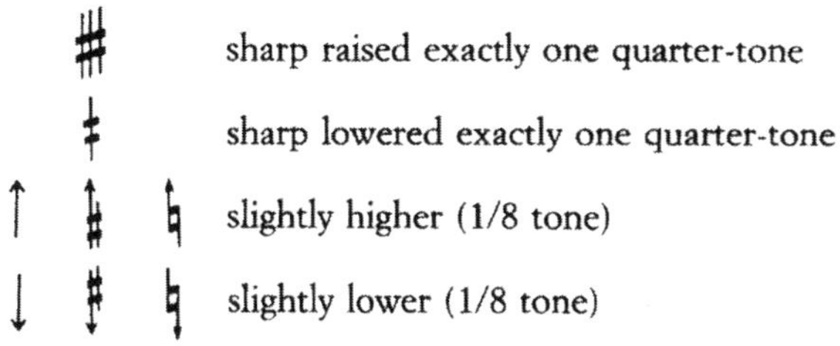

EX. 13.13: Grisey's microtonal notation

The opening pages of the piece (ex. 13.14) create gestures within a harmonic series on E, using E, B, G♯, and F♯ (thus leaving the major third in its 12tet tuning), along with D– (an eighth-tone flat, thus 975 cents as the seventh harmonic), and A and C raised a quarter tone for the eleventh (550 cents) and thirteenth (850 cents) harmonics.

EX. 13.14: Grisey, Prologue for viola solo, opening

As the piece progresses, ever higher harmonics are introduced into the phrases: D♯– quarter tone (31st, approximately 1145 cents), F– quarter tone (35th, 155 cents), C♯–, at 875 cents in place of 873.5 cents), and so on—though after a certain point in the harmonic series, every eighth tone will be an approximation of some harmonic, within 12.5 cents. At one point (ex. 13.15) the viola slides through a sequence of first, third, and eleventh harmonics descending through eighth tones, although the notation doesn't make it immediately clear that's what's happening.

EX. 13.15: Descending phrase from Grisey, Prologue for viola solo

Claude Vivier's *Lonely Child* (1980) uses quarter tones, indicated by upward and downward arrows, as part of a harmonic series–like texture moving in parallel over drones (ex. 13.16). The E↓ in the first chord might be taken as a thirteenth harmonic of G, the F↓, D↓, and G↓ in the next measure as seventh, eleventh, and thirty-first harmonics, respectively, but the quarter-tone movement in upper voices seems more pronounced than any attempt to replicate harmonic series. Yet neither is this a piece in the kind of quarter-tone language used by Hába or Wyschnegradsky, but rather one dealing with pure chord sonority.

Georg Friedrich Haas (b. 1953) has written a work, *limited approximations* (2010), for six pianos tuned a twelfth of a tone apart, for a full 72tet scale, with orchestra. At times it quite audibly builds up harmonic series among its repertoire of unusual sonorities involving tremolo piano chords. Composer Joe Monzo (b. 1962) has developed a notation for 144tet, twelve equal steps to the half step, and wrote his piece *A Noiseless Patient Spider* in 144edo.[28] I wrote in a 1999 review that it "capture[d] with startling clarity the feel of a spider moving through a geometric web of pitches."[29] The tendency to split the half step continues and will doubtless someday go even further.

EX. 13.16: Vivier, *Lonely Child*, mm. 24–30

INTERLUDE M

Some Quarter-Tone Impressions (Hába, Ives, Wyschnegradsky)

In this interlude we will examine, rather cursorily, some quarter-tone usage in works by Hába, Ives, and Wyschnegradsky.

Hába: String Quartet No. 2, Op. 7

The Czech composer Alois Hába was the leading early twentieth-century composer in quarter tone and other equal-tempered idioms of more than twelve pitches. Though some of his larger works are tuned conventionally, his *Matka* (The Mother) of 1927–1929 remains the best-known quarter-tone opera, at least before the much later ones of John Eaton (1935–2015), such as *Danton and Robespierre* (1978). Of Hába's sixteen string quartets, numbers 2 (1920), 3 (1922), 4 (1922), 6 (1950), 12 (1959–60), and 14 (1963) are in a quarter-tone system. Numbers 5 (1923), 10 (1952), and 11 (1957) are in a sixth-tone system (thirty-six pitches to the octave), and numbers 15 (1964) and 16 (1967) are in a 30tet fifth-tone system. The others are tuned conventionally. He also has music for quarter-tone piano, a Suite for quarter-tone clarinet and piano, and a quarter-tone Suite for four trombones, among many other works.

The Second Quartet, op. 7 will give us a picture of quarter-tone writing early in Hába's conception of the style. Hába's own quarter-tone notation, shown in example M.1, was different from the more common notations that have arisen since. I find it a little confusing to read, since the quarter-tone sharp and flat symbols both resemble flats: the quarter-tone sharp symbol has a V-shape to the right, the quarter-tone flat has a curve to the left, so it can be difficult to read quickly which is which, and the quarter-tone sharp too much resembles a flat. In examples M.2–4 below I renotate each passage using more modern notation as available on notation software, shown in the previous chapter (ex. 13.2).

EX. M.1: Hába's quarter-tone notation as provided in the score

The quartet is in four movements played without pause. The piece has a cyclic form in that the two main themes recur from movement to movement, and all of them are characterized by hyperchromatic quarter-tone motion interrupted by larger leaps. Although the general idiom is atonal, all four movements cadence now and again on D, sometimes with dissonant pitches such as A♯ and C♯ added to the tonic D and A. The first theme appears in the violin in measures 1–7 (ex. M.2); it enters again an octave lower in the cello at measure 14, but Hába saves the recapitulation for the end of the fourth movement (transposed down a half step) to reinforce the feel of the entire work being a single movement.

EX. M.2: Hába's String Quartet No. 2, mm. 1–7

One will notice in these opening measures that almost all movement is by contiguous quarter tones, interrupted by the occasional leap of a minor third or more. The exception is the rising scale in the cello in measure 5, which proceeds by steps of three quarter tones (eight equal steps to the octave), and we will find Hába using this scale non-thematically to provide some variety from the quarter-tone motion. In other words, Hába capitalizes on the unfamiliarity of his idiom by using quarter-tone scales with the occasional leap thematically and an 8tet scale for textural variety. Normal scales of half or whole steps are almost entirely absent here. In short, Hába uses his quarter tones structurally, not as decorative adjuncts to a 12tet system.

A rising eight-tone scale in measure 37 ushers in a second, less agitated theme in violin I (ex. M.3), which leaps downward and rises through a scale of one and a half half steps (the interval numbers in the example are expressed in terms of half steps). The accompanying lines make melodic use of this scale in parallel major or minor thirds.

EX. M.3: Hába's String Quartet No. 2, mm. 37–41

The main theme of the following scherzo is based on the notes of the opening theme (ex. M.4).

EX. M.4: Hába String Quartet No. 2, beginning of the scherzo

The Largo movement, naturally, is based on the calmer second theme, sometimes with its downward leap variably extended. The finale transforms the opening theme from 4/4 to 9/8 meter and later, as mentioned, brings the original form of the theme back to close the work. Highly unified by the transformation of two contrasting themes throughout, the work is much in the near-atonal romantic style of the early quartets of Alexander von Zemlinsky and Arnold Schoenberg, with the atmosphere intensified by the quarter tones.

Ives: Three Quarter-Tone Pieces

Charles Ives wrote only one thoroughly quarter-tone work, though he occasionally used quarter tones elsewhere, particularly in his Fourth Symphony (officially 1910–1916 but with new material added until at least 1923). The Three Quarter-Tone Pieces (1923–1924, possibly from earlier materials) were completed for a February 8, 1925, performance arranged by Hans Barth. Ives states that the first and third pieces were intended for a double-manual quarter-tone piano with one player, and the second was written for two pianos a quarter tone apart. The first, he says, "is primarily diatonic, using quarter-tones as passing tones or suspensions,"[1] but he is overly modest here, as the piece plays around with the sonority of two augmented triads, one in the chromatic scale and one in the quarter tone.

The third movement, a chorale, makes more extended use of the chords Ives theorized about in his quarter-tone article, particularly his idea of combining fifths from each scale. One sees at the beginning of example M.5 his first suggested chord, a neutral seventh with (spelling upward in quarter-tone units) 7–7-7. I have renotated the example with quarter-tone notation as though it were for one piano with quarter-tone capacity. The second chord, 7–5–9, recurs as a passing chord, and at the beginning of measure 4 it recurs as a 5–9–5 chord resolving to 7–7-7. Notice the bass harmony anchoring the chord progression in tonic, subdominant, and dominant, and, in measures 7 and 8, the melody ascending to a deliciously ambiguous neutral third.[2]

EX. M.5: Ives, Three Quarter-Tone Pieces, iii, mm. 1–8 (renotated)

At measures 16–18, Ives begins an ostinato to set up a slightly humorous melodic texture in which only the tonic G is at odds with the rest of the quarter-tone pitches (ex. M.6).

EX. M.6: Ives, Three Quarter-Tone Pieces, iii, mm. 16–18 (renotated)

In the closing *maestoso*, Ives quotes "My Country 'Tis of Thee" in a compressed and faintly humorous quarter-tone version in mostly parallel chords (ex. M.7), before ending ambiguously on the neutral third already heard at the end of example M.5.

EX. M.7: Ives, Three Quarter-Tone Pieces, iii, mm. 48–50 (renotated)

Wyschnegradsky: 24 Preludes

Some, at least, of Wyschnegradsky's music has been based on a scale he called the *chromatique diatonisée*, or diatonicized chromatic scale.[3] The scale (ex. M.8) has two segments, one consisting of five half steps, the other comprising six, the two linked at each end by quarter tones.

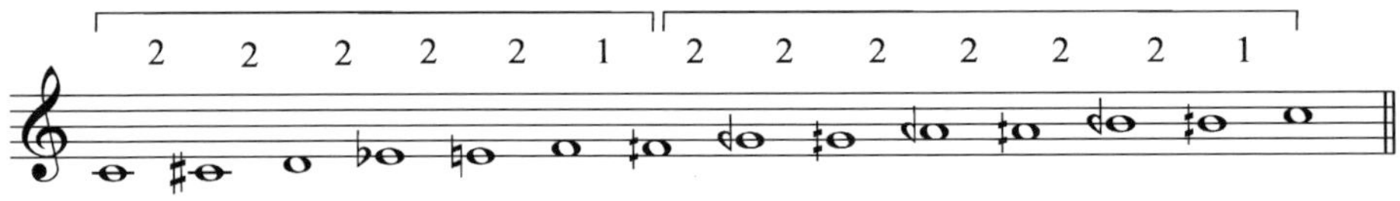

EX. M.8: Wyschnegradsky's diatonicized chromatic scale

The scale has some interesting characteristics in common with the diatonic scale. One is the striking similarity of the interval scheme in quarter tones—2222212222221—to the familiar diatonic half-step scheme of 2212221. Another is that the interval pattern replicates at the major fourth (perfect fourth plus a quarter tone, basically 11/8), so that by transposing it by that interval (eleven quarter tones cycling through the complete twenty-four) you can go through all twenty-four such scales, each transposition necessitating only one pitch change—just as the diatonic scale cycled through the circle of fifths needs only one note changed in the key signature with each move. Wyschnegradsky wrote his 24 Preludes, op. 22 (1934, revised in 1960 and 1970) to cycle through all twenty-four transpositions and added at the start of each prelude the scale transposition he was using. Apparently in the first version he used only those pitches, but in later revisions he added in some non-scale tones, mostly as passing and neighbor notes.[4]

In example M.9, for instance, we have the scale for and opening of Prelude No. 3. Notes from outside the scale are marked with an asterisk; in the first nine measures these include only three passing tones and a grace note. In example M.10, showing the opening of Prelude No. 5, non-scale notes are all passing or neighbor notes, serving to make the descending bottom line even more gradually chromatic.

EX. M.9: Wyschnegradsky, 24 Preludes, No. 3, mm. 1–9

EX. M.10: Wyschnegradsky, 24 Preludes, No. 5, mm. 1–7

Quarter-tone theorist Myles Skinner has found two seminal chords used in Wyschnegradsky's music and calls them the small tonic chord and large tonic chord, respectively (ex. M.11).[5] The small tonic chord is made by starting on the tonic and taking every third note, arriving at a "seventh chord" with a pattern of 6–5–6 in quarter-tones (or 3–2.5–3 in half steps). The large tonic chord is derived similarly, but starting on the eighth note of the scale, so that when given in root position, its upper two notes are a half step higher than those of the small tonic chord. Its interval pattern

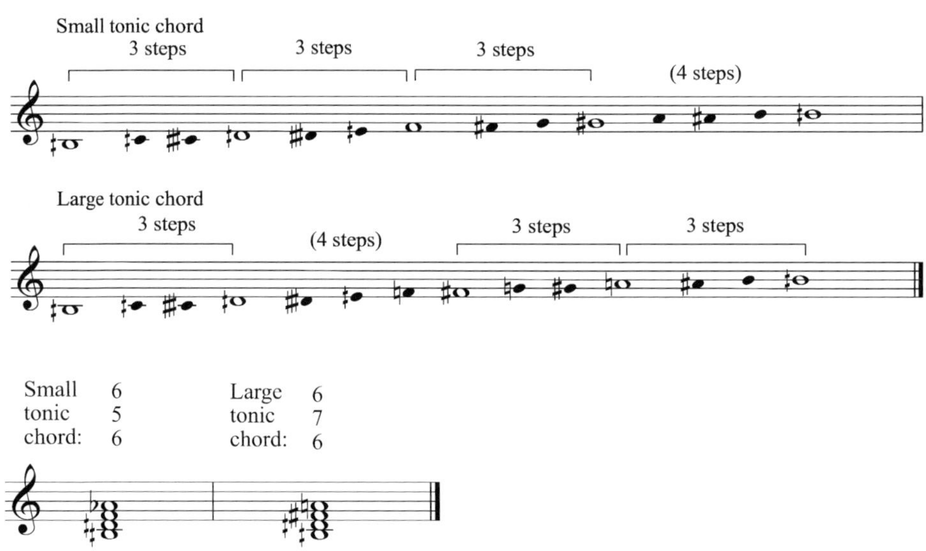

EX. M.11B: Derivation of small and large tonic chords from the diatonicized chromatic scale

in root position is 6–7–6 in quarter tones. However, if one includes the octave, the small chord pattern is 6–5–6–7, the large one is 6–7–6–5, making it clear that they have the same pitch content, only transposed. Like most of Ives's suggested chords, each of these contains two pitches in each of the chromatic scales.

Skinner points out that the tonic chord is outlined by the repeated notes, marked here by asterisks, in Prelude No. 10 (ex M.12). The sizes of the left-hand dyads in numbers of quarter tones are indicated, all quarter-tone intervals.

EX. M.12: Wyschnegradsky, 24 Preludes, No. 10, mm. 16–22

Thus we see some of the strategies that the early quarter-tone composers came up with to enter this strange new world. These same strategies can be generalized to apply to other equal temperaments, and in Interlude N we'll find an analogue to Wyschnegradsky's diatonicized chromatic scale in the 72edo music of Ezra Sims.

INTERLUDE N

Ezra Sims's String Quartet No. 5

Analysis of the large and complex output of Ezra Sims is still in a nascent state,[1] and we can do little to remedy that here. However, I would like to look at the beginning of one work, suggest a means for approaching it, and point out some relatively clear aspects that are not immediately obvious to anyone not steeped in Sims's 72edo notation. That work is his String Quartet No. 5, written in 2001 and premiered in 2003.[2] In a brief program note, Sims says of it:

> The piece proceeds with a Brahms-like development of two basic melodic ideas: one, the paired augmented fourths/diminished fifths relationship; the other, a curling motive around or within some form of a minor third. Its form derives from the deployment of these developments through a sequence of keys centering around C. . . .
>
> It concerns itself—as does all my music since around 1974—with the fact that the asymmetrical 24-note microtonal scale drawn from a 72-note chromatic scale and used at all times in some transposition or other is made up of strictly harmonic intervals. It thereby provides a sense of tonality analogous to that heard in tonal music by use of the diatonic scales.[3]

Example N.1 shows the first thirteen measures. In order to make the pitch structure clearer, I have marked each note with a number from zero to seventy-one, indicating where it falls in a seventy-two-note scale based on C. Thus C = 0, $C_\sharp$ = 6, D = 12, and so on, the other pitches and numbers falling between those.

If we begin with the first eight measures, all seventy-two pitches are not present. Instead, we have the following eighteen-note collection, which I will arrange here as in scalar order:

2 3 12 16 20 23 24 28 32 35 42 46 50 54 58 62 66 70

EX. N.1: Sims, String Quartet No. 5, mm. 1–13

EX. N.1 (CONT.): Sims, String Quartet No. 5, mm. 1–13

This is not the same eighteen-pitch scale outlined in an article by Sims quoted in chapter 13, nor is it the full twenty-four-note scale Sims mentions in the program note (though it is probably a subset of that). But it does have in common with the eighteen-note scale that most of the adjacent intervals are four of the seventy-two steps—that is, third tones, two thirds of a half step. So despite the occasional anomaly (such as the emphasized 24 in measure 3 and the 23 in measure 5), the background grid is a series of third tones, notably in multiples of four from E♭ to the sixth tone above F—12, 16, 20, 24, 28, 32—and another set offset by two from multiples of four from G to a sixth tone above C—42, 46, 50, 54, 58, 62, 66, 70, 2. This incommensurability of third tones in one section of the scale from the third tones in another (separated by a 500-cent perfect fourth, one could say) seems to indicate an influence of, or at least an analogy to, Wyschnegradsky's diatonicized chromatic scale.[4]

More important for our perception of the music, though, are the tritones that Sims mentions, which run through the texture continuously. Almost every interval larger than a minor third is some kind of tritone. I have listed them here with their scale steps and sizes (Vc = cello, Vn1 = violin 1, Va = viola):

Inst.	M.	Tone	Direction	Tone	Size in 72tet steps
Vc	1	35	up	2	39
Vn1	2	70	up	32	34
Va	3	66	up	28	34
Va	3	28	dn	62	38
Vn1	3–4	24	dn	62	34
Vn1	4	58	dn	20	38
Vc	5	28	up	62	34
Vn1	6	58	up	20	34
Vn1	7	12	up	50	38
Vn1	7	46	dn	8	38
Vn1/Vc	9	33	up	71	38
Vn1	10	66	up	30	36
Vn1	11	23	up	58	35
Vn2	11	33	up	71	38
Vc	11	61	up	23	34
Vn2	12	66	dn	32	34
Va	12	26	dn	65	33
Vn2	12	65	dn	32	33
Va	12	65	dn	26	39
Vn2	12	65	dn	32	33
Va	12	65	dn	26	39

We can see, then, that within his displaced 18tet scale (half the scale displaced a sixth tone from the other half) Sims has threaded together, throughout this opening section, a series of tritones of slightly different sizes between thirty-three and thirty-nine 72tet steps (only one of them, in measure 10, actually 600 cents), as the other strings revolve around repeated notes moving only slightly, mostly in third tones. This certainly accords with our listening experience, for this is a tightly focused work, and the tritones stand out strongly from the surrounding microtonal texture. In the subsequent section, the tritones continue in the cello, then cello and viola, then in the two violins, as the other instruments turn around tiny pitch motives.

To drive the point home, we need only cite the opening measures of the third movement (and the three movements proceed without pause), with its interlocking tritones in the violins of 35, 33, 34, and 38 steps respectively (ex. N.2).

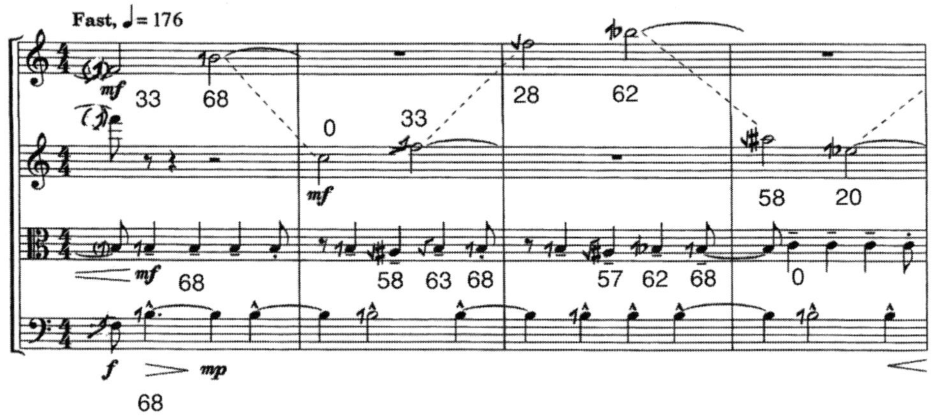

EX. N.2: Sims, String Quartet No. 5, beginning of third movement

This is not the place to attempt an analysis of the entire piece, but I hope this will serve as a quick introduction to the methods and concerns of this fascinating and not yet well-understood composer, one who has enjoyed a widespread underground influence.[5]

CHAPTER 14

A Few Numbers Drawn from Non-Western Musics

Our survey of tuning concepts outside the Euro-American world will be brief and exceedingly uncomprehensive. That I am not an ethnomusicologist is only part of the difficulty. The concept of a microtone is essentially a Western (i.e., European and American) one. For thousands of years, musical traditions of India, Indonesia, Southwest Asia, the Arabic countries, Africa, Japan, the Balkans, and other locations around the globe have used pitches unacknowledged in European music theory. The word "microtone" cannot mean for musicians in these traditions what it means for us. There is, for them, no inherent limitation to thirds and fifths, no natural limit (or minimum) to the number of intervals used. Not being keyboard-based, their musics frequently bask in fluid gradations of tone, not discrete steps. Moreover, the obsession some ethnomusicological researchers have shown with the quantitative sizes of this or that interval is far from universal, especially in recent generations. Some who specialize in these musics rebel against the American and European tendency to try to systematize pitch relationships in a rigid fashion. As ethnomusicologist John Garzoli has written, "Data from the physical sciences that is expressed in numerical terms may be difficult to square with ethnographic and musicological insights that emphasize historical, cultural, and performance factors."[1] Therefore for us to attempt to cover these traditions in more than the most cursory, descriptive fashion would result in anachronism and misrepresentation.

To even try to adequately represent even one of these traditions would require another lifetime of work, not to mention research in far lands of the earth and intensive study of unfamiliar performance practices. However, there are books that purport to include scales and tuning systems from other cultures, some of them written by musicians in those cultures, and since the student interested in our subject so far will doubtless have some curiosity about non-Western systems as well, I have provided here what entrée I can into the harmonic thinking of some selected non-Western worlds, limiting ourselves to the most authoritative sources available. It is important, after all, that the student of microtonality be apprised that the majority of the world's cultures are not limited to the same tuning concepts, interval criteria, and twelve-step scale that dominate European and American music. Consequently I offer only a rough comparative guide of four musical cultures in which the musical encounter between local and colonial projects has been well documented—India, the Arabic world, Indonesian gamelan, and Thai classical music—not to be taken as fairly representative of how those cultures understand their own music. Such information cannot be omitted from a tuning survey, nor can it be taken as gospel.

Indian Classical Tuning

Indian classical music is well known for being couched in a scale of twenty-two steps, or *srutis*, per octave. This does not mean that such music is microtonal in our sense, as though it's performed in twenty-two pitches to the octave. Rather, Indian *ragas*, which are a sort of cross between a mode and a flexible melodic pattern, each employ a subset of the scale, usually seven notes in a certain order. Each has an order in which the scale ascends and another in which it descends.

The traditional tuning of the twenty-two srutis may be more a theoretical construct than a guide to actual performance. Some recent books merely indicate the ragas with Western note names.[2] B. Chaitanya Deva, however, in his 1981 *The Music of India*,[3] gives the ratios of the srutis as in example 14.1 (and most sources that provide

Sol-fege	Ratio	Ratio from previous	Cents	5ths Series	4ths Series
Sa	1/1		0	*	*
	256/243	256/243	90.2		*
Ri	16/15	81/80	117.7	*	
	10/9	25/24	182.4		*
	9/8	81/80	203.9	*	
	32/27	256/243	294.1		*
Ga	6/5	81/80	315.6	*	
	5/4	25/24	386.3		*
	81/64	81/80	407.8	*	
	4/3	256/243	498		*
Ma	27/20	81/80	519.6	*	
	45/32	25/24	590.2		*
	729/512	81/80	611.7	*	
Pa	3/2	256/243	702	*	
	128/81	256/243	792.2		*
Dha	8/5	81/80	813.7	*	
	5/3	25/24	884.4		*
	27/16	81/80	905.9	*	
	16/9	256/243	996.1		*
Ni	9/5	81/80	1017.6	*	
	15/8	25/24	1088.3		*
	243/128	81/80	1109.8	*	
Sa	2/1	256/243	1200	*	*

Ex. 14.1: Ratios and names of the Indian srutis, as given by B. Chaitanya Deva

tunings follow this closely, with minor deviations). Steps Sa and Pa—as they are called in Indian *solfege*, the vocal syllables used to indicate steps of the scale—are the tonic and dominant and are the only diatonic scale steps that are not variable. The astute reader will note that these ratios are all within the five limit and that within each step area defined by a solfège syllable are two pairs (one major, the other minor, in our terminology) separated by a syntonic comma, 81/80. Wolfgang von Schweinitz, adapting a chart from P. Sambamurthy's *South Indian Music*,[4] gives the derivation of the entire system as devised from a series of fifths running in one direction and a series of fourths in the other:

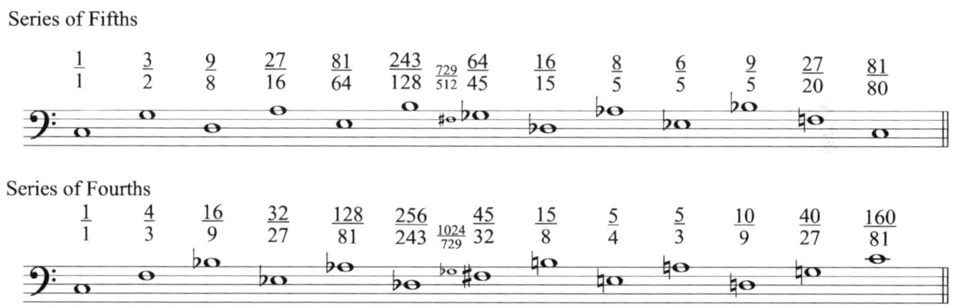

EX. 14.2: The cycles of fourths and fifths upon which Indian srutis are based, as given by von Schweinitz from Sambamurthy's *South Indian Music*

One can see that in each series, the first six notes follow Pythagorean values, and then, to prevent the numbers from getting out of hand, at the small notes a schisma of 32768/32805 (just under two cents) is elided to switch to five-limit numbers for the remainder of the scale. Twenty-five pitches are given for the completeness of the set, but, the tonic C and dominant G reigning supreme, their variants 81/80, 40/27, and 160/81 are not used.

In short, both the series of fifths and the series of fourths yield a twelve-pitch scale that is very close to Pythagorean, though with half the pitches shifted by a schisma to give five-limit values. Also, the dominant (Pa) arrived at in the series of fourths is not used, being too flat. Just as we in the West pick seven notes from our twelve to make our classic modes, Indian classical musicians pick seven out of their twelves to form a raga, though notes drawn from the series of fourths will be a syntonic comma lower or higher (depending on which part of the scale) than those from the series of fifths. Within this system the musicians have a wide range of mode variations associated with a subtle gradation of nevertheless very specific emotions. Incidentally, B. Chaitanya Deva's book documents recordings in which he measured actual performed frequencies against the theoretical system; occasionally a note would deviate by eleven or even fifteen cents, but most were considerably more accurate, providing some evidence that the system is rather closely borne out in practice, or at least used to be at the time.[5]

Chapter 14

Arabic Music

The basis of Arabic traditional music (and I will specifically draw on Egyptian sources here) is a group of modes called *maqam* (plural *maqamat*). Since the mid-eighteenth century, the pedagogy of Arabic music has acknowledged a theoretical division of the octave into twenty-four steps, basically our quarter-tone scale—except that we're dealing with 24edo, since not all potential steps are used in any mode nor are all the steps of equal size, even though they are sometimes explained as if they are. The basic scale of Arabic music (analogous to our major scale) comprises the notes C, D, F, G, and A as we tune them, but an E and B that are a quarter tone flat as in example 14.3. (I am going to continue using modern quarter-tone notation, though Arabic music, while adopting the quarter-tone sharp symbol, uses a flat sign with a slash through the stem for quarter-tone flat.)

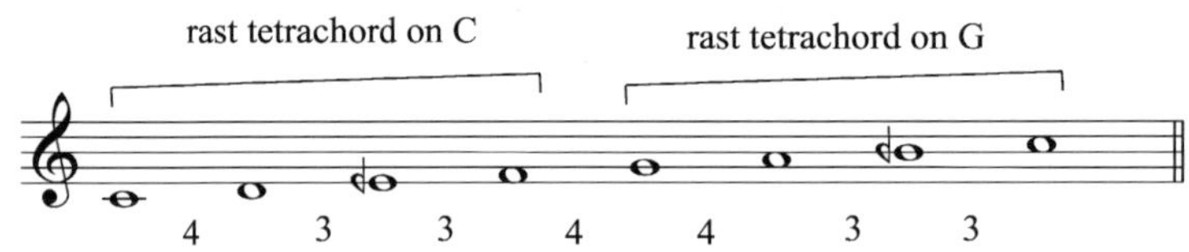

EX. 14.3: Maqam rast

The 4–3–3–4–4–3–3 pattern refers to the number of quarter tones between each two consecutive notes. Note that the tetrachord on G is a transposition of the one on C. The Arabs took over the concept of tetrachords from the ancient Greeks and reintroduced it in theory training in the 1930s.[6]

The scale in example 14.3 is called *maqam rast*, the most prominent of the maqamat, and the first one every student learns. It can be transposed to other scale degrees—the scale on G is G A B↓ C D E F↑ G. The just intonationist will be quick to point out that the E and B a quarter tone flat correspond to 11/9 and 11/6 in pure ratios, but actually it is generally understood that these pitches will be performed slightly sharper than 24edo, as much as 365 cents and 1065 cents, respectively.[7] As in any non-keyboard musical practice, intonation is assumed to be fluid and not grid-based. Accidentals outside the maqam are also common. The predominant ones in maqam rast are D-half-sharp as a neighbor note to the E-half-flat, and also an A-flat as adjunct to the G. Such notes particularly occur just before cadences.

Arabic music theory recognizes at least nine different tetrachords. The *nahawand* tetrachord, for instance, is G–A–B♭–C (found in European Dorian mode), and the *hijaz* tetrachord is G–A♭–B–C, with its augmented second (so often used as a signifier of exoticism in Western music). I give these tetrachords on G because they are sometimes used to replace the conventional upper tetrachord in maqam rast; the names of the resulting maqamat are *suzdilar* and *suznak*, respectively. Maqamat are elaborate melodic formulas, each with its own innumerable characteristics (as medieval European modes sometimes have been assumed to be). One such characteristic is whether a performer begins the maqam on the fifth or upper octave rather than the lower tonic, though such distinctions are not as carefully observed as they once were.[8] Within a composition it is customary to explore the various ranges of the maqam in a certain order, and modulations to different maqamat are expected in a piece of some length.

Some maqamat are achieved by cycling through the basic scale in the manner of medieval modes; within the rast scale above, *maqam bayyati* is the D-to-D scale (D E𝄳 F G A B𝄳 C D), *maqam sikah* the E-half-flat to E-half-flat, *maqam jaharkah* from F to F, and so on. This is only a superficial survey, but Arabic music is more systematic in its tuning theory (and has been for many centuries) than some other world traditions, and what I've presented here should be enough to acquaint the reader with the tuning background.

Indonesian Gamelan

Although they've been among the most popular subjects for world-music study for a century now, the tuning aspects of Balinese and Javanese gamelans—orchestras of mostly percussion instruments— are complicated to approach. First of all, every gamelan is tuned idiosyncratically, and no two are alike; each gamelan orchestra has its own personality, although there are generalizations we can make about the scales. Second, the metallophones (mallet percussion) of the gamelan orchestra are tuned in pairs, and the pairs are intentionally tuned differently from each other. This mistuning creates acoustical beats called *ombah*, or waves,[9] which are responsible for the shimmering and lively quality of the sound. Differences between two notes within one pair are reported to be as much as 6.3 to 9.7 Hz, and instrument builders attempt to achieve a homogenous beating rate throughout the range of the instrument, which means that in a low register the difference between "unison" notes in cents must be more than in a higher register.[10] Third, the struck plates of the metallophones do not vibrate solely at the fundamental but also with a complex spectrum of partials whose physics we are not prepared to cover here. Fourth, tuning the gamelan is an art, and the musicians do not think of it quantitatively; their tuning systems, to quote Donald Lentz, "are atheoretical and do not have their roots in ordered and demonstrable acoustic phenomena."[11] In addition, there are stark differences between Balinese and Javanese gamelan practice. Javanese music makes a greater distinction between the five-note *sléndro* scale and the seven-note *pélog* scale. Balinese music uses both terms, but the popular *Gong kebyar* style tends to use only five notes in either case.[12]

We will begin with the Balinese scale. The five notes of the scale have the names *ding, dong, deng, dung,* and *dang* (in my opinion, a marked improvement over do-re-mi).[13] The sequences ding-dong-deng and dung-dang are what we would call diatonic or chromatic steps, having intervals from 80 to 200 cents. Larger gaps of 350 to 450 cents appear between deng and dung and between dang and the upper octave of ding. Andrew Toth, who published a survey of tunings of forty-nine Balinese gamelans in 1993, distinguished between three forms of the five-note scale: *begbeg* (straight), *tirus* (narrow), and *sedeng* (moderate). Contrary to what we might associate with the names, the begbeg scale has the greatest contrast in interval sizes, with one less than a half step, and the tirus is the smoothest scale, with two whole steps in it; the sedeng is in between. Toth's article, quoted by Michael Tenzer, offers a typical layout of the three comparative scales as in example 14.4.

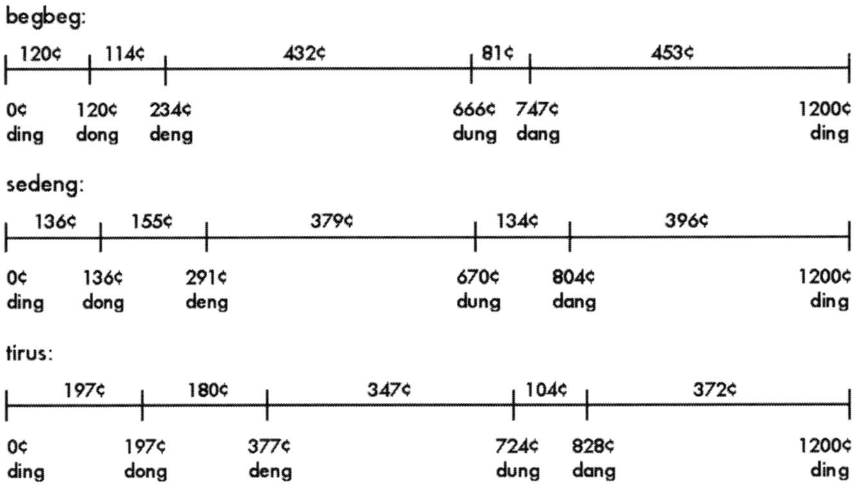

EX. 14.4: Tunings of typical begbeg, sedeng, and tirus scales as given by Toth

The Javanese five-note sléndro scale, on the other hand, has five somewhat evenly spaced pitches, with steps between 231 and 254 cents. Also, octaves are stretched in many Javanese gamelans, to as much as 1230 cents.[14] Javanese pélog scales contain seven notes, unequally spaced. Researchers W. Surjodiningrat, P. J. Sudarjana, and A. Susanto measured seventy-six (out of thousands) of the most highly esteemed gamelans in Yogyakarta and Surakarta (37 sléndro and 39 pélog) and provide cents values for what they consider the "average" Javanese sléndro and pélog tunings, shown with note names in example 14.5.[15] Their charts for the individual gamelans, however, show considerable deviation from these values and also differences among octaves within the same gamelan. Here are three of their sléndro gamelans compared, with

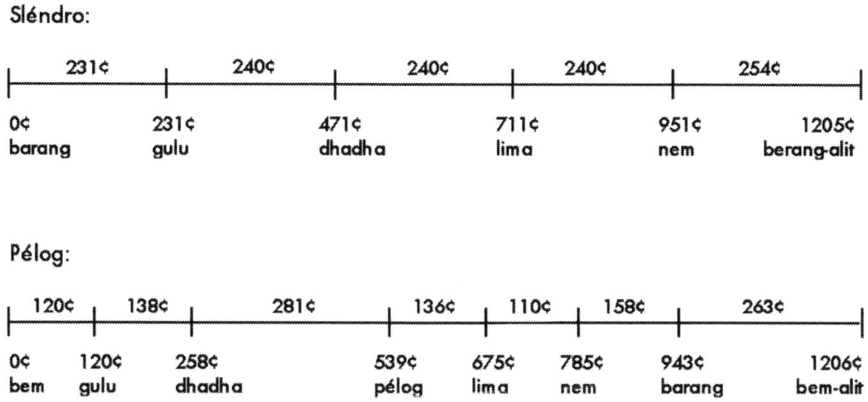

EX. 14.5: Mean tunings of Javanese gamelans as given by Surjodiningrat, Sudarjana, and Susanto

actual pitches in Hertz over three octaves, for which I have applied approximate cent values, begun again at zero for each new octave:

Gamelan Surak

Hz	135	155	176	204	235	
Cents	0	239	459	715	960	
	273	312	357	412	478	
	19	250	484	732	989	
	552	634	727	837	970	
	38	278	515	759	1014	

Gamelan Harjanagara

Hz	133	152	175	202	233	
Cents	0	231	475	724	971	
	270	306	351	404	465	
	26	243	480	724	967	
	540	620	714	822	950	1101
	26	265	509	753	1004	59

Gamelan Pusparana

Hz	137	152	170	194	223	
Cents	0	180	374	602	843	
	261	298	340	391	454	
	–84	145	374	616	874	
	522	600	686	795	910	1050
	–84	157	389	644	878	–74

Since each instrument of the gamelan orchestra may not play through the entire range, these tunings run from one instrument to another, sometimes with very minor discrepancies between instruments. One can see that the first two such gamelans have octaves stretched by 19 and 26 cents, approximately, and that the third has an initial octave smaller than 1200 cents. Next are a couple of pélog scales, with a couple of anomalies (whether in the instruments themselves or in the printing of the results) marked by asterisks:

Gamelan Kancilbelik

Hz	145	156	169	—	215	230	251
Cents	0	127	265	—	682	799	950
	294	315	342	399	434	465	508
	24	143	286	552	698	817	971
	593	638	695	802	870	934	1044
	38	165	313	561	702	825	1018
	1241	1039*	1454	1646	1770	1878	2094
	117	–190	391	606	732	834	1023

Gamelan Harjamulya

Hz	136	147	156	—	203	213	234
Cents	0	135	238	—	693	777	939
	272	293	314	316*	406	429	472
	0	129	249	260	693	789	954
	549	593	630	760	830	876	960
	16	149	254	579	731	825	983
	1124	1213	1313	1542	1691	1790	1987
	56	188	325	604	763	862	1043

One can see that the small-small-large-small-small-small-large interval pattern exists in most octaves, though with considerable variety.

As noted above, the attempt to describe gamelan tuning in terms of ratios is frowned upon by some recent ethnomusicologists, nor would it make much sense to try to apply it above. However, American composer Lou Harrison and his partner, Bill Colvig, have designed American gamelans with just intonation ratios specifically in mind. Their first gamelan, called Old Granddad, is tuned to a Ptolemaic sequence on D. Their later gamelan Si Betty is tuned to the 16th, 19th, 21st, 24th, and 28th harmonics of the same pitch for the sléndro scale and the 12th, 13th, 14th, 17th, 18th, 19th, and 21st for the pélog scale.[16] As of the 1990s there were more than two hundred gamelan ensembles in the United States, and they do not all play only traditional music.

Thai Classical Music

In 1885, at the invitation of the Siamese diplomat Prince Prisdang, Alexander Ellis made a study of Thai fixed-pitch percussion instruments and, in an appendix to his article "On the Musical Scales of Various Nations," stated that they employed a scale of seven equal steps to the octave (7tet).[17] In the decades since, this statement has been frequently challenged for its simplistic inaccuracy, and yet the idea has not been entirely put to rest even in recent years. Some of the caveats that surround the notion include the facts that tuners of Thai percussion instruments tune by ear, with little regard for theory; that (as with gamelan) instruments will differ slightly in tuning from city to city; and that singers, flutists, and string players tend to be intentionally freer with their intonation than the fixed-pitch gongs, xylophones, and metallophones can be. With all of that in mind, we can still apparently make a few generalizations about the typical scale.

Actual 7tet would yield scale steps of 171.43 cents, close to a just interval of 32/29, and there would be little acoustic basis for such a scale. Some Thai musicians believe the scale evolved in the Ayutthaya period (1350–1767), from the attempt to transpose a Chinese-style pentatonic scale onto the fourth- and fifth-scale degrees, necessitating the addition of two more pitches.[18] According to a story told by the distinguished musician Worayot Suksaichon (a former member of the celebrated Siamese Music Ensemble, known in Thai as *Ketkhong damrong sin*), a member of the Thai nobility of that era found the instruments outside his singing range and ordered that the intervals be equalized to allow the traditional melodies to be freely transposed. However far we might want to regard this origin story as merely mythical, it does point to a long history of Thai musicians thinking of their scale steps as at least "functionally rather than acoustically equidistant."[19] (We might compare this to seventeenth-century musicians calling well temperament "equal" when it really isn't.)

One of the problems with the formulation, according to ethnomusicologist John Garzoli, is that Ellis and almost everyone else assumed that the scale fit within a 2/1 octave when in fact Thai octaves (like Javanese) are a little stretched, generally somewhere around 1210 cents.[20] Garzoli republished David Morton's measurements in Hertz of a *ranat ek* (soprano xylophone) and came up with the following interval sizes:

Bar no.	Hz	Cents of interval	Cents from tonic
21	1220	182.4	1217.1
20	1098	165.3	1034.7
19	998	186.6	869.4
18	896	157.7	682.7
17	818	173.5	525.1
16	740	166.9	351.6
15	672	184.7	184.7
14	604	0	0

Measuring the gongs of a specific *khawng wong lek*, Morton arrived at the following pattern in Hertz:

Gong no.	Hz	Cents of interval	Cents from tonic
8	1224	175.5	1228.5
7	1106	184.8	1053.0
6	994	183.6	868.2
5	894	166.6	684.6
4	812	165.4	518.1
3	738	182.9	352.6
2	664	169.7	169.7
1	602	0	0

Garzoli mentions that lists of frequencies taken from other instruments deviate from the 171.43-cent theoretically equal-distance scale by as much as 40, 55 or 70 cents, but it is interesting that he nevertheless continues to use 7tet as an implied standard even while insisting that it never manifests in equal-tempered form (again, European analogues come to mind).[21] It would doubtless be overly Eurocentric to point out that the intervals of 182.4 and 165 cents in these scales come awfully close (in one case exact) to ratios of 10/9 and 11/10, with an effect comparable to Ptolemy's even diatonic scale.

Whatever anachronism and oversimplification I may have inadvertently wandered into here, at least the reader of this volume can now depart under no illusion that European tuning concepts are universal. I console myself with the thought that no musician in an Indian, Arabic, or Indonesian tradition is likely to consult this book for insight into their own theoretical culture. They have more obvious resources available, some listed in the bibliography. Nor, I hope, will any reader take away the impression that they now possess a full understanding of these complex musical practices.

Numbers, on the other hand, are eternal, and unvarying from culture to culture, from eon to eon. I have often taken comfort in the thought that, though all the music I love may someday pass into oblivion, there is no doubt that fifty million years from now, on whatever planet may then possess intelligent life, two tones vibrating at a ratio of three to two will still produce what would have sounded to us like a perfect fifth. There is a bedrock of music theory here that centuries of the accumulated accidents of musical practice cannot efface and whose explication will always continue to render the myriad accretions clearer. "Music," Gottfried Leibniz famously wrote, "is the pleasure the human mind experiences from counting without being aware that it is counting." This book will pass away, but the truth of the principles it attempts to explain will live forever.

CHAPTER 15

Brief Miscellaneous Thoughts

There is no obvious place in this book to mention the fact, but composer Lou Harrison (1917–2003) pioneered a "free style" of just intonation, in which he notated the ratio from each note to the next without regard for sustaining any constancy of pitch or scale throughout. His lovably impractical *Simfony in Free Style* of 1955 (ex. 15.1; Harrison put many of his titles in the invented Esperanto language) requires a large number of specially made flutes to handle all the pitches called for, as well as five diatonic harps that help provide reference pitches for the other instruments. As ratios multiply, the pitch wanders; for instance, the final G in the second line of example 15.1 is no longer the 1/1 G on which the piece started but now 80 cents higher at 288/275. Unsurprisingly, the piece has never been played as intended, and in 1992–1993 just-intonationist composer David Doty (b. 1950) made a computer realization of it under Harrison's direction.[1]

David First (b. 1953) makes music with long, mostly electronic drones that go in and out of tune. As I once wrote about him, "His group starts playing consonant drones that you quickly fall in tune with, then five minutes later they're playing a wildly out-of-tune cacophony, and you can't remember where the change came."[2] First's scores look even simpler and less informative than jazz charts: just whole notes with timings in minutes and seconds along with plus and minus numbers to show how many cents to bend the pitches. This drone aesthetic comes out of American minimalism, but in First's usage it is far more dramatic and mercurial than any other minimalist music. His slow slides from consonance to dissonance and back can truly raise the hair on your neck.

The music of Phill Niblock (b. 1933) uses slowly changing drones as well. Never trained as a musician, Niblock has always notated his music in frequency numbers, cycles per second. For instance, the score to his *Five More String Quartets* (recorded

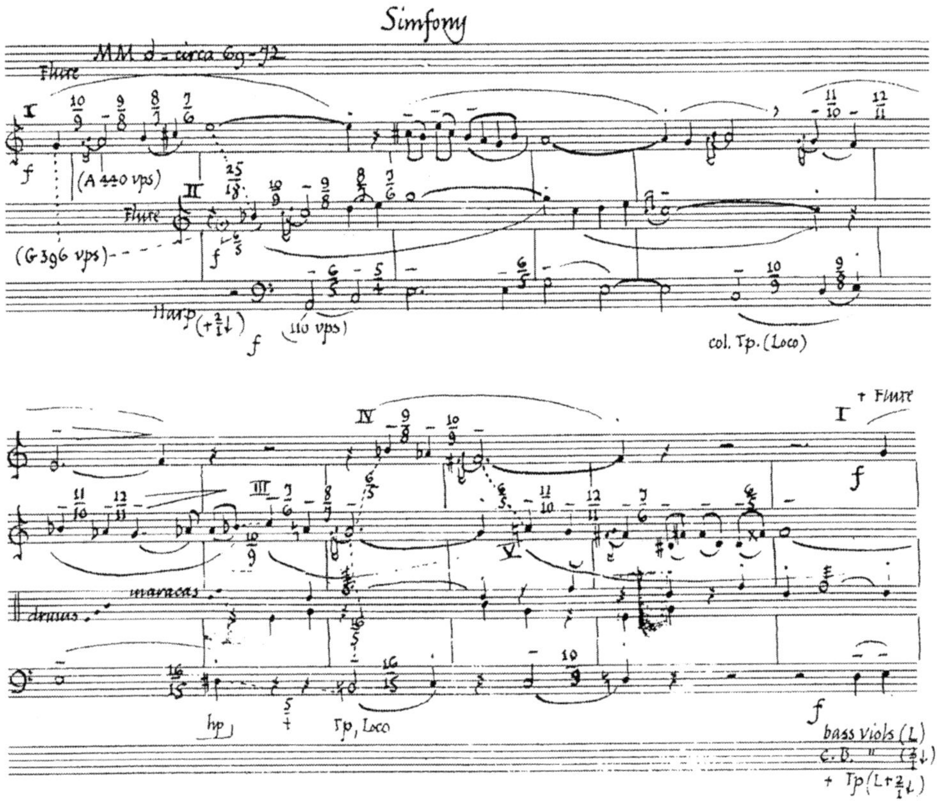

EX. 15.1: Harrison, *Simfony in Free Style*, opening

in 1993) is entirely in numbers. At the beginning the first quartet plays frequencies of 370, 298, 208, and 196 cycles per second; the second quartet, 392, 370, 196, and 92; the third, 392, 185, 208, and 98; and so on. That's 109 cents between the low cello notes, 100 cents between the first violins, and 103 cents between the violas. Over the last few minutes (of twenty-five), all strings gradually move to multiples of 98 cycles per second for a grand final consonance. As with First's, the music can move from massive dissonance to consonance and back so slowly that you can't hear it happening, though here the transformations are far more gradual. The effect can be even more unnerving with three orchestras, as in his *Three Orchids*.

Gloria Coates (b. 1938), an American composer living in Munich since 1969,[3] writes orchestral and chamber music filled with glissandos, slow slides between pitches. She wrote her first string quartet in 1960 entirely in glissandos, exasperating her composition teacher. Her Symphony No. 4, "Chiaroscuro" (1984), has slow glissandos in contrary motion in all the strings playing over, and deliciously obscuring, a quotation of Purcell's "When I Am Laid in Earth" from *Dido and Aeneas* in the winds and brass.

I once compared the effect to a band playing bravely on while the *Titanic* slowly goes down. She even has canons in glissandos. Her effects are quite remarkable.

Elizabeth Brown (b. 1953) also uses glissandos but on a more subtle level. She's a virtuoso on the Japanese *shakuhachi* flute (also the theremin), and the pitch slides in that repertoire are her inspiration. Long held notes in the strings are sometimes indicated to slowly waver up and down a quarter tone in pitch. In performance instructions, she even exhorts performers to sound "like a slightly warped 78 r.p.m. record."[4] This can happen while another instrument is quoting nursery tunes like "London Bridge Is Falling Down," with surreal results.

Once you decide that there is no reason to have only twelve pitches, there are so, so many new effects left to be explored.

Appendix

Selected Equal Temperaments in Cents

Ideal Consonances: 3/2 = 701.96 4/3 = 498.04 5/4 = 386.31 6/5 = 315.64 7/4 = 968.83 11/8 = 551.3

5	6	7	8	9	10	11	12	13	14	15	16	17	18	19
240	200	171.43	150	133.33	120	109.09	100	92.31	85.71	80	75	70.59	66.67	63.16
480	400	342.86	300	266.67	240	218.18	200	184.62	171.43	160	150	141.18	133.33	126.32
720	600	514.29	450	400	360	327.27	300	276.92	257.14	240	225	211.76	200	189.47
960	800	685.71	600	533.33	480	436.36	400	369.23	342.86	320	300	282.35	266.67	252.63
1200	1000	857.14	750	666.67	600	545.45	500	461.54	428.57	400	375	352.94	333.33	315.79
	1200	1028.57	900	800	720	654.55	600	553.85	514.29	480	450	423.53	400	378.95
		1200	1050	933.33	840	763.64	700	646.15	600	560	525	494.12	466.67	442.11
			1200	1066.67	960	872.73	800	738.46	685.71	640	600	564.71	533.33	505.26
				1200	1080	981.82	900	830.77	771.43	720	675	635.29	600	568.42
					1200	1090.91	1000	923.08	857.14	800	750	705.88	666.67	631.58
						1200	1100	1015.38	942.86	880	825	776.47	733.33	694.74
							1200	1107.69	1028.57	960	900	847.06	800	757.89
								1200	1114.29	1040	975	917.65	866.67	821.05
									1200	1120	1050	988.24	933.33	884.21
										1200	1125	1058.82	1000	947.37
											1200	1129.41	1066.67	1010.53
												1200	1133.33	1073.68
													1200	1136.84
														1200

20	21	22	23	24	25	26	27	28	29	31	32	33	34	35
60	57.14	54.55	52.17	50	48	46.15	44.44	42.86	41.38	38.71	37.5	36.36	35.29	34.29
120	114.29	109.09	104.35	100	96	92.31	88.89	85.71	82.76	77.42	75	72.73	70.59	68.57
180	171.43	163.64	156.52	150	144	138.46	133.33	128.57	124.14	116.13	112.5	109.09	105.88	102.86
240	228.57	218.18	208.70	200	192	184.62	177.78	171.43	165.52	154.84	150	145.45	141.18	137.14
300	285.71	272.73	260.87	250	240	230.77	222.22	214.29	206.9	193.55	187.5	181.82	176.47	171.43
360	342.86	327.27	313.04	300	288	276.92	266.67	257.14	248.28	232.26	225	218.18	211.76	205.71
420	400	381.82	365.22	350	336	323.08	311.11	300	289.66	270.97	262.5	254.55	247.06	240
480	457.14	436.36	417.39	400	384	369.23	355.56	342.86	331.03	309.68	300	290.91	282.35	274.29
540	514.29	490.91	469.57	450	432	415.38	400	385.71	372.41	348.39	337.5	327.27	317.65	308.57
600	571.43	545.45	521.74	500	480	461.54	444.44	428.57	413.79	387.10	375	363.64	352.94	342.86
660	628.57	600	573.91	550	528	507.69	488.89	471.43	455.17	425.81	412.5	400	388.24	377.14
720	685.71	654.55	626.09	600	576	553.85	533.33	514.29	496.55	464.52	450	436.36	423.53	411.43
780	742.86	709.09	678.26	650	624	600	577.78	557.14	537.93	503.23	487.5	472.73	458.82	445.71
840	800	763.64	730.43	700	672	646.15	622.22	600	579.31	541.94	525	509.09	494.12	480
900	857.14	818.18	782.61	750	720	692.31	666.67	642.86	620.69	580.65	562.5	545.45	529.41	514.29
960	914.29	872.73	834.78	800	768	738.46	711.11	685.71	662.07	619.35	600	581.82	564.71	548.57
1020	971.43	927.27	886.96	850	816	784.62	755.56	728.57	703.45	658.06	637.5	618.18	600	582.86
1080	1028.57	981.82	939.13	900	864	830.77	800	771.43	744.83	696.77	675	654.55	635.29	617.14
1140	1085.71	1036.36	991.30	950	912	876.92	844.44	814.29	786.21	735.48	712.5	690.91	670.59	651.43
1200	1142.86	1090.91	1043.48	1000	960	923.08	888.89	857.14	827.59	774.19	750	727.27	705.88	685.71
	1200	1145.45	1095.65	1050	1008	969.23	933.33	900	868.97	812.90	787.5	763.64	741.18	720
		1200	1147.83	1100	1056	1015.38	977.78	942.86	910.34	851.61	825	800	776.47	754.29
			1200	1150	1104	1061.54	1022.22	985.71	951.72	890.32	862.5	836.36	811.76	788.57
				1200	1152	1107.69	1066.67	1028.57	993.1	929.03	900	872.73	847.06	822.86
					1200	1153.85	1111.11	1071.43	1034.48	967.74	937.5	909.09	882.35	857.14
						1200	1155.56	1114.29	1075.86	1006.45	975	945.45	917.65	891.43
							1200	1157.14	1117.24	1045.16	1012.5	981.82	952.94	925.71
								1200	1158.62	1083.87	1050	1018.18	988.24	960
									1200	1122.58	1087.5	1054.55	1023.53	994.29
										1161.29	1123	1090.91	1058.82	1028.57
										1200	1162.5	1127.27	1094.12	1062.86
											1200	1163.64	1129.41	1097.14
												1200	1164.71	1131.43
													1200	1165.71
														1200

37		**41**		**43**		**47**		**49**		**53**	
32.43	940.54	29.27	848.78	27.91	809.3	25.53	740.43	24.49	710.2	22.64	656.60
64.86	972.97	58.54	878	55.81	837.21	51.06	765.96	48.98	734.69	45.28	679.25
97.3	1005.41	87.8	907.32	83.72	865.12	76.6	791.49	73.47	759.18	67.92	701.89
129.73	1037.83	117.07	936.58	111.63	893.02	102.13	817.02	97.96	783.67	90.57	724.53
162.16	1070.27	146.34	965.85	139.53	920.93	127.66	842.55	122.45	808.16	113.21	747.17
194.59	1102.7	175.61	995.12	167.44	948.84	153.19	868.09	146.94	832.65	135.85	769.81
227.03	1135.14	204.88	1024.39	195.35	976.74	178.72	893.62	171.43	857.14	158.49	792.45
259.46	1167.57	234.15	1053.66	223.26	1004.65	204.26	919.15	195.92	881.63	181.13	815.09
291.89	1200	263.41	1082.93	251.16	1032.56	229.79	944.68	220.41	906.12	203.77	837.74
324.32		292.68	1121.2	279.07	1060.47	255.32	970.21	244.9	930.61	226.42	860.38
356.76		321.95	1141.46	306.98	1088.37	280.85	995.74	269.39	955.1	249.06	883.02
389.19		351.22	1170.73	334.88	1116.28	306.38	1021.28	293.88	979.59	271.70	905.66
421.62		380.49	1200	362.79	1144.19	331.91	1046.81	318.37	1004.08	294.34	928.30
454.05		409.76		390.7	1172.09	357.45	1072.34	342.86	1028.57	316.98	950.94
486.49		439.02		418.6	1200	382.98	1097.87	367.35	1053.06	339.62	973.58
518.92		468.29		446.51		408.51	1123.4	391.84	1077.55	362.26	996.23
551.35		497.56		474.42		434.04	1148.94	416.33	1102.04	384.91	1018.87
583.78		526.83		502.33		459.57	1174.47	440.82	1126.53	407.55	1041.51
616.22		556.1		530.23		485.11	1200	465.31	1151.02	430.19	1064.15
648.65		585.37		558.14		510.64		489.8	1175.51	452.83	1086.79
681.08		614.63		586.05		536.17		514.29	1200	475.47	1109.43
713.51		643.9		613.95		561.7		538.78		498.11	1132.08
745.95		673.17		641.86		587.23		563.27		520.75	1154.72
778.38		702.44		669.77		612.77		587.76		543.40	1177.36
810.81		731.71		697.67		638.3		612.24		566.04	1200
843.24		760.98		725.58		663.83		636.73		588.68	
875.68		790.24		753.49		689.36		661.22		611.32	
908.11		819.51		781.4		714.9		685.71		633.96	

Anatomy of an Octave

The following is a table of more than 700 pitches within an octave. I provide this because although converting from ratios to cents is easy, doing so the other way presents a problem. When trying to find a suitable ratio for a cents quality, one can divide the number of cents by 1200/(log 2), then take ten (or whatever logarithm base) to that power, which is often possible on a calculator with a (usually secondary) 10^x key. Thus, 701.955 ÷ 3986.3137 = 0.176091259, and $10^{0.176091259}$ = 1.499999999, or 1.5, and 1.5 is obviously 3/2. Other decimal fractions will not so quickly leap to mind. There are mathematical websites that provide decimal-to-fraction converters, with varyingly close approximations, and those can be a godsend. Or, more simply, you can take the value in cents and look down this table to find what reasonably common fractions make a close fit.

The table contains all pitches that meet any one of the following six criteria:

- All ratios between whole numbers 32 and lower
- All ratios between 31-limit numbers up to 64 (31-limit meaning that the numbers contain no prime-number factors larger than 31)
- Harmonics up to 128 (each whole number divided by the closest inferior power of 2)
- All ratios between 11-limit numbers up to 128
- All ratios between 5-limit numbers up to 1024
- Certain historically important ratios such as the schisma and Pythagorean comma

Ratio	Cents	Name, if any	Found in
1/1	0.000	tonic	
32805/32768	1.954	schisma ($3^8/2^{12}$ ÷ 8/5)	
126/125	13.795		
121/120	14.367		
100/99	17.399		
99/98	17.576		
81/80	21.506	syntonic comma	HP; AD
531441/524288	23.460	Pythagorean comma ($3^{12}/2^{19}$)	
65/64	26.841	65th harmonic	
64/63	27.264		
63/62	27.700		
58/57	30.109		
57/56	30.642		
56/55	31.194	Ptolemy's enharmonic	
55/54	31.767		
52/51	33.617		
51/50	34.283		

Ratio	Cents	Name, if any	Found in
50/49	34.976		
49/48	35.697		
46/45	38.051	inferior quarter tone	
45/44	38.906		
128/125	41.059	diminished second (16/15 × 24/25)	AD
525/512	43.408	enharmonic diesis: Avicenna	
40/39	43.831		
39/38	44.970	superior quarter tone: Eratosthenes	
77/75	45.561		
36/35	48.770	superior quarter tone: Archytas	
250/243	49.166		
35/34	50.184	ET quarter-tone approximation	
34/33	51.682		
33/32	53.273	33rd harmonic	HP
32/31	54.964	inferior quarter tone: Didymus	
125/121	56.305		
31/30	56.767	superior quarter tone: Didymus	
30/29	58.692		
29/28	60.751		
57/55	61.836		
28/27	62.961	inferior quarter tone: Archytas	
80/77	66.170		
27/26	65.337		
26/25	67.900	1/3 tone, Avicenna	
51/49	69.259		
126/121	70.100		
25/24	70.672	minor 5-limit half step	AD
24/23	73.681		
117/112	75.612		
23/22	76.956		
67/64	79.307	67th harmonic	
22/21	80.537	hard half step: Ptolemy, Avicenna	
21/20	84.467		HP
81/77	87.676		
20/19	88.801		
256/243	90.225	Pythagorean half step	AD
58/55	91.946		
135/128	92.179	limma ascendant	
96/91	92.601		
19/18	93.603		
55/52	97.104		
128/121	97.364		
18/17	98.955	superparticular ET half-step approximation	

Ratio	Cents	Name, if any	Found in
$2^{1/12}$	100.000	equal-tempered half step	
89/84	100.099	more accurate ET half-step approximation	
35/33	101.867		
52/49	102.876		
86/81	103.698		
17/16	104.955	overtone half step	
33/31	108.237		
49/46	109.377		
16/15	111.731	major 5-limit half step	HP, AD
31/29	115.458		
77/72	116.234		
15/14	119.443	Cowell just half step: NMR	
29/27	123.712		
14/13	128.298		
69/64	130.229	69th harmonic	
55/51	130.721		
27/25	133.238	alternate Renaissance half step	AD
121/112	133.810		
13/12	138.573	3/4 tone: Avicenna	
64/59	140.828		
38/35	142.373		
63/58	143.159		
88/81	143.498		
25/23	144.353		
62/57	145.568		
135/124	147.143		(AD)
49/45	147.428		
12/11	150.637	undecimal "median" half step	HP
59/54	153.307		
35/32	155.140	35th harmonic	
23/21	157.493		
57/52	158.940		
34/31	159.920		
800/729	160.897		AD
56/51	161.915		
11/10	165.004		HP
54/49	168.213		
32/29	170.423		
21/19	173.268		
31/28	176.210		
567/512	176.646		WTP
51/46	178.636		
71/64	179.697	71st harmonic	

Ratio	Cents	Name, if any	Found in
10/9	182.404	minor whole tone	HP; AD
49/44	186.334		
39/35	187.343		
29/26	189.050		
125/112	190.115		
48/43	190.437		
19/17	192.558		
160/143	194.468		
28/25	196.198		
121/108	196.771		
55/49	199.980		
$2^{1/6}$	200.000	equal-tempered whole tone	
64/57	200.532		
9/8	203.910	major whole tone	HP; WTP; AD
62/55	207.404		
44/39	208.835		
35/31	210.104		
26/23	212.253		
112/99	213.598		
17/15	216.687		
25/22	221.309		
58/51	222.667		
256/225	223.463		AD
33/29	223.696		
729/640	225.416		
57/50	226.841		
73/64	227.789	73rd harmonic	
8/7	231.174	septimal whole tone	HP
63/55	235.104		
55/48	235.677		
39/34	237.527		
225/196	238.886		
31/27	239.171		
147/128	239.607		WTP
169/147	241.449		
23/20	241.961		
2187/1900	243.545		AD
38/33	244.240		
144/125	244.969	diminished third (6/5 × 24/25)	
121/105	245.541		
15/13	247.741		
52/45	250.304		
37/32	251.344	37th harmonic	

Ratio	Cents	Name, if any	Found in
81/70	252.680		
125/108	253.076		
22/19	253.805		
51/44	255.592		
196/169	256.596		
29/25	256.950		
36/31	258.874		
93/80	260.677		(AD)
57/49	261.816		
64/55	262.368		
7/6	266.871	septimal minor third	HP
90/77	270.080		
75/64	274.582	augmented second (9/8 × 25/24)	AD
34/29	275.378		
88/75	276.736		
27/23	277.591		
20/17	281.358		
33/28	284.447		
46/39	285.792		
13/11	289.210		
58/49	291.925		
45/38	292.711		
32/27	294.135	Pythagorean minor third	HP; AD
19/16	297.513	overtone minor third	
$2^{1/4}$	300.000	equal-tempered minor third	
25/21	301.847		
31/26	304.508		
105/88	305.777		
55/46	309.357		
6/5	315.641	5-limit minor third	HP; AD
77/64	320.144	77th harmonic	
35/29	325.562		
29/24	327.622		
75/62	329.547		(AD)
98/81	329.832		
121/100	330.008		
23/19	330.761		
63/52	332.208		
40/33	333.041		
17/14	336.130		
243/200	337.148		
62/51	338.125		
28/23	340.552		

Ratio	Cents	Name, if any	Found in
39/32	342.483	39th harmonic	
128/105	342.905		
8000/6561	343.301		AD
11/9	347.408	undecimal “median” third	HP
60/49	350.617		
49/40	351.338		
38/31	352.477		
27/22	354.547		
16/13	359.472		
79/64	364.537	79th harmonic	
100/81	364.807		AD
121/98	364.984		
21/17	365.825		
99/80	368.914		
26/21	369.747		
57/46	371.194		
31/25	372.408		
36/29	374.333		
56/45	378.602		
96/77	381.811		
8192/6561	384.360	Pythagorean “schismatic” third	
5/4	386.314	5-limit major third	HP; AD
64/51	393.090		
49/39	395.169		
44/35	396.178		
39/31	397.447		
34/27	399.090		
$2^{1/3}$	400.000	equal-tempered major third	
63/50	400.108		
121/96	400.681		
29/23	401.303		
125/99	403.713		
24/19	404.442		
512/405	405.866		
62/49	407.384		
81/64	407.820	Pythagorean major third	AD
19/15	409.244		
33/26	412.745		
80/63	413.578		
14/11	417.508		HP
51/40	420.597		
125/98	421.289		
23/18	424.364		

Ratio	Cents	Name, if any	Found in
32/25	427.373	diminished fourth (4/3 × 24/25)	AD
41/32	429.062	41st harmonic	
50/39	430.145		
77/60	431.875		
9/7	435.084	septimal major third	HP
58/45	439.353		
49/38	440.139		
40/31	441.278		
31/24	443.081		(AD)
1323/1024	443.517		WTP
128/99	444.772		
22/17	446.363		
57/44	448.150		
162/125	448.879		
35/27	449.275		
83/64	450.047	83rd harmonic	
100/77	452.484		
13/10	454.214		
125/96	456.986	augmented third (5/4 × 25/24)	AD
30/23	459.994		
64/49	462.348		
98/75	463.069		
17/13	464.428		
72/55	466.278		
55/42	466.851		
38/29	467.936		
21/16	470.781	septimal fourth	HP; WTP
46/35	473.135		
25/19	475.114		
320/243	476.539		AD
29/22	478.259		
675/512	478.492		
33/25	480.646		
45/34	485.286		
85/64	491.269	85th harmonic	
4/3	498.045	perfect fourth	HP; AD
$2^{5/12}$	500.000	equal-tempered perfect fourth	
75/56	505.757		
51/38	509.397		
43/32	511.518	43rd harmonic	
121/90	512.412		
39/29	512.905		
35/26	514.612		

Ratio	Cents	Name, if any	Found in
66/49	515.621		
31/23	516.761		
27/20	519.551		HP; AD
23/17	523.319		
42/31	525.745		
19/14	528.687		
110/81	529.812		
87/64	531.532	87th harmonic	
34/25	532.328		
49/36	533.742		
15/11	536.951		
512/375	539.104		AD
26/19	543.015		
63/46	544.462		
48/35	546.815		
1000/729	547.211		
11/8	551.318	undecimal tritone (11th harmonic)	HP
62/45	554.812		(AD)
40/29	556.737		
29/21	558.796		
112/81	561.006		
18/13	563.382		
25/18	568.717	augmented fourth (4/3 × 25/24)	AD
89/64	570.880	89th harmonic	
32/23	571.726		
39/28	573.657		
46/33	575.001		
88/63	578.582		
7/5	582.512	septimal tritone	HP
108/77	585.721		
1024/729	588.270	low Pythagorean tritone	
45/32	590.224	high 5-limit tritone	AD
38/27	591.648		
31/22	593.718		
55/39	595.149		
24/17	597.000		
$\sqrt{2}$	600.000	equal-tempered tritone	
99/70	600.088		
17/12	603.000		
44/31	606.282		
125/88	607.623		
27/19	608.352		
91/64	609.354	91st harmonic	

Ratio	Cents	Name, if any	Found in
64/45	609.776	low 5-limit tritone	AD
729/512	611.730	high Pythagorean tritone	
57/40	613.154		
77/54	614.279		
10/7	617.488	septimal tritone	HP
63/44	621.418		
33/23	624.999		
56/39	626.343		
23/16	628.274	23rd harmonic	
36/25	631.283	diminished fifth (3/2 × 24/25)	AD
121/84	631.855		
49/34	632.696		
13/9	636.618		
81/56	638.994		
55/38	640.119		
42/29	641.204		
29/20	643.263		
45/31	645.188		(AD)
93/64	646.991	93rd harmonic	
16/11	648.682		HP
51/35	651.771		
729/500	652.789		
35/24	653.185		
19/13	656.985		
375/256	660.896		AD
22/15	663.049		
47/32	665.507	47th harmonic	
72/49	666.258		
25/17	667.672		
81/55	670.188		
28/19	671.313		
31/21	674.255		
189/128	674.691		WTP
34/23	676.681		
40/27	680.449	dissonant “wolf” 5-limit fifth	HP; AD
46/31	683.239		
95/64	683.827	95th harmonic	
49/33	684.379		
52/35	685.388		
58/39	687.095		
125/84	688.160		
112/75	694.243		
121/81	694.816		

Ratio	Cents	Name, if any	Found in
$2^{7/12}$	700.000	equal-tempered perfect fifth	
3/2	701.955	perfect fifth	HP; WTP; AD
121/80	716.322		
50/33	719.354		
97/64	719.895	97th harmonic	
1024/675	721.508		
44/29	721.741		
243/160	723.461		AD
38/25	724.886		
35/23	726.865		
32/21	729.219		HP
29/19	732.064		
84/55	733.149		
55/36	733.722		
26/17	735.572		
75/49	736.931		
49/32	737.652	49th harmonic	WTP
23/15	740.006		
192/125	743.014	diminished sixth (8/5 × 24/25)	AD
20/13	745.786		
77/50	747.516		
54/35	750.725		
125/81	751.121		
17/11	753.637		
99/64	755.228	99th harmonic	
48/31	756.919		
31/20	758.722		(AD)
45/29	760.647		
14/9	764.916	septimal minor sixth	HP
120/77	768.125		
39/25	769.855		
25/16	772.627	augmented fifth	AD
36/23	775.636		
11/7	782.492	undecimal minor sixth	HP; Saf
63/40	786.422		
52/33	787.255		
101/64	789.854	101st harmonic	
30/19	790.756		
128/81	792.180	Pythagorean minor sixth	AD
49/31	792.616		Saf
405/256	794.134		
19/12	795.558		
46/29	798.697		

Ratio	Cents	Name, if any	Found in
100/63	799.892		
$2^{2/3}$	800.000	equal-tempered minor sixth	
27/17	800.910		
62/39	802.553		
35/22	803.822		
51/32	806.910	51st harmonic	
8/5	813.686	5-limit minor sixth	HP; AD
6561/4096	815.640	Pythagorean "schismatic" sixth	Saf
77/48	818.189		
45/28	821.398		
103/64	823.801	103rd harmonic	
29/18	825.667		
50/31	827.592		(AD)
121/75	828.053		
21/13	830.253		
55/34	832.676		
34/21	834.175		
81/50	835.193		AD
125/77	838.797		
13/8	840.528	overtone sixth	
57/35	844.328		
44/27	845.453		
31/19	847.523		
80/49	848.662		
49/30	849.383		
18/11	852.592	undecimal "median" sixth	HP
105/64	857.095	105th harmonic	
64/39	857.517		
23/14	859.448		
51/31	861.875		
400/243	862.852		AD
28/17	863.870		
33/20	866.959		
38/23	869.239		
81/49	870.168		
48/29	872.378		
53/32	873.505	53rd harmonic	
58/35	874.438		
63/38	875.223		
128/77	879.856		
107/64	889.760	107th harmonic	
5/3	884.359	5-limit major sixth	HP; AD
57/34	894.513		

Ratio	Cents	Name, if any	Found in
52/31	895.492		
42/25	898.153		
121/72	898.726		
$2^{3/4}$	900.000	equal-tempered major sixth	
32/19	902.487		
27/16	905.865	Pythagorean major sixth	HP; AD
49/29	908.075		
22/13	910.790		
39/23	914.208		
56/33	915.553		
17/10	918.642		
109/64	921.821	109th harmonic	
46/27	922.409		
75/44	923.264		
29/17	924.622		
128/75	925.418	diminished seventh (16/9 × 24/25)	AD
77/45	929.920		
12/7	933.129	septimal major sixth	HP
55/32	937.632	55th harmonic	
31/18	941.126		(AD)
441/256	941.562		WTP
50/29	943.050		
19/11	946.195		
216/125	946.924		
121/70	947.496		
45/26	949.696		
26/15	952.259		
111/64	953.299	111th harmonic	
125/72	955.031	augmented sixth (5/3 × 25/24)	AD
33/19	955.760		
40/23	958.039		
54/31	960.829		
96/55	964.323		
110/63	964.896		
7/4	968.826	septimal minor seventh	HP; WTP
58/33	976.304		
225/128	976.537		AD
51/29	977.333		
44/25	978.691		
30/17	983.313		
113/64	984.215	113th harmonic	
99/56	986.402		
23/13	987.747		

Ratio	Cents	Name, if any	Found in
62/35	989.896		
39/22	991.165		
55/31	992.596		
16/9	996.090	Pythagorean small min. seventh	HP; AD
57/32	999.468	57th harmonic	
$2^{5/6}$	1000.000	equal-tempered minor seventh	
98/55	1000.020		
25/14	1003.802		
34/19	1007.442		
52/29	1010.950		
88/49	1013.666		
115/64	1014.588	115th harmonic	
9/5	1017.596	5-limit large minor seventh	HP; AD
56/31	1023.790		
38/21	1026.732		
29/16	1029.577	29th harmonic	(AD)
49/27	1031.787		
20/11	1034.996		HP
51/28	1038.085		
729/400	1039.103		
31/17	1040.080		
42/23	1042.507		
117/64	1044.438	117th harmonic	
64/35	1044.860		
4000/2187	1045.256		AD
11/6	1049.363	undecimal "median" seventh	HP
90/49	1052.572		
57/31	1054.432		
46/25	1055.647		
81/44	1056.502		
35/19	1057.627		
59/32	1059.172	59th harmonic	
24/13	1061.427		
50/27	1066.762		AD
63/34	1067.780		
13/7	1071.702		
119/64	1073.781	119th harmonic	
54/29	1076.288		
28/15	1080.557		
58/31	1084.542		
15/8	1088.269	5-limit major seventh	HP; AD
62/33	1091.763		
32/17	1095.045		

Ratio	Cents	Name, if any	Found in
49/26	1097.124		
66/35	1098.133		
$2^{11/12}$	1100.000	equal-tempered major seventh	
17/9	1101.045		
121/64	1102.636	121st harmonic	
125/66	1105.668		
36/19	1106.397		
256/135	1107.821		
55/29	1108.054		
243/128	1109.775	Pythagorean major seventh	AD
19/10	1111.199		
40/21	1115.533		HP
61/32	1116.885	61st harmonic	
21/11	1119.463		
44/23	1123.044		
23/12	1126.319		
48/25	1129.328		AD
121/63	1129.900		
123/64	1131.017	123rd harmonic	
25/13	1132.100		
77/40	1133.830		
52/27	1134.663		
27/14	1137.039	septimal major seventh	WTP
56/29	1139.249		
29/15	1141.308		
60/31	1143.233		(AD)
31/16	1145.036	31st harmonic	
64/33	1146.727		HP
33/17	1148.318		
243/125	1150.834		
35/18	1151.230		
39/20	1156.169		
125/64	1158.941	augmented seventh (15/8 × 25/24)	AD
88/45	1161.094		
45/23	1161.949		
96/49	1164.303		
49/25	1165.024		
51/26	1166.383		
108/55	1168.233		
55/28	1168.806		
57/29	1169.891		
63/32	1172.736	63rd harmonic	WTP

Ratio	Cents	Name, if any	Found in
160/81	1178.494		HP; AD
99/50	1182.601		
125/63	1186.205		
127/64	1186.422	127th harmonic	
2/1	1200.000	octave	

HP = Harry Partch's 43-tone scale
AD = Alain Daniélou's 53-tone scale (65, including ratios in parentheses)
WTP = La Monte Young's *The Well-Tuned Piano*
HNA = Terry Riley's *The Harp of New Albion*
NMR = Henry Cowell's *New Musical Resources*

Conventional Frequencies of Equal Temperament Tuned to A 440

Because it is sometimes helpful in calculating microtonal pitches to be able to compare them with the pitches available on the modern piano, I supply here a list of frequencies, through five octaves, in cycles per second (or Hertz) of the pitches we are used to in an equal-tempered scale as tuned to A 440. For higher octaves, multiply the frequencies in the right-hand column by two or four; for lower frequencies, divide the left-hand column by two or four. For reference, middle C is 261.626 cycles per second (marked with an asterisk).

G♯	103.826	207.652	415.305	830.609	1661.219
G	97.999	195.998	391.995	783.991	1567.982
F♯	92.499	184.997	369.994	739.989	1479.978
F	87.307	174.614	349.228	698.456	1396.913
E	82.407	164.814	329.628	659.255	1318.51
E♭	77.782	155.563	311.127	622.254	1244.508
D	73.416	146.832	293.665	587.33	1174.659
C♯	69.296	138.591	277.183	554.365	1108.731
C	65.406	130.813	261.626*	523.251	1046.502
B	61.735	123.471	246.942	493.883	987.767
B♭	58.27	116.541	233.082	466.164	932.328
A	55	110	220	440	880

NOTES

CHAPTER 1. THE COSMIC JOKE

1. See Alexander Ellis, "On the Calculation of Cents from Interval Ratios," in Hermann Helmholtz, *On the Sensations of Tone* (New York: Dover Publications, 1954), 446–57.
2. Kyle Gann, "Anatomy of an Octave," http://www.kylegann.com/Octave.html.

CHAPTER 2. THE HARMONIC SCALE

1. A *sine tone*, produced electronically, is a pitch heard without any harmonics. Acoustically produced pitches almost always have at least a few harmonics.
2. Marin Mersenne, *Harmonie Universelle*, Paris, Cramoisy, "Traitez des instruments à chords," 210; quoted in Thomas Christiansen, *Rameau and Musical Thought in the Enlightenment* (Cambridge, UK: Cambridge University Press, 2004), 136.
3. Ibid.
4. John Wallis, *Philosophical Transactions XII* (April 1677), cited in Stephen Toulmin, Douglas Bush, James S. Ackerman, and Claude V. Palisca, *Seventeenth-Century Science and the Arts* (Princeton, NJ: Princeton University Press, 1961), 99.

CHAPTER 3. GENERATING SCALES

1. Iamblichus, *The Life of Pythagoras*, trans. Kenneth Sylvan Guthrie, in *The Pythagorean Sourcebook and Library* (Grand Rapids, MI: Phanes Press, 1987), 86.
2. Kenneth Sylvan Guthrie, *The Pythagorean Sourcebook and Library* (Grand Rapids, MI: Phanes Press, 1987), p. 24.
3. Claude V. Palisca, *Humanism in Italian Renaissance Musical Thought* (New Haven, CT: Yale University Press, 1985), 275.
4. Dr. Crotch, "On the Derivation of the Scale, Tuning, Temperament, the Monochord, etc.," *Musical Times*, October 1, 1861.
5. Palisca, *Humanism*, 48–49.
6. Annie Bélis, "Aristoxenus," *Grove Music Online*, http://www.oxfordmusiconline.com/subscriber/article/grove/music/01248.

7. To quote Curt Sachs: "Words like *harmonia, eidos, tonos, tropos, sýstema* were anything but clean-cut and are misleading rather than helpful. As a consequence, the historiography of Greek and Roman music has been particularly exposed to misinterpretation." Curt Sachs, *The Rise of Music in the Ancient World East and West* (New York: W. W. Norton, 1943), 201.

8. Palisca, *Humanism*, 49.

9. See also Curt Sachs, *Rise of Music*, 211.

10. Palisca, *Humanism*, 106; also Warren Anderson and Thomas J. Mathiesen, "Olympus the Mysian," *Grove Music Online*, http://www.oxfordmusiconline.com/grovemusic/view/10.1093/gmo/9781561592630.001.0001/omo-9781561592630-e-0000020337; John Chalmers, *Divisions of the Tetrachord* (Hanover, NH: Frog Peak Music, 1993), 10.

11. Chalmers, *Divisions of the Tetrachord*, 6.

12. Andrew Barker, *Greek Musical Writings: II: Harmonic and Acoustic Theory* (Cambridge, UK: Cambridge University Press, 1989), 271.

13. Actually, what I do is measure the length of the string, draw a line half that length on a piece of paper, divide it into sixty parts with little perpendicular lines as a visual fretboard, and then tape it to the body of the instrument.

14. Sachs, *Rise of Music*, 223. I have seen, in the Metropolitan Museum, an ancient Greek harp shaped in such a way that one could only hold it on his shoulder so that the longest strings were on top.

15. Quoted in Barker, *Greek Musical Writings II*, 311.

16. Ibid., 350 n127.

17. János Kárpáti, "Myth and Reality in the Theory of Chinese Tonal System," *Studia Musicologica Academiae Scientiarum Hungaricae*, T. 22, Fasc. 1/4 (1980), 7; Ernest G. McClain and Ming Shui Hung, "Chinese Cyclic Tunings in Late Antiquity," *Ethnomusicology* 23, no. 2 (1979): 206, 213.

18. See David B. Doty, *The Just Intonation Primer: An Introduction to the Theory and Practice of Just Intonation* (San Francisco: Just Intonation Network, 1993), 49.

19. See, for instance, Llewellyn S. Lloyd and Hugh Boyle, *Intervals, Scales, and Temperaments* (New York: St. Martin's Press, 1978), 53; see also Joe Monzo, "Diesis," http://www.tonalsoft.com/enc/d/diesis.aspx.

20. Another writer who relies on the arithmetic and harmonic means is Nicomachus the Pythagorean (c. 60–120 CE) in his *Manual of Harmonics*, trans. Flora R. Levin (Grand Rapids, MI: Phanes Press, 1994), 107.

Interlude A. Ptolemy and Ancient Greek "Parts"

1. Wilfrid Perrett, "The Heritage of Greece in Music," *Proceedings of the Musical Association* 58 (1931–1932): 85.

2. André Barbera, "Archytas of Tarentum," *Grove Music Online*, http://www.oxfordmusiconline.com/subscriber/article/grove/music/01183.

3. Stefan Hagel, *Ancient Greek Music: A New Technical History* (Cambridge, UK: Cambridge University Press, 2009), 152.

4. Annie Bélis, "Aristoxenus," *Grove Music Online*, http://www.oxfordmusiconline.com/subscriber/article/grove/music/01248.

5. "Eratosthenes," in *Encyclopaedia Britannica*, https://www.britannica.com/biography/Eratosthenes.

6. Lukas Richter, "Eratosthenes," *Grove Music Online*, http://www.oxfordmusiconline.com/subscriber/article/grove/music/08909.

7. Lukas Richter, "Didymus," *Grove Music Online*, http://www.oxfordmusiconline.com/subscriber/article/grove/music/07752.

8. Lukas Richter, "Ptolemy," *Grove Music Online*, http://www.oxfordmusiconline.com/subscriber/article/grove/music/22510.

Chapter 4. The Pythagorean Scale

1. The fraction 3/2 to the –1 power is 2/3, to the –2 power is 4/9, and so on.

2. Euclid, *Sectio canonis*, in Andrew Barker, *Greek Musical Writings II: Harmonic and Acoustic Theory* (Cambridge, UK: Cambridge University Press, 1989), 201–202; Ptolemy, *Harmonics*, in Barker, *Greek Musical Writings II*, 298–300.

3. Ross W. Duffin, *How Equal Temperament Ruined Harmony (and Why You Should Care)* (New York: W. W. Norton, 2007), 19.

Interlude B. Guillaume de Machaut's Notre Dame Mass

1. Wulf Arlt, "Machaut, Guillaume de," *Grove Music Online*, http://www.oxfordmusiconline.com/subscriber/article/grove/music/51865.

2. A student of mine years ago concocted a mnemonic for remembering the mass movements, Kyrie, Gloria, Credo, Sanctus, Agnus Dei: "Kyle Gann Can't Sing Anything." I pass it on.

Chapter 5. The Five Limit, the Second Dimension

1. David Fallows, *Dufay* (London: J. M. Dent & Sons, 1982), 18–19.

2. Frederick Hammond and Peter M. Lefferts, "Odington, Walter," *Grove Music Online*, http://www.oxfordmusiconline.com/subscriber/article/grove/music/20252.

3. Margaret Bent, "Dunstaple, John," *Grove Music Online*, http://www.oxfordmusiconline.com/subscriber/article/grove/music/08331.

4. Craig Wright and Sean Gallagher, "Martin le Franc," *Grove Music Online*, http://www.oxfordmusiconline.com/subscriber/article/grove/music/17928.

5. Henry Partch, *Genesis of a Music* (New York: Da Capo Press, 1974), 373–74.

6. Taken from Claude V. Palisca, *Humanism in Italian Renaissance Musical Thought* (New Haven, CT: Yale University Press, 1985), 263.

Interlude C. Some Modern Five-Limit Notions

1. Terry Riley, liner notes to *The Harp of New Albion*, unpaged, Celestial Harmonies CEL 018/019 (1986).

2. Ben Johnston, "On Sonata for Microtonal Piano," in *Maximum Clarity: Writings on Music*, ed. Bob Gilmore (Urbana: University of Illinois Press, 2006), 185.

3. John Jeffrey Gibbens, "Design in Ben Johnston's Sonata for Microtonal Piano," *Interface* 18, no. 3 (1989): 161–94, DOI: 10.1080/09298218908570544. I recall Johnston giving me the same information.

Chapter 6. Meantone Temperament and the Primacy of Thirds

1. Owen Jorgensen, *Tuning: Containing the Perfection of Eighteenth-Century Temperament, the Lost Art of Nineteenth-Century Temperament, and the Science of Equal Temperament* (East Lansing: Michigan State University Press, 1991), 8.

2. In Margo Schulter's elegant formulation, Aron's instructions "permit a regular 1/4-comma temperament, even if they do not compel it or define it in mathematical terms." Schulter, Yahoo Tuning List, message 29985 (Wed., Nov. 7, 2001, 6:49 pm. Subject: Re 31-EDO and 1/4-comma meantone compared), *Tonalsoft: Encyclopedia of Microtonal Music Theory*, http://www.tonalsoft.com/enc/number/1-4cmt.aspx.

3. Joe Monzo, "Meantone," *Tonalsoft*, http://www.tonalsoft.com/enc/m/meantone.aspx.

4. Giordano Riccati, *Le leggi del Contrappunto dedotte dai fenomeni e confermate col raziocinio*, II, Udine, Biblioteca Comunale, ms. 1026-II, 818, quoted in Patrizio Barbieri, *Enharmonic: Instruments and Music, 1470–1900* (Rome: Il Levante Libreria Editrice, 2008), 208; Barbieri, *Enharmonic*, 209.

5. The 2/7-comma meantone seems to have remained popular for decades; it was also described by Francisco Salinas in his *De musica* (1577), Vincenzo Galilei in his *Discorso intorno all'opere di messer Gioseffo Zarlino da Ghioggia* (1589), Pietro Domenico Cerone in his *El Melopeo y maestro* (1613), Jan van der Elst in his *Den ouden ende nieuwen groundt vande musiicke* (1662), and Lemme Rossi in his *Sistema musico ouero Musica speculativa* (1666). See Joe Monzo, "2/7-Comma Meantone," *Tonalsoft*, http://www.tonalsoft.com/enc/number/2-7cmt.aspx.

6. J. Murray Barbour, *Tuning and Temperament: A Historical Survey* (Mineola, NY: Dover Publications, 2004), 33.

7. Ibid., 32.

8. Ibid., 40–41.

9. John Hind Chesnut, "Mozart's Teaching of Intonation," *Journal of the American Musicological Society* 30, no. 2 (1977): 254–71.

Interlude D. Meantone Examples

1. "Fitzwilliam Virginal Book," *The Oxford Companion to Music*, ed. Alison Latham (Oxford: Oxford University Press, 2002), 464–65.

2. Ibid.

3. Bull seems to have been quite a character personally as well as musically. An archbishop wrote of him, "The man hath more music than honesty and is as famous for marring of virginity as he is for fingering of organs and virginals." Susi Jeans and O. W. Neighbour, "Bull, John," *Grove Music Online*, http://www.oxfordmusiconline.com/subscriber/article/grove/music/04294.

4. The Baroque expert in my music department scoffed when I showed him this editorial annotation.

5. John Hind Chesnut, "Mozart's Teaching of Intonation," *Journal of the American Musicological Society* 30, no. 2 (1977): 254–71.

Chapter 7. Well Temperament and Key Color

1. Edward John Hopkins, "Bach teases Gottfried Silbermann," in *The Organ* (London, 1855), 143; quoted in Hans T. David and Arthur Mendel, eds., *The New Bach Reader: A Life of Johann Sebastian Bach in Letters and Documents* (New York: W. W. Norton, 1998), 410–11. Also referred to in Robert Holford MacDowell Bosanquet, *An Elementary Treatise on Musical Intervals and Temperament, with an Account of an Enharmonic Harmonium Exhibited in the Loan Collection of Scientific Instruments*, South Kensington, 1876 [London: MacMillan & Co. 1876], 31.

2. Quoted in David and Mendel, *New Bach Reader*, 336.

3. George J. Buelow, "Werckmeister, Andreas," *Grove Music Online*, http://www.oxfordmusiconline.com/subscriber/article/grove/music/30123; Owen Jorgensen, *Tuning: Containing*

the Perfection of Eighteenth-Century Temperament, the Lost Art of Nineteenth-Century Temperament, and the Science of Equal Temperament (East Lansing: Michigan State University Press, 1991), 62.

4. Mark Lindley, "Well-Tempered Clavier," *Grove Music Online*, http://www.oxfordmusiconline.com/subscriber/article/grove/music/30099.

5. J. Murray Barbour's *Tuning and Temperament: A Historical Survey* (Mineola, NY: Dover Publications, 2004), originally published in 1951, is probably the most widely consulted source. Also Thomas Donahue, *A Guide to Musical Temperament* (Lanham, MD: Scarecrow Press, 2005).

6. Joe Monzo, "Kirnberger III Well Temperament," *Tonalsoft: Encyclopedia of Microtonal Music Theory*, http://www.tonalsoft.com/enc/k/kirnberger.aspx.

7. Jorgensen, *Tuning*, 173.

8. Cecil Adkins, "Neidhardt, Johann Georg," *Grove Music Online*, http://www.oxfordmusiconline.com/subscriber/article/grove/music/19696. Also Dave Benson, *Music: A Mathematical Offering* (Cambridge, UK: Cambridge University Press, 2006), 193.

9. Barbour, *Tuning and Temperament*, 176; this is the one Barbour calls Neidhardt's Third-Circle No. 1.

10. Jorgensen, *Tuning*, 185–86.

11. Ibid., 284.

12. Ross W. Duffin, "Why I Hate Vallotti (or Is It Young?)," Case Western Reserve University, http://casfaculty.case.edu/ross-duffin/why-i-hate-vallotti-or-is-it-young-3-1.

13. Sometimes the experts come up with slightly different figures. Thomas Donahue, himself a piano tuner, in his *A Guide to Musical Temperament* lists figures that are slightly different from Jorgensen's, though within two cents on every pitch. I compare their results below; the pattern of major thirds (M 3rds) is the same.

		Donahue			**Jorgensen**	
		5ths	**M 3rds**		**5ths**	**M 3rds**
C	0	698.05	392.18	0	697.92	391.69
G	698.05	698.04	394.13	697.92	697.92	393.89
D	196.09	698.04	396.09	195.85	697.92	396.09
A	894.13	698.04	400	893.77	697.92	400.12
E	392.18	700	403.91	391.69	700.12	404.15
B	1092.18	701.955	405.86	1091.81	700.12	405.99
F♯	592.18	701.955	407.82	591.94	701.955	407.82
C♯	94.13	701.955	405.87	93.89	701.955	405.99
A♭	796.09	701.955	403.91	795.85	701.955	404.15
E♭	298.04	701.955	400.01	297.8	701.955	400.12
B♭	1000	700	396.09	999.76	700.12	396.09
F	500	700	394.13	499.88	700.12	393.89

14. Thomas Young, "Outlines of Experiments and Inquiries Respecting Sound and Light," 145, quoted in Jorgensen, *Tuning*, 252.

15. Jorgensen, *Tuning*, 266.

16. Theodor W. Adorno, *Aesthetic Theory* (1970; Minneapolis: University of Minnesota Press, 1998), 23.

17. James Webster, *Haydn's "Farewell" Symphony and the Idea of Classical Style* (Cambridge, UK: Cambridge University Press, 1991), 3.

18. Christian Schubart, *Ideen zu einer Aesthetik der Tonkunst* (1806), quoted in Benson, *Music*, 191.

19. Oskar von Riesemann, *Rachmaninoff's Recollections* (New York: Routledge, 2015), 147.

Chapter 8. Twelve-Step Equal Temperament

1. R. Murray Barbour, *Tuning and Temperament: A Historical Survey* (Mineola, NY: Dover Publications, 2004), 25.

2. Alexander John Ellis, "On the Temperament of Musical Instruments with Fixed Tones," Proceedings of the Royal Society of London, vol. 13 (London: Royal Society, 1864), 418; quoted in Owen Jorgensen, *Tuning* (East Lansing: Michigan State University Press, 1991), 484.

3. Jorgensen, *Tuning* 1.

4. Hermann Ludwig Ferdinand von Helmholtz, *On the Sensations of Tone, as a Physiological Basis for the Theory of Music* (1863; New York: Dover Publications, 1954), 552.

5. Jorgensen, *Tuning* 662.

6. Ibid., 692; William Braid White, *Modern Piano Tuning and Allied Arts* (Boston: Tuners Supply Company, 1953), 68.

7. See Jorgensen, *Tuning*, 568.

8. Edward Quincy Norton, *The Construction, Tuning, and Care of the Piano-Forte* (Boston: Oliver Ditson, 1887), 80.

9. Jorgensen, *Tuning*, 692. White had obtained the beating numbers, however, from a piano technician named Joseph C. Miller, who had calcluated them in 1911.

10. Ibid.

11. Harry Partch, *Genesis of a Music* (New York: Da Capo Press, 1974), 191.

12. Ibid., 192.

Chapter 9. The Seven Limit and Johnston Notation

1. Claude V. Palisca, "Zarlino, Gioseffo," *Grove Music Online*, http://www.oxfordmusiconline.com/subscriber/article/grove/music/30858.

2. Marin Mersenne, *Harmonie Universelle*, Paris, Cramoisy, "Traité des instrumens à chords," quoted in Patrizio Barbieri, *Enharmonic: Instruments and Music, 1470–1900* (Rome: Il Levante Libreria Editrice, 2008), 188–89.

3. Christiaan Huygens, *Oeuvres completes*, 17, 37, quoted in Barbieri, *Enharmonic*, 190.

4. Honorè Fabri, *Physica, id est, scientia rerum corporearum*, II (Lyon: Anysson), 279–80, quoted in Barbieri, *Enharmonic*, 190.

5. Barbieri, *Enharmonic*, 195.

6. Giuseppe Tartini, *Trattato di musica* (Padova: Stamperiadel Seminario, 1754), quoted in Barbieri, *Enharmonic*, 199.

7. Giordano Riccati, *Le leggi del contrappunto dedotte dai fenomeni e confermate col raziocinio*, II; Udine, Biblioteca Comunale, Ms. 1026-III, quoted in Barbieri, *Enharmonic*, 196.

8. Bob Gilmore, *Harry Partch* (New Haven, CT: Yale University Press, 1998), 73–74.

9. See, for instance, David B. Doty, *The Just Intonation Primer: An Introduction to the Theory and Practice of Just Intonation* (San Francisco: Just Intonation Network, 1993), 47.

10. For a dramatic example, listen to the Buffalo Bills sing "Lida Rose" in the 1962 movie of the musical *The Music Man*. They sing the song unaccompanied first, and then the orchestra

enters to accompany them as Shirley Jones sings a counter-melody. As they're forced into 12tet to match the orchestra, the harmony instantly loses its distinctiveness and becomes entirely bland. The disappointment is palpable.

11. "Definition of Barbershop Harmony," Barbershop Harmony Society, http://www.barbershop.org/about-us/definition-of-barbershop-harmony.

12. Marc Sabat, "The Extended Helmholtz-Ellis JI Pitch Notation," 2005, http://www.marcsabat.com/pdfs/notation.pdf.

Interlude F. La Monte Young's *The Well-Tuned Piano*

1. Young kept the tuning of the piece secret for twenty-seven years. When the recording came out, I tuned a synthesizer to the notes of the recording, and when I revealed the fact to him, pointing out that if I could figure it out the tuning was no longer secret, he graciously gave me permission to write an article about it, which I did in "La Monte Young's *The Well-Tuned Piano*," *Perspectives of New Music* 31, no. 1 (1993): 134–62.

2. Ibid.

Interlude G. Ben Johnston's String Quartet No. 4

1. For more detailed information, see Randall Shinn, "Ben Johnston's Fourth String Quartet," *Perspectives of New Music* 15, no. 2 (1977): 145–73. Example G.6 is adapted from Shinn's information.

Chapter 10. The Eleven Limit and the Fourth Dimension

1. Harry Partch, *Genesis of a Music* (New York: Da Capo Press, 1974), 115.

2. Ibid., 126.

3. Patrizio Barbieri, *Enharmonic: Instruments and Music, 1470–1900* (Rome: Il Levante Libreria Editrice, 2008), 180–81.

Interlude H. Harry Partch

1. Bob Gilmore, *Harry Partch: A Biography* (New Haven, CT: Yale University Press, 1998), 60.

2. Henry Cowell, *New Musical Resources* (Cambridge, UK: Cambridge University Press, 1996), 21–23.

3. In his published transcription of Partch's *Barstow: Eight Hitchhiker Inscriptions from a Highway Railing at Barstow, California*, Richard Kassel quite sensibly recentered Johnston's notation around G rather than C, so that pluses were not necessary on As and Fs. Others have followed this convention in Partch transcriptions as well. Coincidentally, Kassel and I were freshmen at Oberlin Conservatory together, and I hadn't heard anything about him in decades when his *Barstow* transcriptions suddenly appeared.

4. Harry Partch, "A Quarter-Saw Section of Motivations and Intonations," in *Bitter Music: Collected Journals, Essays, Introductions, and Librettos*, ed. Thomas McGeary (Urbana: University of Illinois Press, 1991), 196–99.

5. Harry Partch, *Genesis of a Music* (New York: Da Capo Press, 1974), 189; Thomas McGeary, *The Music of Harry Partch: A Descriptive Catalog* (Brooklyn: Institute for Studies in American Music, 1991), 63, 120.

6. Partch, *Genesis of a Music*, 189.

7. For more information on performances and instruments, see https://www.harrypartch.com.

Chapter 11. The Thirteen Limit and Beyond

1. Harry Partch, *Genesis of a Music* (New York: Da Capo Press, 1974), 123.

2. Mayumi Tsuda, *Microtonal Works (1990–2000)*, self-published compact disc, 2001.

3. Kyle Gann, "Key Eccentricity in Ben Johnston's *Suite for Microtonal Piano*," *Thirty-One: Journal of the Huygens-Fokker Society* 1 (Summer 2009): 42–48; http://www.kylegann.com/KeyEccentricity.pdf.

4. Kyle Gann, "The Outer Edge of Consonance: The Development of La Monte Young's Tuning Systems," in *Sound and Light: La Monte Young and Marian Zazeela*, edited by William Duckworth and Richard Fleming (Lewisburg, PA: Bucknell University Press, 1996), 158, http://www.kylegann.com/OuterEdgeofConsonance.pdf.

5. Ibid., 181–84.

Interlude I. Ben Johnston's String Quartet No. 7, Movement 3

1. Timothy Ernest Johnson, *13-Limit Extended Just Intonation in Ben Johnston's String Quartet #7 and Toby Twining's "Chrysalid Requiem," "Gradual/Tract"* (Ann Arbor: UMI Microform, 2008).

2. Ibid., 99–100.

Interlude J. Kyle Gann's *Hyperchromatica*

1. Like La Monte Young's use of E♭ as the key for *The Well-Tuned Piano*, mine was also accidental as the result of transposition, and not intended as an homage or out of any mystical sympathy.

Interlude K. Toby Twining's *Chrysalid Requiem*

1. Timothy Ernest Johnson, *13-Limit Extended Just Intonation in Ben Johnston's String Quartet #7 and Toby Twining's "Chrysalid Requiem," "Gradual/Tract"* (Ann Arbor: UMI Microform, 2008), 143.

2. Ibid.

3. Ibid., 164.

Chapter 12. Non-Twelve-Divisible Equal Temperaments

1. Robert Holford MacDowell Bosanquet, *An Elementary Treatise on Musical Intervals and Temperament, with an Account of an Enharmonic Harmonium Exhibited in the Loan Collection of Scientific Instruments* (South Kensington, 1876 [London: MacMillan & Co. 1876]), 60–68.

2. The 301edo is added at the end. There was apparently some interest in trying out 301edo because there were 301 savarts (see chapter 1) to the octave, so interval size in steps would correspond to logarithms. Bosanquet, *Elementary Treatise*, 64.

3. Hermann L. F. Helmholtz, *On the Sensations of Tone, as a Physiological Basis for the Theory of Music* (1863; New York: Dover Publications, 1954), 480.

4. T. Perronet Thompson, *Theory and Practice of Just Intonation* (London: Effingham Willson, 1850); Bosanquet, *Elementary Treatise*, 22; Helmholtz, *Sensations of Tone*, 474.

5. Darreg's 1994 compact disc *Detwelvulate!*, containing many such pieces, is available from Frog Peak Music.

6. Jonathan Glasier, "Ivor Darreg and Enharmonics," http://www.furious.com/perfect/xenharmonics.html.

7. Ivor Darreg, "New Moods," *Xenharmonic Bulletin* no. 5 (1975), quoted in Glasier, "Ivor Darreg and Enharmonics."

8. "Neil Haverstick: Composer, Guitarist, Author & Instructor," http://microstick.net.

9. For instance, see *Mysteries*, http://microstick.net/microtonal-music.

10. Ervin Wilson, "Letter to Chalmers Pertaining to Moments of Symmetry/Tanabe Cycle," April 26, 1975, http://anaphoria.com/mos.pdf.

11. Paul Erlich, "A Middle Path: Between Just Intonation and the Equal Temperaments," originally published in *Xenharmonikon* 18 (2006): 159–99, http://sethares.engr.wisc.edu/paperspdf/Erlich-MiddlePath.pdf.

12. I'm thankful to composer Juhani Nuorvala for these insights. His *A Spiral Ground* for 22edo harpsichord and violin capitalizes on chord progressions demonstrating such facts (https://soundcloud.com/juhani-nuorvala/a-spiral-ground).

13. Dave Keenan, "Sagittal," http://sagittal.org.

14. Optimized means that the amount of tempering is proportional to the simplicity of the ratio, since simpler ratios are more adversely affected by tempering than are more complex ones; thus here the 3/2 perfect fifth is flattened by about 20.5 cents and the 5/4 major third by about 30 cents.

15. Erlich, "Middle Path," 159–99.

16. After all, certain scales in common use—the octatonic (diminished), the Lydian dominant, the melodic and harmonic minor—cannot be generated by replication of a single interval, and the harmonic minor has three interval sizes (minor, major, and augmented seconds), as do some Indian ragas and Arabic scales. The assumption that scales must be analogous to the diatonic and pentatonic in the range of consecutive step sizes to be valid—or indeed, that a scale is a mandatory starting point for microtonal composition—seems more ideological than empirical.

17. Ervin Wilson, "Letter to Chalmers Pertaining to Moments of Symmetry/Tanabe Cycle," April 26, 1975, quoted in Terumi Narushima, *Microtonality and the Tuning Systems of Erv Wilson* (Oxon, UK: Routledge, 2018), 66.

18. Kraig Grady, "The Wilson Archives," http://www.anaphoria.com/wilsonintroMOS.html.

19. For instance, a harmonic progression illustrating a tempered-out comma by returning to the same pitch through unconventional intervals is called a "pump"; the interval replicated within an octave to introduce new pitches is a "generator," and the octave—though it might be a different interval as well—is a "period"; an exponential array notation (see chapter 11) is a "vector" or "Monzo"; and a "val" is a map of a chain of generators.

Interlude L. Nicola Vicentino's Archicembalo

1. Henry W. Kaufmann, "More on the Tuning of the 'Archicembalo,'" *Journal of the American Musicological Society* 23, no. 1 (1970): 84–94.

2. Quoted and translated in Karol Berger, *Theories of Chromatic and Enharmonic Music in Late 16th Century Italy* (Ann Arbor: UMI Research Press, 1980), 26.

3. Claude V. Palisca, *Humanism in Italian Renaissance Musical Thought* (New Haven, CT: Yale University Press, 1985), 253. As we have seen, there is some dispute about how much the ancients valued, or at least used, the enharmonic genus.

4. Quoted in Jonathan Wild, "Genus, Species, and Mode in Vicentino's 31-Tone Compositional Theory," *MTO* 20, no. 2 (2014), 3.

5. Patrizio Barbieri, *Enharmonic: Instruments and Music, 1470–1900* (Rome: Il Levante Libreria Editrice, 2008), 308, 313, 316; Berger, *Theories of Chromatic and Enharmonic Music*, 22.

6. A sampling: "Vicentino's language leads one to believe that he considers the ratios in his gamut to define more or less equal steps, when they, in fact, do not." Bill Alves, "The Just Intonation System of Nicola Vicentino," *1/1: Journal of the Just Intonation Network* 5, no. 2 (1989): 8–13. "Vicentino's treatise abounds in typographical errors. Sometimes entire parts of sentences are omitted." Kaufmann, "More on the Tuning," 84–94. "It must be admitted that this part of Vicentino's scheme does not make sense." J. Murray Barbour, *Tuning and Temperament: A Historical Survey* (Mineola, NY: Dover Publications, 2004), 118.

7. Alves, "Just Intonation System," 8–13.

8. Kaufmann, "More on the Tuning," 84–94.

9. Barbieri, *Enharmonic*, 319.

10. Berger, *Theories of Chromatic and Enharmonic Music*, 9.

11. I follow Barbieri's renotation here in *Enharmonic*, 320. Barbieri corrects what he says are some typos concerning missing dots, but I believe he makes a mistake himself in the penultimate measure, where he has a B_x and an A in the same chord.

12. Edmond Strainchamps, "Luzzaschi, Luzzasco," *Grove Music Online*, http://www.oxfordmusiconline.com/subscriber/article/grove/music/17234.

13. Lorenzo Bianconi and Glenn Watkins, "Gesualdo, Carlo, Prince of Venosa, Count of Conza," *Grove Music Online*, http://www.oxfordmusiconline.com/subscriber/article/grove/music/10994.

14. Claude V. Palisca, "The Beginnings of Baroque Music: Its Roots in Sixteenth-Century Theory and Polemics," PhD diss., Harvard University, 1954, quoted in Wild, "Genus, Species, and Mode."

15. Barbieri, *Enharmonic*, 310.

Chapter 13. Twelve-Based Equal Temperaments

1. Norman Demuth, "Antonin Reicha," *Music & Letters* 29, no. 2 (1948): 169.

2. Alan Walker, *Franz Liszt: The Final Years, 1861–1886* (Ithaca, NY: Cornell University Press, 1990), 444.

3. Ferruccio Busoni, "Sketch of a New Esthetic of Music," in *Three Classics in the Aesthetic of Music* (New York: Dover Publications, 1962), 93.

4. Ibid., 94.

5. Jiří Vysloužil, "Hába, Alois," *Grove Music Online*, http://www.oxfordmusiconline.com/subscriber/article/grove/music/12113.

6. Andrew McCredie, "Alois Hába (1893–1973)," in Larry Sitsky, ed., *Music of the Twentieth-Century Avant Garde: A Biocritical Sourcebook* (Westport, CT: Greenwood Press, 2002), 190.

7. Vysloužil, "Hába, Alois."

8. Alejandro Madrid, *Julián Carrillo & Sonido 13* (Oxford, UK: Oxford University Press, 2015), 126. "In the last lustrum of the past century, my disciple and friend Eucario Rodriguez of Guanajuato and myself, as a matter of experiment and in a primitive way—lacking proper equipment—tried to see if it were possible to subdivide the semitone. Subdividing a violin string with a razor, we succeeded in hearing sixteen perfectly well-defined sounds between the notes G and A." Carrillo, *Pláticas musicales* 2, no. 6, 262, quoted in Madrid, *Julián Carrillo*,

142. Much later, in 1957, he provided a date: "On July 13, 1895, I made an experiment in Mexico City where I achieved the 1/16th of a tone." His accounts of the "experiment" are plagued by contradictions, and dividing a half step, however finely, falls short of inventing microtonal music, but the assertion has made its way into reference books. Madrid, *Julián Carrillo*, 128, 143.

9. Gerald R. Benjamin, "Carrillo, Julián," *Grove Music Online*, http://www.oxfordmusiconline.com/subscriber/article/grove/music/05018.

10. Madrid, *Julián Carrillo*, 108.

11. Katherine K. Preston, "Barth, Hans," *Grove Music Online*, http://www.oxfordmusiconline.com/subscriber/article/grove/music/A2218612.

12. Charles Ives, *Memos* (New York: W. W. Norton, 1972), 111.

13. Charles Ives, "Some 'Quarter-Tone' Impressions," in *Essays Before a Sonata, The Majority, and Other Writings* (New York: W. W. Norton, 1962), 120.

14. Ibid., 111–12.

15. Ibid., 112–15. I have renotated Ives's suggested chords a little to look more logical.

16. Suzette Mary Battan, "Alois Hába's Neue Harmonielehre des diatonischen, chromatischen, Viertel-, Drittel-, Sechstel- und Zwölftel-Tonsystems," PhD diss., University of Rochester, 1980.

17. Ibid., 113–14.

18. Ivan Wyschnegradsky, *Manual of Quarter-Tone Harmony*, ed. Noah Kaplan (Brooklyn: Underwolf Editions, 2017).

19. Michel Ellenberger, "Wyschnegradsky," http://www.ivan-wyschnegradsky.fr/en/biography.

20. Pascale Criton, "Vyschnegradsky, Ivan Aleksandrovich," *Grove Music Online*, http://www.oxfordmusiconline.com/subscriber/article/grove/music/29509.

21. Catherine Parsons Smith, "Couper, Mildred," *Grove Music Online*, http://www.oxfordmusiconline.com/subscriber/article/grove/music/47044.

22. Douglas Leedy and Johnny Reinhard, "Tucker, Tui St George," *Grove Music Online*, http://www.oxfordmusiconline.com/subscriber/article/grove/music/49199.

23. Gardner Read, *20th-Century Microtonal Notation* (New York: Greenwood Press, 1990), 118.

24. Ibid., 109.

25. Battan, *Alois Hába's Neue Harmonielehre*, 289–91.

26. Ezra Sims, "Reflections on This and That (Perhaps a Polemic)," *Perspectives of New Music* 29, no. 1 (1991): 236–57.

27. Hugues Dufourt, "Musique spectrale: pour une pratique des formes de l'énergie," *Bicéphale*, no. 3 (1981): 85–89.

28. Joe Monzo, "144-Tone Equal-Temperament / 144-edo," *Tonalsoft: Encyclopedia of Microtonal Music Theory*, http://www.tonalsoft.com/enc/number/144edo.aspx.

29. Kyle Gann, "Micro Breweries," *Village Voice*, June 8, 1999, 131.

Interlude M. Some Quarter-Tone Impressions

1. Charles Ives, program note to Three Quarter-Tone Pieces (New York: C. F. Peters, 1968).

2. The correct tuning of the pianos can make or break this piece, and the only recording I've heard that I feel gets the quarter tones absolutely equidistant is the original vinyl on Odyssey.

3. Myles Skinner, "Toward a Quarter-Tone Syntax: Selected Analyses of Works by Blackwood, Hába, Ives, and Wyschnegradsky," http://www.tierceron.com/diss/wysch/wysch.pdf, 147.

4. Ibid., 159.
5. Ibid., 161–69.

Interlude N. Ezra Sims's String Quartet No. 5

1. A signal beginning in that direction is Brian Bartling's master's thesis, "The Microtonal Music of Ezra Sims," https://www.scribd.com/document/326418939/The-Microtonal-Music-of-Ezra-Sims. This thesis contains an analysis of the solo violin piece *All Done from Memory*, though the paper spends more time putting Sims in historic microtonal context than in particular analysis.

2. Although the Fifth Quartet is not commercially available on record, the Pacifica Quartet put up a recording of it at http://arizonachambermusic.org/pieces/string-quartet-no-5. Hopefully it will remain.

3. "String Quartet no. 5," Arizona Friends of Chamber Music, http://arizonachambermusic.org/pieces/string-quartet-no-5.

4. Bartling, "Microtonal Music of Ezra Sims."

5. It strikes me as appropriate to add that Sims is one of the great humorists in twentieth-century music. He has a piano piece charmingly called *Grave Dance*, and a song cycle titled *Brief Glimpses into Contemporary French Literature* whose recurring refrain is "There is no need of Andre Gide." In the 1960s *Baker's Biographical Dictionary of Music and Musicians*, then edited by Nicolas Slonimsky, attributed to Sims a work he hadn't written, a String Quartet No. 2 dated 1962. In 1974 Sims gallantly agreed to ameliorate Slonimsky's embarrassment by writing a piece titled *String Quartet no. 2* (1962), scored for flute, clarinet, violin, viola, and cello. As Sims notes, a title is not necessarily a description, and he cites as precedent the White Knight in Lewis Carroll's *Through the Looking Glass*, whose song was *called* "Haddock's Eyes" even though its *title* was "The Aged Aged Man." The score is dedicated to Slonimsky, "that he (or rather *Baker's*) may now be less in error." Sims also possessed a punchy, direct prose style, and his writings on microtonality, like Partch's, are far more entertaining than the usual fare in the genre.

Chapter 14. A Few Numbers Drawn from Non-Western Musics

1. John Garzoli, "The Myth of Equidistance in Thai Tuning," *Analytical Approaches to World Music* 4, no. 2 (2015), http://www.aawmjournal.com/articles/2015b/Garzoli_AAWM_Vol_4_2.pdf.

2. For instance, T. Viswanathan and Matthew Harp Allen, in *Music in South India: Experiencing Music, Experiencing Culture* (New York: Oxford University Press, 2004).

3. B. Chaitanya Deva, *The Music of India: A Scientific Study* (New Delhi: Munshiram Manohavlal Publishers, 1981), 107.

4. Wolfgang von Schweinitz, "The Classical Indian Just Intonation Tuning System with 22 Srutis Defining the 7 Swaras of Hindu Classical Music," *Plainsound Music Edition*, http://www.plainsound.org/pdfs/srutis.pdf.

5. Deva, *Music of India*, 110.

6. Scott L. Marcus, *Music in Egypt* (New York: Oxford University Press, 2007), 23. The bulk of my discussion is drawn from this book.

7. Ibid., 26–27. Apparently, however, there are some musicians who insist on the equal-tempered version.

8. Ibid., 31–32.

9. Michael Tenzer, *Gamelan Gong Kebyar: The Art of Twentieth-Century Balinese Music* (Chicago: University of Chicago Press, 2000), 31.

10. Ibid., 32.

11. Donald Lentz, *The Gamelan Music of Java and Bali: An Artistic Anomaly Complimentary to Primary Tonal Theoretical Systems* (Lincoln: University of Nebraska Press, 1965), quoted in Roger Vetter, "A Retrospect on a Century of Gamelan Tone Measurements," *Ethnomusicology* 33, no. 2 (1989): 219. Moreover, Vetter goes on, "We might have to accept the fact that the Javanese tuning concepts of sléndro and pélog do not lend themselves to be understood in terms of cents alone. Our continued efforts to reduce Javanese tunings to numerical representations and subject them to Western patterns of analytical logic . . . will add little to our knowledge of the culturally significant factors that surround the art of tuning in Java" (226). Even so, for some of us Westerners, numerical representation is the first step in our understanding something without the benefit of concrete experience.

12. According to Lisa Gold, "By eliminating two of the pitches in the scale, musicians were better able to execute complex, rapid figuration, developing a new virtuosic technique since they no longer had to leap over the 'extra' keys." Lisa Gold, *Music in Bali* (New York: Oxford University Press, 2005), 37.

13. Thus Tenzer; Lisa Gold, in *Music in Bali*, gives the names as *nding*, *ndong*, *ndeng*, *ndung*, and *ndang* (34–35).

14. Edward C. Carterette and Roger A. Kendall, "On the Tuning and Stretched Octave of Javanese Gamelans," *Leonardo Music Journal* 4 (1994): 59, 60, 61.

15. W. Surjodiningrat, P. J. Sudarjana, and A. Susanto, *Tone Measurements of Outstanding Javanese Gamelans in Yogyakarta and Surakarta* (Yogyakarta: Gadjah Mada University Press, 1993), 5, 25, 28.

16. Leta E. Miller and Fredric Lieberman, "Lou Harrison and the American Gamelan," *American Music* 17, no. 2 (1999): 158, 159.

17. Alexander Ellis, "On the Musical Scales of Various Nations," *Journal of the Society of Arts*, 1885.

18. Garzoli, "Myth of Equidistance."

19. Ibid., 10.

20. Ibid., 15.

21. Garzoli also points to some errors caused by confusion with the Isan musical system of northeast Thailand, whose tuning is based on a heptatonic tuning tuned to simple integer ratios. Garzoli, "Myth of Equidistance," 13.

Chapter 15. Brief Miscellaneous Thoughts

1. Leta E. Miller and Frederic Lieberman, *Lou Harrison: Composing a World* (New York: Oxford University Press, 1998), 116–18.

2. Kyle Gann, "Jumping the Groove," *Village Voice*, July 17, 2001, 68.

3. Kyle Gann, "A Symphonist Stakes Her Claim," *New York Times*, April 25, 1999.

4. Kyle Gann, "American Composer: Elizabeth Brown," *Chamber Music* (April 2002): 18–19.

Glossary of Tuning Terms

The following terms may have wider general applications than are needed for this book. We will restrict ourselves to the definitions required for tuning theory.

Arithmetic mean (A + B)/2; the sum of two numbers divided by two, a linear halfway point. Thus the arithmetic mean of 1/1 and 5/4 is (4/4 + 5/4)/2 = (9/4)/2 = 9/8. The arithmetic mean will be closer to the higher pitch than to the lower.

Bearing plan In keyboard tuning, a recipe for the order of intervals tuned in order to achieve a certain temperament.

Beat In a tuning context, the audible pulsation that occurs between two tones very slightly out of tune. In discussions of temperament, the pulsation is more often between the harmonics of two different pitches than between the fundamentals.

Cent (¢) 1/1200 of an octave in perceived pitch difference, or 1/100 of the average size of the common half step. Interval sizes under five cents are difficult for most people to perceive except in certain particular contexts; some people can hear pitch shifts of as little as two cents.

Chromatic In normal usage, pertaining to a scale or musical passage using all twelve pitches of conventional tuning. In expanded non-12tet usage, it might refer to a scale of around twelve steps in which all are employed.

Chromatic half step An interval (augmented unison) between two tones with the same pitch name separated by a flat or sharp, as C and C♯ or B and B♭.

Circulating temperament Early (17th/18th century) term for well temperament.

Comma A general term for the small distance between two close pitches, typically those generated by two different interval calculations.

Consonance Sweetness or intelligibility of pitch relations in a chord or melody. For purposes of this book, the amount of consonance in an interval is directly proportional to the smallness of the whole numbers used to define its ratio, though some approximation is tolerated. For instance, a 5/4 ratio is by definition more consonant than a 7/6, because the numbers are smaller, though the actual interval representing the 5/4 might range between 379 and 392 cents.

cps Cycles per second, the quantity of vibrations a sounding medium makes in one second.

Diatonic Based in a scale of seven pitches to the octave, traditionally the whole-step and half-step pattern (WWHWWWH) of the major scale, though not necessarily excluding the augmented second of the harmonic minor scale. For tuning purposes, we might consider generalizing it to scales in which steps range from about 100 to about 200 steps, in distinction to the smaller steps of the chromatic scale and the larger gaps of the pentatonic.

Diatonic half step A pitch interval of around one hundred cents between two different scale steps (e.g., E and F, A and B♭) of a diatonic scale.

Diesis A rather vague term for a small interval like a comma, originally the diatonic semitone of the Pythagorean scale but given many conflicting definitions since. Without other qualifiers it is sometimes recently defined as the 128/125 interval of 41.1 cents between an octave and three stacked major thirds, $5/4 \times 5/4 \times 5/4$, equaling 125/64.

Dissonance For our purposes, the quality of two or more pitches being representable only by relatively high-numbered ratios. Thus dissonance is relative, and 81/64 is a far more dissonant ratio than the 5/4 that it closely approximates. Historically, however, dissonance is a concept defined contextually, and it need not concern us much here.

edo Short for "equal divisions of an octave"; often with a number, as "22edo" connotes twenty-two equally spaced pitches within an octave. The term "edo" is often used in place of "tet" when a scale is based on an equal-tempered scale, but not all scale steps need be available for use. An example is using 31edo as an approximation for 1/4-comma well temperament when only twelve or sixteen or so of the thirty-one tones are actually necessary for the music.

Enharmonic Functionally equivalent to another pitch notated differently, as on the piano keyboard D♯ is considered the enharmonic equivalent of E♭. For our purposes, many of our scales are distinguished by a lack of enharmonic equivalence, so that D♯ and E♭ are not the same pitch. The concept here is only meaningful in its absence.

Equal temperament The division of an octave (or possibly other interval) into a number of equal intervals. Unmodified, the term most likely refers to the standard twelve-pitch equal temperament of modern piano tuning (12tet), but other equal temperaments are used. The abbreviation is ET, and "tet" is "tone-equal-temperament," so 31tet is a division of the octave into thirty-one equal steps.

Fifth tone A fifth of an equal-tempered whole step, an interval of forty cents, a thirtieth of an octave.

Fundamental The central pitch used as a starting point for a discussion of harmonics or ratios in a particular context.

Genera In ancient Greek music theory, the three types of tetrachords (singular genus) used to create scales. The diatonic genus corresponds to what we today call two whole steps and a half step (such as C–D–E–F). The chromatic genus corresponds to two half steps and a minor third (C–C♯–D–F). The enharmonic genus corresponds to two quarter tones and a major third (C–C𝄲–D♭–F).

Geometric mean The multiplicative average of two numbers, $\sqrt{AB}$. The geometric mean of 1/1 and 5/4, then, is the square root of $(1/1 \times 5/4) = \sqrt{(5/4)} = \sqrt{5}/2$. It gives a pitch that is perceptually exactly between two other pitches.

Harmonic Physically speaking, a tone secondarily sounded by the vibration of 1/2, 1/3, 1/4, and so on, of a vibrating string or column of air. More theoretically, a pitch that vibrates at an integer multiple of an implicit fundamental tone, as C♯ 550 cps and E 660 cps are harmonics of an A at 110 cps. More loosely, we can say that C♯ and E are harmonics of A.

Harmonic mean A kind of average that is the inverse of the arithmetic mean, defined by 2AB/(A + B). For instance, the harmonic mean between 1/1 and 5/4 = (2 × 1 × 5/4)/(1/1 + 5/4) = (5/2)/(9/4) = 5/2 × 4/9 = 10/9. The harmonic mean will be closer to the lower pitch than to the higher.

Harmonic series The potentially infinite string of pitches that are integer multiples of a single frequency, such as 100 cps, 200, 300, 400, 500, 600, and so on to infinity.

Hertz Cycles per second, abbreviated Hz.

Hyperchromatic Pertaining to a scale or music context more noticeably saturated with pitches than a chromatic scale and thus microtonal.

Just intonation A system of tuning in which pitches are defined according to whole-number ratios between frequencies, almost necessarily resulting in scales with unequal scale steps. Just-intonation music involving ratios based on seven, eleven, and so on, is sometimes called *extended just intonation* in order to differentiate it from the just performance of historical music in five-limit tuning; the distinction is not observed in this book.

Kleisma A vague term for a very small discrepancy between two pitches, smaller than a comma. It is defined different ways in different contexts.

Lattice A graphic representation of pitches differentiating them according to the intervals by which they are generated. For instance, a seven-limit (three-dimensional) lattice typically arranges perfect fifth relationships along a horizontal line, major third relationships along a vertical line, and septimal minor seventh relationships along a diagonal line.

Limit In the context of just intonation, the largest prime number involved as a factor in a set of pitches defined as ratios. For instance, 7/5 and 14/9 are within the seven limit, because the ratio numbers involve no prime factors larger than seven. The ratio 14/11, however, is not within the seven limit, because it requires the prime number eleven, which is larger than seven.

Limma A small interval (like a diesis or comma) that is specifically a part left over, as, say, the 256/243 interval that remains when two 9/8s are subtracted from a 4/3.

Logarithm The exponent to which another fixed number, the base, must be raised to produce that number. In terms of this book and tuning theory in general, for instance, the logarithm of 2, base 10, is approximately .30103, since 10 to the .30103 power ($10^{.30103}$) equals 2. Finding the logarithm of a musical ratio between frequencies converts the interval size to its perceived proportion. We multiply .30103 times 1200/log(2) to assign the ratio 2/1 to 1200 cents, and so on with the logarithm of any other ratio. For another common example, log(5/4) × 1200/log(2) = 386.3¢, the perceived size in cents of a 5/4 interval.

Maqam A melodic mode, or scale, of Arabic music, analogous to a raga in Indian classical music.

Meantone A system of temperament in which perfect fifths are narrowed by a few cents in order to achieve more consonant thirds and sixths. Unlike well temperament, it is a regular temperament in that the fifths that are the basis of the system are all the same size. Without a qualifier, the term usually applies to 1/4-comma meantone, in which the fifths are narrowed by one fourth of a syntonic comma in order to achieve perfect 5/4 major thirds. Other sizes have also been widely used, defined by the fraction of the comma subtracted from each fifth.

Meantone fifth A slightly narrowed perfect fifth of from 690 to 700 cents, "squeezed" in order that a sequence of them yield more consonant thirds than in equal temperament.

Quite often the unspecified meantone fifth refers to the 696.6-cent interval found in 1/4-comma meantone temperament.

Meantone intonation Usually in string playing or vocal performance, the convention by which sharps are played or sung flatter than the corresponding enharmonic flat, as C♯ is performed flatter than D♭. Contrasted with Pythagorean intonation, which is the opposite.

Mode For tuning purposes, a scale made by using as its starting point (tonic, final, or fundamental) a note other than the one that might have seemed most logical for that purpose; for instance, in reference to the major scale CDEFGABC, EFGÀBCDE represents a mode (specifically Phrygian) derived from that scale.

Moment of symmetry In the theories of Ervin Wilson, a scale generated by two intervals going out of phase in pitch space to an optimum extent such that only two step sizes result. The equal-tempered major scale, for instance, is generated by perfect fifths (F–C–G–D–A–E–B) being folded back within an octave (C–D–E–F–G–A–B) to the point that all steps are either half steps (100 cents) or whole steps (200 cents).

Monochord An instrument for the measurement of pitch intervals, legendarily invented by Pythagoras, consisting of a sounding string mounted on a sounding board marked into the necessary number of parts.

Neutral In certain contexts, between major and minor. For instance, 11/9 is a neutral (347.4-cent) third between major and minor.

Octave A ratio of 2:1 between the vibrations of two pitches, perceived in many musical cultures as a kind of identity. (Less formally, the ratio can be some higher power of two as well, such as four or eight.)

Otonality Harry Partch's term for a "tonality," or functional group of pitches, based on relationships to a certain pitch, which latter (or a multiple of it) always appears in the denominator of its ratios. Thus, 6/5, 7/5, 8/5, 9/5, and 11/10 are all contained in the 5 otonality. An otonality is Partch's equivalent for a major key extended through further harmonics.

Overtone A harmonic, with the sad distinction that the second harmonic is called the "first overtone"; the third harmonic, the "second overtone"; and so on.

Partial Like overtone, a harmonic, with, again, the sad distinction that the second harmonic is called the "first partial'"; the third harmonic, the "second partial"; and so on.

Parts In ancient Greek music theory, equal divisions of a string or other vibrating medium. On a string divided into sixty parts, forty-five parts (equal 45/60 = 3/4) is the length that will sound a 4/3 perfect fourth above the open string; forty parts will give the 3/2 perfect fifth, and so on. The length of the string made to vibrate, in such cases, is inversely proportional to the pitch frequency, the longest string lengths corresponding to the lowest pitches.

Ptolemaic sequence (so called by Harry Partch), defining in just intonation the most consonant arrangement of the common major scale, 1/1–9/8–5/4–4/3–3/2–5/3–15/8; first found among the ratios of the "intense diatonic" in Ptolemy's *Harmonics*.

Pythagorean comma The small interval difference between pitches arrived at by stacking, above the same pitch, twelve 3/2 perfect fifths and seven octaves, respectively. Its exact ratio is 531441/524288 ($3^{12}/2^{19}$), and its size is 23.46 . . . cents. It is likewise the interval by which six 9/8 major seconds exceed an octave.

Pythagorean intonation Usually in string playing or vocal performance, the convention by which sharps are played or sung sharper than the corresponding enharmonic flat, as C♯ is performed sharper than D♭. Contrasted with meantone intonation, which is the opposite.

Pythagorean major third An interval in the ratio 81/64, with a size of 407.82 cents. The major third above the tonic arrived at by stacking up four perfect fifths.

Pythagorean minor third An interval in the ratio 32/27, with a size of 294.14 cents. The major third above the tonic arrived at by ascending through three perfect fourths.

Quarter tone A half of an equal-tempered half step, an interval of fifty cents.

Raga One of the numerous melodic structures of Indian classical music, inexactly analogous to a scale in Western music but with more built-in traditional subtleties of mood and contour.

Regular temperament A temperament in which the generating intervals are of a consistent size. In meantone, for instance, all the usable perfect fifths are 696.6 cents, unlike well temperament, in which the fifths can vary in size.

Regular Temperament Theory In general, the mathematical theory of regular temperaments; as widely used, the theory of pitch systems generated by two or more interval sizes going out of phase with each other in pitch space. The theory is most often used to generate scales characterized by a maximum efficiency of interval sizes, often based in equal temperaments of various densities.

Savart An alternative, possibly obsolete measure of perceived interval size equaling 3.986 . . . cents. It was once used to simplify logarithm pitch calculations, since the logarithm of 2 is .30103, and there are 301.03 savarts in an octave.

Scale Technically, the pitches of a musical composition or system arranged in order of pitch frequency. The word (originally meaning "ladder") connotes a relatively smooth series of steps from lower to higher or vice versa. (We would be reluctant, for instance, to call C–C♯–D–A♭ a scale, confronted with a piece that used only those pitches.)

Schisma A rather vague term for a discrepancy between pitches smaller than a comma. It is the traditional term for the 32805/32768 interval of only 1.95 cents that separates eight 3/2 perfect fifths plus a 5/4 major third from five octaves. This quantity is also the difference between the Pythagorean and syntonic commas. Other uses of the word, however, are found.

Septemdecimal Derived from the number seventeen. Thus, 17/12 and 24/17 are septemdecimal tritones (603 cents and 597 cents, respectively).

Septimal Derived from the number seven. Thus, 7/4 is a septimal minor seventh, and 27/14 is a septimal major seventh.

Sixth tone A sixth of an equal-tempered whole step, an interval of 33.33 . . . cents; one 36th of an octave.

Subharmonic series A series of pitches defined by the initial pitch being subdivided by the series of integers, such as 600 cps, 300 cps (600/2), 200 cps (600/3), 150 cps (600/4), 120 cps (600/5), and so on. The inverted form of a harmonic series and supposed by Harry Partch and others to be the theoretical basis of minor tonalities, though much more difficult to find in nature.

Superparticular Of the form (N + 1)/N, where N is an integer. Therefore, 3/2, 5/4, and 21/20 are superparticular ratios, but 13/7 and 7/5 are not.

Syntonic comma The ratio 81/80, an interval of 21.506 . . . cents, one of the most important phenomena in the history of tuning theory. It occurs frequently between potential pitches in a five-limit tuning, such as between 5/4 and the Pythagorean major third 81/64, or between 9/8 and 10/9. Because it first appeared in the writings of Didymus, it is sometimes (rarely) called the *comma of Didymus*.

Temper To slightly flatten or sharpen a pure (just-intonation) interval in order to find a compromise pitch that is more consonant to at least two other pitches.

Temperament A system of tuning differentiated from just intonation in which the size of intervals is varied from pure by small amounts, usually to avoid a redundancy of pitches inconveniently close together. Theoretically, the intervals of a temperament are considered irrational ratios (such as a meantone perfect fifth is tempered to the ratio of the fourth root of five). In historical practice, temperament was often achieved intuitively and without exactitude. In modern experimental tunings, the word is most often encountered in the concept of equal temperaments of more or fewer than twelve pitches.

tet Abbreviation for "-tone equal temperament," as 12tet means twelve-tone equal temperament, 31tet has the octave divided into thirty-one equal steps, and so on.

Tetrachord A succession of four pitches filling out the interval of a fourth, almost always a 4/3 perfect fourth, between the highest and lowest ones. For instance, C–D–E♭–F, C–D♭–D–F, and C–D♭–E♭–F are all tetrachords. Two tetrachords, arranged such that the highest note of one is an octave above the lowest note of the other make up an octave scale.

Tonality flux Harry Partch's term for the kinds of subtle harmonic changes that can occur in a microtonal context from notes moving from one chord to another by tiny increments of voice leading.

Tridecimal Derived from the number thirteen. Thus, 13/8 is a tridecimal sixth, and 16/13 is a tridecimal third.

Tritone The interval of around 600 cents that perceptually divides an octave in half. It presents a historical tuning problem because within the five limit there is no simple or obvious ratio that corresponds to it. Mathematically it represents the geometric mean between 1 and 2—namely, the square root of two.

Undecimal Derived from the number eleven. Thus, 11/8 is an undecimal fourth or tritone, and 18/11 is an undecimal neutral sixth (neutral in this sense meaning between major and minor).

Utonality Harry Partch's term for a "tonality," or functional group of pitches, based on relationships to a certain pitch, which latter (or a multiple of it) always appears in the numerator of its ratios. Thus, 5/4, 5/3, 10/7, 10/9, and 20/11 are all contained in the 5 utonality. A utonality is Partch's equivalent for a minor key extended through further subharmonics.

Well temperament Historically, a temperament (irregular) in which all major and minor triads are sufficiently in tune for musical use though not identical in interval sizes. Well temperaments began to be used in the late seventeenth century and dominated much of the eighteenth and possibly early nineteenth century.

Wolf An adjective indicating that an interval is sufficiently out of tune from its common just ratio to create audible beats, traditionally excluding the ratio from accepted usage. The interval most often marked as a wolf is the perfect fifth; the almost-fifth 40/27 has historically been called a wolf fifth because it is 21 cents too flat to sound as consonant as the 3/2 perfect fifth it badly approximates. Other intervals with objectionable beats can be called wolves as well.

Xenharmonic A term coined by Ivor Darreg, theoretically to apply to all tuning systems outside the convention of twelve-pitch equal temperament. In practice it tends to be used by those interested in exotic equal temperaments (as found in Regular Temperament Theory) as an alternative to *microtonal*, since the latter word suggests intervals significantly smaller than a half step, which may not occur in scales based on, say, a 15edo or 16edo framework.

Bibliography

Adkins, Cecil. "Neidhardt, Johann Georg." *Grove Music Online*. http://www.oxfordmusiconline.com/subscriber/article/grove/music/19696.

Adorno, Theodor W. *Aesthetic Theory*. Minneapolis: University of Minnesota Press, 1998. Originally published 1970.

Alves, Bill. "The Just Intonation System of Nicola Vicentino." *1/1: Journal of the Just Intonation Network* 5, no. 2 (1989): 8–13.

Anderson, Warren, and Thomas J. Mathiesen. "Olympus the Mysian." *Grove Music Online*. http://www.oxfordmusiconline.com/grovemusic/view/10.1093/gmo/9781561592630.001.0001/omo-9781561592630-e-0000020337.

Aristoxenus. *On Harmonics* [*Harmonic Elements*]. 1562. In Palisca, *Humanism in Italian Renaissance Musical Thought*. New Haven, CT: Yale University Press, 1985.

Arlt, Wulf. "Machaut, Guillaume de." *Grove Music Online*. http://www.oxfordmusiconline.com/subscriber/article/grove/music/51865.

Barbera, André. "Archytas of Tarentum." *Grove Music Online*. http://www.oxfordmusiconline.com/subscriber/article/grove/music/01183.

Barbieri, Patrizio. *Enharmonic: Instruments and Music, 1470–1900*. Rome: Il Levante Libreria Editrice, 2008.

Barbour, J. Murray. *Tuning and Temperament: A Historical Survey*. Mineola, NY: Dover Publications, 2004.

Barker, Andrew. *Greek Musical Writings II: Harmonic and Acoustic Theory*. Cambridge, UK: Cambridge University Press, 1989.

Bartling, Brian. "The Microtonal Music of Ezra Sims." Master's thesis. New England Conservatory of Music. https://www.scribd.com/document/326418939/The-Microtonal-Music-of-Ezra-Sims.

Battan, Suzette Mary. "Alois Hába's Neue Harmonielehre des diatonischen, chromatischen, Viertel-, Drittel-, Sechstel- und Zwölftel-Tonsystems." PhD diss., University of Rochester, 1980.

Bélis, Annie. "Aristoxenus." *Grove Music Online*. http://www.oxfordmusiconline.com/subscriber/article/grove/music/01248.

Benjamin, Gerald R. "Carrillo, Julián." *Grove Music Online*. http://www.oxfordmusiconline.com/subscriber/article/grove/music/05018.

Benson, Dave. *Music: A Mathematical Offering*. Cambridge, UK: Cambridge University Press, 2006.

Bent, Margaret. "Dunstaple, John." *Grove Music Online*. http://www.oxfordmusiconline.com/subscriber/article/grove/music/08331.

Berger, Karol. *Theories of Chromatic and Enharmonic Music in Late 16th Century Italy*. Ann Arbor: UMI Research Press, 1980.

Bianconi, Lorenzo, and Glenn Watkins. "Gesualdo, Carlo, Prince of Venosa, Count of Conza." *Grove Music Online*. http://www.oxfordmusiconline.com/subscriber/article/grove/music/10994.

Blackwood, Easley. *The Structure of Recognizable Diatonic Tunings*. Princeton, NJ: Princeton University Press, 1985.

Bosanquet, Robert Holford MacDowell. *An Elementary Treatise on Musical Intervals and Temperament, with an Account of an Enharmonic Harmonium Exhibited in the Loan Collection of Scientific Instruments*. South Kensington, 1876. [London: MacMillan & Co. 1876].

Buelow, George J. "Werckmeister, Andreas." *Grove Music Online*. http://www.oxfordmusiconline.com/subscriber/article/grove/music/30123.

Busoni, Ferruccio. "Sketch of a New Esthetic of Music." In *Three Classics in the Aesthetic of Music*. New York: Dover Publications, 1962.

Carrillo, *Julián. Pláticas musicales* 2, no. 6 (1913): 262. Quoted in Madrid, *Julián Carrillo & Sonido 13*. 142

Carterette, Edward C., and Roger A. Kendall. "On the Tuning and Stretched Octave of Javanese Gamelans." *Leonardo Music Journal* 4 (1994): 59–68.

Chalmers, John. *Divisions of the Tetrachord*. Hanover, NH: Frog Peak Music, 1993.

Chesnut, John Hind. "Mozart's Teaching of Intonation." *Journal of the American Musicological Society* 30, no. 2 (1977): 254–71.

Christiansen, Thomas. *Rameau and Musical Thought in the Enlightenment* (Cambridge, UK: Cambridge University Press, 2004).

Ciconia, Johannes. *Nova Musica and De Proportionibus*. Translated by Oliver B. Ellsworth. Lincoln: University of Nebraska Press, 1993.

Cowell, Henry. *New Musical Resources*. Cambridge, UK: Cambridge University Press, 1996.

Criton, Pascale. "Vyschnegradsky, Ivan Aleksandrovich." *Grove Music Online*. http://www.oxfordmusiconline.com/subscriber/article/grove/music/29509.

Crotch, Dr. "On the Derivation of the Scale, Tuning, Temperament, the Monochord, etc." *Musical Times*, October 1, 1861.

Daniélou, Alain. *Music and the Power of Sound: The Influence of Tuning and Interval on Consciousness*. Rochester, VT: Inner Traditions, 1995.

———. *Tabluea Comparatif des Intervalles Musicaux*. Pondicherry, India: Institut Français d'Indologie, 1958.

Darreg, Ivor. "New Moods." *Xenharmonic Bulletin*, no. 5 (1975). Quoted in Glasier, "Ivor Darreg and Enharmonics."

David, Hans T., and Arthur Mendel, eds. *The New Bach Reader: A Life of Johann Sebastian Bach in Letters and Documents*. New York: W. W. Norton, 1998.

Demuth, Norman. "Antonin Reicha." *Music & Letters* 29, no. 2 (1948): 165–72.

Deva, B. Chaitanya. *The Music of India: A Scientific Study*. New Delhi: Munshiram Manohavlal Publishers, 1981.

Donahue, Thomas. *A Guide to Musical Temperament*. Lanham, MD: Scarecrow Press, 2005.

Doty, David B. *The Just Intonation Primer: An Introduction to the Theory and Practice of Just Intonation*. San Francisco: Just Intonation Network, 1993.

Duffin, Ross W. *How Equal Temperament Ruined Harmony (and Why You Should Care)*. New York: W. W. Norton, 2007.

———. "Why I Hate Vallotti (or Is It Young?)." Case Western Reserve University. http://casfaculty.case.edu/ross-duffin/why-i-hate-vallotti-or-is-it-young-3-1.

Dufourt, Hugues. "Musique spectrale: pour une pratique des formes de l'énergie." *Bicéphale*, no. 3 (1981): 85–89.

Ellenberger, Michel. "Wyschnegradsky." http://www.ivan-wyschnegradsky.fr/en/biography.

Ellis, Alexander. "On the Calculation of Cents from Interval Ratios." In *On the Sensations of Tone, as a Physiological Basis for the Theory of Music*, ed. Hermann Helmholtz, 446–57. New York: Dover Publications, 1954.

Ellis, Alexander. "On the Musical Scales of Various Nations." *Journal of the Society of Arts*, 1885.

Ellis, Alexander John. "On the Temperament of Musical Instruments with Fixed Tones," *Proceedings of the Royal Society of London*, vol. 13. London: Royal Society, 1864, 418. Quoted in Owen Jorgensen, *Tuning*. East Lansing: Michigan State University Press, 1991.

Erlich, Paul. "A Middle Path: Between Just Intonation and the Equal Temperaments." http://sethares.engr.wisc.edu/paperspdf/Erlich-MiddlePath.pdf.

Fabri, Honorè. *Physica, id est, scientia rerum corporearum*, II. Lyon: Anysson, 279–80. Quoted in Barbieri, *Enharmonic*, 190.

Fallows, David. *Dufay*. London: J. M. Dent & Sons, 1982.

"Fitzwilliam Virginal Book." *The Oxford Companion to Music*. Edited by Alison Latham. Oxford: Oxford University Press, 2002, 464–65.

Gann, Kyle. "American Composer: Elizabeth Brown." *Chamber Music*. April 2002, 18–19.

———. "Jumping the Groove." *Village Voice*. July 17, 2001, 68.

———. "Key Eccentricity in Ben Johnston's *Suite for Microtonal Piano*." *Thirty-One: Journal of the Huygens-Fokker Society* 1 (Summer 2009): 42–48. http://www.kylegann.com/Key Eccentricity.pdf.

———. "La Monte Young's *The Well-Tuned Piano*." *Perspectives of New Music* 31, no. 1 (1993): 134–62.

———. "Micro Breweries." *Village Voice*. June 8, 1999, 131.

———. "The Outer Edge of Consonance: The Development of La Monte Young's Tuning Systems." In *Sound and Light: La Monte Young and Marian Zazeela*, ed. William Duckworth and Richard Fleming, 152–90. Lewisburg, PA: Bucknell University Press, 1996.

———. "A Symphonist Stakes Her Claim." *New York Times*. April 25, 1999.

Garzoli, John. "The Myth of Equidistance in Thai Tuning." *Analytical Approaches to World Music* 4, no. 2 (2015). http://www.aawmjournal.com/articles/2015b/Garzoli_AAWM_Vol_4_2.pdf.

Gibbens, John Jeffrey. "Design in Ben Johnston's Sonata for Microtonal Piano." *Interface* 18, no. 3 (1989): 161–94.

Gilmore, Bob. *Harry Partch: A Biography*. New Haven, CT: Yale University Press, 1998.

Glasier, Jonathan. "Ivor Darreg and Enharmonics." http://www.furious.com/perfect/xenharmonics.html.

Gold, Lisa. *Music in Bali*. New York: Oxford University Press, 2005.

Grady, Kraig. "The Wilson Archives." http://www.anaphoria.com/wilsonintroMOS.html.

Guthrie, Kenneth Sylvan, ed. *The Pythagorean Sourcebook and Library*. Grand Rapids, MI: Phanes Press, 1987.

Hagel, Stefan. *Ancient Greek Music: A New Technical History*. Cambridge, UK: Cambridge University Press, 2009.

Hammond, Frederick, and Peter M. Lefferts. "Odington, Walter." *Grove Music Online*. http://www.oxfordmusiconline.com/subscriber/article/grove/music/20252.

Helmholtz, Hermann L. F. von. *On the Sensations of Tone, as a Physiological Basis for the Theory of Music*. New York: Dover Publications, 1954. Originally published 1863.

Huygens, Christian. *Oeuvres completes*. Quoted in Barbieri, *Enharmonic*, 188–89.

Iamblichus. *The Life of Pythagoras*. Translated by Kenneth Sylvan Guthrie. In *The Pythagorean Sourcebook and Library*. Grand Rapids, MI: Phanes Press, 1987.

Ives, Charles. *Memos*. New York: W. W. Norton, 1972.

———. "Some 'Quarter-Tone' Impressions." In *Essays Before a Sonata, The Majority, and Other Writings*. New York: W. W. Norton, 1962.

———. Untitled program note to Three Quarter-Tone Pieces. New York: C. F. Peters Corp., 1968.

Jeans, Susi, and O. W. Neighbour. "Bull, John." *Grove Music Online*. http://www.oxfordmusiconline.com/subscriber/article/grove/music/04294.

Johnson, Timothy Ernest. *13-Limit Extended Just Intonation in Ben Johnston's String Quartet #7 and Toby Twining's "Chrysalid Requiem," "Gradual/Tract."* Ann Arbor: UMI Microform, 2008.

Johnston, Ben. "On Sonata for Microtonal Piano." In *Maximum Clarity and Other Writings on Music*, ed. Bob Gilmore, 185–86. Urbana: University of Illinois Press, 2006.

Jorgensen, Owen. *Tuning: Containing the Perfection of Eighteenth-Century Temperament, the Lost Art of Nineteenth-Century Temperament, and the Science of Equal Temperament*. East Lansing: Michigan State University Press, 1991.

Kárpáti, János. "Myth and Reality in the Theory of Chinese Tonal System." *Studia Musicologica Academiae Scientiarum Hungaricae*, T. 22, Fasc. 1/4 (1980).

Kaufmann, Henry W. "More on the Tuning of the 'Archicembalo.'" *Journal of the American Musicological Society* 23, no. 1 (1970): 84–94.

Koch, Albrecht. "J. S. Bach and Gottfried Silbermann: Two Giants in the World of Organ Music." http://www.bach.org.au/index.php/news/blog/j-s-bach-and-gottfried-silbermann-two-giants-in-the-world-of-organ-music.

Latham, Alison, ed. "Fitzwilliam Virginal Book." *The Oxford Companion to Music*. Oxford: Oxford University Press, 464–65. http://www.oxfordmusiconline.com/subscriber/article/opr/t114/e2560.

Leedy, Douglas, and Johnny Reinhard. "Tucker, Tui St George." *Grove Music Online*. http://www.oxfordmusiconline.com/subscriber/article/grove/music/49199.

Lindley, Mark. "Well-Tempered Clavier." *Grove Music Online*. http://www.oxfordmusiconline.com/subscriber/article/grove/music/30099.

Lloyd, Llewellyn S., and Hugh Boyle. *Intervals, Scales, and Temperaments*. New York: St. Martin's Press, 1978.

Madrid, Alejandro. *Julián Carrillo & Sonido 13*. Oxford, UK: Oxford University Press, 2015.

Marcus, Scott L. *Music in Egypt*. New York: Oxford University Press, 2007.

Mathiesen, Thomas J. *Apollo's Lyre: Greek Music and Music Theory in Antiquity and the Middle Ages*. Lincoln: University of Nebraska Press, 1999.

McClain, Ernest G. *The Myth of Invariance: The Origins of the Gods, Mathematics, and Music from the Rg Veda to Plato*. New York: N. Hays, 1976.

———. *The Pythagorean Plato: Prelude to the Song Itself*. New York: N. Hays, 1978.

McClain, Ernest G., and Ming Shui Hung. "Chinese Cyclic Tunings in Late Antiquity." *Ethnomusicology* 23, no. 2 (1979): 206, 213.

McCredie, Andrew. "Alois Hába (1893–1973)." In *Music of the Twentieth-Century Avant Garde: A Biocritical Sourcebook*, ed. Larry Sitsky, 190. Westport, CT: Greenwood Press, 2002.

McGeary, Thomas. *The Music of Harry Partch: A Descriptive Catalog*. Brooklyn: Institute for Studies in American Music, 1991.

Mersenne, Marin. *Harmonie Universelle*, Paris, Cramoisy, "Traité des instrumens à chords." Quoted in Christiansen, *Rameau and Musical Thought*, 136.

———. *Quaestiones celeberrimae in Genesim*. Lvtetiae Parisiorvm: Sumptibus Sebastiani Cramoisy, 1623.

Miller, Leta E., and Fredric Lieberman. "Lou Harrison and the American Gamelan." *American Music* 17, no. 2 (1999): 158, 159.

———. *Lou Harrison: Composing a World*. New York: Oxford University Press, 1998.

Monzo, Joe. "2/7-Comma Meantone." *Tonalsoft: Encyclopedia of Microtonal Music Theory*. http://www.tonalsoft.com/enc/number/2–7cmt.aspx.

———. "144-Tone Equal-Temperament / 144-edo." *Tonalsoft: Encyclopedia of Microtonal Music Theory*. http://www.tonalsoft.com/enc/number/144edo.aspx.

———. "Diesis." *TonalSoft: Encyclopedia of Microtonal Music Theory*. http://www.tonalsoft.com/enc/d/diesis.aspx.

———. "Kirnberger III Well Temperament." *Tonalsoft: Encyclopedia of Microtonal Music Theory*. http://www.tonalsoft.com/enc/k/kirnberger.aspx.

———. "Meantone." *Tonalsoft Encyclopedia of Microtonal Music Theory*. http://www.tonalsoft.com/enc/m/meantone.aspx.

———. "Secor." *Tonalsoft Encyclopedia of Microtonal Music Theory*. http://tonalsoft.com/enc/s/secor.aspx.

Narushima, Terumi. *Microtonality and the Tuning Systems of Erv Wilson*. Oxon, UK: Routledge, 2018.

Nicomachus the Pythagorean. *The Manual of Harmonics*. Translated by Flora R. Levin. Grand Rapids, MI: Phanes Press, 1994.

Norton, Edward Quincy. *The Construction, Tuning, and Care of the Piano-Forte*. Boston: Oliver Ditson, 1887.

Palisca, Claude V. 1954. "The Beginnings of Baroque Music: Its Roots in Sixteenth-Century Theory and Polemics." PhD diss., Harvard University, 1954. Quoted in Jonathan Wild, "Genus, Species, and Mode in Vicentino's 31-Tone Compositional Theory," *MTO* 20, no. 2 (2014).

———. *Humanism in Italian Renaissance Musical Thought*. New Haven, CT: Yale University Press, 1985.

———. "Zarlino, Gioseffo." *Grove Music Online*. http://www.oxfordmusiconline.com/subscriber/article/grove/music/30858.

Partch, Harry. *Genesis of a Music*. New York: Da Capo Press, 1974.

———. "A Quarter-Saw Section of Motivations and Intonations." In *Bitter Music: Collected Journals, Essays, Introductions, and Librettos*, ed. Thomas McGeary, 196–99. Urbana: University of Illinois Press, 1991.

Perrett, Wilfrid. "The Heritage of Greece in Music." *Proceedings of the Musical Association* 58 (1931–1932): 85.

Poletti, Paul. "Just Say Do." http://polettipiano.com/wordpress/?page_id=659.

Preston, Katherine K. "Barth, Hans." *Grove Music Online*. http://www.oxfordmusiconline.com/subscriber/article/grove/music/A2218612.

Read, Gardner. *20th-Century Microtonal Notation*. New York: Greenwood Press, 1990.

Reese, Gustave. *Music in the Middle Ages*. New York: W. W. Norton, 1940.

———. *Music in the Renaissance*. New York: W. W. Norton, 1954.

Riccati, Giordano. *Le leggi del Contrappunto dedotte dai fenomeni, e confermate col raziocinio*, II. Udine, Biblioteca Comunale, Ms. 1026-III. Quoted in Barbieri, *Enharmonic*, 208.

Richter, Lukas. "Didymus." *Grove Music Online*. http://www.oxfordmusiconline.com/subscriber/article/grove/music/07752.

———. "Eratosthenes." *Grove Music Online*. http://www.oxfordmusiconline.com/subscriber/article/grove/music/08909.

———. "Ptolemy." *Grove Music Online*. http://www.oxfordmusiconline.com/subscriber/article/grove/music/22510.

Riley, Terry. Liner notes to *The Harp of New Albion*. Celestial Harmonies CEL 018/019, 1986.

Sabat, Marc. "The Extended Helmholtz-Ellis JI Pitch Notation." MarcSabat.com. 2005. http://www.marcsabat.com/pdfs/notation.pdf.

Rylander, Simon. "The 11 Chords of Barbershop." March 31, 2008. https://www.sunshinetracks.com/chords.pdf.

Sachs, Curt. *The Rise of Music in the Ancient World East and West*. New York: W. W. Norton, 1943.

School of Mathematics and Statistics. University of St Andrews, Scotland. http://www-gap.dcs.st-and.ac.uk/~history/Mathematicians/Archytas.html.

Sethares, William A. *Tuning, Timbre, Spectrum, Scale*. London: Springer Verlag, 2005.

Shinn, Randall. "Ben Johnston's Fourth String Quartet." *Perspectives of New Music* 15, no. 2 (1977): 145–73.

Sims, Ezra. "Reflections on This and That (Perhaps a Polemic)." *Perspectives of New Music* 29, no. 1 (1991): 236–57.

Skinner, Myles. "Toward a Quarter-Tone Syntax: Selected Analyses of Works by Blackwood, Hába, Ives, and Wyschnegradsky." http://www.tierceron.com/diss/wysch/wysch.pdf.

Slonimsky, Nicolas, ed. *Baker's Biographical Dictionary of Musicians*, 5th ed., completely rev. by Nicolas Slonimsky. New York: G. Schirmer, 1958.

Smith, Catherine Parsons. "Couper, Mildred." *Grove Music Online*. http://www.oxfordmusiconline.com/subscriber/article/grove/music/47044.

Spielberg, Lydia. "The Implications of Several Ancient Tunings on Berlin Papyrus 6870, ll 16–19." Unpublished paper, October 2009.

Strainchamps, Edmond. "Luzzaschi, Luzzasco." *Grove Music Online*. http://www.oxfordmusiconline.com/subscriber/article/grove/music/17234.

Surjodiningrat, W., P. J. Sudarjana, and A. Susanto. *Tone Measurements of Outstanding Javanese Gamelans in Yogyakarta and Surakarta*. Yogyakarta: Gadjah Mada University Press, 1993.

Tartini, Giuseppe. *Trattato di musica*. Padova: Stamperiadel Seminario, 1754. Quoted in Barbieri, *Enharmonic*, 199.

Tenzer, Michael. *Gamelan Gong Kebyar: The Art of Twentieth-Century Balinese Music*. Chicago: University of Chicago Press, 2000.

Thompson, T. Perronet. *Theory and Practice of Just Intonation*. London: Effingham Willson, 1850.

Toulmin, Stephen, Douglas Bush, James S. Ackerman, and Claude V. Palisca, *Seventeenth-Century Science and the Arts*. Princeton, NJ: Princeton University Press, 1961.

Vetter, Roger. "A Retrospect on a Century of Gamelan Tone Measurements." *Ethnomusicology* 33, no. 2 (1989): 219.

Viswanathan, T., and Matthew Harp Allen. *Music in South India: Experiencing Music, Experiencing Culture*. New York: Oxford University Press, 2004.

von Riesemann, Oskar. *Rachmaninoff's Recollections*. New York: Routledge, 2015.

von Schweinitz, Wolfgang. "The Classical Indian Just Intonation Tuning System with 22 Srutis Defining the 7 Swaras of Hindu Classical Music." *Plainsound Music Edition*. http://www.plainsound.org/pdfs/srutis.pdf.

Vysloužil, Jiří. "Hába, Alois." *Grove Music Online*. http://www.oxfordmusiconline.com/subscriber/article/grove/music/12113.

Walker, Alan. *Franz Liszt: The Final Years, 1861–1886*. Ithaca, NY: Cornell University Press, 1990.

Wallis, John. *Philosophical Transactions XII* (April 1677). Cited in Stephen Toulmin, Douglas Bush, James S. Ackerman, and Claude V. Palisca, *Seventeenth-Century Science and the Arts*. Princeton, NJ: Princeton University Press, 1961.

Webster, James. *Haydn's "Farewell" Symphony and the Idea of Classical Style*. Cambridge, UK: Cambridge University Press, 1991.

White, William Braid. *Piano Tuning and Allied Arts*. Boston: Tuners Supply Company, 1953.

Wild, Jonathan. "Genus, Species, and Mode in Vicentino's 31-Tone Compositional Theory." *MTO* 20, no. 2 (2014): 1–19.

Wilson, Ervin. "Letter to Chalmers Pertaining to Moments of Symmetry/Tanabe Cycle." April 26, 1975. http://anaphoria.com/mos.PDF.

Wright, Craig, and Sean Gallagher. "Martin le Franc." *Grove Music Online*. http://www.oxfordmusiconline.com/subscriber/article/grove/music/17928.

Wyschnegradsky, Ivan. *Manual of Quarter-Tone Harmony*. Edited by Noah Kaplan. Brooklyn: Underwolf Editions, 2017.

Yasser, Joseph. *A Theory of Evolving Tonality*. New York: American Library of Musicology, 1932.

Index

KYLE GANN is a composer and the Taylor Hawver and Frances Bortle Hawver Professor of Music at Bard College. His books include *Charles Ives's Concord*, *No Such Thing as Silence: John Cage's 4′33″*, and *Robert Ashley*.

The University of Illinois Press
is a founding member of the
Association of University Presses.

University of Illinois Press
1325 South Oak Street
Champaign, IL 61820-6903
www.press.uillinois.edu